Abide with Me

G-4805

Ian Bradley

Abide With Me

The World of Victorian Hymns

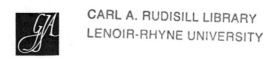

GIA Publications, Inc.

GIA Publications, Inc.
7404 S. Mason Ave., Chicago, IL 60638

ISBN: 1-57999-010-x

GIA Publications, Inc.
exclusive North American distributor.

First published in Britain 1997
by SCM Press Ltd.
9–17 St Albans Place, London N1 ONX

Typeset by Regent Typesetting, London

For my father

who brought me up to know
and love Victorian hymns

'Pull for the shore, sailor'

Contents

Acknowledgments

I have received considerable help in the research and preparation of this book. The archives of *Hymns Ancient and Modern* in Norwich were made available to me through the good offices of Gordon Knights. Richard de Peyer, Curator of Dorset County Museum, kindly allowed me to look at Thomas Hardy's hymn-books and Lilian Swindall supervised my study of them. A Scouloudi Foundation Historical Award helped with the cost of travel to look at archival material.

Several people have significantly contributed to this study by either suggesting new lines of approach or providing information and references to follow up. Francesca Murphy alerted me to Kipling's interest in hymnody and Peter Keating, Kipling's latest biographer, supplied me with several helpful references on this subject. Leon Litvack similarly brought Ruskin's writings on hymns to my notice and Janet Carleton introduced me to D. H. Lawrence's evocative poem 'The Piano'. A doughty trio of Norwich-based Sullivan enthusiasts, Arthur Barrett, John Balls and Richard Cockaday, have greatly assisted my research on the hymn tunes of this particular composer. On a flying visit to Scarborough I was able to pick the brains of Paul Chappell, biographer of Dykes, and Bertram Barnby, author of a recent study on hymnody, *In Concert Sing*, who sadly died just as I was completing my own book. I have also derived much from conversations with Brian Castle, who generously shared the fruits of his research on treatment of the four last things in Victorian hymnody, Peter Coxon, a mine of information on Thomas Hardy's life-long love affair with hymns and psalms, Malcolm Hare, a fellow-enthusiast for Victorian hymn-tunes, and Mervyn Horder.

Pauline Newth sent me a fascinating set of notes taken by one of her ancestors while attending a lecture on hymns in 1897. Sandy Young, minister of Mayfield Salisbury Church in Edinburgh, made available to me his useful comparison of the contents of the first and third editions of *The Church Hymnary*, John Hughes kindly sent me a copy of his paper on 'The Victorian Hymn Tune in Wales' and Alan Duce shared his research on Matthew Bridges. My knowledge of, and interest in, the west gallery tradition was greatly enhanced through attending a conference on the subject held at Clacton in 1995 and organized by Christopher Turner.

Some of the ideas and themes developed in this book were first aired in talks to the Sir Arthur Sullivan Society and in broadcasts on BBC Radio 2. I am grateful to the society's secretary, Stephen Turnbull, and to Clair Jacquiss, producer of 'Abide with me', 'God, the devil and the good tunes' and 'O come, all ye Jacobites', for allowing me to indulge my passion for Victorian hymnody. I am also grateful to the students at Aberdeen University who have taken my courses on 'Singing the faith' and 'the Victorian hymn' and made them so enjoyable, not least because of their spirited singing. I would like to record my special thanks to Fred Stewart, whose enthusiasm for Victorian hymns led him to become my first graduate student working in this area.

I am grateful to those who have allowed me to reproduce material which is in copyright. D. H. Lawrence's poem 'The Piano' from *The Complete Poems of D. H. Lawrence* and excerpts from 'Hymns in a Man's Life' from *D. H. Lawrence: Selected Literary Criticism* are quoted by permission of Laurence Pollinger Limited, the estate of Frieda Lawrence Ravagli and Viking Penguin Inc., New York. Lines from Thomas Hardy's poems, 'A Church Romance', 'Afternoon Service at Mellstock' and 'The Chapel Organist' are quoted with permission from *The Complete Poems of Thomas Hardy* (Papermac) and from his short story 'Absent-mindedness in a Village Choir' from *Collected Short Stories of Thomas Hardy* (Papermac). Extracts from Hardy's novels *The Mayor of Casterbridge, Desperate Remedies, Under the Greenwood Tree, A Laodicean, Tess of the D'Urbervilles, Far from the Madding Crowd* and *The Dynasts* are printed by permission of Macmillan General Books. David Wright's pacifist version of 'Onward, Christian soldiers' is quoted by permission of the author.

Thanks to my good friend Hugo Brunner, this book has found a home with SCM Press. From John Bowden and the staff at the Press I have had strong support and encouragement. My greatest debt of all is to Bernard Massey, editor of the *Hymn Society Bulletin* who knows far more about Victorian hymnody than I ever will. He has read through the entire work in draft and saved me from many howlers. For those that remain, I take sole blame.

Preface

Hymns played much the same role in Victorian culture that television and radio soap operas do today. Popular at all levels of society, including among their enthusiasts those who were sometimes rather loath to admit it, they provoked strongly antagonistic reactions in their detractors. Familiar, pervasive and subtly addictive, they both reassured and shocked, comforted and consoled, and occasionally challenged and disturbed. They exerted a powerful if largely subliminal effect on language, values and attitudes. Derided by critics for their vulgarity, sensationalism and sentimentality, they provided many with companionship, colour and poetry and were a cohesive and unifying force in a society which was in some danger of fragmentation and factionalism. They inspired an extraordinary level of loyalty among their 'fans' who bitterly resented changes to words or tunes and felt a sense of bereavement when old favourites were dropped.

At the risk of straining the analogy towards breaking point, we can perhaps identify a range of styles within Victorian hymnody which correspond to the ethos of particular contemporary soaps. The High Anglican hymns of the Oxford Movement and *Hymns Ancient and Modern*, solid and venerable, though periodically touched up to suit changing tastes, belong as surely as *The Archers* to the reassuring world of rural middle England. At once more gritty and more sentimental, the hymns of Victorian Nonconformity are products of the same bracing yet folksy Northern climate that has sustained *Coronation Street* and *Emmerdale*. More populist and vulgar, the Salvation Army's choruses and adaptations of secular music hall songs belong to the tough metropolitan milieu of *East Enders*. Victorian Scotland had its own couthy and slightly old-fashioned hymns in the style of *Take the High Road*. The gospel songs imported from across the Atlantic with their brash lyrics, their simple message and their catchy tunes perhaps resemble nothing so much as those more recent Antipodean arrivals, *Neighbours* and *Home and Away*, titles which, indeed, could almost have come straight out of Sankey's songbook, although the former perhaps has a touch too much of the social gospel and suggests rather the kind of activist humanitarian hymn which was coming into favour, again under American influence, in the last years of the nineteenth century.

Like soap operas, many hymns are ephemeral, written for the moment and not designed or built for permament survival. Indeed, Victorians often used the medium of hymnody, rather as their successors might write to *The Times* or ring up *Any Answers*, to sound off about contemporary issues. Hymns were provided for every conceivable purpose and occasion. J. M. Neale wrote one for use during a cattle plague. Sir Henry Baker penned one for friendly societies and the *Congregational Church Hymnal* of 1887 printed one to be sung before a parliamentary election. Altogether, it has been estimated that around 400,000 hymns were written between 1837 and 1901.[1] Less than a thousand have survived and are still being sung and perhaps only a hundred or so are likely to attain the status of classics and continue to appear in hymnbooks through the twenty-first century. I offer a personal list of one hundred such classics in Appendix 1 at the end of this book. This might seem a tiny harvest of good grain to winnow from a huge amount of chaff but I doubt very much if the proportion of enduring material which survives from the hymn-writing explosion of the last thirty years will be any greater. I also wonder if its quality, in literary, theological or musical terms, will be as high.

This is where the analogy with soap operas breaks down. Victorian hymnody had its hack scriptwriters and tunesmiths, but it also attracted some of the finest poets and composers of the day. Here is another important difference from our own times. Hymn writing nowadays tends to be seen either as a rather marginal activity or else as a specialist ministry for professional songwriters and church musicians. In the nineteenth century hymns were seen as a central and mainstream literary and musical form. The genre appealed to poets, academics and distinguished classical composers as well as to a host of distinguished amateurs led, in terms of rank at least, by the Prince Consort who composed a number of very passable hymn tunes. It is inconceivable now for a whole variety of reasons to imagine leading politicians writing hymns. Gladstone's 1880 Cabinet, by contrast, contained three distinguished amateur hymnodists: Lord Selborne, the Lord Chancellor, who edited a popular anthology of hymns and contributed a long and learned article on the subject to the *Encyclopaedia Britannica*, the 8th Duke of Argyll, the Lord Privy Seal, who was a talented versifier of the psalms, and the Prime Minister himself whose communion hymn, 'O lead my blindness by the hand' appeared in many twentieth-century hymn books. With strong Nonconformists like Joe Chamberlain, John Bright and W. E. Forster also in this Cabinet, I suspect that conversation before business around the Downing Street table must often have turned to hymns, and perhaps one or two were even sung by the assembled company.

This brings us to another great difference between hymns and soap operas. Watching soaps is an entirely passive experience. Hymns, on the other hand, especially before the age of recordings, radio and television, positively demand participation. At least Victorian hymns do. In the eighteenth century singing in churches was often confined to the choir in the gallery. Nowadays the growth of praise groups and soloists is producing a similar emphasis on performance rather than participation in worship. Like Luther, Victorian writers and composers wrote hymns to be sung by congregations, as, indeed, they were with great gusto and enthusiasm. The Victorian era coincided with a massive upsurge of interest in teaching singing at both school and adult level. Choral societies and glee clubs were started all over the country. Hymn singing was perhaps the greatest beneficiary of this new movement. Whether for reasons of respectability and religious sentiment or simply because they were easier and more fun to sing, it was hymns rather than parlour ballads, folk songs or music hall numbers that most exercised the nation's vocal chords – not just in churches and chapels but in school rooms, at public meetings and social gatherings, in the streets and, most of all, at home in the nursery or parlour.

Now we can pick up the analogy with soap operas again. Like television today, Victorian hymns came directly into the home. They were bound up with family rituals, homecomings and departures, anniversaries and celebrations. Images of home and hearth figure prominently in their verses while their tunes, constructed like part songs, often have the intimacy and emotionalism of parlour ballads. The huge sales of hymn-books suggest that the picture of the Victorian family gathered round the piano or the harmonium on a Sunday evening singing sacred melodies was not a romantic ideal but rather a reality.

It is almost impossible for us to grasp the ubiquity and pervasiveness of hymns in Victorian culture, except again, perhaps, by analogy to the merchandising and franchising spin-offs from television cult series and the related worlds of pop music and professional sport. Their texts appeared on postcards and tombstones, on framed posters to be hung up at home and in school reading books. Their tunes were played by brass bands and barrel organs and formed the largest single category of subject matter for pianola rolls. They were performed by professional singers in recital halls and on concert platforms – Clara Butt largely established her reputation as a soloist in the 1890s through her renditions of 'Abide with me'. Hymns fascinated Victorian novelists from George Eliot and the Brontes to Rudyard Kipling and Thomas Hardy. Composers as varied as Arthur Sullivan and Edward Elgar wove hymn tunes into symphonic and choral pieces.

As a result, hymns came to be known by heart and their distinctive phraseology had an influence on language. Just as expressions such as 'get real' and 'gross' have become standard currency among young people today, so phrases like 'abide with me' and 'say not the struggle naught availeth' passed into common parlance in the late nineteenth and early twentieth centuries. Perhaps the clearest sign that a particular cultural influence has penetrated deep into popular consciousness is when it comes to be parodied. Lewis Carroll knew that his young readers were sufficiently steeped in Isaac Watts' improving hymns for children to appreciate it when he sent them up in *Alice in Wonderland*. When two generations later soldiers in the Flanders trenches thought up songs to keep them going, it was not to parlour ballads or even the music hall that they turned for inspiration but rather to hymn tunes which provided the basis for such favourites as 'We are Fred Karno's Army' and 'We've had no beer, we've had no beer today'.

Like soap operas, Victorian hymns have had a bad press. They have been dismissed as trivial, mawkish, sentimental and shallow. It is certainly true that some of those that are still around today are an acquired taste and have a distinct period flavour. They remind me in many ways of those marble effigies of nineteenth-century deans and bishops that occupy the side aisles of cathedrals – the hands clasped piously in prayer, winged angels in attendance and often a favourite pet at their feet. Many Victorian hymns seem to breathe a similar air of comfortable certainty and ostentatious piety that is alien to the spirit of contemporary Christianity. Where is the sense of the crucifed God, the patripassianism, the sense of vulnerability and ambiguity that has come to dominate late twentieth-century theology?

In fact, these themes are to be found in Victorian hymnody. Some of the most profound expressions of Christian doubt and ambiguity come from this period, including the verses from Tennyson's *In Memoriam* and from Newman's poetry which were among the Victorians' favourite hymns. The themes of darkness and suffering are prominent in many nineteenth-century hymns. Much more so, I would suggest, than in contemporary worship songs and choruses which seem generally to express only spiritual 'highs' and not to plumb the depths of human experience and the struggle to hold on to faith in the face of suffering and evil.

This is an unashamedly enthusiastic study. That does not mean, I hope, that it is uncritical. I am concerned to explain the context in which the Victorian hymn grew up and flourished and to explore this distinctive species from a literary, theological, musical and cultural perspective. Having just assisted in the process of purging the *Church Hymnary* of material that is now due for discarding, I am the first to concede that we are still burdened by some doleful remains from the nineteenth century that we need to commit to the grave as quickly as possible. At the same time, I also think that there are some unjustly neglected Victorian hymns and tunes which deserve rehabilitation. A list of some of them can be found in Appendix 2.

What I am arguing for in this book, above all, I suppose, is a respect for the integrity of the genre. There is growing pressure from a number of directions to tamper with, or discard Victorian hymns in the interests of relevance, inclusive language, accessibility and political correctness. Of course, like all forms of liturgy, hymnody is in a constant state of change and adaptation. To a modern ear, Victorian hymns can seem very anachronistic and archaic in their metaphors, their message and their harmonies. Yet they often have a great richness of imagery, a depth of meaning and a mystery at their heart. These qualities are not particularly prized in our instant, up-front, pick-and-mix post-modern culture, but that is all the more reason why we need to have hymns which express them. We must not be seduced by the vandals who would strip out the beauty and ambiguity from 'difficult' language and replace it with the blandly banal.

This is, of course, where hymns ultimately differ from the soap operas to which some will think I have rather irreverently compared them. The best take their place beside the psalms and the poems of Dante and Milton as amongst the world's greatest sacred verse. By and large, hymns are not written to entertain or boost the audience ratings. They have an altogether nobler and higher purpose, being intended to praise or petition God, convert sinners, sustain the righteous, guide the perplexed, comfort the downhearted, challenge the complacent, wrestle honestly with doubt, celebrate the wonders of creation, teach the basic doctrines of the faith or penetrate the mystery of holiness. They could hardly be further removed from the crude commercialism and materialism, the sexual exploitation and gratuitous violence of so much of what fills our television screens.

Yet we can perhaps come back to one fundamental quality that good popular television shares with many hymns, particularly those from the Victorian era. The best soaps do challenge and even instruct their audiences as well as entertain them. They also have a genuine warmth and an empathy for the whole human condition in all its complexity and vulnerability. The themes that are the stuff of soap opera plots – love, loyalty, conflict, loss and coping with whatever life may throw up – are also at the heart of many Victorian hymns. The treatment may be more restrained, the context spiritual rather than secular, the language more majestic, but the concern with basic human emotion and the sheer business of coping with life is very similar, especially in that significant branch of Victorian hymnody which was subjective and experiential rather than objective and doctrinal.

Let me squeeze one final observation out of the analogy that has dominated this preface and which I promise will not surface again in this book. For better or worse, soaps seem to me to be one of the most distinctive and characteristic cultural products of our age. I think one can say the same about hymns in the Victorian era. The Victorians did not, of course, invent hymns but they did turn them into what they have become throughout the English-speaking world – the folk songs of the church and the most powerful single medium for the transmission of Christian doctrine and the expression of religious feeling, speaking both to committed believers and to the much larger ranks of half-believers. They achieved this by writing verses of great sensitivity and beauty and matching them to tunes of enormous power and compelling singability, by translating and reclaiming the great hymns of the early church and of other Christian traditions, by legitimizing in the main established churches the practice of hymn singing which had hitherto been regarded as a subversive and eccentric activity confined to marginal sects and fringe groups and, last but not least, by inventing the hymn-book as we now know it.

In the Victorians' enormous enthusiasm for hymns we can see the coming together of many of the conflicting values of that complex age – high moral seriousness, sentimentality, populism, evangelical fervour, doubt-laden faith, high literary culture, scholarly antiquarianism, anguished optimism and a strenuous sense of duty. This particularly Victorian passion transcended the barriers of social class, denominational and theological loyalty and political persuasion. It built a bridge between the sacred and the secular and gave people a wonderful store of images, aphorisms and tunes to help them through their earthly pilgrimages. That is certainly more than the most ardent enthusiasts for contemporary soaps would ever claim that they have done for the present generation.

In view of their enormous influence and impact, it is surprising how little attention has been paid to hymns by those writing about Victorian Britain. Some ecclesiastical historians have at least acknowledged that the hymn rather than the sermon provides the most characteristic expression of Victorian Christianity and that hymnody was 'the greatest factor in popularizing Victorian services'.[2] Yet there has been very little serious study of Victorian hymnody from a liturgical, theological or ecclesiological perspective. The failure of literary and cultural historians to engage with the subject is, if anything, even stranger. In the words of one of the few who has:

> It seems indisputable that quantatively the effect of hymns on the Victorian public was more profound than the literary works which traditionally have been mined so assiduously by cultural historians. In sheer volume, the writing of hymns far outweighed the writing of poetry . . . More important, the people whose lives were affected by hymns far outnumber those who were affected by poetry. Only a small percentage of Victorian society read the Greek or Latin poets, or even the more popular Southey or Wordsworth. But hymns were sung everywhere – on street corners, at secular meetings, in the nursery; as well as in the churches and chapels.[3]

My aim in this book is in some small way to atone for the neglect of this subject by historians, theologians, literary and musical critics alike and to accord to the world of Victorian hymns at least some of the attention and admiration that it so manifestly deserves.

Praise, my soul, the King of heaven

The genesis of Victorian hymnody

Hymn singing was a novel experience for most Victorian church-goers, a fact which partly explains why it engendered so much enthusiasm and controversy. Although Methodists, Baptists and Congregationalists had been singing hymns in their services since the mid-eighteenth century, the practice was not officially sanctioned in the Church of England until the 1820s and gradually became the norm in Anglican churches in the following two decades. The Church of Scotland did not stray from the pure paths of metrical psalmody and scriptural paraphrase until the 1870s and English Presbyterians also came late to accepting the legitimacy of singing hymns of human composition in church. Of 279 English Presbyterian congregations surveyed in 1882, 218 were still sticking to metrical psalms only although by the end of the century most were using hymn-books as well. In his book on *Church Music in the Nineteenth Century* Arthur Hutchings comments that 'the spread of congregational hymnody . . . caused the most obvious change in Protestant church music during the century'.[1] It did not reach most Roman Catholic churches until later. The first widely-used Catholic hymn-book (*Arundel Hymns* edited by the Duke of Norfolk) appeared in 1901, the year of Queen Victoria's death.

Hymn singing came to Britain so late because its established churches chose to follow Calvin rather than Luther. Congregational hymn singing was one of the great legacies of the German Reformation. Martin Luther believed that people should sing hymns in their own language and wrote several himself, including the mighty 'Ein' feste Burg'. He also advocated setting them to popular folk tunes. Calvin, on the other hand, allowed only metrical settings of the psalms of David sung to specially composed tunes. This was the route followed by the Protestant churches of the British Isles with their close links to Geneva.

It was to mean that hymns of human composition had virtually no place in British worship for the two hundred and fifty years following the Reformation. The prevailing attitude was summed up in an essay on psalmody written in 1775 by the evangelical Anglican divine, William Romaine: 'I want a name for that man who should pretend that he could make better hymns than the Holy Ghost. His Collection is large enough; it wants no addition. It is as perfect as its Author, and wants no improvement.'[2]

Among the many collections of metrical psalms used in English parish churches, and in Anglican churches in Wales and Ireland, during this period two predominated: the so-called 'Old Version' of Thomas Sternhold and John Hopkins, published in 1562 and the 'New Version' by Nahum Tate and Nicholas Brady which appeared in 1696 but was not widely taken up for another hundred years or so. By the early nineteenth century Tate and Brady's psalms were often bound in with the Book of Common Prayer, giving the 'New Version' semi-official status. Scottish Presbyterians and Episcopalians also leaned heavily on these two collections although they had their own psalters, based more closely on the Anglo-Genevan book of 1561, the most notable of which, produced in 1650 as a result of the work of the Westminster Assembly of Divines, is still in wide use today.

Throughout the seventeenth and for the greater part of the eighteenth century psalms were sung unaccompanied and led by a precentor, normally the parish clerk, who gave out each line before the congregation joined in. The effect of this practice of 'lining out' often left a good deal to be desired. Samuel Pepys complained after attending a Sunday morning service in January 1661 that it had taken an hour to get through a single psalm. This was no doubt due to the extreme slowness with which it was sung, the amount of repetition and the number of very long grace notes and other pieces of ornamentation. Often the clerk found himself effectively singing a solo for lack of congregational enthusiasm. An essay written in 1787 described the situation in those London churches which lacked organ or choir: 'The clerk commences his stave, and goes through it almost wholly unaccompanied, or perhaps joined towards the close, by the feeble efforts of a single voice or two.'[3] Even when they did join in, congregations often seem to have paid very little attention to what was being sung and simply repeated the precentor's words back to him parrot fashion. One story tells of an evening service when the clerk announced 'The light has grown so very dim, I scarce can see to read the hymn' whereupon the congregation,

who were already expecting a long metre couplet, sang those lines back
to him.[4]

The practice of lining out took a long time to die – indeed, it survives
to this day among Gaelic-speaking congregations in the Scottish High-
lands and islands. The Methodist Conference of 1856 voted against a
proposal that it be abolished and the parish church at Wing in
Buckinghamshire still had a clerk lining out psalms and hymns in 1870.
Many English parish churches, however, began to abandon unaccompanied metrical psalm singing led by a precentor in the late eighteenth
century and introduced a choir and instrumentalists who were often
installed in a gallery at the west end of the nave. In large town and city
churches the organ was the preferred instrument of praise – most
Anglican churches in London had organs by 1800 – but in rural areas
the gallery band was generally made up of clarinets, bassoon, flute and
violoncello or bass viol. During the singing of psalms, the congregation
would turn round to face the choir and musicians at the back of
the church. As they gained confidence, gallery choirs extended their
repertoire by singing anthems, often to highly florid fuguing tunes with
imitative entries and repeated lines and phrases.

'West gallery music', as this development has come to be known, was
the dominant tradition in English country churches when Victoria
came to the throne.[5] It is vividly portrayed in the works of a number of
novelists who mourned its passing in favour of organ accompanied
hymn singing later in her reign. Here is George Eliot describing worship
in the fictional church of Shepperton in the early 1830s:

As the moment of psalmody approached, by some process to me
as mysterious and untraceable as the opening of flowers or the
breaking-out of the stars, a slate appeared in front of the gallery,
advertising in bold characters the psalm about to be sung, lest the
sonorous announcement of the clerk should still leave the bucolic
mind in doubt on that head. Then followed the migration of the clerk
to the gallery, where, in company with a bassoon, two key-bugles, a
carpenter understood to have an amazing power of singing 'counter',
and two lesser musical stars, he formed the complement of a
choir regarded in Shepperton as one of distinguished attraction,
occasionally known to draw hearers from the next parish. The innovation of hymn-books was as yet undreamed of; even the New
Version was regarded with a sort of melancholy tolerance, as part of
the common degeneracy in a time when prices had dwindled, and a

cotton gown was no longer stout enough to last a lifetime; for the lyrical taste of the best heads in Shepperton had been formed on Sternhold and Hopkins.[6]

A later Victorian novelist was to write even more lovingly of the old-style psalmody. Thomas Hardy was steeped in the west gallery tradition. His grandfather and father had both played in gallery bands in Dorset churches. Indeed, his father had first caught his mother's eye when she turned in her pew and saw him playing the viol in the gallery of Stinsford Church. He described their encounter in his poem 'A Church Romance (Melstock c.1835)':

> Thus their hearts' bond began, in due time signed.
> And long years thence, when Age had scared Romance,
> At some old attitude of his or glance
> That gallery-scene would break upon her mind,
> With him as minstrel, ardent young, and trim,
> Bowing 'New Sabbath' or 'Mount Ephraim'.[7]

Hardy's novels *Under the Greenwood Tree* and *The Mayor of Casterbridge* give the fullest description that I know of west gallery music in its early nineteenth-century heyday. The impression is of a friendly, slightly disorganized bunch of singers and instrumentalists with a strongly anarchic streak and a determination to resist the clerically imposed authoritarianism of the organ. Hardy makes no bones about their amateurishness and lack of reverence for the sacred atmosphere of the services to which they contributed. They emerge from his pages first and foremost as performers out to have a good time and only secondarily, if at all, as committed to leading God's people in worship and praise. A little known short story published in 1894 but set fifty years or more earlier, 'Absent-Mindedness in a Parish Choir', describes the choir of Longpuddle Church, consisting of a leader on fiddle, bass-viol, tenor fiddle, serpent, clarinet and oboe, who were much in demand for reels and dancing parties 'for they could turn out a jig or a hornpipe out of hand as well as ever they could turn out a psalm, and perhaps better'. During the Christmas season 'they'd been out to one rattling randy after another every night and had got no sleep at all'. The Sunday after Christmas found the choir members back in the gallery of a church so cold that they could hardly sit through the morning service. So for the afternoon service they brought along a gallon of hot brandy and beer, ready mixed 'and by keeping the jar well wrapped in Timothy Thomas's bass-viol bag it kept drinkably warm till they wanted it, which was just a thimbleful in the Absolution, and another after the Creed, and the remainder at the beginning of the sermon'.

Unfortunately, the sermon went on so long that the members of the band fell asleep. At the end of the sermon the parson gave out the evening hymn (Thomas Ken's 'Glory to thee, my God, this night') but there was no sounding out of the tune. Everyone turned expectantly to the gallery and a boy shouted out 'begin, begin'. The church was so dark, and the leader's head so muddled, 'he thought he was at the party they had played at the night before, and away he went, bow and fiddle, at "The Devil among the Tailors", the favourite jig of our neighbourhood at that time'. The rest of the band joined in with gusto and the leader shouted out, 'Top couples cross hands! And when I make the fiddle squeak at the end, every man kiss his pardner under the mistletoe.' The parson was not amused, the squire even less so. He announced that none of the players would ever sound a note in the church again. Later that week he sent for a barrel organ equipped to play 22 new psalm tunes 'so exact and particular that, however sinful inclined you was, you could play nothing but psalm-tunes'.[8]

Barrel organs arrived in many English country churches between 1830 and 1850, usually ousting the gallery bands as in Hardy's story. The band at Puddletown Church near Dorchester, where his grandfather played, and on which he may well have based Longpuddle choir, was replaced by a barrel organ in 1845. These new instruments, which were essentially pipe organs operated by a barrel mechanism with a repertoire of 20 or so common metre psalm tunes, brought a greater regularity and order to congregational psalm singing. In place of the florid gallery melodies a relatively small number of tunes came to be used again and again. They included CAMBRIDGE NEW, immortalized by Hardy in his poem, 'Afternoon Service at Mellstock (*c.*1850)':

> On afternoons of drowsy calm
> We stood in the panelled pew,
> Singing one-voiced a Tate-and-Brady psalm
> To the tune of 'Cambridge New'.[9]

Hardy mentions another favourite psalm tune in *The Mayor of Casterbridge* when he has Michael Henchard call in the pub to which the gallery band repair after the Sunday morning service for 'old Wiltshire – the only tune worth singing – the psalm-tune that would make my blood ebb and flow like the sea when I was a steady chap'.[10] The short metre tune MOUNT EPHRAIM, alluded to in Hardy's poem 'A Church Romance' turns up again in Mrs Gaskell's *Cousin Phillis*, written in 1863-4 but set in rural middle England in the 1840s. It is the melody chosen by Ebenezer Holman, working farmer through the week and pastor of the Independent Chapel at Hornby at the weekend, when he pauses from his labours in the fields in the middle of a Friday after- noon to lead his men in Isaac Watts' 'Come all harmonious tongues'. The scene is witnessed by Paul Manning, clerk to a railway engineer who is building a new branch line through the area:

> He lifted his spade in his hand, and began to beat time with it; the two labourers seemed to know both words and music, though I did not; and so did Phillis: her rich voice followed her father's as he set the tune; and the men came in with more uncertainty but still harmoniously. Phillis looked at me once or twice with a little surprise at my silence; but I did not know the words. There we five stood, bareheaded, excepting Phillis, in the tawny stubble-field, from which all the shocks of corn had not yet been carried – a dark wood on one side, where the wood pigeons were cooing; blue distance seen through the ash-trees on the other. Somehow, I think that if I had known the words, and could have sung, my throat would have been choked up by the feeling of the unaccustomed scene.
>
> The hymn was ended, and the men had drawn off before I could stir. I saw the minister beginning to put on his coat, and looking at me with friendly inspection in his gaze, before I could rouse myself.
>
> 'I dare say you railway gentlemen don't wind up the day with singing a psalm together,' said he; 'but it is not a bad practice – not a bad practice.'[11]

It is significant that the instigator of this impromptu piece of open-air hymn singing should have been the pastor of an Independent Chapel, for it was the Independents, followed closely by other Dissenting groups, who first broke the stranglehold of metrical psalmody in Britain and pioneered the practice of singing hymns. Many Dissenters also remained deeply attached to unaccompanied psalm singing, as is clear from this extract from another of Mrs Gaskell's novels, *Ruth*, written in 1853, which describes a chapel service in rural Cheshire:

> The country people came in, sleeking down their hair, and treading with earnest attempts at noiseless lightness of step over the floor of

the aisle; and, by and by, when all were assembled, Mr Benson followed, unmarshalled and unattended. When he had closed the pulpit door and knelt in prayer for an instant or two, he gave out a psalm from the dear old Scottish paraphrase, with its primitive inversion of the simple perfect Biblical words; and a kind of precentor stood up, and, having sounded the note on a pitch-pipe, sang a couple of lines by way of introducing the tune; then the congregation stood up, and sang aloud.[12]

From the mid-eighteenth century onwards, however, a growing number of dissenting congregations had begun to add hymns to their repertoire, both in their chapel services and more particularly at open-air meetings. They were not short of high quality material to use. The eighteenth-century religious revival produced the two founding fathers of English hymnody who continue to rank as its most prolific and distinguished exponents. Isaac Watts wrote some 600 hymns and Christianized versions of the psalms, many for use by his Independent congregation at Mark Lane Chapel, London. Charles Wesley's output was even greater and is said to have totalled some 6,500 hymns, a good number of which, like the immortal 'O for a thousand tongues', were written for the great open-air rallies at which he and his brother John preached in the 1740s and 50s. Members of other denominations also played a significant part in the development of English hymnody. John Nuttall, minister of the Baptist Chapel at Lumb in Rossendale, Lancashire, did much to encourage and improve congregational singing, for example. One of the first hymn-books produced in England was published in 1764 for use in the Countess of Huntingdon's Chapels. Significantly, the earliest hymn-book in Scotland was to come from an equally small and marginal source, being published in 1792 by the tiny Relief Church which had broken away from the Church of Scotland thirty years earlier.

The first major denominational hymn-book was the *Collection of Hymns for the Use of People called Methodists* which John Wesley put together in 1780, claiming not altogether unreasonably that within its pages were contained 'all the truths of our most holy religion, whether speculative or practical'.[13] If Methodism was born in song, it also nurtured some of the most vigorous and committed hymn singers throughout the nineteenth century for whom hymns were powerful expressions of personal faith and devotion. The Wesley brothers' own verses, which formed by far the largest element in Methodist hymnody,

were often intensely emotional and dramatic, dealing with their conversion experiences, and lending themselves to fervent, heart-felt singing
and appropriation by their followers. Hymns became central to
Methodist worship and they were not just confined to chapel services,
being sung out of doors at great open-air meetings, at street corners, in
the workplace and pre-eminently at home.

Several of the groups which split away from the main Wesleyan body
in the early nineteenth century earned nicknames on account of the
heartiness of their singing. The Independent Methodists, who began in
Lancashire in 1805-6, were known as the 'Singing Quakers'. Singing
also featured prominently among the 'diversity of pious exercises' at the
open-air meeting on Mow Cop, Staffordshire, in 1807 which gave birth
to Primitive Methodism, some of whose early followers were dubbed
'Ranters' for singing in the streets of Belper, Derbyshire. Primitive
Methodists, the most solidly working-class of all nineteenth-century
British denominations, developed a distinctive hymnody which was
genuinely popular and vulgar in the best sense of the word. Like the
Gaelic prayers from the Outer Hebrides collected by Alexander
Carmichael in the *Carmina Gadelica* and so much in vogue now,
Primitive Methodist hymnody interwove the themes of work and
worship, the secular and the sacred. The members of this particular
branch of the Methodist family probably did as much as anyone in the
nineteenth century to establish hymn singing as an everyday activity for
all times and places. As the preface to one of its later hymnals proclaimed, 'Primitive Methodists do not require hymns for public worship
only; they need them for the sick chamber, for the marriage feast, for
funerals, for journeys by sea and land, for various social gatherings, for
the home sanctuary, for personal and private use, for praising the Lord
"secretly among the faithful" as well as in the "great congregation".'[14]
Such was the enthusiasm with which working people took up this
invitation that an anonymous anti-Methodist tract complained in 1805
that the typical labourer was returning from his daily toil and taking 'his
wife and children from the wheel and other useful employments in the
house' in order that they might sing hymns together.[15]

Alongside its emotional intensity and earthiness, Methodist hymnody
also had an important educative purpose and a significant theological
agenda. The Wesleys saw hymns as a vehicle for teaching Christian
doctrine. They wrote their verses to set out and explain the key articles
of the faith, to counter what they saw as bad teaching (such as
Calvinistic concepts of election and limited atonement) and to promote

particular doctrines which they championed, such as the notion of sanctification. As we shall see, this didactic, credal dimension to hymnody was to be particularly dear to the Victorian heart, especially to the hearts of Victorian Anglicans and those who wrote hymns for children. Methodism not only supplied the wider Victorian church with some of its key principles about the importance and purpose of hymns. It also provided compellingly singable tunes which were widely taken up by other denominations, even though many Anglicans remained rather sniffy about them. Several of the psalm tunes which Thomas Hardy became so attached to as a boy in Stinsford Church, and whose disappearance from Church of England worship he mourned, had non-Anglican origins. MOUNT EPHRAIM was written in the 1760s by Benjamin Milgrove, a shop-owner who was precentor at the Countess of Huntingdon's Chapel in Bath, and NEW SABBATH, which first appeared in 1802, was the work of Thomas Phillips, a Methodist brush-maker from Bristol. Both these tunes appeared regularly in Methodist hymnals throughout Victoria's reign although most Anglican collections rejected them. The same was true of a group of particularly lively fuguing tunes in the west gallery tradition whose Nonconformist and proletarian pedigree has kept them out of many Church of England collections to this day. They include the magnificent LYNGHAM, written for a Methodist village choir in Northamptonshire in 1803 by Thomas Jarman, a Baptist tailor, CREDITON, WARSAW and CRANBROOK (long used for 'While shepherds watched' but later hi-jacked for 'On Ilkley Moor Baht'at'), which were all the work of Thomas Clark, a cobbler and precentor at a Wesleyan Chapel in Canterbury, SAGINA by Thomas Campbell, first published in 1825, and MADRID which was written by a Nottinghamshire stocking maker, William Matthews.

In fairness, it should be said that John Wesley himself was not over-enamoured of the gallery tradition and the fuguing tunes which his followers chose for their hymns. His diary entry following a visit in 1768 to a parish church in Neath, where he had been invited to preach by the churchwardens, reveals a clear distaste for their imitative entries and repeated phrases.

Greatly disgusted at the manner of singing. 1. Twelve or fourteen persons kept it to themselves, and quite shut out the congregation: 2. These repeated the same words, contrary to all sense and reason, six or eight or ten times over: 3. According to the shocking custom of modern music, different persons sang different words at one and the same moment: an intolerable insult on common sense, and utterly incompatible with any devotion.[16]

It is not difficult to find examples in early nineteenth-century hymnody and psalmody of the practice that so offended Wesley whereby phrases, words or syllables were reiterated to fit a particular tune. One hymn began 'Stir up this stu, stir up this stu, stir up this stupid heart of mine' (which inevitably became 'stir up this stew') while a popular anthem, 'O for a mansion in the sky', which for obvious reasons became known as the spinster's prayer, began 'O for a man, O for a man'. Other unfortunate openings included 'My poor pol, my poor pol, my poor polluted heart' and 'Oh take thy mourning pil, Oh take thy mourning pil, Oh take thy mourning pilgrim home'. The tunes mentioned above, however, do not lend themselves to this kind of vain repetition any more than the earlier HELMSLEY (c.1765), which has justly been described as 'probably the greatest musical achievement of Methodism' and which even Anglican hymn-book editors (though not those responsible for the early editions of *Hymns Ancient and Modern*) have been magnanimous enough to concede is the perfect accompaniment for 'Lo, he comes with clouds descending'. Interestingly, the burgeoning of provincial, amateur, Nonconformist talent which produced these great Methodist melodies seems to have come to an end at the beginning of the Victorian era. The last of the great tunes which belong to this distinctive tradition, the thrilling DIADEM, was composed by James Ellor, an 18-year-old hat-maker, for the choir of the Wesleyan Methodist Chapel at Droylsden near Manchester in the year of the Queen's accession.

The contribution of Methodism in sowing the seeds for the full flowering of Victorian hymnody has been acknowledged by Erik Routley, the greatest authority on hymns in the twentieth century. 'Before about 1840', he writes, 'we still talk either of "psalm tunes" or of "Methodist hymns". Thereafter, it is, with an affectionate or patronizing air according to one's temperament, simply "hymns".'[17] We can also turn again to novels for confirmation of the extent to which in the pre-Victorian period hymn singing was seen essentially as a Dissenting or Methodist activity. To some extent, indeed, this perception continued throughout the nineteenth century. Although I have not made anything like a systematic trawl through all the sources – there is room for a thesis here if it has not been done already – I have the strong impression that when

Victorian novelists mention hymn singing (as they often do), the great majority of their references are to non-Anglicans doing the singing and to verses by Wesley or Watts being sung. George Eliot's *Adam Bede*, published in 1859 but set at the turn of the century, is a case in point. Although the novel begins with the eponymous hero, who is an Anglican, singing Bishop Ken's morning hymn as he carves a mantelpiece in the carpenter's shop where he works, it is the singing of two Methodists, Dinah Morris and Adam's brother Seth, to which the author alludes much more frequently and, indeed, that provide her story with some of its most moving movements. The first is when Dinah has finished preaching on the village green and says 'Let us sing a little, dear friends'. At this a stranger, who has looked on fascinated by her sermon, turns his horse aside and rides away 'and as he was still winding down the slope, the voices of the Methodists reached him, rising and falling in that strange blending of exaltation and sadness which belongs to the cadence of a hymn'.[18]

Later, Seth expresses his love for Dinah by turning to the words of a hymn by Isaac Watts.

Perhaps I feel more for you than I ought to feel for any creature, for I often can't help saying of you what the hymn says –

In darkest shades if she appear,
My dawning is begun;
She is my soul's bright morning-star,
And she my rising sun.[19]

Two further hymnological references in *Adam Bede* both quote from the hymns of Charles Wesley. Seth is portrayed walking home on a frosty February morning, 'mentally repeating one of his favourite hymns – he was very fond of hymns'. The particular verse which comes to his mind is 'Dark and cheerless is the morn, unaccompanied by thee' from 'Christ whose glory fills the skies'.[20] Later Dinah cheers herself as she is cleaning out Adam's cottage by singing 'Eternal Beam of Light Divine'.[21]

Wesley is also chosen for what is surely the most extensive quotation from hymnody to be found in any Victorian novel. Charlotte Bronte's *Shirley*, published in 1849 but set around 1811-2, describes the scene in Briar Chapel, 'a large, new, raw, Wesleyan place of worship':

As there was even now a prayer-meeting being held within its walls, the illumination of its windows cast a bright reflection on the road, while a hymn of a most extraordinary description, such as a very

Quaker might feel himself moved by the spirit to dance to, roused cheerily all the echoes of the vicinage. The words were distinctly audible by snatches: here is a quotation or two from different strains; for the singers passed jauntily from hymn to hymn and from tune to tune, with an ease and buoyancy all their own.[22]

The 'quotation or two' that follows consists of two pages of verses from hymns which are to be found in *The Collection of Hymns for the Use of the People Called Methodists*. Valentine Cunningham, who has pains-takingly identified the sources from which they come, has suggested on the evidence of slight mistakes over the shapes of some stanzas that Charlotte Bronte was quoting from memory rather than copying the hymns out of a book.[23]

The Bronte sisters provide an interesting example of Anglicans whose interest in hymns was largely kindled by Methodists. Their father, Patrick, although a Church of England clergyman, was well-disposed towards Methodism and attended the Methodist Chapel at Hawarden for Sunday evening worship. Tabitha Aykroyd, the live-in servant at the rectory for thirty years, was a devout Methodist and taught the sisters many Methodist hymns. A poem written by Anne Bronte in 1842 was dedicated to the great eighteenth-century evangelical Anglican poet, William Cowper, whose verses were to find their way into virtually every Victorian hymnbook:

> Sweet are thy strains, Celestial Bard.
> And oft in childhood's years
> I've read them o'er and o'er again
> With floods of silent tears.[24]

The fact that Anne Bronte writes of reading rather than singing Cowper's verses reminds us that even in a pro- Methodist and evangelical Anglican household, the singing of hymns was still regarded in the early years of Victoria's reign as a somewhat unseemly activity which smacked too much of subjective emotionalism and enthusiasm. The process by which hymns came to be acceptable to the established churches of England and Scotland was long and gradual. It began with the introduction of freer metrical versions of the psalms, notably Isaac Watts' Christianized verses such as 'Jesus shall reign where'er the sun' which abandoned literal adherence to scripture. In 1781 the General Assembly of the Church of Scotland, bowing somewhat reluctantly to pressure from evangelicals, agreed that metrical psalms could be supplemented by paraphrases of other parts of scripture, opening the way for the singing in church of 'O God of Bethel', 'Behold, the mountain of the Lord' and 'The race that long in darkness pined'. In fact, the paraphrases were never formally authorized – the 1781 Assembly simply allowed their temporary use by congregations if ministers approved – but this did not stop them catching on and winning their way into the Scottish heart. The book in which they were contained, and which was soon bound in with the Scottish Psalter, also included five hymns, among them Joseph Addison's 'The spacious firmament on high' and 'When all Thy mercies, O my God!'

A small number of hymns had also achieved semi-official recognition in the Church of England by the beginning of the nineteenth century. Prayer books were often bound together with Tate and Brady's Psalter and a collection of around a dozen hymns. One from 1816 includes 'Hark! the herald angels sing' for Christmas Day, three Easter hymns including 'Jesus Christ is risen today' and four communion hymns, among them Philip Doddridge's 'My God, and is thy table spread?' as well as metrical versions of the Lord's Prayer, the Apostles' Creed, the Magnificat and the Nunc Dimittis. Also to be found in this small collection are the morning and evening hymns of Bishop Ken, 'Awake, my soul, and with the sun' and 'Glory to thee, my God, this night', which we have already encountered respectively being sung by Adam Bede and being mistaken for a jig by the drunken gallery musicians of Longpuddle. Ken's evening hymn seems, in fact, to have been very commonly sung at evensong (which was often held in the afternoon) well into Victoria's reign, particularly in rural parish churches. Thomas Hardy's first published novel, *Desperate Remedies* (1871), has a description of this hymn being sung at the afternoon service at Carriford Church as experienced by the heroine, Cytheria Graye. From her square pew she 'looked at all the people as they stood and sang, waving backwards and forwards like a forest of pines swayed by the gentle breeze; then at the village children singing too, their heads inclined to one side, their eyes listlessly tracing some crack in the old walls, or following the movement of a distant bough or bird with features petrified almost to painfulness'.[25] Another vivid account of 'Glory to thee, my God, this night' being sung in a church service which was otherwise without hymns is provided by the children's author, Juliana Ewing, possibly drawing on her childhood experience in the 1840s and 50s in the vicarage at Ecclesfield, Yorkshire:

When the sermon was ended, and I had lost sight of the last grass-
hopper in my hasty rising, we found that there was to be a hymn. It
was the old custom of this church so to conclude Evening Prayer. No
one seemed to use a book – it was Bishop Ken's evening hymn, which
everyone knew, and, I think, every one sang . . . It sounded strangely
above the nasal tones of the schoolchildren, and the scraping of a
solitary fiddle.[26]

Another testimony to the enduring popularity of this hymn comes
from the recollections of William Walsham How, one of the greatest
Victorian hymn-writers. Shortly after taking up his first incumbency in
the Shropshire village of Whittington in 1851, he visited an elderly
couple who told him of their nightly routine.

The old man and me, sir, never go to bed without singing the Evening
Hymn. Not that I've got any voice left, for I haven't, and as for him,
he's like a bee in a bottle; and then he don't humour the tune, for he
don't rightly know one tune from another, and he can't remember the
words neither; so when he leaves out a word, I puts it in, and when I
can't sing I dances, and so we gets through it somehow.[27]

There was, of course, no ban on members of the established churches
singing hymns at home or at prayer meetings and other gatherings. It
was at such occasions that many English Anglicans and Scottish
Presbyterians first encountered the musical and spiritual delights of a
world beyond the bounds of metrical psalmody. It was, indeed, for use
at prayer meetings that Cowper's verses had been published together
with those of his great friend and collaborator, John Newton, in 1779 in
a volume entitled *Olney Hymns*. They were also much used at services
in schools, hospitals and other charitable institutions. Two early
nineteenth-century hymns which were to become firm favourites with
Victorian congregations, 'Praise the Lord! Ye heavens adore him' and
'Lead us, Heavenly Father, lead us' were written respectively for the
London Foundling Hospital and the London Orphan Asylum.
    Undoubtedly one of the factors which persuaded clergy in the Church
of England to introduce hymns into Mattins and Evensong was the
desertion of worshippers to the chapels of other denominations where
the singing, and indeed the whole style of worship, was much brighter
and livelier. As early as the 1760s, the Archbishop of Canterbury,
Thomas Secker, had pointed to the dreariness of a diet made up exclusively of metrical psalms and demanded that 'Something must be done

to put our psalmody on a better footing; the Sectarists gain a multitude of followers by their better singing' and in 1790 Beilby Porteus, Bishop of London, told the clergy of his diocese that of all the aspects of worship in the Church of England none was 'at so low an ebb' as the psalmody.[28] In similar vein, John Venn, rector of Clapham, and a leading member of the famous evangelical sect which included William Wilberforce and Sir Robert Grant, author of 'O worship the King', wrote to a friend in 1802: 'I am persuaded that the singing has been a great instrument in the Dissenters' hands of drawing away persons from the church, and why should not we take that instrument out of their hands?' Practising what he preached, Venn introduced congregational hymns and more singable versions of the psalms into his services. When attendance at Clapham Parish Church subsequently improved he was quite sure that this was at least in part attributable 'to the improved state of our singing which has been the means of keeping many from the meetings who were allured to go by the excellence of the music'.[29]

It was no coincidence that evangelical clergymen like Venn led the way in introducing hymns into Church of England services. They were closer than other Anglicans both theologically and liturgically to the Dissenters and Methodists. They were also heirs to the Evangelical Revival of the mid-eighteenth century which had produced such great Anglican poets as Cowper, Newton and Toplady, whose verses cried out to be sung. John Venn's father, Henry, Vicar of Huddersfield from 1759-71, was one of a number of evangelical clergy in Yorkshire who pioneered the reintroduction of chanted canticles and psalms and managed to persuade congregations to join in the Magnificat and Te Deum, which had hitherto been the exclusive preserve of the choir. Several incumbents started writing hymns and anthems and composing tunes specifically for congregational use. Prominent among them were John Darwall, Vicar of Walsall from 1769 to 1789, who wrote a new tune for each of the psalms, including the jaunty melody that now bears the name DARWALL's 148th, and T. O. Bartlett, Rector of Swanage from 1817 to 1841. In the words of Nicholas Temperley, the leading modern authority on the music of the English parish church: 'As a group the evangelicals opposed the vicarious psalmody that had developed both in town and country during the eighteenth century, and restored to the people their right to take part in the singing of praise. It was through them that both the hymn and the chanted psalm became accepted parts of congregational worship in the Church of England'.[30]

Not surprisingly, it was the activities of an evangelical clergyman which led to the lifting of the Church of England's prohibition on singing hymns in services. Thomas Cotterill, Vicar of St Paul's Church in Sheffield, produced a small hymn-book for his congregation in 1810. Nine years later he expanded it to include 367 hymns. He was greatly helped by James Montgomery, a radical journalist in Sheffield and the author of many hymns, including 'Stand up and bless the Lord' and 'Angels from the realms of glory'. A group within Cotterill's congregation objected to their vicar's innovation and took the matter to the York Consistory Court. The dispute was referred to the Archbishop of York, who ruled in 1820 that Cotterill's book must be withdrawn, but gave his blessing to a smaller collection of 146 hymns which he personally approved and paid for to be printed. 'The Archbishop's Selection', as it came to be known, was taken up by a good number of churches in the North of England and went through 29 editions. Thus, in a classic piece of Anglican compromise, the practice of hymn-singing was officially authorized in the Church of England, at least in its northern province, and at the same time kept under strict episcopal control.

Bishops in the southern province took rather longer to accept the legality of hymn singing in their churches. In the same year that the Archbishop of York brought out his hymn-book the Archbishop of Canterbury refused to authorize a highly orthodox and liturgically correct collection of hymns written and adapted by the High Anglican Reginald Heber for the weekly services of the church's year and the Bishop of Peterborough condemned the use of hymns in services as illegal. It was not until the first decade of Victoria's reign that hymns became fully accepted in the Church of England, and even then there were bishops and others who remained opposed to their use. In 1840 a correspondent to the *British Critic* fulminated:

> There cannot be a more miserable bondage than to be compelled to join in the so-called hymns which, rising and spreading from the conventicles, now infest our churches. They are full of passionate and exaggerated descriptions of moods of mind and unqualified descriptions of spiritual experience.[31]

It was partly because of the strength of this lingering opposition that Anglicans lacked a major national denominational hymn-book for so long. The great majority of the forty hymn-books which John Julian lists as having been produced in the Church of England between 1800 and 1840 were highly localized publications, produced by enthusiastic incumbents for their own congregations. By contrast, several of the main Nonconformist bodies produced comprehensive hymnals in this period which were used throughout the country. Wesleyan Methodists retained the 1780 collection as their core book, adding a supplement in 1831. Primitive Methodists produced their own 'Large Hymnbook' in 1825. Baptists sang from a range of books, depending on their theological persuasion. Those of a strict and Calvinistic bent tended to use either the selection of hymns first published in 1814 by William Gadsby, minister of a Baptist Chapel in Manchester, or a hymnal published for Particular Baptist congregations in 1828. More liberal Baptists sang from either the *Union Collection of Hymns* of 1827 or the *General Baptist Hymnbook* of 1830. From 1836 Congregationalists had their own hymn-book, a fine collection of 620 hymns compiled by Josiah Conder, the editor of the *Eclectic Review*. The nearest equivalent to these books in the Church of England was the *Church Psalmody* compiled by Edward Bickersteth, Vicar of Watton, and published in 1833. It proved enormously popular, selling 150,000 copies within a few months of its publication, but its use was largely confined to evangelical parishes and it never achieved the status of a comprehensive national Anglican hymnal. For the most part hymns were being introduced to Anglican congregations on an *ad hoc* basis by evangelical clergy like John Rashdall, who after one month as curate in sole charge of Orby in Lincolnshire decided to replace metrical psalmody with hymn singing 'as more simple, and liked by the poor'.[32]

The extent to which the introduction of hymns into Church of England services was perceived as essentially an evangelical activity is clearly brought out in George Eliot's story 'Amos Barton' in her *Scenes of Clerical Life*. The reign of the west gallery minstrels at Shepperton Church with their psalms and exuberant anthems is brought to an abrupt end with the arrival in the 1830s of 'a zealous Evangelical preacher'. Very different from the much-loved previous incumbent, Mr Gilfil, 'who smoked very long pipes and preached very short sermons', this new unnamed vicar introduces a new regime of long sermons and the supplanting of the Old and New Versions of the Psalms by the hymn-book. His successor, Amos Barton, another evangelical, continues these undesirable innovations, being in the words of one disgruntled parishioner 'a confounded, methodistical, meddlesome chap . . . all for hymns and a sort o'music as I can't join in at all'.[33] Barton causes particular offence when he silences the traditional wedding psalm (Psalm 133) which had been spontaneously sung in church for every newly-married couple for generations 'and gave a hymn out himself to some meeting-house tune'.[34] The tune is later revealed to be LYDIA which another parishioner complains he is always hearing as he passes the Independent Chapel.

This last incident introduces us to one of the fascinating by-ways of English hymnody and, indeed, of the English class system. Amos Barton's parishioners were not alone in protesting about a tune because of its non-Anglican origins and connotations. I have elsewhere pointed to that extraordinary and unique feature of English life (it does not apply to anything like the same extent in the rest of the United Kingdom) whereby you can tell someone's denominational upbringing, and by implication also something of their background and social class, by what tune they use for certain hymns – 'O for a thousand tongues' and 'All hail the power of Jesu's name' are particular giveaways in this respect, both having distinct Anglican and Nonconformist tunes.[35] Snobbery has sadly intruded its way into hymnody as into so many other areas of life. At least it is good to know that some Anglican congregations were not as snooty about LYDIA as those at Shepperton. It is one of the tunes Thomas Hardy pencilled in the Psalms section of his Prayer Book as having been used at Stinsford Church. He also refers to his father playing it on the viol during his time in the gallery band at Puddletown, suggesting that this fine vigorous common metre tune must be older than its first known appearance in a collection of psalm and hymn tunes in 1844. In *The Return of the Native* Hardy describes it being used for a particularly rousing rendition of Psalm 133. The tune is used twice in the 1983 Methodist *Hymns and Psalms* and also features in the new Baptist hymnal, but I am sorry to say that it is still missing from virtually every Anglican hymn-book.

The contribution made by evangelical Anglicans and Dissenters in the early nineteenth century to the development of English hymnody was enormous. They established the hymn as a vehicle for expressing personal devotion and expounding sound doctrine. They promoted congregational singing and ensured that the naves as well as the galleries of churches were ringing with the sound of music. They composed rousing and thrilling tunes which enhanced the dramatic power and effect of the great poetry which came out of the Evangelical Revival. Set to these vigorous melodies, the verses of Isaac Watts and Charles Wesley, William Cowper and John Newton, Augustus Toplady and Philip Doddridge, were to be among the Victorians' favourite hymns and remain hugely popular today. Yet had only Evangelicals and Dissenters been promoting it in this period, hymn singing would never have become quite as central an activity in Victorian religious life as it did. What really established the hymn as the characteristic expression of Victorian religious sentiment, and as the icon of the Victorian church, was its championship by those in the High Church and Oxford movements.

We have already encountered one of the first and most important High Church enthusiasts for hymnody in the person of Reginald Heber, vicar of Hodnet in Shropshire from 1807 to 1823. Soon after his installation, he asked a friend where he could get hold of Cowper and Newton's *Olney Hymns* – 'some of them I admire much, and any novelty is likely to become a favourite, and draw more people to join in the singing'.[36] In his Sunday services Heber introduced hymns to illustrate the Bible readings prescribed in the Book of Common Prayer for that particular day. In that way, he circumvented two of the main objections to hymns from the High Church point of view – that they failed to reflect the church's calendar and had no liturgical underpinning or relationship with the Prayer Book. Heber's demonstration that they could in fact be used to enhance liturgical propriety and were not simply expressions of individual feeling and subjective emotion did much to win Anglican converts to hymns from beyond the ranks of the evangelicals.

Drawing on material that he had gathered for his services at Hodnet and which he had first published in the evangelical periodical, the *Christian Observer*, Heber set about producing a book which would provide appropriate hymns for every Sunday and festival of the church's year. All the 98 hymns in the collection had impeccable Anglican credentials – 57 were his own compositions and a further 13 were written by his friend, Henry Hart Milman, son of a baronet, Eton and Oxford educated, Vicar of St Mary's, Reading, and a future Dean of St Paul's. Addison, Cowper, Dryden, Pope, Sternhold and Hopkins and Bishop Ken were all represented and not a single non-Anglican figured in the list of contributors. Heber admitted to having some 'high church scruples against using (hymns) in public', but in the preface he pointed out that the hymns, which were designed to be sung between the Creed and the sermon, each had some reference to the Collect and Gospel prescribed for the day they were set. They were, he suggested, preferable to 'a few verses of the Psalms, entirely unconnected with the peculiar devotions of the day, and selected at the discretion of the clerk or organist'.[37]

Heber was well aware of the reception his book was likely to receive in many quarters and was defensive and cautious about promoting it. He assured prospective users that 'no fulsome or indecorous language has been knowingly adopted; no erotic addresses to Him whom no unclean lips can approach; no allegory, ill understood and worse applied'. When he wrote to the Bishop of London in 1820 seeking episcopal approval for the project, his tone was distinctly grovelling.

I began this work with the intention of using it in my own Church, a liberty which, I need not tell your Lordship, has been, for many years back, pretty generally taken by the clergy, and which, if custom alone were to be our guide, would seem almost sufficiently authorised. Thus the morning and evening hymn of Bishop Ken are, in country parishes, almost universally used. Hardly a collection is made for charitable purposes without a hymn being sung . . .

Under these circumstances, my Lord, I feel I am taking a great liberty, but one for which I hope I shall be pardoned, in requesting to know whether you think it possible or advisable for me to obtain the kind of permission for the use of my hymns in Churches as was given to Tate?[38]

In fact, the Bishop of London refused to authorize the hymn-book and, as we have already seen, Heber got an equally negative response from the Archbishop of Canterbury. It was not until 1827, a year after Heber's death from drowning in a swimming pool where he was seeking to cool off from his duties as Bishop of Calcutta, that his widow was given permission to publish the collection. They were to be an important quarry for later hymn-book editors. Three of Heber's own compositions 'Holy, Holy, Holy', written to be sung on Trinity Sunday, 'Brightest and best of the sons of the morning', for Epiphany, and 'From Greenland's icy mountains', for use before a collection made for the Society for the Propagation of the Gospel, were to become firm Victorian favourites, as was Milman's Palm Sunday contribution, 'Ride on, ride on, in majesty'.

Another book published in 1827 by a High Churchman of a rather different hue was also to provide the Victorians with some of their best-loved hymns. Like Heber's collection, John Keble's *The Christian Year*, was designed to provide a devotional lyric for every Sunday and major festival in the church's calendar, including the commemorations of King Charles the Martyr and the Gunpowder Plot. Unlike Heber, however, the young Gloucestershire curate who was soon to be at the centre of the Oxford Movement did not write his verses to be sung. They were intended, in Owen Chadwick's memorable phrase, 'not for the congregation but for the soul at his bedside'.[39] Although Keble himself used the word 'hymns' to describe his work, he was very uneasy about having it published. He consulted a number of friends on the matter, including Samuel Taylor Coleridge and Richard Hurrell Froude, who felt that there was 'something which I should call Sternhold-and-Hopkinsy about the diction'.[40] After much agonizing, Keble decided to publish his collected devotional poems anonymously. *The Christian Year* became a Victorian best-seller. By the end of the century it had gone through more than 170 editions and sold over half a million copies. No book of secular poetry came near to matching its popularity. Five years before his death eleven of Keble's poems were put into *Hymns Ancient and Modern*, among them 'New every morning is the love', 'Blest are the pure in heart' and 'Sun of my soul, Thou Saviour dear'.

The fact that Keble wrote his verses for private devotional use rather than congregational singing indicates the unease that was still felt in High Church circles about hymns on the eve of the Victorian era. Some clergy were happy to countenance the new movement towards freer congregational singing in services, provided that it remained solidly based on the psalms. A case in point is Henry Francis Lyte, who in 1834 published *The Spirit of the Psalms*, a collection of metrical versions of the psalms to fit every Sunday of the church year, among them 'Praise, my soul, the King of heaven' (Psalm 103), 'God of mercy, God of grace' (Psalm 67) and 'Pleasant are thy Courts above' (Psalm 84). Like the verses of Heber and Keble, Lyte's work displays a cultivated, literary quality which distinguishes it from some, though by no means all, of the hymns of eighteenth and early nineteenth-century evangelicalism and Dissent. In his seminal work, *The English Hymn*, Louis Benson has gone so far as to identify a distinct genre, 'the literary hymn', exemplified particularly in the writings of Heber, Keble and Milman. He sees it as a product of the Romantic movement and points out that such figures as Coleridge, Shelley and Wordsworth also wrote hymns. Indeed, Wordsworth's 'The Labourer's Noon-day hymn' which begins 'Up to the throne of God is borne' was much used in village schools well into the Victorian period.[41]

The literary quality of these early High Church hymns is certainly striking. It was to remain an important element in the next wave of High Church hymnody but even more crucial were matters ecclesiological, theological and historical. What really made hymn singing not just respectable but positively valued within this part of the Church of England in the early years of Victoria's reign was its enthusiastic espousal by those in the van of the Oxford Movement. Tractarians found themselves in total agreement with evangelicals in wanting to get rid of metrical psalms and disorderly gallery choirs. They differed, however, over what should replace them. Where evangelicals wanted lively congregational hymns of experiential faith expressing the doctrines of conversion and atonement, Tractarians dreamed of robed choirs intoning the chants of the early church. For them, metrical psalms were an unappealing product of the Reformation. Better by far to restore the traditional psalmody of the church, chanted, preferably in Latin, to Gregorian or other modes. At the heart of the Oxford Movement was a desire to return to the catholicity, universality and doctrinal orthodoxy of the pre-Reformation church. How better to express this than by singing again, to ancient melodies, the Latin and Greek office hymns of the early Christian centuries and the verses of Ambrose, Augustine and later mediaeval lyricists? Antiquarian research revealed that hymns had been an integral part of both the Mass and the daily offices in the mediaeval Catholic Church. It was as a vehicle for catholicizing Anglican worship that Tractarians seized on hymnody and made it a key element in their crusade to sweep away everything modern and reformed.

One of the first results of this new-found High Church enthusiasm for hymn singing was the production in 1836 of *Psalms and Hymns Adapted to the Services of the Church of England*. The work of W. J. Hall, Vicar of Tottenham, 'The Mitre', as it came to be known because of the suitably episcopal symbol on its cover, included 400 hymns and psalms and sold over four million copies. The opening years of Victoria's reign also saw the appearance of a number of significant Tractarian-inspired collections of ancient hymns in new English translations. John Henry Newman had pointed to the Church of England's neglect of Latin hymnody in his *Tracts for the Times* in 1836. His fellow Tractarians lost no time in remedying this deficiency. First off the mark was John Chandler, Vicar of Witley in Surrey, whose *Hymns of the Primitive Church*, published in 1837, included his very free translation of a Latin lyric which was to become the popular Advent hymn 'On Jordan's bank the Baptist's cry'. He was closely followed by Richard Mant, Bishop of Down and Connor, who brought out *Ancient Hymns from the Roman Breviary for Domestic Use* later in the same year. Although the bulk of this book was made up, as its title suggests, of translations from Latin originals, Mant also appended a number of his own compositions, one of which, 'Bright the vision that delighted', was destined to give generations of children puzzled amusement as to who or what was Judas' ear. In 1839 Isaac Williams, a leading Oxford Tractarian and close friend of Newman and Keble, published *Hymns translated from the Paris Breviary* and in 1849 Edward Caswall, who two years earlier had followed Newman out of the Church of England and joined his oratory at Birmingham, produced *Lyra Catholica, containing the Hymns at Vespers, Compline and Benediction, with those in the Office of the Blessed Virgin and in the Missal.* Despite its strongly Romish flavour, this last collection was to furnish Victorian Anglicans with a clutch of favourite hymns including 'Days and moments, quickly flying', 'Jesus, the very thought of Thee', 'My God, I love Thee, not because I hope for heaven thereby' and 'When morning gilds the skies' as well as a particularly fine translation of the *Stabat Mater*, 'At the Cross, her station keeping'.

Not all of these translations were made for use in public worship. Nor were the verses on which they were based always quite as primitive and ancient as they were made to appear. The Paris Breviary from which Williams took his hymns, for example, dated only from 1736 and several of Caswall's translations were based on seventeenth and eighteenth-century originals. Nonetheless, the effect of the work of these men, and of others who followed in their wake, was to make available to the growing Catholic wing of the Church of England a body of hymnody with impeccably Catholic credentials for liturgical use. There was still resistance in certain quarters to singing ancient hymns in English. Newman catered for such purists with his two volumes of *Hymni Ecclesiae* (1838) which printed the original Latin texts. By the 1850s, however, most High Church Anglicans had come round to the idea of congregations singing hymns in the vernacular.

One man did more than anyone else to persuade his fellow Tractarians of the liturgical and theological value of singing hymns in English. Interestingly, he himself underwent a complete change of heart on the subject of hymnody. Like so many of those at the forefront of the Oxford Movement, John Mason Neale was brought up in an evangelical home and reacted strongly against the hymns that he had been forced to learn as a child. In 1840, as the 22-year-old chaplain of Downing College, Cambridge, he wrote to a friend of his 'general dislike of hymns'.[42] He felt that they encouraged a dangerously subjective emotionalism and often peddled false doctrines. His particular anathema was the work of Isaac Watts which he regarded as far too personal and experiential. It was, indeed, this hostility that inspired Neale's own first venture into hymnody. Realizing that whether he liked it or not, hymns were gaining in use and popularity, he wrote a set of verses in 1843 'to free our poor children from the yoke of Watts'.[43] The tone of his *Hymns for Children* was as didactically Catholic as that of Watts was evangelical:

> I am a little Catholic,
> And Christian is my name,
> And I believe in Holy Church
> In every age the same.

> And I believe the English Church
> To be a part of her,
> The Holy Church throughout the world
> That cannot fail or err.

It was, however, as an antiquarian and an ecclesiologist rather than as a children's versifier that Neale was to have most impact on Victorian hymnody. In 1839 he was instrumental in founding the Cambridge Camden Society, later the Ecclesiological Society, which became one of the main agencies for promoting the liturgical principles of the Oxford Movement and putting them into practice in parish churches up and down the land. One of the great enthusiams of its members was the recovery of the ancient office hymns of the Church and they regularly gathered to sing them in the original Latin. A favourite venue for these antiquarian singing sessions was the parlour of Brasted Rectory in Kent where the rector, Dr W.H. Hill, another enthusiast, 'would approach the piano with hands clasped, his grand old sculptured face lighted up with holy fire, like a medieval saint out of a stained glass window, and there lift up his voice in O *Lux beata, Vexilla Regis*, or *Aeterna Christ Munera*'.[44] Hill's curate at Brasted, Benjamin Webb, was equally committed to preserving these ancient verses in their original Latin versions and deeply uneasy about those Tractarians who translated them into English and wanted to jump on to the hymn-singing bandwagon. He wrote to Neale in 1849, accusing him of having failed to cast off 'the slough of Evangelicalism':

> I am more and more convinced that the age of hymns has passed. Happy are those who can use the Latin ones; with our vernacular we

have lost our privilege . . . the translation into English has reduced everything to common sense – the curse or glory (as you choose) of our present ritual . . . I doubt, in short, the possibility of the language of common life, in such an age as this, being fit for this sort of composition.[45]

Neale had no time for this kind of obscurantist antiquarianism. Pointing out that Tractarians were quite happy with the Prayer Book in English, he asked Webb, 'why should Hymns be less Catholick than prayers and, therefore, why English Hymns less Catholick than English prayers?'[46] Through the force of his arguments, and because of his own undoubted scholarship and attachment to both the spirit and the letter of the ancient Latin hymns (of which he himself produced an original language edition in 1851), he succeeded in winning round fellow members of the Ecclesiological Society to his position. Indeed, he persuaded them to sponsor him in a major project which involved translating the hymns of the early church and publishing them together with the original ancient melodies.

Altogether, Neale produced four major volumes of English hymns either translated from or based on ancient originals. *Medieval Hymns and Sequences* appeared in 1851 and was closely followed by the first part of *The Hymnal Noted*. This was the main project sponsored by the Ecclesiological Society and involved collaboration with Thomas Helmore, Master of the Choristers at the Chapel Royal and Chaplain-in-Ordinary to Queen Victoria, who edited the music. The Hymnal, the second part of which came out in 1854, provided in vernacular and accessible form 105 hymns and melodies that had been sung in English churches before the Reformation. It was taken up in a number of Tractarian parishes – three London churches used it as their only hymn-book until 1895 – but its main impact was as a source book for later hymnal editors. In 1862 Neale completed his work with *Hymns of the Eastern Church*. This book broke new ground in translating hymns from the Greek rather than the more common Latin. Neale had a strong attachment to the Orthodox tradition and hoped for close rapprochement and eventual reunion between the Anglican and Eastern Orthodox churches. He felt that by translating the early hymns of the Eastern Church he could bring something of the richness of Orthodox liturgy and spirituality to English-speaking Christians.

Neale felt that his work created a solid foundation for Anglican hymnody that was orthodox, catholic, objective and doctrinally sound as well as deeply devotional. While highly scholarly in his approach, following the exact measure and rhythm of the original wherever possible, he had a natural poetic talent and a facility for clear expression which made his translations popular with Victorian Christians of virtually every denomination and theological hue. Two of his freest translations, which were virtually his own original compositions, 'Art thou weary, art thou languid?' and 'Safe home, safe home in port', appealed enormously to the religious taste of his contemporaries. Despite his own Catholic sympathies, which were to land him in deep trouble with his own bishop, he was sensitive enough to Protestant feeling to play down the central role accorded to the Virgin Mary in much ancient and Orthodox hymnody. Indeed, he ran into considerable criticism among Roman Catholics for toning down or ignoring the Roman doctrines in the hymns he translated. Among his most enduring contributions to English hymnody are 'Christ is made the sure foundation', 'Jerusalem the golden', 'Come ye faithful, raise the strain', 'The day of resurrection, earth tell it out abroad', 'Of the father's love begotten' and his original Christmas carols 'Good King Wenceslas' and 'Good Christian men, rejoice'.

Thanks to Neale, hymn singing now became an Anglo-Catholic as well as an evangelical passion within the Church of England. Whereas in the 1820s and 1830s it had been evangelical clergy who had replaced the old-style metrical psalmody with congregational hymns, in the 1840s and 1850s it was predominantly Tractarian incumbents who swept away the old gallery musicians and introduced organs and robed choirs to lead the singing. Once again we can turn to fiction for confirmation and illustration of this trend. The arrival of a Tractarian at Stinsford Church in the early 1840s spelt doom for the gallery band in which Thomas Hardy's father played. The novelist almost certainly had this in mind when he described the tussle between the new organ-loving vicar of Mellstock and the old church musicians in *Under the Greenwood Tree*. The hero of Samuel Butler's *The Way of All Flesh*, Ernest Pontifex, returns to his father's church in the mid-1860s and notes 'that the ever receding tide of Evangelicalism had ebbed a stage lower'. Among the signs of creeping high churchmanship that he notices are his father's abandonment of Geneva bands and adoption of a surplice, the disappearance of psalms with complex orchestral accompaniment in favour of chanted canticles and the arrival of *Hymns Ancient and Modern*.[47] As Nicholas Temperley has pointed out, the practice of hymn singing was now firmly embedded in the services of the

Church of England.

The adoption of hymnody by the Tractarians, who eventually carried with them the more reluctant high churchmen, meant that hymns were now an established part of Anglican worship, accepted with enthusiasm by all parties within the Church. Whatever difficultie there might be in persuading congregations to chant the psalms of sing the responses, there was no doubt that they could sing the hymns.[48]

'The playing of the merry organ, sweet singing in the choir'

Musical and cultural influences

The fact that Victorian congregations could sing hymns – and sing them very well – owed a good deal to a musical revolution in mid-nineteenth-century Britain which was just as important in its effects on worship in general, and hymnody in particular, as the Evangelical Revival and the Oxford Movement. The old régime of gallery bands performing to largely passive congregations did not just offend the theological and liturgical sensibilities of the clergy. It was also anathema to a new breed of musical educators who exemplified the Victorian passion for cultural improvement and popular participation. They were at one with Evangelicals and Tractarians in deploring the dreariness of much metrical psalmody, the vulgarity of the florid gallery anthems with their instrumental accompaniments and the practice of congregations sitting and for the most part remaining silent for the musical parts of services. In place of these old ways the reformers championed the ideal of full-blooded congregational hymn singing to organ accompaniment as the main musical feature of worship. That this became the norm in the great majority of churches during the middle decades of Victoria's reign was a tribute to the vigour and success of the crusade that these musical missionaries mounted to popularize communal singing and establish the organ as the proper instrument for Christian praise.

It is not difficult to find criticisms of the poor musical standards prevailing in churches of all denominations in the 1820s and 30s. A contributor to the *Congregational Magazine* of 1825 complained of 'vociferation' and 'nasal twang' in congregational singing.[1] An important treatise on the state of music in the Church of England, published in 1831 by John Antes La Trobe, curate at St Peter's, Hereford, complained that psalms were sung too slowly and to unseemly settings. He cited the inappropriate use of the melody of 'Drink to me only with thine eyes' which appeared as PROSPECT in several church tune books. La Trobe listed the main evils of contemporary practice as 'singing out of tune, frequently too flat, with a nasal twang, straining the voice to an unnatural pitch, introducing awkward drawls and tasteless ornaments . . . thus the solemn chords of a good tune are most crudely frothed into absurd decorations'. He singled out for particular condemnation 'the scream, the pert snap, the buzzing bass, the rude and violent pronunciation and the deafening thump of the timekeeper, which resembles that of the tilt-hammer of some furnace'.[2] The first volume of Vincent Novello's *The Psalmist*, which appeared in 1835 and was among the earliest of several publications that attempted to provide good, singable hymn tunes for congregational use, commented that the only people who cared about singing in church were 'the Wesleyans and Dissenters', but went on to complain that they had 'generally degraded its quality by the admission of light and trivial music'.[3]

There had, in fact, been moves on the part of several churches to improve the standard of singing in the late eighteenth and early nineteenth centuries. The Methodists, as we have already seen, led the way with hearty and uninhibited congregational participation in tunes like LYNGHAM and HELMSLEY. In the Church of Scotland, too, the old painfully slow style of singing, with every verse lined out, had given way in many places to a brisker and more musical rendition of the psalms with congregations singing in four-part harmony. The instigator of this new method was an English Methodist, Thomas Channon, a soldier stationed with Government troops in Aberdeenshire in the aftermath of the Jacobite rebellions. Initially this new 'scientific singing', as it came to be known, aroused considerable opposition from traditionalists and there were dramatic scenes in several Aberdeen churches when congregations singing in the old and slow way tried to drown out the more vigorous tempi being set by Channon's followers. Gradually, however, the reformers won and, as part of a general choral revival in early nineteenth-century Scotland, several churches started choirs. An important centre of this new movement for better musical standards in the Kirk was St George's Church, Edinburgh, where the minister from 1814 to 1831, Andrew Thomson, was an accomplished composer. His psalm tune, ST GEORGE'S, EDINBURGH, is still used to accompany the verses of Psalm 24 which are sung at the 'great entrance' of the elements at communion services in the Church of Scotland. In 1823 Thomson appointed a talented musician, Robert Smith, as precentor and leader of psalmody at St George's. Smith composed a number of tunes which have some affinity with the fuguing tunes of the gallery tradition and Methodism but are altogether more restrained and sober, among them INVOCATION which is still regularly used for the metrical version of verses three to five of Psalm 43 ('O send thy light forth and thy truth').

The Church of England also experienced a movement for 'correct singing' in this period but it was sporadic and not altogether beneficial in its effects. While most country churches retained their gallery bands, in towns and cities choirs were introduced, often made up of children from local charity schools. Although their contribution to worship was often limited both in volume and musicianship, Anglican diffidence on the part of the congregation often meant that choir members were the only people singing in church. As late as 1843 John Hullah, one of the most important of the musical reformers of the early Victorian period, complained that in most Anglican churches 'Congregations generally do not sing at all . . . The praise of God is left to the charity children – it is not genteel to sing in church.'[4]

To remedy the sorry state of music in most churches reformers like La Trobe and Hullah proposed the introduction of properly-trained choirs, pipe organs and simpler and more dignified hymn tunes. These were also dear to the hearts of clergy influenced by the Oxford Movement and in many places Tractarians and musical reformers worked hand in hand to eliminate metrical psalmody, instrumental bands and barrel organs. Perhaps the most striking result of their collaboration was the appearance in parish church chancels of robed or surpliced choirs singing services of a kind that had hitherto been heard only in cathedrals. The first English parish church to have a choir of this kind was probably St Mary Magdalene in Newark on Trent in 1814. Leeds Parish Church followed suit four years later and in 1841 introduced daily sung services on the cathedral pattern. In Ireland John Jebb, Vicar of Coleraine, started choral services in his church in 1834. In London the choral revival initially centred on the Margaret Chapel, Marylebone where in 1839 the incumbent, Frederick Oakeley, introduced the chanting of psalms to Gregorian tones and Anglican chant, the singing of Tudor settings of the communion service and the use of printed leaflets with hymns for feast days. Among those who worshipped at the Chapel was the young William Ewart Gladstone who commented that the worship was at once devout and hearty and also expressed his appreciation that the sermon never lasted more than twenty minutes. Oakeley was hounded out of the Church of England for his ritualistic practices and converted to Roman Catholicism in 1845. The Margaret Chapel, re-built as All Saints, Margaret Street, remained a centre of Anglo-Catholic worship. The organist, Richard Redhead, composed several highly successful tunes including PETRA.

The introduction of robed and trained chancel choirs did not necessarily encourage congregational hymn singing. Indeed, in many ways they were just as much wedded to a performance ethic as the old gallery choirs had been and their repertoire was often even more arcane and inaccessible. This was not surprising given the largely antiquarian agenda that motivated some of the leading figures in the choral revival. Just as the more romantic Tractarians looked longingly back to the liturgy and ecclesiology of the Middle Ages, so musical purists wished to reinstate in everyday worship the pure sound of Gregorian plainsong and the chants used for psalms and canticles in mediaeval cathedrals. Much effort went into digging out and publishing ancient tunes and chants. One of the first compilations of such material was produced in 1827 by John Goss, organist of St Luke's Chelsea and subsequently organist at St Paul's Cathedral for thirty-four years. In 1836 William Crotch, first Principal of the Royal Academy of Music, brought out a volume of *Psalm Tunes selected for the use of Cathedrals and Parish Churches*. He hoped his work would foster a general return to ancient melodies in worship and an abandonment of the more recent tunes 'made out of songs, glees and quartetts'.[5] In 1847 William Havergal, who had devoted himself to researching mediaeval church music after a carriage accident forced him to give up his clerical duties at Astley in Worcestershire, published *Old Church Psalmody*. Perhaps the supreme exemplar of this antiquarian-restorationist school was Thomas Helmore, master of the choristers of the Chapel Royal, who produced the *Psalter Noted* in 1849 and subsequently collaborated with J. M. Neale, finding suitably ancient tunes for his translations of Latin and Greek hymns.

Several of the leading figures in the choral revival that took place in the Church of England between 1830 and 1870 had no desire to see this restored treasury of ancient music restricted simply to choirs. They had a vision of congregations singing William Merbecke's settings of the communion service, intoning psalms to mediaeval chants and even tackling plainsong. To some extent this dream was realized. Many Victorian congregations did take up Merbecke and the chanting of prose psalms and canticles. Indeed, they remained the staple fare of

Anglican worship until the 1960s and 70s. However, the main result of the choral revival, as its leading historian, Bernarr Rainbow, has demonstrated, was, in fact, further to separate choir and congregation and to foster the development of a distinct repertoire of church music which was for trained singers only. In part this unintended development came about because of a split within the ranks of church musicians. While Oakeley, Redhead and Helmore, whose *Manual of Plainsong* was published in 1849, hoped that a revived Gregorian plainchant would become the mainstay of congregational singing, another group, led by S. S. Wesley, organist at Leeds Parish Church from 1842, and E. J. Hopkins, organist at the Temple Church, London, favoured Anglican prose chant confined to the choir as found in cathedrals.[6] In the event, the cathedral pattern of sung services, with canticles, psalms and anthems, became the model which many parish church choirs sought to follow while congregations prefered to sing hymns to modern tunes. The movement towards cathedral-style choirs in parish churches was given a considerable boost in 1856 when Sir Frederick Gore Ouseley founded St Michael's College, Tenbury Wells, as a model choir school and training establishment with daily choral services. The same year saw St Paul's Cathedral and Westminster Abbey bow to public taste and introduce services largely shorn of elaborate choral adornments and consisting of prayers, a sermon and several hymns.

Although church choirs rapidly developed their own brand of élitism and performance mentality, they did often provide a lead and stimulus for more congregational participation in worship. Their arrival often coincided with the introduction of hymns, as at the Margaret Chapel where Frederick Oakeley's successor, George Cosby White, produced a book of *Hymns and Introits* in 1852. Another notable London Tractarian church where the role of the choir was very much seen as being to lead and encourage congregational singing was St Matthias, Stoke Newington, where W. H. Monk was organist from 1852. It is noticeable that two of the greatest Victorian hymn-writers were strong supporters of the new parish choir movement. One of William Walsham How's first actions when he became rector of Whittington in 1851 was to get rid of the church's barrel organ and replace it with a choir of seven boys in Eton collars and blue ties whom he often accompanied himself on the flute. John Ellerton introduced a surpliced choir, with the girl members in white dresses, to his last parish, White Roding in Essex, when he moved there in 1885.

The replacement of the old west gallery bands by the much more 'churchily' clad choirs in their prominent pews in front of the altar was almost certainly the most visible result of the choral movement that began just as Victoria came to the throne. It was not, however, as important for fostering congregational hymn singing, and for the whole development and prominence of the Victorian hymn, as was another less obvious but more widespread movement in British musical life that took place at the same time. The first two decades of Queen Victoria's reign saw a burst of musical education and an explosion of popular interest and involvement in choral singing unparalleled before or since. In part this was the result of a Government initiative. As part of a wider drive for national education, Lord Melbourne's Whig administration sponsored mass weekly singing classes in London's Exeter Hall from 1839 to 1841. The moving spirit in this venture was Dr James Kay, first Secretary of the Committee of the Privy Council for Education. He had been greatly influenced by a lecture given on the 'Use of Singing as Part of the Moral Discipline of Schools'. Kay was convinced that singing would improve the morals of schoolchildren and so of the nation. The classes which he organized were aimed particularly at school teachers. To teach them he hired John Hullah, organist at Croydon Parish Church, whose concern at the silence of most congregations during the sung parts of services we have already noted. Hullah had made a special study of methods of vocal instruction in Paris and he brought to the task of teaching singing a new and distinctive technique as well as dashing good looks, an almost permanently cheerful disposition and a fund of anecdotes with which he spiced his lessons. His popularity and influence were enormous. By the end of 1841 it was estimated that over 50,000 working-class children in London were learning singing from teachers taught by him. Altogether, over the twenty years that he taught singing, more than 25,000 people passed through his classes.

John Hullah was also closely involved in another important early Victorian educational venture to promote singing which was more 'churchy' in its emphasis. In 1841 the Church of England set up its first national training establishment, St Mark's College, Chelsea, to train teachers for the National (i.e. Church of England) primary schools that were being set up across the country. Singing – and especially choral singing in the context of the standard Anglican service – was put at the heart of the curriculum, not surprisingly, perhaps when this was in the hands of the college's Vice Principal and precentor, Thomas Helmore. Hullah was engaged to teach the singing classes and the college's alumni went out across England, fired with his enthusiasm to teach singing in schools and often to set up choirs in their local parish churches.

It was not just Anglicans who were touched by the choral revival and the new enthusiasm for singing. F. W. Faber, who like Oakeley switched from Anglican to Roman orders in the 1840s, introduced popular English congregational hymns, many written by himself, into his otherwise exclusively Latin evening services at the London Oratory (later the Brompton Oratory) which he established in 1849. While few other Roman Catholics followed his lead, Nonconformists were not surprisingly in the forefront of moves to popularize communal singing and encourage congregations to develop greater musical expertise. Congregationalists were particularly active in both of these areas. John Curwen, pastor at Plaistow in Essex from 1844 to 1867, developed and promoted the tonic solfa system which had been invented by Sarah Ann Glover, a Norwich schoolmistress, in the early 1830s. He used the system to teach singing in his own chapel and in local schools and lectured on its benefits around the country. In 1853 he was instrumental in founding the Tonic Solfa Association and in 1862 the Tonic Solfa College. In 1867 Curwen resigned from his charge and established a printing and publishing business to make solfa material more widely and cheaply available. Curwen's interest was always first and foremost in teaching people to sing in church and particularly in encouraging the habit among Sunday School pupils. *The Child's Own Hymn Book* that he compiled in 1846 went through several enlargements and was one of the most widely-used hymnals in Victorian Sunday Schools.

Another leading enthusiast for improved singing in church was Thomas Binney, minister of King's Weigh House Chapel in London from 1829 and the leading Congregational minister in the capital during the early decades of Victoria's reign. In 1848 he wrote an essay on 'The service of song in the House of the Lord', which argued for an end to the old practices of lining out hymns and psalms, using precentors and pitch pipes and accompanying the praise on stringed and wind instruments. Following his lead and under his influence, the ministers of many urban Congregational churches introduced organs and robed choirs. The one at Rusholme Road Congregational Church in Manchester was trained and conducted by Charles Dickens' sister, Fanny Burnett, and her husband, Harry. More rural and remote congregations were not left untouched by the movement for better singing. John Waite, a blind Congregational minister, established himself as an itinerant singing master and visited Nonconformist chapels across the country promoting harmonized hymn singing. The Church of England also had similiar travelling musical evangelists, the most notable being Thomas Helmore's brother, Frederick, who went round parish churches teaching congregations to sing in parts and setting up choirs. Collections of hymn and psalm tunes were published to satisfy the demand from newly musically literate choirs and congregations. Among the most popular were the *Church Hymn and Tune Book*, produced in 1852 by Henry Gauntlett and W. J. Blew, and *Congregational Church Music*, which Binney edited in 1853.

The movement to improve singing in church even had its own pressure group which used the tactics of lobbying and pamphleteering more usually associated with bodies like the Anti-Corn Law League. The Society for Promoting Church Music was the brainchild of Dr Robert Druitt, a Mayfair medical practitioner who in 1845 wrote *A Popular Tract on Church Music, with Remarks on its Moral and Political Importance*. Like Dr Kay, Druitt was convinced of the moral benefits conferred by learning to sing and he sought to build on the work of Hullah at Exeter Hall. The society which he set up concentrated especially on promoting singing among children and amateur adult choirs and on improving music in worship. His approach was conservative and austere. Believing that church music should be 'chaste, severe and simple in style', he argued strongly for ancient texts and melodies in hymnody rather than modern ones. 'They who would hope to join the saints above . . . would rather cling to the words which their forefathers in the faith sung before them.'[7] For all his antiquarianism, however, Druitt was passionately committed to the principle of congregational singing and had no truck with the idea of choirs as a separate entity from the rest of the worshipping community. Indeed, he advocated the distribution of choir members throughout the body of the congregation to encourage good singing and deplored their segregation in the chancel. Although he tirelessly lobbied clergy and choir leaders on the benefits of this practice he persuaded few if any of them to implement it.

In its other more general aims, however, Druitt's crusade was more successful. The medium which he primarily used to promote it was the society's journal, *The Parish Choir*, which appeared from 1846 to 1851 and had a wide circulation. What made the journal a particularly good buy for the newly-formed parish church and chapel choirs across the country was the fact that each issue contained a generous amount of music, including hymn and psalm tunes, anthems, Gregorian tones, responses and canticles. *The Parish Choir* also set down four key principles which were to be very important for the development of Victorian hymnody. Firstly, it decreed that congregational singing should be in unison. Although this went against the efforts of the itinerant teachers like John Waite and Frederick Helmore to encourage four-part singing on the part of congregations, it established a note of realism and stressed the simplicity and accessibility of hymns to the musically untrained majority of church-goers. In fact, many Victorian congregations did happily sing hymns in harmony and, as we shall see, the distinctive Victorian hymn tune was written very much with part singing in mind. At the same time, however, the kind of tunes which the Victorians wrote and favoured for hymns also lent themselves to unison singing and were eminently accessible and appealing to non-musical people. This stress on accessibility is also evident in two of the other key principles laid down in the pages of *The Parish Choir*, that the melody should always be clearly marked (in distinction to the west gallery tradition where the melody was generally in the tenor line and often could not be clearly heard) and that its compass should be within the natural limits of the human voice. The Society for Promoting Church Music was determined that there should be no more straining for high notes and no more growling basses among those lifting their voices in praise of God. Its overall aim for more seemly and reverential music in church is evidenced in the fourth and final principle laid down in its journal, that metrical psalmody should henceforth be confined to tunes in common time, rather than the triple time often employed in the west gallery tunes.

By the late 1860s the great majority of churches of all denominations in England and Wales (Scotland took a little longer to embrace the new ways) had abandoned precentors, pitch pipes and instrumental bands. Metrical psalms had largely given way to hymns with congregations standing to sing them. Choirs robed either in surplices (in Anglican churches) or more sober academic-style gowns (in Nonconformist chapels) sang four-part anthems and often chanted prose psalms and canticles. The anarchic atmosphere of the west gallery bands with their complex fuguing tunes and lengthy orchestral 'symphonies' had been replaced by a style of music that was more controlled, more solemn and more reverential. Nothing, perhaps, contributed more to this new heavier, more solemn and 'churchy' atmosphere of worship than the installation of massive pipe organs, their ornate cases embellished with angelic trumpeters and positioned, like the choir, in a much more prominent and eye-catching place than had been occupied by the bassoons and bass viols of the gallery band.

Prior to Victoria's accession in 1837 the majority of places of worship in Britain did not have organs. Over the next sixty years they were installed in virtually every church and chapel in the country. Those that could not afford a full pipe organ settled for a harmonium. Technological progress probably played as big a part as liturgical or musical pressures in effecting this revolution. New production techniques brought down prices while also greatly increasing tone quality and range. Organs featured prominently in the Great Exhibition of 1851, the *pièce de résistance* being an instrument with three manuals and seventy speaking stops made by Henry Willis. Their evident craftsmanship and suitability for ornamentation and decoration appealed to the tastes of those caught up and influenced by the arts and crafts movement. The huge wave of new church building, and the fad for altering and 'restorating' the interiors of existing churches that characterized the mid-Victorian era made it much easier than it might otherwise have been to construct new organ galleries. The last decades of Victoria's reign saw further technological improvements with the introduction of electrically-blown organs. Some rural congregations retained their instrumental ensembles – Holmer Green Baptist Chapel in Buckinghamshire still had a string quartet in the gallery in 1939 – but they were increasingly regarded as anachronistic oddities. In the remote diocese of Truro, 211 parishes had organs by 1895 and only 18 were left with bands.

Pipe organs were championed by Tractarian clergy and musicians alike for their liturgical propriety and beneficial effects on the quality of music making in church. Sir Frederick Ouseley told the 1874 meeting of the Church Congress that the introduction of an organ or harmonium was the single most important step that could be taken to improve the music in a church 'because it enabled the band to be suppressed'.[8] He had no time for the half-way house of barrel organs, with their mechanical actions and severely limited repertoire of tunes, and compared them to oriental prayer wheels. The status of the organ received a considerable boost with the Bach revival that took place in the mid-nineteenth century and the popularity of works for the instrument by Mendelssohn and Liszt. In 1864 the College of Organists was founded by Richard Davidge Limpus to promote the art of organ playing and choir training. Its system of examinations, introduced in 1866, did much to enhance the prestige of organists and improve standards of church music.

The takeover of the organ as the main instrument of Christian praise was important for the development of Victorian hymnody. The pitch-pipe and mechanical barrel organ went naturally with metrical psalms sung to a limited range of relatively simple tunes. The clarinets, bassoons and strings of the gallery band favoured florid fuguing tunes with their repetitive entries and polyphonic passages. Pipe organs and harmoniums produced a sound that was at once more solemn and distinctively ecclesiastical and also richer in harmonic resources, encouraging the composers of Victorian hymn tunes to indulge in lush chromaticisms. More than any other factor, perhaps, it was the ubiquity and popularity of organs in Victorian churches and chapels that defeated the hopes of the pioneers of the choral revival for a return to the purity of Gregorian chants and early plainsong melodies. It was not to accompany their austere tones that wealthy patrons and congregational boards had installed state-of-the-art two- or three-manual instruments with full pedal boards and swell. They and their organists were as excited and enthusiastic as schoolboys playing with their first model railways. They wanted to show off all the tricks and versatility of their new technological toys. Nothing did that better than Victorian hymn tunes with their sentimentality and harmonic prodigality.

Organs were not universally welcomed into nineteenth-century churches and chapels. Indeed, their arrival could be the occasion for major protests and secessions. The installation of one of the first organs in a Methodist church, at Brunswick Chapel in Leeds in 1827, led directly to the loss, either through expulsion or secession, of 1000 members who formed a new group, the Protestant Methodists. Yet before long they too had bowed to fashion and put an organ in their own chapel.[9] In 1848 a Congregational minister and journalist, John Campbell, expressed his sadness that every chapel in the West Riding now had an organ and fulminated against the sacred concerts that were held to 'open the organ'.[10] Scots held out longest against the 'kist o' whistles' which was seen as a Devilish, or even worse a Popish, innovation. It was not until 1863 that the first organ was installed in a Protestant church in Edinburgh – and significantly it was a Congregational rather than a Presbyterian church that broke the ice. The first Church of Scotland parish church, Greyfriars in Edinburgh, followed suit two years later. The United Presbyterian Church banned organs until 1872 and Glasgow Cathedral did not get one until 1879. When a two-manual instrument was installed in Elgin Parish Church in 1874, three members of the congregation took their appeal against it right up to the General Assembly where their case was rejected by a majority of ten to one. This effectively marked the end of serious opposition in Scotland, and over the next two decades organs were installed in the great majority of churches belonging to the three major Presbyterian denominations – the Church of Scotland, the Free Church and the United Presbyterians.

The introduction of robed chancel choirs in place of the old gallery musicians caused equal if not greater protests in several English parish churches. When in 1842 the vicar of Cottenham, near Cambridge, announced that he intended to form a proper choir 'his endeavours were met, as is usual in such cases, by a rebellion in the choir, and a voluntary withdrawal of all the singers, together with their fifes, fiddles, clarionets, double basses, etc. This was followed by a silence of some months.'[11] Some reformers were surprised by the extent of the hostility to their innovations. 'You can scarcely conceive the violence of the opposition, and the love that exists for the fiddle and clarionet,' wrote a correspondent to *The Parish Choir* in 1846.[12] Others counted themselves lucky if they lost only a few of their congregation. Henry Wilberforce was considerably relieved when just three farmers and an evangelical curate walked out when he introduced a choir into the chancel of his church at East Farleigh, near Maidstone.[13]

The fierce opposition that often greeted the introduction of organs and choirs stemmed not so much from an objection to these things in themselves but an intense dislike of what they represented and a strong feeling of loss amounting almost to a sense of bereavement over the passing of the world of the gallery bands. The musical innovations were associated, quite rightly, with the onward march of Tractarianism and with other practices unwelcome to the Protestant mind such as eastward-facing priests in full vestments at communion services. Organs and choirs exemplified a new clerical control over all aspects of worship and a solemn authoritarianism that contrasted unfavourably in many people's eyes with the cheerful anarchy of the old gallery days. They were also seen as part of a wider movement to replace a democratic and populist musical culture with a much more élitist and regulated regime which was essentially high-brow and rather stuffy.

This sense of the loss, through deliberate policy, of an important aspect of communal working-class folk tradition is classically expressed in Thomas Hardy's novel *Under the Greenwood Tree*, first published in

1872. The plot of this book centres on the upset caused by the determination of the vicar of Mellstock to dispense with the services of the
old church musicians and replace them with an organ. There is no doubt
where Hardy's sympathies lay in the dispute. In the preface to the 1896
edition of the book, written when the gallery tradition had been well
and truly killed off by the unstoppable progress of choirs and organs, he
felt compelled to pen his own obituary tribute to the old order.

> One is inclined to regret the displacement of these ecclesiastical
> bandsmen by an isolated organist or harmonium player; and despite
> certain advantages in point of control and accomplishment which
> were, no doubt, secured by installing the single artist, the change has
> tended to stultify the professed aims of the clergy, its direct result
> being to curtail and extinguish the interest of parishioners in church
> doings. Under the old plan, from half a dozen to ten full-grown
> players, in addition to the numerous more or less grown-up singers,
> were officially occupied in the Sunday routine, and concerned in
> trying their best to make it an artistic outcome of the combined
> musical taste of the congregation. With a musical executive limited,
> as it mostly is limited now, to the parson's wife or daughter and the
> school-children, or to the school-teacher and the children, an impor-
> tant union of interests has disappeared.[14]

Thomas Hardy was not the only Victorian novelist to lament the
ousting of gallery choirs by determined reformers and autocratic clergymen. Writing 'Amos Barton' in 1857, George Eliot expressed equivocal
feelings about the new organ which was 'the crowning glory, the very
clasp or aigrette of Shepperton church adornment'.

> Immense improvement! says the well-regulated mind, which uninter-
> mittingly (sic) rejoices in the New Police, the Tithe Commutation
> Act, the penny post, and all guarantees of human advancement, and
> has no moments when conservative-reforming intellect takes a nap,
> while imagination does a little Toryism by the sly, revelling in regret
> that dear, old, brown, crumbling, picturesque inefficiency is every-
> where giving place to spick-and-span new-painted, new-varnished
> efficiency . . . Mine, I fear, is not a well-regulated mind: it has an
> occasional tenderness for old abuses; it lingers with a certain fond-
> ness over the days of nasal clerks and top-booted parsons.[15]

It is noticeable that both Hardy and Eliot hint at deep underlying
cultural factors behind the changes in church music. Historians of music

have been inclined to agree that the transition from west gallery psalmody to congregational hymnody led by choir and organ probably owed as much to urbanization, greater mobility, technological progress and other social factors as to the enthusiasms of Tractarians and musical reformers. Social and cultural historians, on the other hand, have tended to see the changes as resulting more specifically from a clerical conspiracy to stamp out a potentially anarchic popular culture and replace it with a more authoritarian and elitist form of worship. Echoing Hardy's comments, they have seen elements of class struggle and ideological conflict in the battles over the introduction of choirs, organs and hymn-books, with Oxbridge educated clergymen seeking to impose high culture and individualist values on working people steeped in a populist and communitarian folk tradition of worship. I have even heard the dreaded term 'cultural imperialism' used about the efforts to introduce hymn-books into mid-nineteenth century churches.[16]

There is no doubt that the introduction of organs, choirs and hymns into churches did represent an assertion of clerical control over all aspects of worship. This was certainly how these innovations were often viewed by congregations. Even the first tentative moves towards singing hymns rather than psalms were interpreted as an unwelcome sign of a new determination to own the liturgy, as is clear from this recollection of what happened in Bideford Parish Church in the 1840s:

> We were told to bring a pencil to church on some Sunday afternoons so that after sermon we could write out the words of hymns on the fly-leaves of our Prayer Books. The Rector dictated 'Sun of my Soul' from Mr Keble's book and 'Lead, kindly light', and people didn't altogether like this . . . especially those who could not write. Some said the Rector was an old Pusey and some said he was a Methody.[17]

It is clear that the introduction of hymns went hand in hand with attempts by clergy to stamp out popular practices in the general area of church music which they regarded as irregular and irreverent. Perhaps the most striking example of this is the attempted suppression of the funeral anthems which mourners had traditionally sung at the grave-side. These anthems, which often had lively fuguing tunes and expressed distinctly pagan sentiments, were particularly disliked by Tractarians who shared Keble's feeling that mourners should 'better in silence hide their dead and go than sing a hopeless dirge'. The tradition of singing a psalm at the graveside also seems to have declined, or been suppressed. Pasted into the back of Thomas Hardy's hymn-book are verses from

Tate and Brady's version of Psalm 90, 'Thou turnest man, O Lord, to dust' under the heading 'Stinsford Church – the Graveside hymn of this parish down to about 1840'. In his poem 'The Rash Bride' Hardy describes the Mellstock choir standing at the graveside of a young widow and singing the same psalm to the tune ST STEPHEN 'as was the custom then'. In fact, funeral songs and anthems do not seem to have disappeared altogether – one of the liveliest,'The Vital Spark', based on a poem by Pope, remained very popular throughout the second half of the century. Mourners got round the clerical ban by waiting around the churchyard until the clergy had left and then regrouping at the graveside to sing.

To some extent the efforts to replace these unofficial and un-authorized songs with proper hymns sung from an authorized hymn-book were part of a more general trend towards greater regulation and order. The fact was that worship in many churches, and especially rural Anglican parish churches, was badly in need of discipline and control. If contemporary accounts of what went on are to be believed, the behaviour of those responsible for the music was sometimes boorish and bordering on the blasphemous. One parish clerk sang the services with a quid of tobacco wedged in his cheek, punctuating his liturgical utterances by spitting from the lower deck of the pulpit after each Amen. In several churches the altar was regarded as a convenient shelf for choir members' coats, hats and sticks. J. M. Neale was appalled when in the middle of the first evening service he took as vicar of Crawley, Sussex, in 1842, the churchwarden climbed up on the altar in order to open the east window.

Part of the reason for this lack of reverence and decorum in worship was the almost complete divorce that existed between the said and sung parts of the service. The latter were left entirely to the gallery band and the parish clerk. Indeed, the clergy often absented themselves from the church during the singing of psalms and anthems and retired to the vestry to polish up their sermons or read a book. The musicians recipro-cated by choosing psalms to express disapproval of the sermon and switching off during those parts of the service taken by the minister. One Sussex gallery musician confessed that during the sermon he counted the windows while 'the cobbler wiped his clarinet dry wi' a big red han'kerchief and the smith he tooned his big fiddle'.[18] The divide between clergy and musicians was reinforced by the fact that the gallery in which the latter sat often had curtains which could be drawn during periods of protracted prayer and preaching, allowing the occupants to chat or play cards. The following confessions by 'an old singer' which appeared in *The Parish Choir* in 1848 suggest that John La Trobe was quite justified when he castigated the members of gallery bands for 'want of reverence in the House of God, fondness for display, obstinate rejection of advice and bad taste'.[19]

> On assembling, (and it is not seldom that the singers come in quite late, after the service has begun,) there is the How d'ye do? what are we to have today? how did people say the hymn went last Sunday evening? and similar gossip to be discussed. The books are to be found and sorted; Mr.A. must be told to mind such a point, where the tenor leads; Mr. B. cautioned not to sing too loud, &c. Mr. C. has not got a part; so a leaf must be torn out of one of the music-books, and it must be copied with a pencil; so they sit and crouch together, holding a whispering chat till the time comes for the grand display. Then curtains are withdrawn; they come forward and sing their parts. The psalm over, the curtains are closed: and they sit down again and criticize the thing they have just done. Thus the time is beguiled till the next psalm; then follows the sermon, when one or two shirk out; others sit, and sleep, or talk, or peep between the curtains at the ladies in the congregation.
>
> In fact, the occupants of these galleries do not, for the most part, come to praise God, or pray; they come to sing, either for the gratification of a musical taste, or for the gratification of vanity, or for pay . . . As for leading the congregation, it is the last thing your gallery singers dream of. They ridicule the idea; and render the thing as impossible as they can.[20]

Some enthusiasts for the gallery tradition have suggested that the above may, in fact, have been written by the editor of *The Parish Choir* himself for propaganda purposes.[21] Although that is not impossible, its description of happenings and attitudes in the gallery is confirmed by other more clearly authenticated stories and reminiscences which similarly point to the performance ethic motivating the old church bands and their almost total lack of interest in leading congregational praise or in the devotional aspects of worship. Hardy's romanticized picture of an essentially democratic and communal institution needs serious qualification. In reality, the gallery bands were often highly élitist groups who operated as self-regulating oligarchies, limiting membership to certain trades and often only to the members of a handful of families. They were certainly fiercely independent and could often be highly disruptive as John Smith, the rector of Camerton, near Bath, found out in 1822.

> During the evening service the church was crowded; and the singers, who have been in a state of constant intoxication since yesterday, being offended because I would not suffer them to chant the service after the first lesson, put on their hats and left the church. This is the most open breach of religious decorum I have ever witnessed.[22]

The disgruntled singers repaired to the Red Host public house where they decided to sing in future at the Methodist meeting house, where the gallery was enlarged to accommodate them. What their new hosts made of their fondness for the demon drink is not recorded. At least Smith got rid of his troublesome singers. In other churches they stayed on to cause the maximum havoc. When a newly-appointed vicar in the parish of Aldingbourne in Sussex decided to introduce a sermon at Mattins, the choir effectively sung him out:

> Knowing that there was never much time to spare for the parson to have his lunch and make the journey to Oving (where he was also incumbent) between the two services, on the first Sunday that he went into the pulpit to preach they started singing the 119th psalm, and refused to stop when the would-be preacher wished. In vain the vicar looked up at the gallery and held up his written discourse, in vain he coughed and hum'd and ha'd; the singers would look at nothing but their 'Old Version'. Verse after verse they bawled out, lustily and slowly, till at last the vicar's patience and time were completely exhausted, and he had to climb down, literally and metaphorically, and leave the church without delivering a discourse at all.[23]

It was doubtless with such incidents in mind that John La Trobe expressed his view that 'had the taming and bringing into order of a country choir been appointed for one of the labours of Hercules, he would have lost his reward'.[24] It is not surprising that clergy with a genuine desire to improve the devotional atmosphere of worship in their churches, whatever their theological and liturgical persuasions, often felt the dismissal of the old choir to be an essential first step. The presence of robed choirs in the chancel where they could clearly be seen by priest and people did undoubtedly signal a new determination by clergy to own and control the whole liturgy. Yet they were acting as much in the interests of the congregation as for their own self-aggrandisement. Similarly, while the introduction of organs and hymn-books brought greater order and standardization into church services, and indicated a desire for higher musical standards and more exalted language, this was as much a reflection of more refined literary and musical tastes on the part of the church-going population at large as of clerical élitism and cultural imperialism. The fact was that many people felt increasingly uncomfortable about offering their praises to God in verses such as that sung in a charity service in London and quoted in the May 1846 issue of *The Parish Choir* as an example of the worst of the old gallery tradition:

> And ever in this calm abode
> May Thy pure Spirit bc, *rit be*,
> And guide us in the narrow road
> That terminates, *minates* in Thee.

An old member of the band at Falmer Church in Sussex was surely right to reflect that its demise in 1864 was due above all to the 'disdain, shall I say contempt, with which a more educated public regarded our old compositions with their repeat and twiddle'.[25]

So while hymns, like organs and choirs, were to some extent a clerically imposed innovation, they also had strong popular support. Congregations had been largely excluded from the musical parts of worship during the reign of the gallery musicians. That people wanted to sing devotional words to strong tunes was indisputable. Books of religious verse, such as John Keble's *The Christian Year*, achieved phenomenal sales, as we have already seen. Interest in and enthusiasm for singing was booming, inspired by the new teaching methods of John Hullah and John Curwen. Choral societies were being set up all over the country and families were gathering round pianos in suburban drawing rooms to sing parlour ballads and sacred solos. The Methodists had already demonstrated how effectively devotional verses could be married to stirring melodies. Victorian hymn writers and composers of hymn tunes wanted their work to be popular in the sense of being singable and accessible in a way that had not been true of the elaborate fugues and repeats of eighteenth-century psalm tunes which, in the words of Nicholas Temperley, 'seem quite deliberately designed to exclude the congregation from taking part in their performance'.[26]

The introduction of hymns as a major feature in the services of all the main Christian denominations was in many ways a profoundly democratic and popular movement. The fact that the same verses were being sung to the same tunes in Eton College Chapel and Westminster Abbey

as at the Rusholme Street Congregational Church brought a new egali-
tarian and ecumenical dimension to worship. More importantly, hymns
sung by congregations in their own language to tunes which they found
immediately appealing and which became familiar friends embodied the
Lutheran principle of the priesthood of all believers. It is true that these
hymns and tunes were for the most part written and chosen by an
educated élite, but they rapidly came to be owned by those who sang
them. Indeed, many took on the status of national folk songs and were
jealously protected and defended when any alteration of either words
or tune was subsequently mooted. Far from being an unpopular
imposition, hymns probably kept people going to church who might
otherwise have deserted it. The distinguished historian of worship,
Horton Davis, is quite certain that 'the greatest factor in popularizing
Victorian services was the hymnody'.[27]

Hymns belonged to a new régime in worship which was undoubtedly
more serious and 'churchy' than the old one. You wouldn't find
organists and robed choirs playing and singing at weddings and dances
as the old gallery bands had. Church music was now more dignified and
distinctly ecclesiastical, more separate from the everyday secular world.
This, of course, was part of a much more general trend towards
respectability, decorum and earnestness which characterizes the whole
early and mid-Victorian age. Undoubtedly something was lost in these
changes. The old gallery tradition had a vigour, a spontaneity and an
enthusiastic and infectious vulgarity which the more disciplined robed
choirs and organists lacked. Thanks to the efforts of the West Gallery
Association and other revivalist groups, we can now see how many
good tunes were lost, particularly in Anglican worship, with the move
away from the old style psalms and anthems. Nonconformists were
happier about keeping the best of the gallery tunes. Within the Church
of England they fell victim to a cultural snobbery and purism which
does seem excessive. Once again, we can turn to Hardy for evidence of
this. In the opening chapter of his novel A Laodicean (1881), George
Somerset, a young architect, brought up in a church whose gallery band
had been ousted by a Tractarian incumbent, is out on a country walk.
From a remote Baptist Chapel he hears the notes of a once-familiar
hymn tune.

> It was his old friend the 'New Sabbath', which he had never once
> heard since the lisping days of childhood, and whose existence, much
> as it had been to him, he had till this moment forgotten. Where the

'New Sabbath' had kept itself all these years – why that hearty melody had disappeared from all the cathedrals, parish churches, minsters and chapels-of-ease that he had been acquainted with during his apprenticeship to life, and until his ways had become irregular and uncongregational – he could not, at first, say. But then he recollected that the tune appertained to the old west-gallery period of church-music, anterior to the great choral reformation and the rule of Monk – that old time when the repetition of a word, or half-line of a verse, was not considered a disgrace to an ecclesiastical choir.[28]

Perhaps the most revealing literary lament for the robustness and gutsiness of the old unreformed pre-Victorian world of church music comes from the pages of Samuel Butler's *The Way of All Flesh*.

Gone now are the clarinet, the violoncello and the trombone, wild minstrelsy as of the doleful creatures in Ezekiel, discordant but infinitely pathetic. Gone is that scare-babe stentor, that bellowing bull of Bashan the village blacksmith, gone is the melodious carpenter, gone the brawny shepherd with the red hair . . . They were doomed and had a presentiment of evil, even when I first saw them, but they still had a little lease of choir life remaining, and they roared out 'Wicked hands have pierced and nailed him, pierced and nailed him to a tree' but no description can give a proper idea of the effect. When I was last in Battersby church there was a harmonium played by a sweet-looking girl with a choir of school children around her, and they chanted the canticles to the most correct of chants, and they sang Hymns Ancient and Modern.[29]

That passage points to an important and little noticed aspect of the triumph of the hymn. It replaced a male-dominated culture of church music by one in which women and children predominated. Hardy hints at the same point in his preface to *Under the Greenwood Tree*. Just as Butler talks of the 'sweet-looking girl with a choir around her', so Hardy complains of 'a musical executive limited . . . to the parson's wife or daughter and the school-children'.[30]

It may be going too far to characterize the gallery tradition as a macho culture. There were, however, very few women in the old bands and the blacksmiths, shoemakers and other artisans who made up the majority of their members belonged to a distinctly masculine world. In the new régime of organs, harmoniums and robed choirs, women stood at least on an equal footing with men and probably predominated. The keyboard was considered a much more lady-like instrument than the bass viol or the bassoon. Indeed, the great Victorian enthusiasm for learning and playing the piano which contributed so much to the general upsurge of music-making at home and provided a ready supply of keyboard players for churches and chapels was an overwhelmingly female phenomenon. A popular broadside ballad singled it out as one of the main changes in the family life of 'The new-fashioned farmer':

> The farmers' daughters used to work all at the spinning wheel, sir;
> Now such furniture as that is thought quite ungenteel, sir.
> Their fingers they're afraid to spoil with all such kind of sport, sir,
> And sooner than a mop or broom they'd handle a piano-forte, sir.[31]

Playing the organ or singing in a choir was considered seemly for ladies in a way that taking part in the gallery band, with its coarse language and frequent trips to the pub, was not. To some extent chauvinistic attitudes lingered in the new régime and women church musicians continued to be treated as second-class citizens even when they were filling the most demanding jobs and performing them very well. This is evident from Hardy's poem, 'The Chapel Organist', about a brilliant organist hounded out of her post at a Nonconformist Chapel when it is discovered that she is pregnant, and from the condescending comment in the Church of England Quarterly Review of 1857 that 'the wives and sisters of the clergy form an excellent staff of organists, where there are no funds to secure professional help'.[32] In general, however, the changes in church music associated with the triumph of the hymn opened up new possibilities and opportunities to women, not least, as we shall see, in the area of hymn writing, and played a not insignificant role in female emancipation and liberation. They may also have encouraged femininity in a rather different way. For its critics, the Victorian hymn, and even more the Victorian hymn tune, exhibited the worst excesses of sentimentality and emotionalism and was often decried for its effeminacy. In fact, of course, many Victorian hymns were robustly manly and exude muscular Christianity. There is no doubt, however, that the tender sentiments and ballad-like tunes which distinguish some of the most characteristic products of the genre do belong, like robed choirs, to a more feminine world than the vigorous fuguing anthems of the gallery tradition.

The mention of school children in both Hardy's and Butler's descriptions of the new world of hymn singing point us to another very important cultural factor behind its spread. Churches were not the only place where the Victorians encountered hymns. They made their first and arguably their most profound impact at infant school and in the nursery. The child-centred orientation of so many Victorian hymns will be considered in chapter 4. It is, of course, just one aspect of the Victorians' idolization of children which placed them on a plinth as little angels and established a whole cult of childhood innocence which lasted long into the twentieth century. For the moment, let us just content ourselves with noticing that it was as children that most people first experienced hymns and assimilated, consciously or unconsciously, their powerful images and metaphors. Upper-class children sang them with their governesses at home and in the chapels of their boarding schools. Middle-class children learned them in the nursery, at church every Sunday morning and around the piano in the drawing-room on Sunday evenings. Working-class children sang them at elementary school and heard them at street corner missions, played on street pianos and brass bands and wafting from public houses and mission halls.

The institution that did more than any other to promote the hymn-singing habit among the young was the Sunday School. By 1888 three out of every four children in England were attending Sunday Schools and the proportion was much the same in the rest of the United Kingdom. There they learned to sing, generally by the tonic solfa method which had its origins in a meeting held in Hull in 1841 and attended by Sunday School teachers concerned to find a simple way of teaching their young charges to read music. With the development of action songs and dramatized choruses, singing became an immensely enjoyable Sunday School activity. We can return to Samuel Butler's *The Way of All Flesh* for proof of this. As a young curate in London, Ernest Pontifex invites Sunday School children to his rooms on Sunday evenings and lets them sing hymns and chants – 'they like this'.[33]

Home was also a very important nursery for the hymn-singing and the hymn-learning habit. Once again, the female influence was significant. Victorian autobiography abounds with descriptions of hymns learned at the knees of mothers and nannies. In one of the most poignant passages in *Father and Son,* Edmund Gosse recalls singing, as a seven year old, one of Toplady's hymns with his ailing mother (see p. 211). It was never too young to start learning hymns. When in 1895 the journalist W. T. Stead asked for people to send him the names of hymns that had helped them, one respondent sent a list of 23 hymns which he had memorized before he was four. One of the most familiar scenes in Victorian novels is of children learning hymns to recite at family gatherings and entertainments. Henry Fairchild, the hero of Mrs Sherwood's *The Fairchild Family*, memorized hymns as part of his lessons and then joined with the rest of the family in singing them when visitors came. *The Way of All Flesh* contains a marvellous description of the children of a middle-class clerical family singing hymns to a visitor as a special treat (see p. 210), while in *Father and Son* Gosse recalled a tea party at the Browns, a Baptist family who kept a haberdashery shop, at which the children repeated hymns, 'some rather long . . . but all very mild and innocuously evangelical'.[34] In Mrs Gaskell's *North and South* the heroine, Margaret Hale, visits the Higgins family in their tiny millworkers' cottage to find their young son repeating a Methodist hymn 'far above his comprehension in language, but of which the swinging rhythm had caught his ear, and which he repeated with all the developed cadence of a member of Parliament'.[35] Lucy Snowe, the narrator in Charlotte Bronte's novel *Villette*, reports a conversation between sixteen-year-old Graham Bretton and the young Pauline Home:

> 'Have you learned any hymns this week, Polly?'
> 'I have learned a very pretty one, four verses long. Shall I say it?'
> 'Speak nicely, then: don't be in a hurry.'
> The hymn being rehearsed, or rather half-chanted, in a little singing voice, Graham would take exception to the manner, and proceed to give a lesson in recitation.[36]

The process of memorizing hymns in the family and the schoolroom created a powerful shared oral culture. The verses which were learned came originally from books, and notably from two eighteenth-century classics, Isaac Watts's 1715 collection of *Divine and Moral Songs for the Use of Children*, Charles Wesley's *Hymns for Children* (1763), which gave the Victorians their picture of 'Gentle Jesus, meek and mild', and two pre-Victorian collections by female authors, Ann and Jane Taylor's *Hymns for Infant Minds* (1810) and Anne Shepherd's *Hymns Adapted to the Comprehension of Young Minds* (1836). These were supplemented by a torrent of hymn-books for children published during the second half of the nineteenth century. It was through oral transmission, via mothers, grandmothers, nursemaids and teachers, however, that most children learned hymns. This method reinforced their central place in the Victorian cult of the home and the sanctification of the family and it also confirmed their role as carriers of moral values and teaching aids to instruct the young in catechetical principles and the basic doctrines of the Christian faith. Victorian hymn-writers consciously produced verses for children that might stay with them throughout their lives. John Ellerton published his *Hymns for Schools and Bible Classes* in 1859 in the hope of 'storing the minds of our young people with words of praise which may be of value to them all their lives, not merely in childhood'.[37]

It was the shared childhood experience of memorizing them at home and school, reinforced by their repetition by adults in the context of public worship, that made hymns the folk song of Victorian Britain. They combined elements of the nursery rhyme, the parlour ballad and the national air as well as the worship song and devotional chorus. Significantly, churchmen and others were often alerted to the enormous potential power of hymns by noticing their hold on children. We have already noted how J. M. Neale was converted from his initial opposition to hymn singing when he saw the extent of the influence that Watts' gloomy Calvinism had on young minds through this source and realized that the only way of combating it was to write hymns of his own with a different doctrinal perspective. In his book, *Deeds of Faith: Stories for Children from Church History*, Neale made much of the power of hymns to inspire people to action, quoting the story of the Emperor Louis who was moved to order the release of an imprisoned archbishop when he heard him singing the Palm Sunday hymn 'Gloria, laus et honor'. Seeking to persuade the reluctant Scots to adopt hymns in church in 1848, William Alexander, an Edinburgh Congregational minister, pointed to their didactic value:

> In every proper hymn, there is an embodiment of some great principle or idea of a devotional kind; this is set forth in a poetical or at least rhythmical form, and the words thus put together, being sung to an attractive tune, the idea not only comes to be familiar to the mind, but what is of more importance, it comes to be surrounded with agreeable associations, which tend to make us love it, and cling to it.[38]

Their ability to teach lessons and point morals, especially in respect of what Alexander called 'the younger and less instructed part of our congregations' was a key component in the Victorian love affair with hymns. Thanks to the way they permeated childhood experience, they were also embedded deep in the collective consciousness, bound up with memories and feelings of nostalgia. Of the impact and power of this new medium the Victorians were in no doubt. In the words of the preface to one of the many huge-selling collections of hymns and sacred songs (in its 12,000th edition by 1863):

Next to the Bible itself, hymns have done more to influence our views, and mould our theology, than any other instrumentality whatever. There is a power in hymns which never dies. Easily learned in the days of childhood and of youth; often repeated; seldom, if ever, forgotten, they abide with us, a most precious heritage amid all the changes of our earthly life. They form a fitting and most welcome expression for every kind of deep religious feeling: they are with us to speak of Faith and Hope in hours of trial and sorrow; with us to animate to all earnest Chrstian effort; with us as the rich consolation of individual hearts, and as one common bond of fellowship between the living members of Christ's mystical body.[39]

3

'There is a book, who runs may read'

The making of Victorian hymn-books

The hymn-book, in its characteristic modern form with each hymn provided with a particular tune, ranks alongside the penny post and the
railway system as a great Victorian invention embodying the quest for
order, efficiency and ease of communication. From modest origins as a
tool of reforming clergy wishing to improve congregational worship, the
hymn-book became one of the central institutions of Victorian religion,
defining the identity of different denominations and church parties and
providing a handbook for doctrine and devotion which, if sales provide
any indication, had more influence and impact than any other category
of publication.

The development of Victorian hymnody in fact depended to a considerable extent on the other two inventions mentioned above. The provision of a cheap and efficient postal system enabled material to be
gathered, proofs circulated and hymn-books distributed on a nation-
wide basis and greatly helped what was in effect a cottage industry
largely carried out by country clergymen in remote rectories. The penny
post also contributed in a more direct way to popularizing hymns. One
of its offshoots was the development of the picture postcard. James
Bamforth of Holmfirth, Yorkshire, whose brilliant exploitation of this
new medium earned him the title 'King of the Magic Lantern Slides',
made his name and his fortune by producing cards with the text of
hymns like 'Abide with me' and 'Lead, kindly light' printed on a
suitably melodramatic background.

The railways were if anything even more important to the development of Victorian hymnody. The most influential hymn-book of the age,
Hymns Ancient and Modern (hitherto referred to as *A & M*) was conceived in a carriage of the Great Western Railway. The line to Hereford
played a key role in the book's gestation, linking its Leominster-based

editor, Henry Baker, with contributors and taking him to regular
editorial committee meetings at the Langham Hotel in London. Returning by train to Durham after a week of such meetings at 'the Hymn and
Tune manufactory, Portland Place', J. B. Dykes penned his tunes for
'Just as I am' and 'The Son of God goes forth to war'. Sending them
later to *A & M*'s musical editor, W. H. Monk, he wrote: 'I have since
thought it over, and slightly modified my railway version.'[1] It is appropriate that there should be a Victorian hymn which tells the entire
Christian story in railway language. 'The line to heaven by Christ was
made' can be read on a tombstone in the south porch of Ely Cathedral
erected in memory of two railwaymen killed in 1845.

Making hymn-books ranks alongside butterfly collecting and
fossil hunting as a favourite pastime of Victorian country clergy. A
correspondent to the *English Churchman* in 1862 deplored 'this hymn-
book-making-age' and complained that 'every clergyman now-a-days
seems to pride himself on having "*his own*" selection of hymns, compiled probably by his wife and eldest daughter, and the music selected
perhaps by some young "Tommie" (simpleton) who has just learned to
play a double-chant, and sing boy-alto in his school choir'.[2] Far from
being seen as a chore, the lengthy committee meetings needed to com-
pile hymn-books were regarded by those involved as a delight, affording
the pleasures of clerical company as well as antiquarian research and
joint liturgical endeavour. J. M. Neale declared that meetings of the
committee which produced the *Hymnal Noted* provided 'some of the
happiest and most instructive days of my life'.[3] An indication of the con-
viviality that surrounded such gatherings is given in a letter to Baker
from Francis Murray, another key member of the team that produced
A & M, proposing a meeting at his Chislehurst rectory to discuss
progress on the new book: 'I will promise not to drench you with cider
or ginger beer as I did last time.'[4]

I doubt if even the great 'hymn explosion' of the last thirty years has
produced the volume of new hymn-books that appeared in the
Victorian age. The British Library catalogue of printed books lists over
1200 hymn-books published between 1837 and 1901. The *Literary
Churchman* commented in 1880 that over the previous fifty years the
Church of England alone had produced an average of one new hymnal
a year. Although many of these were for relatively limited and local
circulation, the major hymnals achieved huge sales which put them at
the top of the Victorian best-seller lists. Leading the field was *Hymns
Ancient and Modern* which sold steadily at the rate of around 3000

copies a week for thirty-five years and clocked up total sales of over thirty-five million by the end of the century. In 1896 the journalist W.T. Stead estimated that more than two million hymn-books were sold in Britain each year.

Victorian hymn-books display a remarkable range of approach and subject matter. They include a number of collections for supporters of particular political causes and pressure groups. Abolitionists had *Hymns for Anti-Slavery Prayer Meetings*, published in 1838, followers of Robert Owen used *Social Hymns for the use of the Friends of the Rational System of Society* (1840), while Chartists sang from *Democratic Hymns and Songs* (1849) with its clarion cry:

> Hark! millions cry for justice, Lord,
> A little rest, a little corn.[5]

It is a sign of the hold that hymn singing came to have over the Victorians that it was taken up by groups whose beliefs and ethos were far removed from those of church and chapel. Among the most unlikely hymn singers were adherents to the rationalist ethical movements that sprang up in the latter part of the century. One of the main books they used, *Hymns of Progress*, was published in 1883 to promote singing at meetings of the Progressive Association and provide a selection of hymns 'neither directly founded on theological conceptions, nor yet directly antagonistic to such conceptions, but dealing solely with the largest and simplest aspects of human life, human love and human hope'.[6] Within its pages the Evangelical Bonar ('He liveth long who liveth well') nestles uncomfortably close to the Broad Church Kingsley ('Still the race of hero-spirits/Pass the lamp from hand to hand') while Tennyson ('Ring out, wild bells, to the wild sky'), Clough ('Say not the struggle naught availeth'), Longfellow, Lowell, Whittier and Shelley sit alongside improving doggerel on the themes of work and duty.

> Work! it is thy brightest mission,
> Work! all blessings centre there;
> Work for culture, for the vision
> Of the true and good and fair.
>
> Onward, brothers, march still onward,
> Side by side and hand in hand,
> Ye are bound for man's true kingdom,
> Ye are an increasing band.[7]

Such sentiments were not, of course, confined to progressive rationalists and earnest secularists. They are to be found in good measure in another very different type of Victorian hymn-book, the collections produced for use in public school chapels. The first school hymn-books, produced by Rugby in 1824 and Leeds Grammar School two years later, were largely service books composed of psalms and anthems. It did not take long, however, for the new hymn-singing habit to catch on in schools. By 1843 Rugby had 56 hymns in its collection. Harrow produced its first chapel hymn-book in 1855, Marlborough in 1856, Repton in 1859, Wellington in 1860, Clifton in 1863, Sherborne in 1867 and Uppingham in 1874. By 1897 the Rugby hymn-book had grown to include 360 items. In his seminal study, *The Public School Phenomenon* Jonathan Gathorne-Hardy has argued that 'hymns bound the public schools together'.[8] Certainly this particular world produced a distinct corpus of hymns and hymn tunes – robust, uplifting and brimming with Christian manliness and the ideal of strenuous service. The experience of singing in chapel every morning undoubtedly helped to foster a shared upper-middle-class culture which survived at least until the 1960s. Like those responsible for *Hymns of Progress* the compilers of public school hymnals realized that communal singing could reinforce values and create fellowship and recognized hymn-writers as 'the prophets and psalmists of today who bring to the children of today the most real and life-giving inspirations'.[9]

Collections aimed at young people make up easily the largest single category of hymn-book published in the second half of the nineteenth century. Those who think of the youth market as a modern phenomenon are clearly unaware of the extent to which Victorian hymnal publishers targeted Sunday schools and parents and created a huge demand for collections of hymns for children. Several of the best-selling hymn-books fall into this category, notably Mrs C. F. Alexander's *Hymns for Little Children* which went through more than a hundred impressions in the fifty years after its first appearance in 1848. The sick-bed provided another niche market which was identified and catered for with great success. Charlotte Elliott's *The Invalid's Hymn Book* (1835) was one of the first and most successful forays into this field – by 1855 it had sold over 13,000 copies. J. M. Neale also entered this market in 1843 with his *Hymns for the Sick* which included special hymns for those suffering a sleepless night, in great bodily pain, with a high fever, troubled by consumption or being forced to spend a Sunday in bed. Neale produced a further collection of *Hymns for the Sick-room* in 1860 which went through numerous reprintings. Mrs Alexander also wrote a number of hymns in this vein, including one somewhat reminiscent of 'All things bright and beautiful' where 'the rich man in his castle' is transformed into 'the sick man in his chamber'.

Hymn-books could be big business. The *Congregational Hymn Book*, produced in 1836 under the editorship of Josiah Conder to supplement Watts' *Psalms and Hymns*, sold over 116,000 copies in nine years and provided the Congregational Union with a major part of its revenue. Indeed, historians of Congregationalism are agreed that profits from the book prevented the denomination from facing bankruptcy in the middle of the century. The proprietors of *Hymns Ancient and Modern*, most of whom were country clergymen, each drew an annual dividend well in excess of £300 and often considerably more. In 1891 it was over £1000. It was little wonder that their enthusiasm for bringing out new editions was regarded by critics as a money-spinning device which was not justified on other grounds.

Hymn-books sold so well because they were bought not just by churches but by individuals for use at home. They appeared at a time of rapidly rising literacy as a result of advances in education, and appealed to a public that had a seemingly insatiable appetite for reading, particularly devotional works. Their compact size and variety of material made them ideal for taking on journeys, carrying to and from church and reading in bed. As such they became the constant companions of their owners who used them as much for personal devotion at home as for singing in church. Many hymn-books catered for this by dividing their contents into two separate sections. The *Congregational Hymn Book*, for example, contained 500 hymns for public worship and 120 for private devotion. There was also a booming market in anthologies of hymns which were solely designed to be read at home as devotional poems. *The Book of Praise from the Best English Hymnwriters*, compiled by Lord Selborne and published by Macmillan in their Golden Treasury series, was reprinted three times in the three months following its publication in October 1862 and went through another seven impressions in the next fifteen years.

The notion of hymns as a species of English literature was not confined to the compilers of collections for reading at home. Some of those responsible for hymn-books intended for use in worship took a similarly high view of their material. Perhaps the most literary of all Victorian denominational hymnals was the Unitarian *Hymns for the Christian Church and Home* compiled by James Martineau in 1840. Its preface makes much of the close relationship between art and worship and declares its aim as being 'to substitute for the poor and low thoughts of ordinary men, the solemn and vivid images of things invisible that have revealed themselves to loftier souls'.[10]

It is easy to perceive on what principle of selection a compiler of hymns must proceed, who is impressed with this idea of the relation between poetry and worship. His rule will be simply to take those poems which appear to shed forth, with the greatest genuineness and force, the emotions of a mind possessed with the religious or mysterious conception of God, of life and death, of duty, of futurity.[11]

Martineau's hymnal also offers a fascinating example of the extent to which editors were prepared to alter the words of hymns to fit the doctrinal position of their own denomination or party. To make them suitable for Unitarian use, the verses of Watts, Wesley, Newton, Cowper, Doddridge, Heber, Keble and Montgomery are all carefully doctored to remove any suggestion that Jesus is the son of God and any trace of the name of Christ. Thus 'Hail to the Lord's Anointed' becomes 'Receive Messiah gladly', while 'Christ, from whom all blessings flow' is changed to 'Lord, from whom all blessings flow'. Martineau was by no means the only hymnal editor to take liberties with classic texts. Those of an opposite persuasion were equally capable of altering the lines of well-known hymns to beef up their christological content. John Keble did exactly this shortly before his death when he rewrote 'Guide me, O thou great Jehovah' for *The Sarum Hymnal* so that it became 'Guide us, Thou whose name is Saviour'.

As hymns and hymn-books increasingly came to carry distinct theological messages, so their publication engendered greater controversy. Perhaps the most heated row over a Victorian hymn-book was the one that erupted in Congregational circles following the publication of a small book of hymns entitled *The Rivulet* in 1855. It was savagely castigated in the religious press, and especially in the columns of the Congregationalist *Christian Witness* for its deistic and rationalistic character and for lacking any evangelical piety. The author, Thomas Toke Lynch, who had written the hymns primarily for use by the congregation in Grafton Street, London, which he pastored, sought to defend his use of nature imagery and his departure from the fierce and gloomy Calvinism of Watts, whose work he insisted he was seeking to supplement and not supplant. The fierce debate which ensued split the

Congregational Union down the middle and at one stage seemed to threaten its continued integrity.[12]

Most of the hymn-books produced for Nonconformist congregations in the early Victorian period were much less controversial and divisive. Indeed, they increasingly reflected a desire by the main denominations to clarify their identity and bring greater uniformity and standardization into worship. In Nonconformity, as in Anglicanism, the coming of hymn-books was bound up with moves for more clerical control over the liturgy and with broader trends in the direction of order and centralization. For non-Anglican churches the hymn-book came to take on something of the authority and status that the Prayer Book had in the Church of England and became an important bearer and symbol of denominational identity. The 1850s saw this process happen in a number of churches. In 1851 the General Baptist Association formally adopted a hymn-book for use in its churches. The Particular Baptists followed suit by authorizing a volume entitled *Hymns and Psalms* in 1858. The Primitive Methodist Conference approved a collection of 852 hymns in 1854 and the 1858 assembly of the Congregational Union authorized publication of the *New Congregational Hymn Book*. This work, the first Congregational hymnal to be produced as an alternative rather than a supplement to Watts's *Hymns and Psalms*, was the fruit of considerable labour by a committee that had met for three hours every week over the previous three years under the able leadership of Henry Allon, minister of the Union Chapel, Islington.

The 1850s were also a productive decade for hymn-book makers within the Church of England. In 1852 SPCK entered the field with a collection simply entitled *Hymns* which sold 360,000 copies in its first ten years. The *Salisbury Hymn Book* of 1857 was the result of collaboration between another enthusiastic aristocratic amateur, Horatio, 3rd Earl Nelson, and John Keble. On the evangelical side, Edward Bickersteth, Vicar of Christ Church, Hampstead, extended his father's *Christian Psalmody* of 1833, turning it into a volume of *Psalms and Hymns Based on the Christian Psalmody* which appeared in 1858. In keeping with the practice of the time, these collections printed only the words of hymns. Tunes were published in separate books and were not linked with particular hymns. Among the most widely-used Anglican collections of tunes were the *Church Tune Book* produced by Henry Gauntlett in 1852 and Richard Redhead's *Church Hymn Tunes for the Several Seasons of the Year* (1853) in which PETRA made its first appearance. Nonconformist hymn-books were similarly nearly all words-only at this stage and were supplemented by tune books, of which the *Congregational Psalmist* of 1858, also co-edited by Gauntlett, was one of the most important.

No single Anglican hymnal had established the authority which was coming to be exerted by the major authorized Nonconformist collections by the end of 1850s. The five parish churches in central Nottingham were typical in each using a different hymn-book. It was out of a desire on the part of certain clergymen for greater uniformity and higher standards in hymnody in the Church of England that the idea for *Hymns Ancient and Modern* was born. It began with a conversation on a train journey in the summer of 1858 between two clerical hymn-book compilers, William Denton, Vicar of St Bart's, Cripplegate, whose *Church Hymnal* had been published in 1853, and Francis Murray, Rector of Chislehurst, who was joint editor of a *Hymnal for Use in the Church of England* (1852) which had already gone through three editions and sold 20,000 copies. After discussing the plethora and the generally poor quality of contemporary Anglican hymn-books, the two men agreed how good it would be if 'present editors should unite in abandoning, as far as they could, interest in their books and unite in an endeavour to promote *one* good one'.[13]

Denton and Murray set about recruiting others to this self-sacrificial cause. They began by approaching George Cosby White, who had compiled a volume of *Hymns and Introits* in 1852, and Sir Henry Baker, baronet and Vicar of Monkland, Herefordshire, who was working on his own hymn-book. This led to a meeting with other interested parties at St Barnabas, Pimlico, where White was curate-in-charge. A committee, numbering around twenty, was formed, with Baker as secretary, and an advertisement placed in the High Church newspaper, *The Guardian*, in October 1858:

> To the clergy and others interested in hymnology. The Editors of several existing HYMNALS being engaged, with others, in the compilation of a book which they hope may secure a more general acceptance from Churchmen, would be very thankful for any suggestions from persons interested in the matter.[14]

This appeal provoked a huge response, predominantly from country clergymen, many of whom were engaged in producing their own hymn-books. These they now selflessly gave up, sending the material that they had collected to Baker. Others sent samples of their own work for consideration by the editors of the projected new volume – among them

William Whiting, master of the Quiristers at Winchester College, who submitted the manuscript of a hymn that he had written for one of his charges who was due to sail to America. Revised by the compilers, who reversed the order of Whiting's opening stanza, 'Eternal Father, strong to save' was destined to become one of the most popular of all Victorian hymns.

Much of *A & M*'s later success was undoubtedly due to the way in which the project remained closely bound to the constituency which had originally fostered it. The making of *A & M* was never taken over by bishops or members of the ecclesiastical establishment. It remained firmly in the hands of parish clergymen, the majority of them from rural areas, who were close to their congregations and sensitive to the needs and requirements of ordinary churches like their own. They predominated among the group of eleven proprietors who took over the running and management of the project from the original committee in 1860, putting up their own money to finance the book's publication and later drawing substantial annual dividends as a result of its spectacular sales. In all its aspects, the making of *A & M* was very much a clerical enterprise – there were virtually no laymen involved even in the business side of the operation – but that again was one of its strengths. It was a book made by and for working clergymen with a very practical purpose, as is clear from its full original title *Hymns, Ancient and Modern, for Use in the Services of the Church.*

Although those behind the new hymn-book were of broadly Tractarian persuasion, they were determined that it should not simply reflect a party position. They set out to include the best of evangelical and non-Anglican hymnody as well as recently-translated material from the early church. The very title, 'Ancient and Modern', supposedly thought up by William Henry Monk, who occupied the post of 'musical co-adjutor', was a proclamation of catholicity. So was the declaration of Sir Henry Baker that the book would include hymns 'that would be suitable for singing in mission rooms, at lectures in cottages or meetings of brotherhoods'.[15]

The painstaking way in which the compilers of *A & M* went about their task of selecting and editing material epitomizes the high seriousness with which the Victorians took the whole subject of hymns. It also reflects the meticulous standards of Baker, who acted as chairman of the proprietors and *de facto* editor-in-chief throughout the 1860s and early 1870s. Great care was taken to test out the suitability and popularity of material being considered for inclusion in the new book. Hymns were sent out to a wide range of clergy for their comments and a specimen booklet containing 50 hymns was circulated in 1859 before the first words-only edition with 273 hymns appeared in December 1860, to be followed by a complete music edition with words and tunes printed together in March 1861. An appendix in 1868 added a further 130 hymns and a revised edition in 1875 contained a total of 473 hymns. A further supplement was added in 1889 to include material for festivals and missions as well as a number of hymns by Wesley and other eighteenth-century writers which had not been included in earlier editions.

The early editions of *A & M* look very austere to modern eyes. As with *The Times* in its high-minded heyday, the principle of anonymity ruled and neither authors nor composers were named. For the 1875 edition this principle was relaxed to the extent that their names appeared in the index but they were not credited in the body of the book until the standard edition of 1922. In 1883 Henry Gauntlett's widow took the proprietors to court for their failure to print her husband's name at the top of each of his tunes. She claimed that when he had assigned the copyright of ten of his tunes for the original edition for five guineas it was on the understanding that his name would appear at the head of each tune. In fact, no evidence could be adduced to prove that Gauntlett had dissented from the principle of anonymity and his widow's attempt to gain an injunction stopping publication of his tunes was turned down by the High Court.

The first edition maintained an even balance between ancient and modern material. Some 46% of its contents were translations from ancient Greek and Latin sources while 36% were from nineteenth-century English writers. A further 13% came from pre-nineteenth-century English sources and 4% were translations from German hymns. Subsequent supplements tilted the balance progressively in favour of modern hymns, a process started by the 1868 Appendix which included the work of leading contemporary hymn writers such as Mrs Alexander, Christopher Wordsworth, William Bright and Godfrey Thring. In the 1875 edition translated hymns from the early church made up just 31% of the total, and the proportion of original contemporary hymns had risen to 53%, although the most represented authors, aside from Baker, remained the translators, Neale, Chandler and Caswall with over 100 hymns between them (see Table 1 on p. 79). The broad nature of the editorial policy was indicated by the presence of several hymns by John Henry Newman and his fellow-convert to Rome, Frederick Faber, alongside old evangelical favourites like 'Rock of Ages' and 'When I survey the wondrous Cross'.

The book's publication provoked predictably mixed reactions from different wings of the church. The very breadth of *A & M* caused it to be attacked for being both too evangelical and too Catholic. Some critics found the style too sentimental and populist while others castigated it for being too highbrow and dryly liturgical.

The proprietors got an early taste of the criticism that would be meted out from what might be called the literary lobby when they received a fifteen-page letter from a Mr Priest of Lincoln's Inn in response to the specimen edition sent out early in 1860. He complained of the tendency to doggerel, prosaic expression, feebleness of expression and the 'schoolboy-like structure of many of the lines and sentences'. His own criterion was clear: 'No piece should be admitted into such a collection which is not finished English poetry.'[16] Others, however, felt that the collection was too literary. Prebendary J. H. Lester, secretary of the Lichfield Church Mission, called for 'simple English bred words, sentences direct in construction, and metaphors drawn from actual life. Such language as

> Crown him the Lord of years
> The Potentate of time
> Creator of the rolling spheres
> Ineffably sublime

is out of place. How simple is the General Confession in the prayer book compared with this'.[17]

The issue of literary versus popular language was bound up with the wider question of whether certain kinds of hymn were appropriate for inclusion in a volume provided for services of worship in the established church. Once again Mr Priest led the attack:

> Has the effect, for congregational use, of passages such as the following been carefully weighed:
>
> > There Jesus shall embrace us,
> > There Jesus be embraced.
>
> Such passages are of frequent occurrence and in the earlier days of the Church movement would, I think, have been looked upon with uneasiness, from their want of 'reserve'. Public service need not be cold and heartless but surely, even the most perfunctory service is

better than the obtrusion of *personal* feeling either by the congregation or clergy.[18]

A good many Tractarians felt that the compilers of *A & M* were
altogether too keen on evangelical hymns of an over-subjective and
emotional kind. Their view was clearly stated in a review of the first
edition in *The Ecclesiologist* which laid down as one of six key
principles for hymn-book compilers that 'The subject of the hymns
should be God and the wonders of nature or grace, rather than the
emotions of the individual worshipper'.[19] The Bishop of Oxford was
one of those who felt that Baker and his colleagues had deviated from
this principle:

> I should have been disposed to question the fitness of introducing a
> class of *sentimental* hymns, such as 'Hark, hark, my soul'. I should
> have preferred that the book should consist mainly of hymns suitable
> for worship, dwelling on the majesty and mercy of God, rather than
> on experiences and feelings of men. Bishop Heber's Trinity Sunday
> hymn (Holy, holy, holy) is just what I mean.[20]

Among these brickbats the compilers must have been relieved to
receive a number of complimentary letters applauding their courage in
including evangelical hymns. Frances Ridley Havergal wrote to express
her delight that her work had been taken up in a High Church hymnal.
Edward Husband, compiler of the *Mission Hymnal* (1874) encouraged
Baker to stick to his guns and resist the siren voices of the Tractarians
calling for more reserve and liturgical correctness: 'I am one of a large
and increasing body of men in the Church of England who . . . like a
hearty, fervid hymn.'[21]

The objection that *A & M* strayed too far in an evangelical direction
by including hymns of a personal, sentimental nature was nothing, however, to the counter-charge that it was too Romish. This accusation was
most strongly stated in a tract by James Ormiston, Vicar of Old Hill,
near Dudley, published by the Church Association. Entitled 'Hymns
Ancient and Modern and Their Romanizing Tendency', it accused the
book of teaching mariolatry, idolatry, transubstantiation, baptismal
regeneration, prayer for the dead and salvation by human works.
Numerous popish phrases were identified, including 'octaves', 'introit',
'altar' and 'penitential tears' and the author detected behind the book a
'Jesuitical stratagem', seeing its successive editions as 'a progressive
scheme for Romanizing the congregations of our land'.[22]

Less hysterical but equally uneasy reactions came from senior clergy on the evangelical wing of the church. The Archdeacon of Shrewsbury was concerned that some of the material proposed for the 1868 appendix 'exceeds in many particulars the teaching of our church and is even startling to very high churchmen', and the Archdeacon of Bedford wrote to Baker: 'May I ask you to take care that the new edition shall be very carefully examined in regard to doctrine. A letter of "Anglicanus" in the *Churchman* of January 2 1868 has drawn attention to four lines which are very likely to be interpreted in a Romish sense. This would pervert *Hymns Ancient and Modern* from having almost a national character.'[23]

The accusation that *A & M* was a popish plot was not helped when one of the proprietors, W. H. Lyall, seceded from the Church of England to Rome in 1878 and refused to resign. Another proprietor wrote: 'The presence of a Romanist among the Managers would hopelessly ruin the book when known.'[24] Baker pursued a protracted and increasingly acrimonious correspondence with Lyall, but although it took some years to secure his resignation, the reputation and sales of the book do not seem to have suffered greatly in consequence.

Communion hymns which went beyond traditional Anglican eucharistic doctrine were a particularly sensitive issue among the proprietors. The inclusion of 'Now, my tongue, the mystery telling', which was based on Neale and Caswall's translation of Aquinas' office hymn *Pange, lingua, gloriosi corporis mysterium* for the feast of Corpus Christi, led directly to the resignation of one of the original members of the committee. Francis Pott, Rector of Northill, Bedfordshire, felt that 'it defines what the Church of England has purposely left undefined'.[25] He was specifically worried that it hinted at transubstantiation and suggested that Christ was received by every communicant whereas the Church of England held that the wicked only received the outward sign of his body. Edward Caswall's 'Days and moments quickly flying' provoked considerable unease when it first appeared in the 1868 appendix. Its last verse was felt by some to suggest the doctrine of purgatory. In one of many letters of protest to the compilers, a Suffolk incumbent wrote: 'I dare not put into the hands of my people a tremendous statement, which as *a matter of fact*, is not in the Prayer Book.'[26] The offending verse was, in fact, dropped from the 1875 revised edition.

The compilers took all these objections extremely seriously and frequently altered hymns which they felt were doctrinally dubious.

Particular care was taken to excise the perceived mariolatry in Faber's hymns. His translation of the *Stabat mater dolorosa* originally began:

> O come and mourn with me awhile;
> See, Mary calls us to her side;
> O come and let us mourn with her,
> Jesus, Our Love, is crucified.

This was both too Catholic and too emotional for Baker and his moderate Anglican colleagues who toned it down considerably:

> O come and mourn with me awhile;
> O come ye to the Saviour's side;
> O come, together let us mourn;
> Jesus, Our Lord, is crucified.

Faber's 'Faith of our Fathers' was also drastically pruned. The third stanza, which began 'Faith of our Fathers! Mary's prayers/Shall win our country back to Thee!', was bound to be unacceptable in any Protestant hymn-book. The editors of the Unitarian *Hymns for the Church of Christ* had rewritten it as 'Faith of our Fathers! Good men's prayers/ Shall win our country all to Thee!' but the compilers of *A & M*, setting a precedent that was to be followed by subsequent Anglican hymnal editors, deemed it safer to remove the offending stanza altogether.

It was not just hymns hinting at Romish doctrine that were doctored by the editorial committee. Over-emotional and excessively erudite language was also censored. The first edition omitted the verse from J. M. Neale's 'Brief life is here our portion' about Jesus being embraced, which had so offended Mr Priest in the pre-publication specimen copy. Some of Neale's other translations were altered on grounds of intelligibility. The phrase 'Holy Sion's acceptation' in 'Christ is made the sure foundation' was thought to be rather obscure and was changed to 'Holy Sion's help for ever'. The stark imagery of Toplady's 'Rock of Ages' was toned down with the lines 'Foul, I to the fountain fly/ Wash me, Saviour, or I die' being excised and 'When my eye-strings break in death' being changed to the more genteel 'When my eyelids close in death'. A verse of 'Abide with me' was also omitted because it was felt to be too personal:

> Thou on my head in early youth didst smile;
> And, though rebellious and perverse meanwhile,
> Thou hast not left me, oft as I left Thee,
> On to the close, O Lord, abide with me.

Sometimes hymns were altered to make them conform more closely to scripture. A line in William Chatterton Dix's 'As with gladness men of old' had the wise men coming 'to that lowly manger bed'. The compilers felt that this was not consonant with the clear statement in St Matthew's Gospel that by the time they came to see him, Jesus was a young child and his family were living in a house. They changed it to 'Saviour, to thy lowly bed' despite the author's objection that their attitude was 'rather hyper-critical. In all art representations of the adoration our Lord is on a manger bed.'[27] One shudders to think what they would have done to 'Away in a manger' with its references to lowing cattle and the non-crying baby Jesus. That particularly unscriptural American Christmas hymn has, in fact, never been allowed to sully the pages of *Hymns Ancient and Modern*.

The extent to which the compilers altered hymns to satisfy their doctrinal and stylistic scruples rankled with some authors and led one to comment that *A & M* really stood for 'Hymns asked for and mutilated'. Many contributors, however, were prepared to accept the minor changes made to their work and were impressed by the compilers' unfailing courtesy and meticulous attention to detail. No other hymn-book has surely ever been compiled with so much care and consultation. Proposed new hymns for inclusion were sent out to academic theologians and literary experts for correction and comment. Francis Palgrave, compiler of the *Golden Treasury* and himself a hymn writer, advised on felicity and dignity of language. Particularly thorny issues were referred to the leading experts in the field. A distinguished team of theologians, including E. B. Pusey, Bishop Christopher Wordsworth and William Bright, Regius Professor of Ecclesiastical History at Oxford, were consulted in 1874 as to the propriety of retaining the word 'husband' in John Newton's 'How sweet the name of Jesus sounds'. All hymns proposed for inclusion in the 1889 edition and supplement were submitted for scrutiny to the Archbishop of Canterbury, E. W. Benson.

The most difficult doctrinal issue that faced the proprietors of *A & M* surfaced in 1897 and concerned the acceptability of hymns which seemed to argue that some Christians by-passed the normal process of dying and rising again on the Day of Resurrection by going straight to heaven. Some of these were of impeccable evangelical pedigree, like Isaac Watts' 'There is a land of pure delight', Charles Wesley's 'Let saints on earth in concert sing' and Catherine Winkworth's hymn for children's funerals, 'Tender shepherd, Thou hast stilled'. It was, however, the more Catholic-inclined hymns which suggested a direct ascent to heaven on the part of the saints which particularly concerned the compilers. When word got round that they were considering dropping them from the next edition, there was a concerted protest from High Church clergy who threatened to change hymn-books if these 'radical changes in a Protestant direction' were made.[28] The compilers responded characteristically by setting up a high-powered committee 'upon hymns on heaven and kindred subjects'. After taking soundings from a number of theologians it concluded that 'there is no Scriptural warrant for assuming that any of the departed Saints are risen or will rise from the dead before the General Resurrection at the Last Day; or that it is possible for human beings to enter into full fruition of heavenly blessedness without the Resurrection of the Body. We should not wish, therefore, to see the book include any hymns which appear distinctly to teach the contrary.'[29]

There was, of course, a danger that a hymn-book designed to be a force for unity in a body as broad and diverse as the Church of England would end up by pleasing no one and offending everyone. An early sceptic predicted that *A & M* would never take off and argued that no one could produce 'a hymnal to suit all tastes, or to be universal'.[30] Yet other voices sounded encouragement. In the midst of a welter of conflicting correspondence in the *Church Times* when a new edition was being mooted, with some wanting more Catholic hymns and others fewer, some urging a broader theological approach and others a narrower one, a letter appeared that must have given some consolation to the beleaguered proprietors:

> One of your correspondents says a thousand hymns would not be too many for the required book. Why, Sir, a million would not meet all the fads, likes, dislikes, tastes, requirements, opinions and 'views' of the entire body of clergy and laity of the Church of England, and then how on earth is an ordinary mortal to carry such a book around with him? . . . All things considered, I would respectfully urge, let well alone.[31]

Along with all the criticisms and complaints, the compilers also received many heartfelt letters of thanks from country clergymen confirming that the book did, indeed, fulfil the need and cater for the constituency for which it was produced. One of the most striking, dating from 1876, came from a Dorset incumbent who reported that before the introduction of the book his church had a barrel organ with just three tunes and two chants. The congregation numbered just twelve, of whom only three regularly took communion. Many of his parishioners had deserted the church and taken to worshipping in Dissenting chapels that flourished because of their much livelier hymns. Introducing *Hymns Ancient and Modern* had changed the situation dramatically: 'They had singing at church, they could join in it, it was easily musical and varied and the tunes which they took to especially were many of those of Mr Dykes. Now I have no Dissent here – Congregation up to 150, communicants to 25.'[32] The sales figures suggested that this story was repeated in parishes right across the country. The first edition sold over four and a half million copies within eight years and demand was so great for the 1889 edition that one million copies were dispatched by the publishers on the day of publication. One of the reasons for these high sales was undoubtedly the proprietors' decision to produce a cheap version of the book. Containing words and tunes, it sold for just fourpence. The Free Churches took up this idea and both the Baptists and Congregationalists brought out penny hymnbooks in 1867. This was an important development which encouraged the individual purchase of hymnals for use at home as well as bulk buying by churches, schools and other organizations.

The spectacular initial success of *A & M* did not deter other Anglican bodies from bringing out rival hymnals. Indeed, it may well have stimulated them by greatly boosting the transition from psalmody to hymn singing in the Church of England and creating a much bigger Anglican market for hymn-books. Three major new Anglican collections appeared in the early 1870s: *The Hymnal Companion to the Book of Common Prayer*, edited by Edward Bickersteth and firmly in the evangelical tradition established in his own and his father's earlier volumes; *Church Hymns*, published by SPCK and edited by William Walsham How, John Ellerton and Robert Brown-Borthwick, Vicar of All Saints, Scarborough; and *The Hymnary*, a High Church volume produced by William Cooke, Canon of Chester Cathedral and Benjamin Webb, Vicar of St Andrews, Wells Street, London. Attempts to prevent the appearance of these rival publications came to naught despite the intervention of J. B. Dykes, whose tunes had contributed so much to *A & M*'s appeal, and who sought to persuade Joseph Barnby, Webb's organist at Wells Street and musical editor of *The Hymnary*, simply to produce a tune book, arguing that there was no need for another full-scale hymn-book and expressing the hope 'please God that it may be so arranged that there be no Hymnal quarrelling'.[33]

The proliferation of new Anglican hymn-books meant that throughout the 1870s and 80s there continued to be no uniformity in the hymnody of the Church of England. An enquiry in 1872 revealed that in one Worcestershire town thirteen different hymn-books were in use in the parish churches. In the same year *The Literary Churchman* calculated that altogether around 200 hymnals were being used in the Church of England. Gradually, however, three books emerged as clear favourites and one in particular established a position of unassailable dominance. A survey of London churches in 1880 indicated that 421 were using *A & M*, 124 Bickersteth's *The Hymnal Companion* and 78 the SPCK's *Church Hymns*. Only six used *The Hymnary*, five *The Hymnal Noted* and just one was still left with Tate and Brady.[34] By 1894 a comprehensive census revealed that although 269 different hymnals were still in use across the Church of England as a whole, over 97% of all churches sang from one of the 'big three' books. Of these, *A & M* was by far the most popular, being found in over 10,340 churches (70% of the total). Well behind came *The Hymnal Companion* and *Church Hymns* which were used respectively by 1478 and 1426 churches.[35]

The rise of *A & M* to this dominant position encouraged a feeling in some quarters that it should be formally recognized as the authorized hymn-book for the Church of England. It already had some official status, having been adopted for use in the Army and Navy. The idea of authorization by the Church was first mooted by the Bishop of Ely in 1871 in the Convocation of Canterbury. The idea came up again in 1893 and a committee of Convocation was set up to investigate the matter. It expressed the hope that when the three most widely used hymn-books next came up for revision, their compilers might co-operate with Convocation to produce a single authorized hymnal. However, after a lengthy debate in both the Upper and Lower Houses of Convocation in April 1894 it was decided that 'it was not expedient to take any steps which would tend to interfere with the liberty of clergy and congregations in respect to the use of hymns'.[36]

In fact, there was little enthusiasm either within the Church or among the proprietors of *A & M* for giving it official authorization on the pattern of the major Nonconformist hymnals. The diversity of approach to theology and worship and the strength of party feeling ruled out, as it would surely still rule out today, the acceptance of a single authorized hymn-book in the Church of England. Evangelicals continued to cling to *The Hymnal Companion* which remained in use until the 1960s when it was replaced by other books from the same stable. An indication of the extent of High Church opposition to the production of a single official hymn-book can be gauged from the tone of a correspondent to the *Church Times* in 1897 who foresaw 'a new and watered down edition taking from it all distinctive teaching, and reducing it to the level of the undenominational teaching of our Board-school system'.[37] The proprietors of *A & M* were also unhappy at the thought of their book being taken over by Convocation. Cynics suggested that this was because it would deprive them of a considerable revenue. This may well have been a factor in their opposition to such a move but there was too a feeling that church committees and bureaucracies were not the best places to produce hymn-books. George Cosby White, who had taken over from Baker as chairman of the proprietors, was also surely right to warn that any attempt to produce an authorized hymn-book for the Church of England would 'open the floodgates of controversy'.[38]

In many ways *Hymns Ancient and Modern* did not need an official imprimatur. As early as 1865 it was being bound in with the Book of Common Prayer, replacing the New Version of the Psalms as its approved and accepted companion. Its use in so many churches, together with its undoubted quality and authority, gave it the status of a national institution. Its influence outside Anglican circles, which was considerable, was almost certainly enhanced by the fact that it was not the authorized hymn-book of the established church. Freedom from interference and control by the church authorities enabled the proprietors to keep *A & M* as the main innovative force and principal standard-setter for all denominations in the field of hymnody throughout the second half of Victoria's reign.

Within the Church of England *A & M*'s most important achievement was almost certainly to complete and consolidate the triumph of hymn singing over psalmody. It is significant that both Thomas Hardy and Samuel Butler represent the book's introduction in parish churches as marking the death-knell of the old west gallery tradition. *A & M* contained just one psalm from the Old Version of Sternhold and Hopkins, 'All people that on earth do dwell', and two from the New Version of Tate and Brady, 'As pants the hart for cooling streams' and 'Through all the changing scenes of life', from which, as Hardy lost no time in pointing out, 'the most poetical verse' was omitted, a crime which he took as confirming 'the usual ineptness of hymn-selectors'.[39] The widespread take-up of *A & M* in English parish churches hammered the final nail into the coffin of metrical psalmody. In its place came chanted prose psalms and hymns drawn from the liturgies of the early church, the outpourings of the Evangelical Revival and the work of contemporary writers. Baker and his colleagues achieved their aim of getting Anglican congregations to sing hymns ancient and modern. Perhaps even more importantly, by combining the best of different traditions in a single volume, they introduced evangelicals to the riches of Eastern and mediaeval spirituality and kept Tractarians from going down the road of narrow antiquarianism, as they would had they clung to *The Hymnal Noted*.

The single most important and enduring contribution which *A & M* made to British hymnody, as influential in Nonconformist circles as it was within Anglicanism, stemmed from its radical innovation of giving each hymn its own particular tune. The proprietors' determination to end the free-for-all approach encouraged by the production of separate volumes for hymns and tunes expressed itself not just in the way that their book was laid out, with verses and melody printed together on the same page, but also in their rigid refusal to allow other hymn-books to detach a tune from the hymn to which it had been assigned in *A & M*. This revolutionary principle was not without its critics, prominent among them being Edward Bickersteth who protested that he had been 'accustomed since my childhood to have the same tune sung to many hundred hymns'.[40] It was, however, almost universally accepted and taken up by subsequent hymn-book compilers and came to be one of the most important factors in promoting both the popularity and the power of hymns in late Victorian Britain.

What Baker and his associates had grasped, of course, was the extent to which the language and message of a hymn was enhanced and reinforced if it was always sung to the same tune. They recognized the power of a strong and distinctive melody not just to underline the words of a hymn but to implant them deep in the human subconscious and act as a trigger for their subsequent recall. By providing a good, singable tune for each hymn, and for that hymn only, they established that indissoluble association between particular words and music which was at the heart of the Victorian love affair with hymns and which turned them into a kind of folk song for the British.

Many of the marriages of words and tunes effected by 'those cunning old match-makers', as the compilers of *A & M* have justly been dubbed, have remained indissoluble to this day. Some involved newly written hymns and melodies, like 'Eternal Father, strong to save' to MELITA and 'The King of love my shepherd is' to DOMINUS REGIT ME. In other cases an existing hymn was given a specially written new tune, as in the

case of NICAEA for Heber's 'Holy, Holy, Holy' and EVENTIDE for Lyte's
'Abide with me'. *A & M* also coupled well-established old hymns,
which had previously been sung to a whole variety of different tunes,
with a single traditional melody, often drawn from the psalm tune
repertoire of the sixteenth and seventeenth centuries. Examples of such
couplings are Watts' 'O God, our help in ages past' with ST ANNE and
'While shepherds watched their flocks by night' with WINCHESTER OLD.
The links forged in *A & M* were taken up by virtually every subsequent
hymnal with the result that it became impossible to think of a particular
hymn, still less to sing it, without its accompanying tune.

This process, for which William Monk must take much of the credit,
had its down-side. Inevitably it led to a greater degree of standardization and uniformity in church music. Those who lament the passing of
the old gallery tradition see the pairing of particular hymns and tunes as
a piece of centralizing authoritarianism which eroded variety and
spontaneity and sacrificed local and regional traditions on the altar of
national uniformity. This is the view of Vic Gammon: 'The hymn-book,
which often took the place of the individually-compiled manuscript, is
at once an authority and a more alienated form. In the widespread
acceptance of *Hymns Ancient and Modern* after 1861 we see the
national and standard triumphing over the local and various.'[41] Another
accusation which has some truth in it is that *A & M* and its successors
greatly limited the range of tunes available for use in church worship.
The tunes which Monk and Baker chose to accompany their hymns
were almost all of one type. They were solid four-part tunes which
moved at a sedate pace and eschewed the lively fuguing style and imitative entries of the gallery tunes. Only one tune in *A & M*, ADESTE
FIDELIS, retained any hint of the old ways.

The new style of hymn tune was not without its critics. A clergyman
complained of the 1875 edition that 'the tendency is toward the modern
part-song and even the sentimental ballad' while Hardy gave poetic
expression to his view that *A & M* had sanitized and emasculated
vigorous old tunes in his 'Apostrophe to an Old Psalm Tune':

> I met you first – ah, when did I first meet you?
> When I was full of wonder, and innocent,
> Standing meek-eyed with those of choric bent,
>   While dimming day grew dimmer
>   In the pulpit-glimmer.

Much riper in years I met you – in a temple
Where summer sunset streamed upon our shapes,
And you spread over me like a gauze that drapes,
    And flapped from floor to rafters
    Sweet as angels' laughters.

But you had been stripped of some of your old vesture
By Monk, or another. Now you wore no frill,
And at first you startled me. But I knew you still,
    Though I missed the minim's waver,
    And the dotted quaver.[42]

In general, however, the new respectability and decorum that Monk and Baker had brought to hymn singing was welcomed. Their tunes might be more reserved and restrained than the old gallery melodies but they were also a lot easier for congregations to sing. The proprietors were inundated with requests from other hymn-book editors for permission to use their tunes. Dr Thring put in a request to reproduce a string of copyrighted melodies, headed by EVENTIDE and NICAEA, for a combined hymnal he was putting together for Uppingham and Sherborne schools. When Baker gently suggested to him that public schools might give up producing their own hymnals and use *A & M* instead, however, he was give a headmasterly rebuff: 'I fear you will find the task of stopping Hymn Books a serious one. Schools especially with their very singular congregations will not easily accept an external dictum that a large miscellaneous collection is suited for them.'[43] Free Church hymn-books from the 1860s onwards generally adopted *A & M*'s tunes, either dropping their old ones or relegating them to appendices. They also took up the practice of printing hymns and tunes together. The first Methodist book to be produced in this form came out from the Wesleyans in 1877. The General Baptists followed suit in 1879 with a massive volume containing 920 hymns, the English Presbyterians in 1882 with *Church Praise* and the Primitive Methodists in 1889.

Perhaps the most enthusiastic Free Church disciple of the new approach pioneered by *A & M* was Dr Henry Allon, minister of Union Chapel, Islington, and editor of *The Congregational Psalmist* which first appeared in 1858 with new editions in 1868, 1875 and 1886. Allon had long been an enthusiast for congregational hymn singing, believing that 'worship is a sacrifice to God, not to musical art . . . I do demand that it be, not a choir to which people must listen, but a congregational song in which people may join – a worship, not of priests, but of the whole church.'[44] He put this principle into practice at Union Chapel where 'no hymn, chant or anthem is sung in which the congregation does not join. The idea . . . is that the whole congregation shall sing from music-books in four-part harmony. The choir, technically so called, is therefore only part of the singing congregation; its function is simply to lead it.'[45] Allon was greatly taken by the singability and emotional power of the tunes chosen for *A & M*. Writing to Baker to ask permission to reproduce them in his Congregational hymnals, he noted that 'some of the tunes really double the devotional power of the hymns with which they are connected' and singled out for special praise Dykes' tunes for Horatius Bonar's 'I heard the voice of Jesus say' (VOX DILECTI) and John Ellerton's 'Saviour, again to Thy dear name we raise' (PAX DEI).[46] The extensive correpondence between the two men preserved in the *A & M* archives, which begins in sweetness and light, betrays a gradual worsening of relations which reveals the extent of doctrinal and ecclesiological tensions between Nonconformity and the Establishment. In 1879 Allon was refused permission by Baker to use Neale's 'Christian, dost thou see them' on the grounds that 'he said he knew we would not sing the last two lines of the second verse without alteration (Smite them by the virtue/Of the Lenten fast)'.[47] Considerable offence was taken at a hostile article by Allon on established churches in *The British Quarterly Review* in January 1881 and what had begun as a mutual admiration society ended with the *A & M* proprietors banning Allon from using any of their copyright tunes. Despite this rebuff, however, Allon remained a firm devotee of Anglican hymnody and believed that the development of the congregational hymn had brought the worlds of Nonconformity and Establishment closer:

> In the Anglican Church the neglected hymn has become prominent in congregational worship, in the Puritan churches worship has developed in aesthetic forms. The art-music of ritual worship has deepened and broadened into Congregational song, while the rude fervour of Evangelical hymn singing has developed higher art-expression. Both tendencies have thus combined to produce what is perhaps a more consentaneous and extended culture of the worship of the congregation than the Church of Christ has ever known.[48]

Allon was not without critics in his own church. In a fascinating article Clyde Binfield has shown how his evangelical populism offended more liberally and intellectually minded Congregationalists. Allon's argument that 'the hymns of the Church, like the Ballads of the nation are for popular lyrical use, and are to be tested not by mere literary canons, but by the power of their devotional inspiration' particularly irritated William Garrett Horder, minister of Wood Green Congregational Church. He believed that hymns should be of a high poetic and literary quality and eschew doctrine: 'Rhymed prose dealing with theological doctrine is not a hymn . . . Doctrine should be spoken from the pulpit, not sung from the pew.'[49] This philosophy, which echoes the views of James Martineau, informed Horder's *Congregational Hymns* of 1884. Although it reflected a more literary and intellectual approach than Allon's *Congregational Psalmist Hymnal* of 1886, it drew equally heavily on *Hymns Ancient and Modern* for words and particularly for tunes. The two most frequently used composers in Horder's collection were those two *A & M* stalwarts, E. J. Hopkins and J. B. Dykes.

Congregationalists were, indeed, particularly active in the hymn-book making business in the 1880s. Another prominent figure on the liberal wing of the church, John Hunter, minister of Wycliffe Chapel, Hull, produced a volume of *Hymns of Faith and Life* in 1886. The following year an official *Congregational Church Hymnal*, sanctioned by the Congregational Union, appeared under the editorship of George Barrett, minister of Princes Street, Norwich, where the proprietor and many of the staff of the nearby Colman's mustard factory worshipped. It must stand as one of the most comprehensive hymn-books ever produced by a major denomination. Every conceivable occasion in church life is catered for, including meetings of ministers, elections of deacons, dedications of organs and flower festivals (for which one of the hymns provided, William Tarrant's 'Long ago the lilies faded' seems a touch inappropriate). The 'Christian Missions' section alone has seven subsections with special hymns covering their necessity, prayer for their success, anticipation of their final success, missions to the Jews, colonial missions, home missions and the departure of missionaries.

Scottish churches were noticeably slower than their English counterparts to adopt hymn-books. The first of the three main Presbyterian churches to do so were the United Presbyterians, who authorized a hymn-book for use in public worship in 1851. Ten years later, following lobbying from evangelicals, the General Assembly of the Church of Scotland for the first time approved a hymn-book. *Hymns for Public Worship*, as it was known, was replaced in 1870 by the *Scottish Hymnal*, a broadly based collection consciously modelled on *A & M*. Its adoption was something of a victory for the rising liturgical and Scoto-Catholic movement within the Kirk, but there was still deep suspicion in

many quarters about singing hymns and a good number of congregations stuck exclusively to the metrical psalter. The difficulties faced by
those trying to introduce hymnody into the services of the established
Church of Scotland are well illustrated in two letters sent to *A & M*'s
proprietors by Scottish ministers. The first, written in 1873 by
Alexander Brown of Aberdeen to request permission to use the tunes of
Dykes, 'our favourite composer', remarked plaintively, 'In Scotland we
have no organs in our church to assist the voices.'[50] The second came
from A. H. K. Boyd, parish minister in St Andrew's and chairman of the
Church of Scotland's hymn committee:

> If you knew the amount of vulgar and stupid bigotry which we in the
> Scotch Kirk who desire to bring in Catholic hymns have had to fight
> with, I am sure you would sympathise with us and help us. At my
> week-day services, for years, I used H.A.M. (which was quite illegal):
> and you will see our Hymnal is wonderfully like yours, considering it
> had to be approved by the General Assembly.[51]

Ironically, the church which produced incomparably the greatest
Scottish hymn-writer was the most reluctant to allow hymns in its
services. Horatius Bonar's 'I heard the voice of Jesus say' was one of the
great 'hits' of *Hymns Ancient and Modern* and several of his other
hymns were to become firm Victorian favourites. Yet he was not
allowed to hear them sung in the church where he was a minister for
over twenty years. Although the Free Church of Scotland authorized the
use of hymns in public worship in 1872, it was left to individual Kirk
Sessions to decide whether they would have them for their own congregations. The Session of Chalmers Memorial Free Church at Grange in
Edinburgh, where Bonar ministered from 1866 to 1889, was one of
those which resolved to sing only psalms.

The great breakthrough in Scottish hymnody came in 1893 when the
three main Presbyterian churches set up a joint hymnal committee. It
was a significant ecumenical initiative which has been seen as the
significant first step towards the reunion of the churches which took
place in 1929. The committee was augmented in 1894 by representatives from the Presbyterian churches of England, Ireland and the
Empire. Like the compilers of *A & M*, they went about their task with
enormous care, combing through more than fifty books for suitable
material and sending out several drafts for comment and reaction before
finalizing their choice. Despite his Anglican background, Sir John
Stainer was the committee's unanimous choice for the post of musical

editor. He set about his work with relish, writing 15 new tunes for the book and commissioning 31 others from contemporary composers.

The *Church Hymnary* appeared in 1898, making it the last great denominational hymn-book of the Victorian era. It is interesting and instructive to compare it with the 1875 edition of *Hymns Ancient and Modern*. What is perhaps most striking is the similarity between these two books, separated as they are by more than two decades and by a deep denominational and national divide. They have many of the same hymns set to the same tunes, a tribute to the strong influence that *A & M* had on nearly every hymn-book that followed it. They also share a breadth of style and subject matter which would have been unthinkable at the beginning of Victoria's reign. Indeed, this was a matter of pride for the once stern and unbending psalm-singing Presbyterians responsible for *The Church Hymnary*: 'The object which the Committee steadily pursued throughout its labours was to produce a collection of hymns which should be truly catholic, including representatives of every branch of the church in its roll of authors, and comprehensive as a book must be which is intended for use in various churches and congregations'.[52]

There are, of course, clear differences between the books which reflect the distinctive perspectives of their makers. This is perhaps most marked in the matter of layout. While *A & M* takes an emphatically liturgical approach, beginning with morning and evening hymns and then running through the church's year with a large section of general hymns and special sections devoted to sacraments and saints' days, *The Church Hymnary* adopts a more thematic and theological scheme. It begins with hymns on the subject of God: His attributes, works and word, which includes sections on The Holy Trinity, Christ, the Holy Spirit, the Holy Scriptures and the Gospel. This is followed by a section on the Christian Life with subheadings like 'Holiness and Aspiration', 'Brotherly Love' and 'Trust and Resignation'. Then under a third general heading of 'The Church' come hymns for different seasons and sacraments. This difference of approach is perhaps most clearly marked in the way hymns about death are treated. *A & M* puts them firmly in a section labelled 'Burial of the Dead' while *The Church Hymnary* divides them between 'Death and Resurrection' and 'Heavenly Glory'.

Some of the differences between the two books can be put down to the time gap in their publication. The last twenty-five years of the nineteenth century saw a huge rise in Sunday School attendance and hymn singing among children. This is almost certainly one of the main reasons

---

Table 1

Most represented writers in two major hymn-books

Hymns Ancient and Modern 1875 edition (473 hymns)	*The Church Hymnary* 1898 edition (625 hymns)
1 J. M. Neale (48 appearances)	1 Horatius Bonar (17 appearances)
2 Henry Baker (31)	2 William Walsham How (16)
3 John Chandler (25)	3 Mrs C.F. Alexander (15)
4 Edward Caswall (21)	4 John Ellerton (14)
5= John Ellerton (11)	5= Frances Havergal (12)
Mrs C. F. Alexander (11)	Catherine Winkworth (12)
7 Isaac Williams (10)	Henry Baker (12)
8= John Keble (9)	8= J. S. B. Monsell (10)
Christopher Wordsworth (9)	Christopher Wordsworth (10)
10 F. W. Faber (7)	10 J. M. Neale (5)

These ten authors contributed 40% of the hymns in the book.	These ten authors contributed 20% of the hymns in the book.

---

why *The Church Hymnary* has 96 hymns for children against just 17 in the 1875 *A & M*. As Table I shows, its contents were less dominated by a small group of authors. One clear reason for this is the much smaller number of translations from ancient sources in the Presbyterian volume and the consequent relegation of Neale, Caswall and Chandler from the leading position that they occupied in *A & M*. It also reflects a general trend, which we have already noted in respect of successive editions of *A & M*, away from ancient hymns and towards the work of contemporary authors. For the compilers of *The Church Hymnary* this was a matter of conscious policy: 'While careful to retain hymns which familiar usage had endeared to the members of the several Churches, the Committee made room as far as possible for new hymns which were of intrinsic merit, and fitted to enrich the collection with fresh material of congregational praise.'[53]

Both books have one very significant feature in common which distinguishes them very clearly from their modern successors. A significant proportion of their contents is the work of contemporary authors and composers. In the case of *The Church Hymnary*, 105 of the 650 hymns (16%) were the work of living writers (this does not include translations) and 240 of the 650 tunes (37%) were the work of living composers. The comparable figures for the current (third) edition are 59 out of 695 hymns (8%) and 75 out of 695 tunes (11%). It was not uncommon for over two-thirds of the contents of Victorian hymnals to be the work of living writers. The proportion in most modern hymn-books seldom rises above a quarter and is often substantially less. It is time to see what sort and condition of men and women were those eminent Victorians who supplied the great hymn-book industry and off whose capital we are still substantially living today.

4

'For all the Saints who from their labours rest'

Victorian hymn-writers

The Victorians took a high view of hymn writing both as an art form and as a vocation. In part this stemmed from their realization of the immense power and influence of this particular medium of communication. 'Let me write the hymns of a Church', declared the great Congregational preacher, R. W. Dale, 'and I care not who writes the theology.'[1] Moved by the singing of 'Rock of Ages' at W. E. Gladstone's funeral in 1898, A. C. Benson reflected: 'To have written words which should come home to people in moments of high, deep and passionate emotion; consecrating, consoling, uplifting . . . there can hardly be anything worth better doing than that.'[2] Men of letters as well as churchmen respected hymn writers as toilers in a branch of literature that was notoriously difficult. A brief hymn beginning 'O man, forgive thy mortal foe' inserted into a children's play, *The Promise of May*, by Alfred Tennyson in 1882 won the plaudits of Benjamin Jowett, the formidable master of Balliol College, Oxford, who pressed him to write more. The Poet Laureate declined, telling Jowett's friend, Robert Warren, the President of Magdalen College, that 'a good hymn is the most difficult thing in the world to write. In a good hymn you have to be both commonplace and poetical.'[3]

There was, in fact, no shortage of poets keen to try their hand at writing hymns in the nineteenth century. Among them were five recipients of university prizes for poetry (Henry Lyte, H. H. Milman, F. W. Faber, Edward Caswall and J. M. Neale), a Professor of Poetry at Oxford (John Keble) and a Poet Laureate (Robert Bridges). Other literary figures who successfully wrote hymns, several of which are to be found in modern collections, included Anne Bronte ('Believe not those who say'), Charles Kingsley ('From thee all skill and science flow'), Thomas Hughes ('O God of truth, whose living word'), Francis Palgrave ('O thou not made with hands'), Walter Scott, whose translation of the *Dies Irae* was included in Heber's 1827 hymnal and Thomas Carlyle, who was responsible for the finest and most durable translation of Luther's *Ein' Feste Burg*, 'A safe stronghold our God is still'. Journalist hymn-writers included William Canton, a sub-editor and leader-writer on the *Glasgow Herald* ('Hold thou my hands') and James Montgomery, editor of the radical Sheffield newspaper, *The Iris*, ('Stand up and bless the Lord' and 'According to thy gracious word').

This roll-call underlines the fact that in the Victorian period, unlike our own, hymn writing was very much within the mainstream of literary activity. Another important difference from today, when the composition of hymns and worship songs has increasingly become the preserve of specialists and professionals, is the great contribution made by amateur hymn writers. Virtually all of those who wrote hymns in the nineteenth century did so as a sideline from their main occupation. A number of them were distinguished academics. They include two Regius Professors at Oxford, William Bright, who wrote numerous hymns including 'And now, O Father, mindful of the love', and Arthur Stanley ('Oh master, it is good to be'); the Professor of Greek at Edinburgh, J. S. Blackie ('Angels holy, high and lowly'); a Reader in Ecclesiastical History at Oxford, Edwin Hatch ('Breathe on me, breath of God'); and the author of the standard critical commentary on the Greek New Testament, Henry Alford ('Come, ye thankful people, come'). There was also a clutch of hymn-writing schoolmasters, prominent among them H. Montagu Butler, headmaster of Harrow and author of that quintessentially public-school hymn, 'Lift up your hearts, we lift them Lord to thee', Henry Twells, headmaster of Godolphin School ('At even, when the sun was set'), George Bourne, headmaster of Chardstock College ('Lord enthroned in heavenly splendour'), Arthur Campbell Ainger, assistant master at Eton ('God is working his purpose out'), Henry James Buckoll of Rugby ('Lord behold us/dismiss us with thy blessing') and Andrew Young, principal teacher of English at Madras College, St Andrews ('There is a happy land, far, far away'). The delightfully named Folliott Sandford Pierpoint, author of one of the 'greenest' hymns in the English language ('For the beauty of the earth'), should perhaps also be added to this list. He spent most of his life living in Somerset on a small patrimony which he occasionally supplemented with a little classics teaching.

Politicians made a notable contribution to nineteenth-century hymnody. We have already noted the impressive hymnological expertise gathered together in Gladstone's second Cabinet. The Grand Old Man himself regularly whiled away quiet hours on the Front Bench by translating the hymns of Cowper and Toplady into Latin, Greek and Italian. Sir John Bowring, Radical MP for Kilmarnock and later Governor of Hong Kong, penned 'In the cross of Christ I glory', Philip Pusey, Liberal MP for Berkshire, 'Lord of our life and God of our salvation', Robert Grant, Tory MP for Inverness, Norwich and Finsbury and Governor of Bombay, 'O worship the King', and Charles Horne, Liberal MP for Ipswich, 'For the might of thine arm we bless thee'. John Frederick Stainer, Chief Examiner in the Passport Office and author of the Processional Easter Day hymn 'Daystar on high', provides an interesting example of a hymn-writing civil servant. The peerage and landed aristocracy were also well represented. Perhaps the most colourful figure from this world was Sir Edward Denny who owned the whole town of Tralee but forsook ancestral Anglicanism for the Plymouth Brethren and lived in a small cottage in Islington where he devoted himself to studying prophetical books and composing religious verses.

Several other professions are represented in the great pantheon of Victorian hymn-writers. James Edmeston, an architect, wrote more than 2000 hymns, including the enduring 'Lead us heavenly Father, lead us'. One of the most succesful of all Victorian children's hymns, 'There's a friend for little children', was written by an Isle of Wight ironmonger, Albert Midlane. William Chatterton Dix, the author of 'Alleluia! sing to Jesus' and 'As with gladness men of old', started his career as a stationer in Bristol and went on to become manager of a marine insurance company in Glasgow. Charles Mudie, founder of the famous circulating library that became a Victorian institution, published a book of devotional verses several of which were taken up as hymns. Oswald Allen, manager of the Kirkby Lonsdale branch of the Lancaster Banking Company, produced a collection of 148 hymns during a particularly severe winter which confined him to the house.

It would be wrong to gain the impression from these lists that hymn writing was predominantly a lay occupation. Most of the new material that appeared in Victorian hymn-books was supplied by clergymen, the great majority of them Anglicans. This was hardly surprising. The Free Churches already had a substantial body of hymns on which to draw. It was in the Church of England, which had come so recently to hymn singing and taken to it so enthusiastically, that the demand for new material was greatest. Its clergy responded by pouring out a torrent of verse which sought that tricky balance Tennyson had identified between the poetical and the commonplace and often added a large dose of the devotional and the doctrinal for good measure.

Much of this work was done in the studies of rural vicarages and rectories. The following list identifies where twenty of the most popular and prolific hymn-writers among nineteenth-century Anglican clergy were based when they wrote their best-known work.

Henry Alford, vicar of Wymeswold, Leicestershire ('Come ye thankful people, come', 'Ten thousand times ten thousand')

Henry Baker, vicar of Monkland, Herefordshire ('The King of love my Shepherd is')

Sabine Baring-Gould, curate of Horbury, West Yorkshire ('Onward, Christian soldiers')

John Ernest Bode, rector of Castle Camps, Cambridge ('O Jesus, I have promised')

Ernest Edward Dugmore, vicar of Parkstone, Dorset ('Almighty Father of all things that be')

John Ellerton, vicar of Crewe Green, Staffordshire ('The day thou gavest, Lord, is ended')

Lewis Hensley, vicar of Hitchin, Hertfordshire ('Thy kingdom come, O God')

William Walsham How, rector of Whittington, Shropshire ('For all the Saints')

John Keble, curate of Hursley, Hampshire ('Blest are the pure in heart', 'Sun of my soul, Thou Saviour dear')

Henry Francis Lyte, perpetual curate of Brixham, Devon ('Abide with me', 'Praise, my soul, the King of heaven')

Henry Hart Milman, vicar of St Mary's, Reading ('Ride on, ride on in majesty')

J. S. B. Monsell, vicar of Egham, Surrey ('Fight the good fight')

John Mason Neale, warden of Sackville College, East Grinstead, Sussex ('Christ is made the sure foundation', 'Jerusalem the golden', 'The day of Resurrection')

Charles Oakley, rector of Wickwar, Gloucestershire ('Hills of the North rejoice')

Francis Pott, curate of Ticehurst, Sussex ('Angel voices ever singing')

George Hunt Smyttan, rector of Hawksworth, Nottinghamshire ('Forty days and forty nights')

Samuel Stone, curate of Windsor, Berkshire ('The Church's one foundation')

Godfrey Thring, rector of Alford, Somerset ('Fierce raged the tempest o'er the deep')

Isaac Williams, curate of Bisley, Surrey ('Be thou my guardian and my guide')

Christopher Wordsworth, vicar of Stanford-in-the Vale, Berkshire ('Gracious Spirit, Holy Ghost', 'O day of rest and gladness')

It is significant that the great majority of these leading clerical hymnodists served in rural parishes at the time they were writing their most significant and influential hymns. This is a point which might seem to support those who have criticized Victorian hymnody in general, and the Anglican hymnody of *Hymns Ancient and Modern* in particular, for its romantic and archaic rural bias and failure to engage with the pressing social issues raised by rapid industrialization and urban squalor. Only a handful of those listed above did have first-hand knowledge of this side of Victorian life. Christopher Wordsworth spent a third of each year at Westminster, Charles Oakley moved to St Paul's, Covent Garden, and John Ellerton's Crewe Green parish took in the works of the London and North Western Railway. He is said to have thought up a good number of the 86 hymns that he wrote while he was there during his nightly walks to and from the Mechanics' Institute, where he conducted evening classes for the railway workers.

It is also significant that the great majority of clerically composed hymns were the work of ordinary parish clergymen and not of those further up the ecclesiastical hierarchy. There were very few hymn-writing bishops in the Victorian church. Richard Mant, who held a number of Irish sees from 1820 to 1848, translated several hymns from the early church and was responsible for puzzling generations of children with his apparent reference to 'the sight of Judah's ear' in 'Bright the vision that delighted'. In most cases, however, hymn writing seems to have been given up by those who donned the episcopal cope and mitre. Edward Bickersteth wrote the stirring 'For My sake and the Gospel's, go' when he was Bishop of Exeter but most of his work in this field, including the production of the *Hymnal Companion to the Book of Common Prayer* and his fine hymn 'Peace, perfect peace, in this dark world of sin' belonged to the period when he was an incumbent in Hampstead. William Maclagan similarly wrote most of his hymns, including 'Lord, when Thy Kingdom comes, remember me' before he became Bishop of Lichfield in 1878, while Edward Benson's great period of hymnological activity long pre-dated his elevation to the see of Canterbury and belonged to his days as a schoolmaster at Rugby and Wellington. Two leading Victorian hymn-writers became bishops, William Walsham How of Wakefield and Christopher Wordsworth of Lincoln, but they wrote very few hymns during their episcopates.

This underlines another interesting point about the hymn-writing habits of Victorian clergy which, as we shall see, also applies to the hymn tune writing habits of Victorian composers. Perhaps rather surprisingly, it was predominantly a young man's occupation which was engaged in at the beginning rather than the end of a career. In the case of musicians, it was often a way of making relatively easy money before a reputation had been established. This was much less of a factor among hymn-writing clergy, although the prospect of financial reward may not have been entirely absent from the thoughts of pale young curates sending their carefully turned verses off to editors and compilers. One might have thought that hymns would come more naturally out of the quieter, more reflective and more leisured days towards the end of a ministry than from its busier earlier years but this was emphatically not the case. Many of the abiding hymns of the Victorian age were penned when their authors were in their late twenties and early thirties. Typical in this respect is 'Onward, Christian soldiers', written when Sabine Baring-Gould was thirty and a busy West Yorkshire curate. Significantly, nearly all of his hymns come from this period in his life. His later, more leisured years – all forty of them – as rector and squire of Lew Trenchard on the edge of Dartmoor saw him turn his attention to collecting folk-songs like 'Widdicombe Fair' and largely forsake writing hymns.

Some clergy went on writing hymns throughout lives that were spent in the quiet calm of a rural backwater. Perhaps the prime example of this breed was Sir Henry Baker, the chief begetter of *Hymns Ancient and Modern*, who spent twenty-six years comfortably installed as both vicar and squire of Monkland in Herefordshire. With just 200 souls in the parish to care for and substantial private means, Baker could afford to devote most of his time and talents to writing hymns and compiling hymn-books. He lived in a large country house specially designed by G. E. Street with private chapel and organ and with two cottages built in the grounds for the use of the organist and choirmaster. Several other clerical hymn writers led a similarly settled and untroubled rural exis- tence – Allen Chatfield whiled away his forty-eight years as vicar of another tiny Herefordshire parish, Much Marcle, by translating the 'songs and hymns of the earliest Greek Christian poets and bishops' into English verse. Three other prominent translators of the hymns of the early church found themselves in obscure rural retreats more by force of circumstance than by choice. Richard Littledale had to give up his duties at St Mary the Virgin, Soho, because of ill health and spent the rest of his life living quietly in the country translating and writing hymns. Isaac Williams slunk away from his Oxford fellowship when he failed to succeed John Keble as Professor of Poetry because of his extreme Tractarianism, and went first as curate to Keble's brother, Thomas, in Devon and then as rector of Stinchcombe, Gloucestershire. J. M. Neale lived as a virtual exile in East Grinstead for the last twenty years of his short life (he died at 48), eking out an existence on a pittance of £27 a year. For most of the period he was barred from administering the sacrament or saying the divine office by a bishop who disliked the 'spiritual haberdashery' involved in Neale's introduction of a rood screen and vested altar with cross and candlesticks in the chapel of the college where he was warden.[4] At least this enforced leisure gave Neale and his fellow Tractarian scholars the time to devote themselves to the important work of translating and promoting the hymns of the early church.

Although few led quite such secluded lives as this Tractarian trio, virtually all the hymn-writing clergy in the Victorian Church of England shared a privileged and socially exclusive background. Educated at public schools and Oxbridge, their experience was far removed socially if not culturally from many of those who enthusiastically sang their verses at church and chapel on Sunday mornings and evenings. Some did attempt to bridge the gap – How was known as the 'omnibus bishop' throughout his time at Wakefield because of his endearing habit of regularly travelling by bus. Some of the most socially concerned hymns of the late Victorian and early Edwardian period were, in fact, written by some of the most upper-class clergy. Henry Scott Holland, author of that great Christian socialist anthem, 'Judge Eternal, throned in splendour', was an old Etonian who became Precentor of St Paul's Cathedral and Regius Professor of Divinity at Oxford. The truth was that there were few genuinely working-class hymn-writers in any denomination, still less in Anglicanism. The Salvation Army and the Primitive Methodists produced some and their hymn-books contained a number of verses by working men. Ebenezer Elliott, a Rotherham foundry worker's son who became a prominent Chartist and Anti-Corn

Law campaigner, achieved considerable fame with his hymn 'When wilt thou save the people' which became an anthem for working-class radicals and reformers. On the whole, however, hymn writing was a middle-class and upper-middle-class occupation in Victorian Britain and did not attract many devotees from lower down the social scale.

If Anglican authors constituted an élite, at least socially, then the representatives of the other great stronghold of clerical hymn-writers, Scottish Presbyterianism, came of more solidly bourgeois stock. Like their Anglican counterparts, the leading Scottish hymn writers were parish ministers. Unlike them, however, they served predominantly in urban and city charges. By far the most successful and prolific was Horatius Bonar ('I heard the voice of Jesus say', 'Thy way, not mine, O Lord', 'Light of the world, for ever, ever shining') who ministered to Free Church congregations in Kelso and Edinburgh. From the same church came Walter Chalmers Smith ('Immortal, invisible, God only wise'), who served in Glasgow and Edinburgh, and James Drummond Burns, who wrote 'Hushed was the evening hymn' and 'At thy feet, our God and Father' while he was minister of a Free Church of Scotland congregation in Hampstead. Three of the most prominent hymnodists in the established Church of Scotland had highly demanding and effective ministries in what would now be called inner-city areas: Robert Murray McCheyne ('When this passing world is done' and 'Jehovah Tsidkenu') in Dundee and John Ross MacDuff ('Christ is coming! let creation from her groans and travails cease') and Norman Macleod ('Courage, brother! do not stumble') in Glasgow. George Matheson, the blind author of 'O love that wilt not let me go', 'Make me a captive, Lord' and the marvellously inclusive 'Gather us in, thou love that fillest all', ministered first in the Clyde resort of Innellan and then in Edinburgh. The only truly rural figures among leading nineteenth-century Scottish hymn writers were Peter Grant, who wrote hymns and spiritual songs in Gaelic during a forty-one-year pastorate at the Baptist Church at Grantown-on-Spey, and John Brownlie, minister of the United Free Church in Portpatrick, Wigtownshire, who translated a number of hymns from the Greek, including a cento from Gregory Nazianzen's Hymn to Christ, 'O Light that knew no dawn', that was widely taken up in many churches.

This group of Scottish hymnodists encompassed a particularly broad range of theological position and churchmanship. With one or two notable exceptions, most of the hymn-writing clergy in the Church of England tended towards moderate High Churchmanship. On the whole, the hymns of nineteenth-century Anglican evangelicalism were written by laymen, and more especially, as we shall see, by laywomen. This was also true, though to a lesser extent, of those that reflected liberal Broad Churchmanship. The situation in Scotland was rather different with clerical authors supplying hymns representing all the main traditions. Bonar and McCheyne wrote from an unashamedly evangelical perspective, Matheson and Macleod from a liberal one, in the latter's case tempered by a strongly catholic liturgical sense, while Brownlie was closer in interest and outlook to some of the English Tractarians.

Although there was relatively little congregational hymn singing in Roman Catholic churches before 1900, a quartet of Victorian priests wrote hymns that were widely taken up by Protestants. All four were converts from Anglicanism, as, of course, was John Henry Newman, whose own work, which was not intended for congregational use, will be considered later in this chapter. Two were primarily translators of hymns from the early church. Edward Caswall, who gave up the living of Stratford-sub-Castle, Wiltshire, in 1847 and later joined Newman's Birmingham Oratory as a priest, produced 'When morning gilds the skies', 'Jesus, the very thought of Thee' and 'My God, I love Thee, not because I hope for heaven thereby'. Frederick Oakeley, the former incumbent of the Margaret Chapel who became a canon of Westminster Cathedral, was responsible for 'O come, all ye faithful'. Matthew Bridges, who converted to Roman Catholicism in 1848 and spent much of his life in Canada, wrote 'Crown him with many crowns' and 'Behold the Lamb of God'. The most prolific of the four, Frederick William Faber wrote a number of highly popular original hymns including 'My God! how wonderful thou art', 'Faith of our fathers', 'O come and mourn with me awhile' and 'There's a wideness in God's mercy'. He came from a similar background to many Anglican hymn-writers, having been educated at Harrow and Oxford where he was known as 'Water-lily Faber' because of a poem *The Cherwell Water-Lily*, in which he apostrophized that flower as a type of virgin love and purity. As rector of Elton in Huntingdonshire he wrote romantic poetry and indulged in ritualistic practices but it was as a Roman Catholic priest in London, where he established a branch of Newman's Birmingham order that was to develop into the Brompton Oratory, that he wrote his hymns. He was anxious to promote congregational singing among Roman Catholics and was unhappy with the existing diet of translated hymns from the early church since 'they do not express Saxon thoughts and feelings, and consequently the poor do not seem to take to them'.[5]

Although his own compositions were enthusiastically sung by those attending Mass at his church in the Brompton Road, they were not widely taken up in the Roman Catholic Church. Purged of their Mariolatry, however, they found their way into most Anglican and Nonconformist hymnals.

Compared to the hymnodic output of clergy in the Anglican, Scottish Presbyterian and Roman Catholic churches, the contribution made by Free Church ministers to Victorian hymnody seems very small. The fact is that most Nonconformist congregations were still relying heavily on eighteenth-century hymns, especially those of Watts and Wesley, and saw little need to supplement them. Within the Victorian Free Churches hymn writing seems to have been more of a lay than a clerical activity. Perhaps the denomination in which it was most popular was Unitarianism. As we shall see later, the most significant contribution from this direction was made by Americans. Unitarian hymn-writers in Britain included two radical political figures whom we have already encountered, Sir John Bowring and Ebenezer Elliott, William Gaskell, husband of the novelist and himself a distinguished minister and academic in Manchester, and Sarah Adams, whose 'Nearer, my God, to thee' ranked high in the Victorian Top Ten.

Mrs Adams was one among a particularly talented and prolific group of women hymn-writers in the nineteenth century. On the face of it, female authors contributed only a small proportion of the contents of Victorian hymn-books – just 10% in the case of the 1875 edition of *Hymns Ancient and Modern* and a little under 20% in the 1898 edition of *The Church Hymnary*. Yet among hymns by contemporary authors, the proportion written by women was very much higher and in certain categories, notably Sunday School songs and hymns for children, they were in an overwhelming majority. There were few other walks of life in which the contribution made by women was so prominent, or so openly acknowledged. As we have already seen, hymn singing was seen very much as a female activity and, in a church culture that was overwhelmingly male dominated, hymnody provided women with a rare outlet for expressing their creative talent and giving voice to their spirituality.

A good number of Victorian women hymn writers were either the daughters or the wives of clergymen. Emma Toke, author of the Ascensiontide hymn 'Thou art gone up on high', falls into both categories, being the daughter of the Bishop of Kilmore and wife of the Vicar of Godington Park, near Ashford, Kent. Caroline Noel ('At the name of Jesus') was daughter of the vicar of Romsey, Hampshire. Other clergy daughters who achieved fame as hymn-writers include Frances Havergal, Dorothy Gurney and Anne Shepherd, author of *Hymns Adapted to the Comprehension of Young Minds*. Charlotte Elliott ('Just as I am, without one plea') was the grand-daughter of Henry Venn of Huddersfield and had two clergymen brothers, one of whom was the father of Emily Elliott ('Thou didst leave thy throne and thy kingly crown'). Cecil Frances Alexander's husband was a priest, and later bishop, in the Church of Ireland, Jemima Thompson ('I think when I read that sweet story of old') married Samuel Luke, a Congregational minister in Bristol, and Anne Ross Cousin ('The sands of time are sinking') was the wife of a minister in the Free Church of Scotland.

It is tempting to categorize Victorian women hymn-writers into two distinct types – the sickly spinster who pours her frustration into highly-charged verse of an intensely emotional and evangelical hue, and the robust and active wife and mother who writes with more objectivity and control. It is certainly the case that many of the best and most popular female hymn-writers led lonely lives dogged by ill health. Jennette Threlfall ('Hosanna, loud hosanna') was the victim of two accidents which left her a hopeless invalid. Adelaide Anne Procter, a close friend of Dickens, who turned her hands to parlour ballads as well as to hymns such as 'My God, I thank thee, who hast made the earth so bright', endured considerable suffering before dying at the age of 38. Elizabeth Clephane, author of 'Beneath the Cross of Jesus I fain would take my stand' and 'There were ninety and nine that safely lay', died at the same age after being bedridden for many years. Catherine Hankey wrote 'Tell me the old, old story' in 1866 when 'I was weak and weary after an illness, and especially realizing what most of us realize, that simple thoughts in simple words are all that we can bear in sickness.'[6] Another chronic invalid, Charlotte Elliott, opened up a lucrative new 'niche market' with her *Invalid's Hymn Book* (1835) and *Hours of Sorrow cheered and comforted* (1836). Caroline Noel surely put some of her own suffering into *The Name of Jesus, and Other Verses for the Sick and Lonely* (1861).

Perhaps the most productive of this group of sickly spinsters was Frances Havergal, whose hymns include 'Who is on the Lord's side', 'I am trusting Thee, Lord Jesus', 'Jesus, Master, whose I am' and 'Take my life and let it be consecrated, Lord, to thee'. The sense of submission and resignation conveyed in these last three titles is found in many hymns written by women in the Victorian period. It is the theme of 'Just as I am' and of the best-known hymn of another chronic invalid with clerical connections, Eliza Alderson, sister of J. B. Dykes – 'And now, beloved Lord, my soul resigning'. Frances Havergal, commenting on the subject matter and message of her own hymns, said that her favourite name for Christ was Master because 'it implies rule and submission, and that is what love craves. Men may feel differently but a true woman's submission is inseparable from deep love.'[7] This sense of submissiveness often went alongside a high degree of subjectivity and emotionalism, even among those women who enjoyed rude health and happy marriages. Anna Waring, brought up as a Quaker but later an Anglican, who devoted herself to prison visiting, produced a stream of highly personal and subjective hymns, the most enduring of which, 'In heavenly love abiding', is a statement of utter resignation to the God who will protect the individual believer from the storm that roars without. Anne Cousin was to live to the age of 82 but that did not stop her when she was just 33 from penning one of the most maudlin of all Victorian hymns, 'The sands of time are sinking'.

It has been claimed that the only truly objective hymn written by a woman in the nineteenth century is Caroline Noel's 'At the name of Jesus'. This does seem a rather sweeping statement. There is surely a strong measure of objectivity in the writings of two women who emphatically do not fit into the 'sickly spinsters' category, the redoubtable Mrs Alexander and Dorothy Gurney, whose 'O perfect Love, all human thoughts transcending', despite its gloriously sentimental tune by Barnby, is a straightforward enough evocation of the joys of Christian marriage which for the most part steers clear of gushing emotionalism. There is also a good deal of objectivity to be found in the translations of German hymns which were made by women writers in the mid-nineteenth century.

It is interesting that while the Latin and Greek hymns of the early church were worked on almost exclusively by male Tractarians, the important corpus of post-Reformation German hymnody was almost entirely translated by women whose outlook could best be categorized as Broad Church. Outstanding among them was Catherine Winkworth, the daughter of a silk manufacturer who spent her early life in and around Manchester where she was profoundly influenced by William Gaskell. Although she never renounced Anglicanism, she flirted with Unitarianism and was friendly with James Martineau as well as being a disciple of Charles Kingsley and F. D. Maurice. With her sister Susanna she spent substantial periods in Germany and both girls were encouraged to take up translating German spiritual classics by Baron

Karl Josias von Bunsen, Prussian Minister in London from 1841 to 1854. While Susanna concentrated on theological works and translated large numbers of sermons and tracts from the Reformation era, Catherine took up hymns which she translated at the rate of one a day in her home in Alderley Edge. Her collection, *Lyra Germanica*, appeared in two parts – the first, *Hymns for the Sundays and Chief Festivals of the Christian Year* in 1855 and the second, *The Christian Life*, in 1858. Although initially offered as devotional verses for individuals to read at home, her translations soon came to be taken up for congregational singing and were wedded in hymn-books to the great German chorale tunes that had often accompanied the originals. In 1863 Catherine Winkworth herself produced *The Chorale Book for England* with melodies edited by Mendelssohn's pupil William Sterndale Bennett. She also wrote *Christian Singers of Germany* (1869), a detailed commentary on German hymn writing from the ninth to the mid-nineteenth century. It is to her that we owe 'Now thank we all our God' and 'Praise to the Lord, the Almighty, the King of Creation'.[8]

Several other women were involved in translating hymns from the German. Frances Cox, an Oxford spinster, who was also influenced by Baron Bunsen, brought out a collection of *Sacred Hymns from the German* in 1841 which included a translation of an Easter hymn by Christian Gellert that became the basis of 'Jesus lives! thy terrors now'. Catherine Dunn produced a volume of *Hymns from the German* in 1857. Four years later Jane Campbell, daughter of the rector of St James's, Paddington, translated a peasants' song from a late eighteenth-century sketch about farming in North Germany to produce the ever-popular harvest hymn, 'We plough the fields and scatter'. Two sisters who were staunch members of the Free Church of Scotland, Jane and Sarah Borthwick, collaborated on *Hymns from the Land of Luther*, published in four volumes between 1854 and 1862. Their best known translation is almost certainly 'Be still, my soul: the Lord is on thy side'.

The field most clearly dominated by women writers was that of hymns for children. Most of the great Victorian Sunday School favourites come from female hands – a high proportion, like 'Jesus loves me, this I know' and 'Jesus bids us shine with a pure, clear light' originating from the other side of the Atlantic. Once again the influence of the sickbed is evident: 'Thine for ever! God of Love' was written in 1847 by Mary Maude for her Sunday School class at St Thomas's Church, Newport, Isle of Wight, where her husband was vicar, during a period of protracted illness. So, too, is the note of dependence and submission clearly evident in 'Loving shepherd of thy sheep' and 'Saviour, teach me day by day', two of the many hymns penned by Jane Leeson, an active member of the Catholic Apostolic Church who wrote her verses during services as 'prophetical utterances' apparently under the prompting of the Holy Spirit, and produced a stream of books, including *Infant Hymnings*, *Hymns and Scenes of Childhood*, *The Child's Book of Ballads* and *Songs of Christian Chivalry*. Not all the seemingly gentle Victorian ladies who wrote children's hymns were in fact quite as mild, obedient and good as their verses might suggest. Jemima Thompson, who penned the intensely and infectiously senti- mental 'I think when I read that sweet story of old' was also responsible for turning out viciously splenetic anti-Catholic propaganda in such novels as *The Female Jesuit* (1851). One wonders how she squared this with her longing in the hymn for the time 'when the dear little children of every clime / shall crowd to His arms and be blest'.

One name dominates the children's section of Victorian hymn-books. Mrs Alexander continues to be remembered today chiefly for children's hymns like 'All things bright and beautiful', 'There is a green hill far away' and 'Once in royal David's city' although her St Andrew's Day hymn 'Jesus calls us! o'er the tumult' and her translation of St Patrick's Breastplate, 'I bind unto myself today' are also still popular. Previous generations knew her as the author of 'Every morning the red sun / Rises warm and bright' and 'We are but little children weak' with its improving injunction, 'O, day by day, each Christian child / Has much to do, without, within'. Cecil Frances Humphreys wrote most of her hymns before her marriage at the age of 32 to a moderate Tractarian clergyman, William Alexander, who was to end his dazzling ecclesiastical career as Archbishop of Armagh and Primate of all Ireland. The daughter of an English army officer, she was born in Dublin in 1818 and spent much of her childhood mixing with the Anglo-Irish aristocracy. When she was seven her father became agent to the Earl of Wicklow and it may well have been the grand houses and the almost feudal society of southern Ireland that inspired the much-criticized and much-misunderstood verse of her best-known children's hymn about the 'rich man in his castle' and 'the poor man at his gate'.

Although the prevailing ethos of the upper-class Anglo-Irish society in which she grew up was evangelical, Frances Humphreys was touched and excited by the Oxford Movement. Her first book of children's hymns, *Verses for Holy Seasons*, which came out in 1846, was dedicated to John Keble whom she prevailed on to provide a brief preface for her second and most successful collection, *Hymns for Little Children*, which appeared in 1848 and went through more than a hundred impressions in the next fifty years. The profits from it went to an institute for the deaf at Strabane which she was instrumental in founding. Although her sympathies probably lay with moderate Tractarianism, however, there is no particularly Catholic or party feel to her hymns. They are, indeed, for the most part a model of theological objectivity and simplicity in expounding the essential points of biblical and credal orthodoxy. Where other more evangelical women wrote hymns to evangelize and convert, or to express in deeply personal and subjective terms their own relationship with God and Christ, Frances Humphreys sought simply to teach. For her, hymns were primarily catechistical aids. She wanted above all to implant in the minds of the young through simple verse the essential doctrines of the Christian faith. This aim underlay her 1848 volume which was based on the church catechism and provided fourteen hymns to explain the different sections of the Apostles' Creed. 'All things bright and beautiful' was written to amplify and explain the phrase 'I believe in God the Father Almighty, Maker of heaven and earth', 'Once in Royal David's City' for 'I believe in Jesus Christ . . . who was born of the Virgin Mary' and 'There is a green hill far away' for 'He was crucified dead and buried'.

This essentially didactic view of the hymn-writers' craft was shared by many other Victorian practitioners, especially Anglicans, who saw their work primarily as educating people in the basic doctrines of the faith and defending credal orthodoxy. Instilling good behaviour in children was another principle that motivated Frances Humphreys and many of her hymn-writing contemporaries. Her third collection, published in 1849, was entitled *Moral Songs*. It is full of improving injunctions and homilies.

> Do no sinful action,
> Speak no angry word,
> Ye belong to Jesus,
> Children of the Lord.
>
> Christ is kind and gentle,
> Christ is pure and true,
> And His little children
> Must be holy too.

It comes as something of a shock to turn from this piece of pious moralizing to the angry language of a hymn written to be used in the Church of Ireland in the aftermath of the Disestablishment brought about by Gladstone's first Government in 1869. This is the voice of Mrs Alexander, defender of the principle of church establishment and wife of a bishop who had been deprived of his seat in the House of Lords as a result of the Liberal legislation.

> Look down, O Lord of heaven, on our desolation!
> Fallen, fallen, fallen is now our Country's crown,
> Dimly dawns the New Year on a churchless nation,
> Ammon and Amalek tread our borders down.[9]

Mrs Alexander was by no means the only prominent nineteenth-century hymn-writer to be moved to put pen to paper by an event or trend that seemed to threaten the future of the church and the maintenance of sound doctrine. Philip Pusey wrote 'Lord of our life, and God of our salvation' to warn of the challenge facing the church from without and within:

> See round Thine ark the hungry billows curling;
> See how Thy foes their banners are unfurling;
> Lord, while their darts envenomed they are hurling.

Pusey wrote of this hymn: 'It refers to the state of the Church – that is to say, of the Church of England in 1834 – assailed from without, enfeebled and distracted within, but on the eve of a great awakening.'[10]

Like the creeds of the early church, Victorian hymns were often seen by their authors as vehicles for defining and defending orthodoxy and promoting sound doctrine. Like the creeds also, they were often inspired by perceived heresies which they sought to correct. We have already noted how J. M. Neale gave up his initial hostility to congregational hymnody and began writing hymns himself to counter the malevolent influence of Watts' verses on children. His decision to take up hymn writing may also have been a response to the Gorham judgment of 1850 where the Judicial Commission of the Privy Council upheld the appeal of a clergyman whose bishop had found him unsound on the doctrine of baptismal regeneration and refused to institute him. This is certainly the view of Dr Leon Litvack, the author of an important recent study on the great Tractarian translator:

> The Gorham judgment provided the impetus for Neale's belief that
> the Church of England was about to commit itself to heresy; perhaps

he saw himself as saviour of his Church. He knew, both from his Evangelical upbringing and his familiarity with the state of affairs in other Christian communions, that hymn singing had a popular appeal. Here was an easily accessible, popular method of instilling what he considered to be 'right' Christian doctrine into Anglicans.[11]

Another heresy case that rocked the Anglican world fifteen years later provided the direct impetus for at least two hymns which continue to be widely sung today. John Colenso, Bishop of Natal, was deposed from his see by Archbishop Gray of Capetown, for challenging the traditional Mosaic authorship of the first five books of the Old Testament and questioning the doctrine of eternal punishment. As in the case of Gorham, his appeal was upheld by the Judicial Committee of the Privy Council and as a result Colenso continued to remain a bishop. Among the traditionalists who rallied behind Archbishop Gray's defence of orthodoxy were Henry Baker, who wrote 'Lord, thy word abideth' to defend the principle of biblical infallibility against the rising tide of liberalism represented by Colenso and the authors of the infamous 'Essays and Reviews' of 1860, and Samuel Stone, who penned his great hymn of church defence, 'The Church's one foundation', which found its way into the 1868 Appendix of *A & M* and became, in the words of a late twentieth-century champion of his work, 'the Battle Hymn of the Anglican Communion', still widely sung long after the Colenso affair has been forgotten.[12]

Hymn-writers found heresy in different guises, of course, depending on their own theological and denominational persuasion. Whereas F.W.Faber wrote 'Faith of our Fathers' in the hope of reversing the whole misguided Protestant experiment and returning the British to their Catholic roots, R.J.Leslie, Vicar of Holbeach, St John, had a very different agenda, as evidenced in the verses he sent to Baker in 1875 which, not surprisingly, did not find their way into *A & M*:

> We are English Catholics,
>   Who own no sway of Rome,
> The Church is universal,
>   And our part here at home.
>
> O! if heretics and sects
>   Their jarring work would cease,
> And if Popery were gone,
>   What bliss was here and peace!

Others had a much more eirenic and ecumenical purpose in writing or translating hymns. J. M. Neale saw hymnody as the principal means of effecting his great goal of a reconciliation between Anglicanism and Eastern Orthodoxy. Through translations of early Greek hymns like 'The day of Resurrection' and 'Come, ye faithful, raise the strain' he sought to give British Christians a flavour of the exuberance of the Orthodox Easter. George Matheson expressed his broad and inclusive faith in 'Gather us in, Thou Love that fillest all'. For every Victorian hymn expressing a partisan or polemical view, there are far more written out of a deep sense of piety and devotion. Many are clearly the products of hours spent in private prayer such as that engaged in by Horatius Bonar whose 'voice of earnest pleading from behind the locked study door, pleading continued for hours, formed one of the most sacred memories of the home circle'.[13]

Inspiration for hymns came in many forms. Most commonly it was a passage of scripture or sermon but it could also be a work of art. At least two great Victorian hymns were directly inspired by paintings: William Walsham How's 'O Jesu, thou art standing' by Holman Hunt's 'The Light of the World' and Lionel Muirhead's 'The Church of God a Kingdom is' by van Eyck's 'The Adoration of the Lamb'. Illness could also be a source of inspiration – and not just to those sickly spinsters whom we encountered earlier. J. H. Newman wrote 'Lead, kindly light' while suffering from a high fever and lying in the cabin of an orange-boat that was taking him back from Italy. When asked later to explain the imagery of the verses he referred to 'the transient states of mind which come upon one when homesick, or seasick or in any other way sensitive or excited'.[14] Edward Bickersteth wrote 'Peace, perfect peace' at the bedside of a dying friend one Sunday afternoon.

At a more mundane level, several hymns were written to fit particular tunes that the authors could not get out of their heads. Finding that Phoebe's song 'Were I thy bride' from Gilbert and Sullivan's opera, *The Yeoman of the Guard* kept floating into his mind, William Canton wrote a hymn, 'Hold thou my hands' to fit it. He commented later 'these words seemed to grow into it and out of it'.[15] 'There is a happy land' came to Andrew Young while on holiday in Rothesay on the island of Bute. He was spending an evening at the house of a friend who was playing tunes on the piano. One in particular charmed him and he was told that it was an Indian air called 'Happy Land': 'It immediately occured to me that such a melody could not fail to be popular in Sunday Schools, if wedded to appropriate words.'[16] The following morning he rose early and thought up the hymn as he walked in the garden. During a stagecoach journey through Somerset, Jemima Thompson could not get a Greek tune called 'Salamis' out of her head. 'It was an hour's ride and there was no other inside passenger. On the back of an old envelope I wrote in pencil the first two verses (of "I think when I read that sweet story of old") in order to teach the tune to the village school supported by my stepmother.'[17]

Hymns were, indeed, written in a fascinating variety of places and circumstances. Archibald Charteris, Professor of Biblical Criticism at Edinburgh University, wrote 'Believing fathers oft have told' on a steamer taking members of the Church of Scotland Young Men's Guild on an excursion across Lake Como in 1889. John Ellerton was not alone in finding that the muse came to him on evening walks. Although the words of Albert Midlane's best-known hymn, 'There's a friend for little children', apparently came to him during a particularly busy day in his ironmonger's shop, he composed many of his other sacred verses during walks round the ruins of Carisbroke Castle – 'the twilight hour, so dear to thought, and the hushed serenity then pervading nature, have often allured my soul to deep and uninterrupted meditation, which, in its turn, has given birth to lines which, had not these walks been taken, would never probably have been penned.'[18] Arthur Stanley, who as Dean of Canterbury from 1851 to 1855 did much to initiate and develop congregational singing in the Cathedral, was another who composed hymns while perambulating. Others found that the muse came to them when they were engaged in more sedentary occupations. Henry Twells is said to have written 'At even when the sun was set' while invigilating an exam at Godolphin School. Perhaps, although it strictly belongs to a later chapter, this is also the place to record that Bishop Strong of Oxford managed to compose a passable tune for 'Praise to the Holiest in the height' during a meeting of the university's Hebdomadal Council.

The time taken to write a hymn also varied enormously from author to author. Some agonized over their compositions and spent long hours in revising and polishing them. Not that a substantial input of effort was always a cause for weariness – Thomas Gill, a Unitarian who later moved to evangelical Anglicanism, described the day in 1868 on which he wrote 'We come unto our Father's God' as 'almost the most delightful of my life. Its production employed the whole day and was a prolonged rapture.'[19] Others turned out hymns with remarkable speed. Reginald Heber took just twenty minutes to produce four verses of

'From Greenland's Icy Mountains' one Saturday morning when his father-in-law asked him for a suitable hymn for a service in Wrexham Parish Church the following day at which the collection was to be in aid of the Society for the Propagation of the Gospel in Foreign Parts. 'O perfect love, all human thought transcending' (another hymn to be inspired by a tune – in this case Dykes' STRENGTH AND STAY), which Dorothy Gurney wrote in 1883 for her sister's wedding, was finished in less than quarter of an hour. Frances Havergal wrote 'Golden harps are sounding' on the back of an envelope in ten minutes while waiting in the playground of a Birmingham infants' school. Sabine Baring-Gould confessed towards the end of his life that he had 'knocked off' 'Onward, Christian soldiers' in much the same time.[20] The work of translation could also be swift. When J. M. Neale visited John Keble in 1856 he took the opportunity while his host was out of the room for a few minutes to translate one of the poems from *The Christian Year* into Latin. He then persuaded Keble on his return that this was an ancient hymn which he had unwittingly plagiarized.

Speedy composition is not, of course, necessarily incompatible with divine inspiration, witness George Matheson's account of how 'O love that wilt not let me go' came to him as he was sitting in his manse one evening in 1882:

> Something had happened to me which was known only to myself and which caused me the most severe mental suffering. The hymn was the fruit of that suffering. It was the quickest bit of work I ever did in my life. I had the impression rather of having it dictated to me by some inward voice than of working it out for myself. I am quite sure the whole work was completed in five minutes, and equally sure it never received at my hands any retouching or correction.[21]

A good number of hymns were written to order or specially commissioned for particular occasions. 'Onward, Christian soldiers' falls into this category, having been penned by the young Sabine Baring-Gould for an outdoor Whit Sunday children's procession. Those who object to its supposed militarism are perhaps unaware of the fact that it was never intended for use in church. Those missionary hymns that also cause such unease today because of their perceived racism and imperialism often belonged in a similar category, as in the case of 'From Greenland's icy mountains', and were not written to be sung at regular Sunday services. Some hymns that were written for very specific occasions have survived well and proved easily adaptable to more general use. A good example is 'Almighty Father of all things that be', which Ernest Dugmore produced for the opening of a small industrial exhibition in his Dorset parish. Others failed even to be accepted by those who had commissioned them. A harvest hymn written by John Ellerton in 1882 at the request of the Church of England Temperance Society was rejected as unsuitable, perhaps not surprisingly when it contained the line 'All praise to Thee for corn and wine' and the verse:

> Thy sun and shower bring back the hour
> Of Cana's gracious sign,
> Where warm on Southern vineyard slopes
> The mellow clusters shine.

Ellerton struck a more suitable note in a hymn written in the same year for the opening of a workmen's coffee tavern:

> What is earth itself? an Inn
> Where we wait our time to go;
> Business, pleasure, care, and sin
> Through the doors pass to and fro.[22]

Ellerton was called upon more than most to provide instant and appropriate hymnodic accompaniments to events both local and national. It is hardly surprising that he occasionally lapsed into doggerel, as in this children's hymn for the Queen's jubilee in 1887:

> Dusky Indian, strong Australian,
> Western forest, Southern sea,
> None are wanting, none are alien,
> All in one great prayer agree –
> God save the Queen![23]

Was there an element of hack work in the production of so many hymns to order? The fact that several well-known ones first appeared in the pages of popular newspapers might suggest that hymn-writing was regarded as a superior kind of journalism. James Montgomery wrote 'Angels from the realms of glory' for a Christmas Eve number of the *Iris* and the solemn Lenten hymn 'Forty days and forty nights' made its first appearance somewhat incongruously in the *Penny Post* in March 1856. Yet there is very little impression among even the most prolific hymn writers of a casual attitude to their work. The phenomenon found across the Atlantic of writers who were contracted by publishers to produce a certain number of hymns each month was unknown in Britain.

Even those who mixed hymnody with the composition of more lucrative parlour ballads took considerable pains with their sacred verses. Adelaide Anne Procter seems to have taken as much trouble with 'My God, I thank thee, who hast made the earth so bright' as she did with 'The Lost Chord'. Some hymns were undoubtedly dashed off quickly for use on a particular occasion and regarded as essentially disposable items, but many were the fruit of careful drafting and polishing and were offered to the church in the hope that they might prove useful over a considerable period of time.

It was, of course, the editors of hymn-books who sorted the wheat from the chaff and determined what should be preserved in hard covers and take its place in the canon of authorized hymnody. On the whole, they did their job well and ensured that the ephemeral and the awful was not passed down to posterity. When Edward Plumptre submitted 'Thy hand, O God, has guided' for inclusion in the 1889 supplement of *A & M*, the compilers wisely cut out a verse which began:

> God bless our merry England,
>   God bless our Church and Queen,
> God bless our great Archbishop,
>   The best there's ever been.

The *A & M* archives provide a fascinating insight into how Victorian hymn-writers regarded their work. They are especially illuminating on attitudes towards the vexed subjects of copyright and alteration of texts. A majority of authors took a generous and self-effacing line and regarded their work as public rather than private property. Francis Pott declared his strong feeling 'that hymns and other devotional writings are – or ought to be – an exception to the laws of copyright and property. They are I think written *pro bono Ecclesiae* and ought to be considered as public Church property.'[24] Horatius Bonar told the editors of *A & M*: 'You are welcome to the use of my hymns. As to the charge, it seems to me of little moment, and you can do with it as you like.'[25] J. M. Neale displayed a similarly generous attitude. Indeed, the compilers' policy of wherever possible securing the copyright in hymns they used caused problems for several authors who were used to freely granting permission to all those who sought to reproduce their work. William Whiting responded to a request to assign the copyright of 'Eternal father, strong to save' to the proprietors of *A & M*: 'I have always given not sold the right to use that as well as any other of my hymns which have been asked for, and have refused all offers to purchase that or any other right . . . The only profit I have had is the satisfaction of knowing that I have written anything which has proved of service in Divine Worship.'[26] In the event the proprietors bought the copyright of 'Eternal father' for two guineas which gave them the exclusive use of it and meant that all other hymn-book editors wishing to include it must approach them and not the author.

Some writers were more proprietorial about their work. Perhaps the most awkward of those with whom the proprietors of *A & M* had to deal was Christopher Wordsworth. When they approached him to ask if eight of his hymns could be used in the 1868 appendix, he objected on both doctrinal and financial grounds. He demanded to know which other hymns would be appearing in the appendix since he was uneasy about being associated with 'erroneous and dangerous doctrine, introduced into the service of the Church, by means of hymnody'.[27] He also feared that sales of his book, *The Holy Year*, would suffer if hymns from it appeared in *A & M* and asked in compensation that he should share in the profits of the new appendix. Wordsworth continued to be a thorn in the flesh of the proprietors, constantly complaining about the way his hymns were treated and vital stanzas omitted.

The alteration of words in hymns was, as now, a particularly sensitive issue. James Montgomery described it as 'the Cross, by which every Author of a hymn, who hopes to be useful in his generation, may expect to be tested, at the pleasure of any Christian brother, however incompetent or little qualified to amend what he may deem amiss in one of the most delicate and difficult exercises of a tender heart and an enlightened understanding'.[28] Once again, most hymn-writers were prepared to submit with a good grace to the editorial emendations made to their verses in the interests of felicity of expression or intelligibility. W. D. Maclagan, sending his 'In the gloomy realms of darkness' to the editors of the 1875 edition of *A & M*, wrote: 'I have no tenderness for my literary children so you may criticise freely.'[29] John Ellerton wrote detailed notes on all his hymns to explain why he had chosen certain words but was quite prepared to see them changed: 'Anyone who presumes to lay his offering of a song of praise upon the altar, not for his own but for God's glory, cannot be too thankful for the devout, thoughtful and scholarly criticism of those whose object it is to make his work less unworthy of its sacred purpose.'[30] J. M. Neale raised no objections when phrases in 'Christ is made the sure foundation' were altered because they were thought to be too obscure. He was, however, prepared to dig in his heels over other proposed alterations. His translation of the Latin hymn *Ad cenam Agni providi* ('The Lamb's high banquet call to share') contained the line 'and tasting of his roseate Blood', a reasonable rendering of the original Latin *cruore eius roseo*. When the editors of *A & M* changed this to 'crimson blood' he objected that this weakened the force of the message that Jesus gave his last drop of blood to save the world – 'as everyone knows, the last drainings of life-blood are not crimson, but of a far paler hue: strictly speaking, roseate. Change the word, and you eliminate the whole idea'.[31] A compromise was reached and the phrase became 'precious Blood'.

Some authors made several alterations to their hymns at the request of the editors of different hymnals. Sabine Baring-Gould was prevailed on by the compilers of the *Fellowship Hymn Book* to change the phrase 'one in hope and doctrine' in 'Onward, Christian soldiers' to the rather more accurate 'one in hope and purpose', and in a similar mood of realism the editors of the 1904 edition of *A & M* persuaded him to alter 'we are not divided' to the more accurate 'though divisions harass'. There is a story that when an evangelical Archbishop of York objected to the cross being carried in a procession at Dalton at which Baring-Gould was present, he promptly changed the last line of the refrain to 'With the Cross of Jesus/Left behind the door'. However, a letter written after his death suggests that this episode was invented by his son to satisfy an American newspaper reporter avid for anecdotes about the hymn.

No hymn went through more alterations during its author's lifetime than J. H. Newman's 'Lead, kindly light'. The author himself had no say in any of them. He was not consulted when Horatius Bonar put his verses, which had been written for private devotional use, into a hymnbook in 1845. Bonar added a more distinctively christological focus to the hymn by altering its first line to 'Lead, Saviour, lead amid the encircling gloom' and, sensing that no congregation would understand the expression 'I loved the garish day' he changed it to 'I loved the glare of day'.[32] These two lines were further altered in subsequent hymnbooks. A volume produced for use in the American Episcopal Church in 1860, for example, began the hymn 'Send, Lord, thy light amid the encircling gloom' and continued 'I loved day's dazzling light'. Newman's verses were rather less mutilated in Unitarian hymn-books, although even they could not cope with the 'moor and fen' in the third verse which they turned into 'dreary doubts'. It was, of course, the fact that Unitarians could sing Newman's verses so easily that made many hymn-book editors feel that they needed changing and given a more clearly christocentric focus. When Edward Bickersteth included 'Lead, kindly light' in his *Hymnal Companion to the Book of Common Prayer* in 1870 it was with an extra verse of his own tagged on the end to dispel the mood of doubt that prevailed in the original:

> Meantime along the narrow rugged path
> Thyself hast trod
> Lead, Saviour, lead me home in childlike faith,
> Home to my God,
> To rest for ever after earthly strife
> In the calm light of everlasting life.'[33]

Newman was not alerted to this additional verse, which so substantially altered both the tone and meaning of his poem, until four years after Bickersteth's book appeared. His protest was remarkably restrained: 'It is not that the verse is not both in sentiment and in language graceful and good, but I think you will see at once how unwilling an author must be to subject himself to the inconvenience of that being ascribed to him which is not his own.'[33] Bickersteth responded by promising that in the next edition of the *Hymnal* he would make clear that the fourth stanza was not by Newman but he vigorously defended his editorial initiative, pointing out that the original verses did not make a hymn and required the addition if they were to be sung in church. Once again, Newman's response was a model of forbearance: 'I agree with you that these verses are not a hymn, nor are they suitable for singing, and it is this which at once surprises and gratifies me, and makes me thankful that, in spite of their having no claim to be used as a hymn, they have made their way into so many collections.'[34]

It is ironic that 'Lead, kindly light', which had not been written with congregational singing in mind, should have become one of the Victorians' most popular hymns. As Owen Chadwick reflects, 'Newman himself must have been one of the minority of Englishmen who never heard it sung.'[35] It was, of course, by no means the only poem originally intended for private devotional use which was taken up by hymnal editors. By the end of the nineteenth century more than a hundred of John Keble's verses were to be found in hymn-books. The great majority of them came from *The Christian Year*, which, as we have seen, was only published after much soul-searching by the author. Keble himself never gave his own reaction to the huge popularity of the hymns made out of verses in his 1827 collection such as 'New every morning is the love' and 'Sun of my soul, Thou Saviour dear', although in later years he could bear no reference to the book in his presence. He collaborated with Newman in 1836 to produce a book of verses, *Lyra Apostolica*, which, while again predominantly intended for private devotional use, became, in the words of Henry Scott Holland, 'the song book of English Catholicity, in its most militant and defiant mood'.[36] Keble also published a metrical version of the psalms in 1839 and wrote some verses specifically for congregational singing, including 'Lord, in thy name thy servants plead' for the 1857 *Salisbury Hymn Book*.

Other distinguished poets found their verses widely taken up and sung as hymns. Despite his reticence about joining the ranks of hymn writers, Tennyson found himself in the hymn-books as the author of the very popular 'Strong son of God, immortal love' and 'Sunset and evening star', taken respectively from his 1850 epic *In Memoriam* and his poem 'Crossing the Bar' written when he was 80.[37] Even the work of avowed atheists was quarried to provide material for congregational praise. Given a suitably 'churchy' setting by J. B. Dykes, verses by William Morris, 'From far away', were included in the Christmas section of some hymn-books.[38] Several churchmen also had the experience of seeing lines that they had never intended to be sung appearing in hymnals. Norman Macleod wrote 'Courage brother! do not stumble' as an exhortatory poem to conclude a lecture he delivered to young men in London in 1858. Set to a particularly stirring tune by Sullivan, it was to become a favourite hymn in Scottish and Non-conformist circles. When Sir Henry Baker decided to include William Bright's verses 'And now, O Father, mindful of the love' in the Communion section of *A & M*, the author felt obliged to confess: 'The verses were composed without the faintest thought of their being used congregationally.'[39]

On the whole, authors were pleased to see their work in hymn-books. Quite apart from being flattered at the wider circulation that their verses would be given, they shared the general enthusiasm of the age for the whole enterprise of hymn singing. It is significant and wholly characteristic that as well as inventing the hymn-book, the Victorians also invented hymnology, the academic study of hymns. One of the main manifestations of this interest was the production of annotated editions of the major hymn-books with extensive notes on the sources and background of hymns. The first such volume dates from 1845. An annotated edition of the first edition of *A & M* appeared in 1867 and in 1881 John Ellerton brought out one for *Church Hymns*. The 1875 edition of *A & M* was served by a *Historical Companion* which came out in 1889, the year that also saw the publication of William Garrett Horder's important and pioneering study, *The Hymn Lover: An Account of the Rise and Growth of English Hymnody*, a labour of love by a man who claimed to own a copy of every hymn book ever published. An 1891 volume entitled *Scottish Church Music* dealt with the contents of seven Scottish hymn-books and in 1899 Dr John Brownlie produced *Hymns and Hymn writers of the Church Hymnary*. Learned articles on hymnology appeared in religious and literary journals and general encyclopaedias. Most impressive of all was the 1500 page *Dictionary of Hymnology* produced by John Julian in 1892. The fruit of nearly thirty years' research by the vicar of a remote Yorkshire parish, it represents the consummation of the Victorian love affair with hymns and the respect and recognition accorded to those who wrote them.

5

'Tell me the old, old story'

Themes in Victorian hymns

Generalizations about Victorian hymns abound. They are seen as shallow and sentimental, comfortable and complacent, full of militaristic imagery and triumphalism and exuding the xenophobic nationalism and class consciousness of Britain's imperial high noon. Plenty of hymns do display these traits, it is true, but there are others which express doubt and uncertainty, grapple with complex and difficult theological issues and present a radical and disturbing reading of the Gospel.

The fact is, of course, that Victorian hymnody is a vast and varied body of material about which it is very hard to generalize. Some important distinctions within the genre can be made from the outset. Lionel Adey, in his significant study *Class and Idol in the English Hymn*, distinguishes learned and popular hymnody. In the former category he places the hymns of Anglicanism, Presbyterianism, Congregationalism and Unitarianism which are for the most part characterized by doctrinal objectivity, a stress on the themes of social service and responsibility and the portrayal of work as a vocation or fulfilment. The hymns of Methodists (and especially Primitive Methodists), Baptists, the Salvation Army and the mission halls and revivalist movements of the latter part of the century are more dramatic and personal, stressing deliverance from a world that is seen as full of drudgery, and concentrating rather on the hope of heaven. For Adey class provides the key to distinguishing two dominant and apparently contradictory trends in Victorian hymnody: 'Hymn book religion divided along class lines into working class *Eros*, God experienced in family life and love, alienation from work and ambition, and ruling-class *Agape*, sacrificial self-giving in work for neighbour and nation.'[1]

I have some reservations about the validity of this distinction. One problem with it, which Adey himself acknowledges, is the very small number of Victorian hymns that are genuinely popular in origin, in the sense of having working-class authorship, as against the huge number which became popular by destination. The enthusiastic take-up of hymn singing by the respectable classes tended to blur the distinction between the learned and the popular. As Adey himself observes, 'Wesleyan hymns bawled lustily by miners in the eighteenth century came to be sung decorously by schoolmistresses and small businessmen in the nineteenth.'[2] It is, in fact, possible to point to genuinely working-class hymns which stressed an activist social gospel and did not display the escapism and other-worldliness of Adey's popular hymnody, just as there were verses from the learned tradition which idolized family life and portrayed heaven as home.

Perhaps a more important distinction to make about the tone and themes of Victorian hymns relates to the period from which they come. The Victorian age was a very long one and however settled and secure it may seem in comparison with our own, it encompassed enormous changes in terms of theological, ecclesiastical and cultural trends and preoccupations. A hymn written in the late 1830s is likely to have a very different feel and flavour from one penned around 1900. Lionel Adey sees the learned and popular traditions in hymnody coming together in the late nineteenth century in the context of increasing social stability and prosperity. At the same time, and partly as a result of this congruence, he discerns the increasing intrusion of secular themes into hymns and the transference of religious veneration to the idols of family, nation state and nature. In *Make a Joyful Noise unto the Lord: Hymns as a Reflection of Victorian Social Attitudes*, Susan Tamke notes a similar process of secularization, or at least of humanization, taking place in the hymnodic portrayal of Jesus which moves away from the intensely physical blood-soaked imagery of the eighteenth century towards the notion of friend, brother and role model. This, of course, is in part a reflection of a significant shift in theological emphasis during the Victorian period from atonement to incarnation. It is significant that most of the great Passion and Easter hymns date from before the mid-1860s. There are also clear hymnic echoes of the movement from the Christ of faith to the Jesus of history. Susan Tamke also notes, in contrast to Adey, a move in the latter part of the nineteenth century away from the complacent imperialism of early Victorian mission hymns towards a much greater expression of the social gospel and an appreciation of the value of Christian humility. My own findings, and the evidence presented later in this chapter, tend to support this view.

Some general statements can be made about the tone of Victorian hymns as a whole. The first is their tendency towards the doctrinal and didactic. This is especially noticeable when they are compared to the hymns of the eighteenth century. Whereas Watts, Wesley and the other hymn-writers of the Evangelical Revival poured their own personal experience of salvation into their verses, their Victorian successors struck a more objective note and wrote to expound orthodox doctrine. Their style was more reserved and liturgical, their hymns designed to instruct people in the faith rather than to bring sinners to repentance. Instruction, rather than conversion, was the great object of Victorian hymnody.

One of the products of this approach was the large number of hymns that concentrated on exploring central articles of the Creed. In the unlikely event of the formularies of Nicaea and Chalcedon ever being lost, it would be perfectly possible to reconstruct them in all their intricacy by recourse to Victorian hymnody. Some hymns, like the four-teen written for children by Mrs Alexander in 1848 (see p. 95), were, of course, explicitly intended to elucidate specific aspects of the creed. Others, like Neale's 'Christ is made the sure foundation', with its ringing affirmation of the consubstantial and co-eternal nature of the Trinity, and Newman's 'Firmly I believe and truly' with its acknowledg-ment of 'Manhood taken by the Son', tackle the more complex doctrines of perichoresis and hypostasis. These are expressions of intellectual belief and assent to sound doctrine as much as of saving faith. This is not to say that Victorian hymns were dry and impersonal. Indeed, another consequence of the stress on instruction and imparting sound doctrine was the production of a good number of narrative hymns which retold biblical stories in vivid detail – James Burns' 'Hushed was the evening hymn' on the Lord's call to Samuel and Mrs Alexander's 'The Shepherd now was smitten' on the conversion of St Paul are fine examples of this now largely discarded genre. These narra-tive hymns often ran to a considerable length. Sabine Baring-Gould wrote to the proprietors of *A & M* in 1873 imploring them not to shorten his nine-verse Easter hymn, 'O sons and daughters, let us sing' which told the story of the Resurrection: 'It is very popular with children and with villagers. I have found it useful for conveying the whole story to the memory of ploughboys and the like.'[3]

This didactic strain is, of course, most marked in children's hymns.

Several tackled difficult or complex doctrines – Emily Elliott's 'Thou didst leave thy throne and thy kingly crown' is one of the few hymns of any age which seeks to expound kenotic theory. More commonly, however, children's hymns pursued the easier path of preaching moral exhortation and good behaviour. This was another area of hymnody in which the approach altered significantly over the course of the Victorian period. Initially, the methods used to inculcate moral principles were often pretty crude, as witnessed by verses which appeared in a hymn-book issued in 1831 by the National Society, the body that supervised all Church of England schools:

> Children, never tell a lie:
> Don't you know that when you die,
> God for every lie you tell
> May remove your soul to Hell?

> On the holy Sabbath day
> Christian children must not play;
> They who do this day profane
> Soon may dwell in fire and pain.[4]

This kind of language was a hangover from the wilder excesses of eighteenth-century evangelicalism and was to have less and less of a place in the more genteel atmosphere of Victorian hymnody. It is true that many Victorian children continued to be brought up on the hell-fire imagery of Isaac Watts' hymns that had so disturbed J. M. Neale. A volume of *Questions with Answers Taken from Dr Watts' Hymns for Children* was being used for catechistical exercises by many infants' schools in the late 1830s and 1840s. To the question 'Does God see you, and know all you say' the children were drilled to reply 'There's not a sin that we commit / Nor wicked word we say / Unrecorded in God's dreadful book.'[5] However, this kind of approach steadily lost favour in the face of the Victorian idolization of childhood. In the words of Lionel Adey: 'Between the early and mid-Victorian periods the balance tilted from the depravity of childhood to its consecration, from threat and prohibition to sentimentality, from God the Hanging Judge to God the Friend of Children or Jesus our Elder Brother.'[6]

This shift of emphasis did not indicate any weakening of the didactic impulse. Rather it betokened an appreciation of the fact that children were more likely to be encouraged than frightened into good behaviour and that the carrot was more effective than the stick. It also went hand in hand with the increasing emphasis on instruction rather than evangelism. Children were seen first and foremost as pupils to be taught rather than as unregenerate rascals to be snatched from the devil. This philosophy is perfectly expressed in the advertisement for *Hymns for Infant Minds* (1876) which promised that its hymns are 'calculated in every instance to win to what is good by love rather than deter from what is evil by terror'.[7] It also underlies the approach of Mrs Alexander, whose hymns were brimfull of moralizing ('Little children must be quiet/ When to holy Church they go/ They must sit with serious faces/Must not play or whisper low) but never threatened hell fire and brimstone. Rather the teaching was by example – 'Christian children all must be/mild, obedient, good as he' – and by the promise of heavenly reward – 'Who shall go to that bright land? All who do the right'.

For all this softer approach, however, there was one stark subject that Victorian hymn-writers did not try to tone down or make more palatable, whether they were writing for adults or children. Another set of Mrs Alexander's verses for the young brings us face to face with the topic that is found more than any other in Victorian hymns:

> Within the churchyard, side by side,
>   Are many long low graves;
> And some have stones set over them,
>   On some the green grass waves.

> Full many a little Christian child,
>   Woman, and man, lies there;
> And we pass by them every time
>   When we go in to prayer.

> They cannot hear our footsteps come,
>   They do not see us pass;
> They cannot feel the bright warm sun
>   That shines upon the grass.

> They do not hear when the great bell
>   Is ringing overhead;
> They cannot rise and come to church
>   With us for they are dead.

There is no getting away from the centrality of death as a theme in Victorian hymnody. In an important monograph Brian Castle has pointed to the frequency with which Victorian hymns deal with or refer to the four last things of death, heaven, hell and judgment.[8] The concentration on these subjects stands in marked contrast to their almost complete absence from modern hymns and hymnals. The *Congregational Psalmist Hymnal* of 1886, for example, contained a section on 'Death and the Grave' which included fourteen hymns with substantial additional sub-sections of material dealing with the death of a minister and the death of a child. Its current successor, the United Reformed Church's *Rejoice and Sing* (1991) does not even have a section on funerals, let alone on death. Of the 638 hymns in the 1889 edition of *A & M*, 89 dealt primarily with the experience of death and dying. One would be hard put to find a single hymn on these themes in the current (1984) *Hymns Ancient and Modern New Standard*, certainly not the lone entry in the 'Funeral and Commemoration' section, a translation from the Swahili which is wholly ethereal. The contrast is even more striking in the area of children's hymns. It is almost impossible to think of a contemporary chorus or worship song for young people which even touches on the experience of death. They are almost relentlessly cheerful and up-beat. Victorian children's hymns, on the other hand, frequently evoked death-bed scenes, graphically describing 'the feeble pulse, the gasping breath, /the clenched teeth, the glazed eye'.[9] It was not surprising that, like other sensitive souls brought up to sing lyrics such as these week after week, Janet Hogarth, the journalist daughter of a Lincolnshire vicar, for ever connected hymns with the fear of death.

The fact is, of course, that death was a much more common experience for Victorian children than it is for young people today. Rates of infant mortality remained frighteningly high throughout the nineteenth century with fifteen of every hundred babies dying within a year of their birth. Diseases like scarlet fever, diphtheria and tuberculosis carried off many older children. Victorian hymn-writers were not being morbid or macabre in dwelling so often and so graphically on the subject of death, especially in the context of verses aimed at the young. They were acknowledging and confronting what was undoubtedly one of the most widespread and disturbing experiences of Victorian childhood. In so doing, indeed, they were displaying a good deal more relevance and social awareness than their successors today. How many contemporary hymns treat the equivalent harsh realities of child abuse, drugs and AIDS?

Much of the concentration on death in Victorian hymns sprang from a sincere desire to make some sort of theological and pastoral sense out of a profoundly upsetting process which took so many children suddenly away from their parents and siblings. The attempt to bring consolation and hope to those suffering bereavement or contemplating their own mortality may well have lain at the root of what were perhaps the most widespread 'heresies' perpetrated in Victorian hymns, the portrayal of the passage from this world to the next as relatively swift and effortless and the inclination to favour the sub-Christian notion of the immortality of the soul over the more biblical but more difficult concept of resurrection and a tendency towards universalism. We have already noted the unease felt by the proprietors of *A & M* about hymns that seemed to deny the doctrine of general resurrection and suggest an immediate transition to heaven at death (pp. 67–68). Among those deemed suspect on this count was J. M. Neale's immensely popular 'Safe home, safe home in port!' and the much more evangelically inclined J. D. Burns' 'The Apostle slept':

> So when the Christian's eyelid droops and closes
>   In nature's parting strife,
> A friendly Angel stands where he reposes,
>   To wake him up to life.
>
> He gives a gentle blow, and so releases
>   The spirit from its clay;
> From sin's temptations, and from life's distresses,
>   He bids it come away.

The ubiquity of this kind of language certainly seems to confirm Brian Castle's view that 'there was a preference for the immortality of the soul rather than the resurrection of the body in the Victorian understanding of the afterlife'.[10] Yet the latter doctrine was taken extremely seriously by Victorian hymn-writers and hymnal editors. Both the 1870 *Scottish Hymnal* and the *Church Hymnary* of 1898 had substantial subsections on the theme of 'Death and Resurrection'. The 1887 *Congregational Church Hymnal* included separate sections on 'Death', 'The Rest after Death', 'The Resurrection' and 'The Final Glory of Heaven'. Sabine Baring-Gould and Christopher Wordsworth both penned verses which imaginatively expounded the difficult doctrine of bodily resurrection ('On the Resurrection morning' and 'Alleluia, Alleluia, hearts to heaven and voices raise'). I suspect that an unease about the prevailing belief in immortality may well have lain behind clerical attempts to suppress the popular funeral anthems sung by mourners at the graves of their loved ones. Certainly 'The Vital Spark', Alexander Pope's ode which climbed to the top of the west gallery pops on the basis of its jaunty fuguing tune by Edward Harwood, makes not even the merest nod to the orthodox Christian doctrine of death and resurrection and suggests rather the soul flying out of the body and being instantly liberated. Its suppression may have had less to do with 'High Church aestheticism and disdain for popular cultural practices' than with a high-minded desire to discourage the spread of a comforting but erroneous doctrine.[11]

There were, in fact, a good number of hymn-writers who chose to ignore the advice of Sir Garnet Wolseley, the swashbuckling hero of Victorian imperialism, that a hymn should have 'plenty of consolation and not too much theology'.[12] Many Victorian hymns are packed with theology, sometimes of a complex and unsettling kind which engages with some of the most problematic passages in the Bible. In 'It is finished! blessed Jesus', written for the 1875 edition of *A & M*, William Maclagan tackled the whole difficult subject of the state of Jesus between crucifixion and resurrection. Erik Routley rightly points to Christopher Wordsworth's 'Alleluia, Alleluia, hearts to heaven and voices raise' as 'one of the few hymns which have come to terms with the mysterious passages about the seed and the harvest in St John xii. 24 ff. and 1 Corinthians xv. 37, 42-4'.[13] Another complex scriptural image, Paul's picture of creation groaning and travailing, was picked up by J. M. Neale for his hymn for use in times of cattle plague and by John Ross MacDuff, minister of Sandyford Parish Church, Glasgow, for his thrilling 'Christ is coming, let creation/From her groans and travails cease'. Scottish writers in particular wrestled with theological paradoxes and problems, supreme among them George Matheson with his exploration of the Christian contradiction of the One in whose service we find perfect freedom in 'Make me a captive Lord, and then I shall be free' and the extraordinary depth of 'O love that wilt not let me go' with its radical anticipation of twentieth-century process theology in its conception of life beyond death.

If Victorian hymns about death were often theologically profound, they also display deep pastoral sensitivity. The funeral hymns of John Ellerton in particular are surely some of the finest ever written and display the compassionate approach of a parish minister seeking to bring genuine comfort to church-goer and non-church-goer alike while holding fast to the difficult doctrine of general resurrection. This balance is particularly well struck in the final verse of 'Now the labourer's task is o'er':

> 'Earth to earth, and dust to dust,'
> Calmly now the words we say,
> Leaving him to sleep in trust
> Till the Resurrection-day.
> Father, in Thy gracious keeping
> Leave we now thy servant sleeping.

Another of Ellerton's hymns, originally written for the burial of children but reworked for use at the funerals of those who were not regular church-goers, exemplifies the breadth and inclusivity found in so many great Victorian hymns in its message that those who die unregenerate and beyond the bounds of the church are not dead to God:

> God of the living, in whose eyes
> Unveiled thy whole creation lies;
> All souls are Thine; we must not say
> That those are dead who pass away;
> From this our world of flesh set free,
> We know them living unto Thee.

Disturbed by the universalist implications of this hymn, the proprietors of *A & M* sought revisions from the author to give a greater emphasis on judgment and election. Ellerton refused and his hymn appeared in only one edition of the book (that of 1889) before being removed, though it has lasted longer in other hymnals. His defence of it is a moving apologia for the hymn-writing parish minister seeking to meet a real pastoral need.

> I do not *deny* Hell, or *assert* Purgatory; I merely say that the soul which departs from the body does not depart from the range of God's love. Surely it is recalling the worst side of doctrinal Calvinism to assert this only of those few whom we can honestly call faithful Christians. The belief that *all live with Him* is the only belief which can justify the Church in expressing hope in the Burial Service over all whatsoever their lives who are not formally excommunicate. Most of our funeral hymns either presuppose that the deceased was an eminent saint, or else say nothing which can give hope and comfort to mourners at the very moment when their hearts are most ready to receive the Gospel of God's love . . . If then you think it wise, in deference to the Protestant mind, to withdraw all suggestion of a possibility of mercy in the future life for the great mass of our

parishioners, it would be I think better for you to cancel the hymn
... I am afraid I cannot alter it without destroying it.[14]

Ellerton's broad-minded inclusivism was shared by several of the greatest Victorian hymn-writers and was by no means the sole preserve of middle-of-the-road Anglicans. It is there in the Roman Catholic Faber's 'There's a wideness in God's mercy' with its splendid affirmation 'For the love of God is broader than the measures of man's mind', and the Presbyterian Matheson's 'Gather us in, thou love that fillest all'. It is possible to trace a general reaction on the part of Victorian hymn-writers against the notions of limited atonement and eternal punishment held by their eighteenth-century predecessors. Hell featured less and less in successive hymn-books throughout the period. In the 1889 edition of *A & M* it was mentioned in just 15 of the 638 hymns and only in four of those was it conceived of primarily as a place of pain and punishment. Heaven, by contrast, was the subject of more than 100 hymns and ranks as one of the most popular themes in Victorian hymnody generally.

The evocation of heaven was particularly common in children's hymns. It is the subject of by far the longest sub-section of hymns for the young in the *Church Hymnary* of 1898. I suspect that two factors already noted explain its prominence – the pastoral urge to address natural and widespread anxieties about death and its aftermath and to provide reassurance in an age of high child mortality and the urge to use hymns to teach lessons and point morals. One can see them both coming together in Thomas Bilby's 'Here we suffer grief and pain', a favourite hymn for Victorian children to be taught to memorize (Hardy has Tess Durbeyfield's young brother, Abraham, learning it at his National School) :

> All who love the Lord below,
> When they die, to heaven shall go,
> And sing with saints above.
>
> Little children will be there,
> Who have sought the Lord in prayer,
> From every Sabbath school.
>
> Teachers, too, shall meet above,
> And our pastors, whom we love,
> Shall meet to part no more.

The prospect of being reunited with teachers was not necessarily very attractive, of course. In the world of improving fiction pious children might repeat these verses on their death-beds, as in the 1855 novel *Alice Grey*, but in real life they came in for rather less reverential treatment, like this version produced by the boys of one Yorkshire village:

> Here we suffer grief and pain -
> Over the road they're doing the same,
> Next door they're suffering more
> Oh, won't it be joyful when we part to meet no more.[15]

This dual sense of heaven as a reward for those who love God in this world and a place where people will be reunited after death is strongly conveyed in several of the most popular and enduring Victorian children's hymns. They also give it a precise, almost concrete location and paint a picture of a happy home packed with happy children, as in Jemima Thompson's 'I think when I read that sweet story of old'

> In that beautiful place He is gone to prepare
> For all who are washed and forgiven;
> And many dear children are gathering there,
> For of such is the kingdom of heaven.

The same imagery infuses Albert Midlane's 'There's a friend for little children':

> There's a home for little children
> Above the bright blue sky,
> Where Jesus reigns in glory,
> A home of peace and joy.
> No home on earth is like it,
> Or can with it compare,
> For every one is happy,
> Nor could be happier there.

Perhaps the most significant word here is 'home'. The image that recurs again and again in the depiction of heaven in Victorian hymns is that of the happy home, with work over for the day, the table spread and the family gathered together. The Free Church of Scotland's *Home and School Hymnal* (1893) was by no means unusual in heading its selection of funeral hymns 'Homegoing'. Nor was this just a feature of verses aimed at children. Adult hymns also dwelt on the homely pleasures and happiness of heaven, prominent among them Henry Lyte's 'Pleasant are thy courts above', Andrew Young's 'There is a happy land, far, far away', Henry Baker's 'There is a blessed home', F. W. Faber's 'O Paradise! O Paradise', Christopher Wordsworth's 'Hark, the sound of holy voices' and J. M. Neale's 'Safe home, safe home in port'. Heaven is portrayed as a place, to quote Godfrey Thring's 'Saviour, blessed Saviour', 'Where no pain nor sorrow/ Toil nor care is known'. The blissful state of those who dwell there is contrasted sharply with the miserable existence of those left toiling on earth, even if all are united in the great communion of saints:

> We by enemies distrest -
> They in Paradise at rest;
> We the captives – they the freed-
> We and they are one indeed.[16]

Does this amount to a dangerously escapist dualism in which this world is seen as a wholly evil place which it is the Christian's business to have as little to do with and get through as quickly as possible? Certainly such a view might be deduced from the sharp contrast of the four immensely popular hymns that J. M. Neale extracted from the writings St Bernard of Cluny, 'The world is very evil', 'Brief life is here our portion', 'For thee, O dear, dear country' and 'Jerusalem the golden'. Yet Victorian hymnody is not dualistic. Indeed, much of it has a strongly incarnational flavour. One can hardly level an accusation of hating the world against those who produced such holistic and creation-centred hymns as 'All things bright and beautiful', 'For the beauty of the earth' and 'Almighty Father of all things that be'. If Victorian hymn-writers were not preoccupied with the evil of earthly existence, however, they were very struck by its transitoriness. This is a theme that recurs again and again, often being contrasted with the security and permanence of heaven.

> The roseate hues of early dawn,
>   The brightness of the day,
> The crimson of the sunset sky,
>   How fast they flee away!
> Oh! for the pearly gates of heaven!
>   Oh! for the golden floor!
> Oh! for the Sun of Righteousness
>   That setteth nevermore![17]

In many ways it seems strange that in a society which was so dynamic and a culture so optimistic, most hymn-writers should have remained wedded to a static Aristotelian view of God as the 'unmoved mover' and equated all change with corruption and decay. Victorian hymnody produces remarkably few statements of optimistic belief in progress. Indeed, the only one I can think of is A. C. Ainger's 'God is working his purpose out', which was written at the end of the period in 1894. Much more common are references to the transitoriness and disintegration of worldly things contrasted with the permanence and changelessness of God, most memorably of course in those immortal lines 'Change and decay in all around I see: /O Thou who changest not, abide with me' and 'So be it, Lord! Thy throne shall never, /Like earth's proud empires, pass away'.

Pilgrimage, rather than progress, was the ideal that gripped Victorian hymn-writers. It was, of course, much more compatible with a sense of the world as not being the final destination. Thomas Potter's 'Brightly gleams our banner' spoke of 'waving wand'rers onward / to their home on high' while the compilers of A & M produced a translation from the Latin which proclaimed 'Strangers and pilgrims here below, / We seek a home above'. This could easily slip over into a negative world hating dualism as it had in a well-known (and just pre-Victorian) hymn by Thomas Taylor:

> I'm but a stranger here,
> Earth is a desert drear,
>   Heaven is my home;
> Danger and sorrow stand
> Round me on every hand:
> Heaven is my fatherland,
>   Heaven is my home.

Stressing the theme of pilgrimage did not necessarily involve denouncing the world and preaching a gospel of quietist non-involvement in its affairs. It could, indeed, lead in the opposite direction. Some of the greatest Victorian pilgrim hymns were exhortations to perseverance and calls to action, like Neale's 'O happy band of pilgrims', Baring-Gould's 'Through the night of doubt and sorrow', Henry Alford's 'Forward! be our watchword' and Norman Macleod's 'Courage, brother! do not stumble'. Horatius Bonar regarded the brevity of human life as a reason for engaging in the world rather than just sitting back and longing for heaven:

> 'Tis not for men to trifle! Life is brief,
>   And sin is here.
> Our age is but the falling of a leaf –
>   A dropping tear.
> We have no time to sport away the hours;
> All must be earnest in a world like ours.[18]

Calls to be up and doing sound through several of Bonar's hymns, notably 'Make use of me, my God!', 'Go, labour on', 'Work, for the time is flying' and 'Make haste, O man, to live'. Other hymns with a similar theme include Thomas Lynch's 'Dismiss me not Thy service, Lord', Faber's 'Workman of God, O lose not heart' and Ellerton's 'Behold us, Lord, a little space', one of the few Victorian hymns to allude to the workplace ('Thine is the loom, the forge, the mart'), with its clear articulation of the doctrine of *laborare est orare*:

> Work shall be prayer, if all be wrought
>   As Thou wouldst have it done;
> And prayer, by Thee inspired and taught,
>   Itself with work be one.

Interestingly, some of the most powerful hymnodic endorsements of the gospel of work come from women writers: Jane Borthwick's 'Come, labour on! No time for rest till glows the western sky!', Charlotte Elliott's 'Christian, seek not yet repose', Mary Hasloch's 'Christian, work for Jesus' and Annie Walker's 'Work, for the night is coming' with its injunction 'Fill brightest hours with labour,/Rest comes sure and soon'. The same conjunction of work and rest occurs in the opening lines of one of Godfrey Thring's hymns: 'Work is sweet for God has blest/ Honest work with quiet rest'.

Rest is, indeed, another prominent theme in Victorian hymnody. It is not the rest of idleness and inactivity, however, but rather the well-earned reward promised by Jesus to those who have fought the good fight and find themselves weary and spent. Matthew 11. 28-30 provided inspiration for several very popular hymns, including Jane Borthwick's 'Rest, weary soul', William Chatterton Dix's 'Come unto me, ye weary', J. M. Neale's 'Art thou weary, art thou languid?' and, of course, Bonar's 'I heard the voice of Jesus say/Come unto me and rest'. It is no coincidence that the word 'weary' features prominently in the first verse of all these hymns. I suspect that a word count would reveal it to be one of the most frequently used terms in all Victorian hymnody. We are

back to the pastoral sensitivity of the hymn-writers and their consciousness of the many lives worn down by tiredness and cares. Like death, the
theme of sickness looms much larger in Victorian hymn-books than in
modern collections. As we might expect, it was taken up especially by
those women writers who themselves suffered chronic ill-health and
who were ever ready to draw a lesson and point a moral from their
experiences.

> Sickness is a school severe,
> Where the soul (in childhood here)
> Wayward 'neath a milder sway,
> Learns to think, and learns to pray.
> Blest and wise its discipline,
> There the teacher is divine.
>
> . . . .
>
> I thank thee more that all my joy
>   Is touched with pain:
> That shadows fall on brightest hours,
>   That thorns remain;
> So that earth's bliss may be my guide,
>   And not my chain.[19]

The dominant note struck in the many hymns about illness and
suffering is that of resignation. J. M. Neale's 'In Sickness' begins: 'Thy
Will be done, I still would say, / Whate'er that Will may be'. Bonar, in
'Thy way not mine, O Lord', prays 'Choose thou for me my friends, /
My sickness or my health'. The same sentiment underlies those two
great hymns of self-dedication, Charlotte Elliott's 'Just as I am' and
Frances Havergal's 'Take my life and let it be consecrated, Lord, to
Thee', and is particularly powerfully expressed by Catherine Wink-
worth:

> Whate'er my God ordains is right:
>   His will is ever just;
> Howe'er he orders now my cause,
>   I will be still and trust.
>   He is my God;
>   Though dark my road,
> He holds me that I shall not fall;
> Wherefore to Him I leave it all.

There is, of course, a thin dividing line between resignation, obedience and utter trust in God and a passive and abject submissiveness which meekly accepts manifest injustice and oppression. There is no doubt that the qualities of resignation and obedience are much lauded in Victorian hymns, especially those aimed at the young. This is the moral, and the prayer, that J. D. Burns draws from his retelling of the story of Samuel in 'Hushed was the evening hymn':

> Oh, give me Samuel's mind,
>   A sweet, unmurmuring faith,
> Obedient and resigned
>   To Thee in life and death.

Resignation to the will of God, however, does not necessarily mean grovelling submission to a particular social or political order that fosters inequality or injustice. Victorian hymn-writers have often been accused of either unconsciously or quite deliberately blurring the distinction and preaching passive acceptance on the part of the poor of a highly hierarchial and unjust social order. Indeed, they have been held guilty of compounding the crime by perpetrating the heresy that inequality is ordained by God. The latest to make this accusation, David Konstant, Roman Catholic Bishop of Leeds, recently described the infamous (and now almost universally discarded) verse of 'All things bright and beautiful' about 'the rich man in his castle' and 'the poor man at his gate' as 'one of the most dreadful, even unintentionally wicked commentaries on society'.[20]

In fact the point that Mrs Alexander was seeking to make in this verse was not that God made some high and some lowly but rather that his grace is equally available to all, whatever condition they find themselves in. This is put more clearly in a verse from one of her earlier hymns:

> The poor man in his straw-roofed cottage,
>   The rich man in his lordly hall,
> The old man's voice, the child's first whisper,
>   He listens, and He answers all.

One could say, indeed, that Mrs Alexander's message here, far from being about the divine ordaining of inequality, is rather about God's indifference to human distinctions of rank and wealth. It is, however, undeniable that in another children's hymn she does come much closer to preaching submissiveness and consecrating the *status quo*.

> Day by day the little daisy
> Looks up with his yellow eye,
> Never murmurs, never wishes
> It were hanging up on high.
>
> And the air is just as pleasant,
> And as bright the sunny sky,
> To the daisy by the footpath
> As to flowers that bloom on high.
>
> God has given each his station:
> Some have riches and high place,
> Some have lowly homes and labour;
> All may have His precious grace.
>
> And God loveth all His children,
> Rich and poor, and high and low;
> And they all shall meet in heaven
> Who have served Him here below.

Several of the themes that we have already identified as central to Victorian hymnody are prominently displayed here – a broad inclusive theology, a stress on the love rather than the wrath of God and a focus on heaven as the place where all will meet. Yet what strikes us most forcibly today is the apparent message that social inequality is divinely ordained. Stephen Wilson has argued that the legitimizing of the existing social order is, in fact, the dominant theme of Victorian hymns in general, and those found in *A & M* in particular. He finds that 223 of the 638 hymns in the 1889 edition present submissiveness as an important Christian virtue and sees the prevailing attitude epitomized in the Ember Day hymn, 'The earth, O Lord, is one wide field' with its lines 'And give their flocks a lowly mind / to hear and to obey'.[21]

It is certainly true that many Victorian hymns breathe an air of social conservatism. They are gentle rather than angry, reflecting the calm and secluded atmosphere of the country rectory rather than the chaos and squalor of the city slum or factory. This is, of course, what we would expect given the background of the great majority of their authors. As Erik Routley has pointed out, on the whole Victorian hymn-writers were ' a set of men whose lives were abundantly serene and without traces of dramatic conversion and spiritual tumult. In the nineteenth century the F. W. Robertsons and F. D. Maurices, the men of urgency and action, did not write the hymns.'[22] In Anglican writers especially serenity could spill over into complacency and into the heresy of ecclesiolatry. Worship of the church as an institution was a besetting temptation for Victorian hymn-writers, even one as accomplished as J. M. Neale:

> The good old Church of England!
>   With her priests throughout the land,
> And her twenty thousand churches,
>   How nobly does she stand!
> Dissenters are like mushrooms,
>   That flourish in a day;
> Twelve hundred years, through smiles and tears
>   She hath lasted on alway!

At least this piece of Anglican chauvinism never found its way into any hymn-book. Hymnal editors did sometimes exercise censorship in the interests of what would now be called political correctness. The infamous verse of 'All things bright and beautiful' was dropped from the first edition of the *Church Hymnary* in 1898 although it appeared in the 1889, 1904 and 1916 editions of *A & M*. On the whole, however, those responsible for compiling the hymnbooks of the major churches were reluctant to include verses which questioned prevailing social and economic conditions and expressed a theology of liberation and radical change. Ebenezer Elliott's 'When wilt thou save the people', first published in a Sheffield newspaper in 1832 and sung widely first at Chartist demonstrations and later in labour churches and at Pleasant Sunday Afternoon meetings, was taken up by the Methodists and Congregationalists but resolutely excluded from the hymnals of the established churches of England and Scotland. 'God is our Guide!', written in prison by George Loveless, one of the Tolpuddle Martyrs, and Edward Osler's 1836 rewriting of Watts, 'Come, let us search our hearts, and try/If all our ways be right' were similarly cold-shouldered. There were hymns being written comparatively early in Victoria's reign that expressed anger and indignation over inequality and injustice, but they remained confined to collections produced by radical reforming groups such as *Democratic Hymns and Songs* (1849), which included this biting attack on the churches' indifference to social problems:

Our streets are filled with woe;
  Starvation and distress;
And widows' tears are seen to flow
  For children, fatherless.

And yet the priests declare
  We must contented be!
But by our country's wrongs, we swear,
  Our country shall be free.

By comparison, the hymns written by F. D. Maurice's Anglican Christian Socialist disciples in the 1840s and 1850s, which did find their way into respectable mainstream hymn-books, seem very pallid affairs. It is difficult to discern much righteous anger or crusading zeal in Thomas Hughes' 'O God of truth, whose living word' or Charles Kingsley's 'From thee all skill and science flow', although the latter does at least introduce a social element to the Gospel message by stressing the importance of caring for the sick and desolate. The first significant Anglican hymn calling for a radical change of direction in society was probably 'Thy kingdom come, O God', written by Lewis Hensley, Vicar of Hitchin, in 1867. On the whole, even the Broad Churchmen who were more influenced than most by Christian Socialism still clung to a broad and comfortable credo with more than a touch of complacency – none more so than Arthur Stanley writing in 1873:

Give us homes serene and pure,
Settled freedom, laws secure;
Truthful lips and minds sincere,
Faith and love that cast out fear:
Grant that light and life divine
Long on England's shores may shine;
Grant that people, Church and Throne
May in all good deeds be one.

Fifteen years later a Christian Socialist of a very different background and hue was penning verses that reflected much more anger and much more engagement with the problems of the people. Edward Carpenter's 'England arise! the long, long night is over' belonged firmly in the tradition of 'When wilt thou save thy people'.

Over your face a web of lies is woven,
  Laws that are falsehoods pin you to the ground,

Labour is mocked, its just reward is stolen,
  On its bent back sits Idleness encrowned.
    How long, while you sleep,
    Your harvest shall It reap?
Arise, O England, for the day is here!

Significantly, Carpenter's hymn did not appear in any mainstream late Victorian hymn-book but was confined to the pages of collections produced by socialist societies. These tended towards Unitarianism in their theology and eschewed dogmatic and christocentric hymns. The first hymn-book published by the Labour Church in 1892 contained only one hymn (by Whittier) in which Jesus was mentioned. An ethical socialist hymnal published in Newcastle in 1893 similarly eliminated all specifically Christian references and substituted the impending reign of love for the coming of God's kingdom.

Sometime, when right comes uppermost
  The old wrongs all must die,
Pure love will conquer evil's host,
  And all his pow'r defy:
Then there shall be no starving poor
  Begging the rich for bread,
Peace will unlock the prison door,
  All shall be cloth'd and fed.[23]

Although showing no inclination to use these and similar verses being sung in socialist and labour circles from the 1880s onwards, those compiling hymn-books in the closing years of Victoria's reign often complained of the lack of hymns on the plight of the poor. Their efforts to commission verses on the themes of social and economic justice tended to produce rather patronizing results, like this hymn 'for a service for working men' by Canon S. R. Hole of Newark in the 1889 supplement to *A & M*:

Sons of labour, dear to Jesus,
  To your homes and work again;
Go with brave hearts back to duty,
  Face the peril, bear the pain,
Be your dwellings ne'er so lowly,
  Yet remember by your bed,
That the Son of God most Holy
  Had not where to lay His head.

Even with its essentially conservative message, this was a rarity among hymns in the mainstream collections in actually mentioning and being addressed to working men. Even rarer were hymns advocating communitarian values of mutual care and social responsibility. When Percy Dearmer became Secretary of the Christian Social Union in London in 1894 he found it very hard to find suitable hymns to use at mid-day services at St Edmund's, Lombard Street: 'We could find in the book used in the church no hymns that were concerned with man's duty to his neighbour; and we grew weary of the doleful tune and depressing words of "Thy kingdom come, O Lord". We wanted hymns that expressed faith and hope.'[24] Ten years later the editors of the new edition of *Hymns Ancient and Modern* apologized for the dearth of hymns on social conditions: 'The defect lies largely with the composers of our hymns and not with the compilers of the collections . . . few hymn writers apparently have been inspired by the social and national aspects of Christianity which appeal so largely in our time'.[25]

In fact, the compilers of the 1904 edition of *A & M* were able to find one very powerful hymnodic expression of Christian socialism by an Anglican clergyman, 'Son of God, eternal Saviour' written in 1893 by Somerset Corry Lowry, vicar of North Holmwood, Surrey. They might also have included Henry Scott Holland's 'Judge eternal, throned in splendour' which had first appeared in 1902 in the pages of *The Commonwealth*, the journal that he edited to promote the social application of the Christian faith. It was to be the Edwardian age – that great era of progressive social reform which laid the foundations of the Welfare State – that saw the fullest and finest expression of the Christian social gospel in hymnodic form, most majestically, perhaps, in G. K. Chesterton's 'O God of earth and altar' which appeared in *The Commonwealth* in 1906. It was from this period that Percy Dearmer took many of the hymns that he put into his 'Social Service' section of *Songs of Praise* (1931), the first hymn-book to have such a category. Yet alongside more recent verses, like Laurence Housman's 'Father eternal, ruler of creation' and Clifford Bax's 'Turn back, O Man, forswear thy foolish ways', he also included the hymns of Ebenezer Elliott and Edward Carpenter that had so long been excluded from major collections and even found a poem by Kingsley with an urgent and prophetic tone, 'The day of the Lord is at hand', which had not appeared in any nineteenth-century hymn-book.

Alongside social conservatism, Victorian hymns are often accused of plugging triumphalist militarism and xenophobic imperialism. Stephen

Wilson identifies these as major themes in the hymns in the 1889 edition of *A & M* and Lionel Adey's computer word search suggests that those hymns that offer military images for Christian life come overwhelmingly from the nineteenth century.[26] I am myself dubious as to whether the language of Victorian hymnody was, in fact, excessively militaristic. If we are talking about references to Christians taking up swords and putting on armour, then we have to say that the Bible is also militaristic. Many Christian traditions have used the imagery found in Ephesians 6. 10-18, not least the gentle and spiritually sensitive Celts with their *lorica* tradition exemplified in the verses we know as 'St Patrick's Breastplate'. Actual analysis of the language of the much-maligned 'Onward, Christian soldiers', which was written, as we have seen, for an outdoor children's parade and not for use in normal church worship, shows that military imagery is used only in a metaphorical sense. The church is portrayed as being 'like a mighty army' but never as an army itself. Owen Chadwick has pointed out that the Victorian hymns which do contain military imagery are mostly the products of a specific and short period in the early 1860s.[27]

The charge that Victorian hymns sometimes displayed a chauvinistic and xenophobic nationalism is more difficult to refute. Several writers of children's hymns slipped into this particular heresy, although few perhaps quite as whole-heartedly as Ann and Jane Taylor in these verses which first appeared in *Hymns for Infant Minds* (1876).

> I thank the goodness and the grace
>   Which on my birth have smiled,
> And made me, in these Christian days,
>   A happy English child.
>
> I was not born, as thousands are,
>   Where God was never known;
> And taught to pray a useless prayer
>   To blocks of wood and stone.
>
> I was not born a little slave,
>   Beneath a burning sun,
> To wish I were but in a grave,
>   And all my labour done.

Missionary hymns, that distinctively Victorian genre which has been discreetly banished from modern hymn-books, were particularly prone to the danger of patronizing other cultures and preaching an imperialistic doctrine of Anglo-Saxon supremacy. Heber in 'From Greenland's icy mountains' and Charles Oakley in 'Hills of the North rejoice' came close to espousing this position and portraying benighted heathens in Africa and India crying out to the British to free their lands from error's chains. Yet there were also hymns that acknowledged that heathens were not only to be encountered among the dusky natives of far-off lands. J. A. Todd's 'Hark the voice of Jesus crying' reminded children that:

> If you cannot cross the ocean,
> And the heathen lands explore,
> You can find the heathen nearer,
> You can help them at your door.

Patriotism, rather than nationalism, is perhaps the characteristic theme of those hymns written about home and country. The dividing line between these two positions is very difficult to draw and to modern ears I suspect there is a disturbingly chauvinistic and xenophobic feel to several of the hymns that the Victorians would have considered as perfectly proper expressions of loyalty to Queen and country. A good example is still to be found in some current hymn-books, including the *Church Hymnary*:

> Lord, while for all mankind we pray,
> Of every clime and coast,
> Oh, hear us for our native land,
> The land we love the most.

Significantly, this verse was penned by John Wreford, a Unitarian, for Queen Victoria's accession in 1837. A whole crop of hymns written for royal occasions and anniversaries, and now largely forgotten, expound a similar theme of Britain as a chosen and favoured nation. Arthur Stanley's 'Let us with a gladsome mind', quoted above (p. 126) was written for use on 20 June, 1873, the 36th anniversary of the Queen's accession. John Ellerton, whom we have already encountered in this mood, had produced a similarly florid piece of patriotic sentiment three years earlier:

> Praise to our God, whose bounteous hand
> Prepared of old our glorious land,
> A garden fenced with silver sea,
> A people prosperous, strong and free!

This particular hymnodic genre reached its apogee, as might be expected, during the celebrations of the golden and diamond jubilees of Victoria's accession. A booklet of specially commissioned hymns was produced for the 1887 jubilee with contributions from Ellerton, Baring-Gould, Bickersteth ('God of our fatherland') and S. J. Stone ('God of supreme dominion'). For the 1897 jubilee How produced 'O King of kings, whose reign of old' which greatly appealed to Arthur Sullivan, who set it to music (see p. 168), but angered many Scots because of the Anglo-centrism of its second verse:

> Oh Royal heart with wide embrace
>   For all her children yearning!
> Oh happy realm, such mother-grace
>   With loyal love returning!
> Where England's flag flies wide unfurl'd
>   All tyrant wrongs repelling,
> God make the world a better place
>   For man's brief earthly dwelling.

By far the most significant and surprising verses to come out of the Diamond Jubilee celebrations of 1897 were written by Rudyard Kipling at the request of *The Times*. 'Recessional' has a definite hymnodic quality. Partly inspired by the great naval review at Spithead, it might be expected to be full of imperial echoes and patriotic pride. Yet the Poet Laureate of the Empire, as he has been dubbed, chose rather to call his countrymen to humility and repentance. In the words of Kipling's latest biographer, Peter Keating, ' "Recessional" is virtually a compilation of Biblical allusions, quotations and echoes. Like "The Song of the English" (an earlier poem which also had a hymn-like quality), it is based on the assumption that God has made a special covenant with England, but whereas the earlier poem had centred on the forging of the covenant, "Recessional" points to its possible collapse.'[28] Kipling took his refrain from Moses's words of warning to the people of Israel in Deuteronomy 6.12: 'Then take heed lest you forget the Lord, who brought you out of the land of Egypt.'

> God of our fathers, known of old,
>   Lord of our far-flung battle line,
> Beneath Whose awful hand we hold
>   Dominion over palm and pine,
> Lord God of hosts, be with us yet,
> Lest we forget – lest we forget.

The tumult and the shouting dies,
   The captains and the kings depart;
Still stands Thine ancient sacrifice,
   An humble and a contrite heart.
Lord God of hosts, be with us yet,
Lest we forget – lest we forget.

Far-called, our navies melt away,
   On dune and headland sinks the fire;
Lo, all our pomp of yesterday
   Is one with Nineveh and Tyre!
Judge of the nations, spare us yet,
Lest we forget – lest we forget.

The note of national humility sounded in Kipling's 'Recessional' is
not exceptional in late Victorian hymnody. It is worth recalling that
Ellerton's great evening hymn, chosen by Queen Victoria herself to be
sung at churches across the British Isles on 20 June 1897, carries the
reminder that earth's proud empires, presumably including even the
British one on which the sun never sets, do, in fact, pass away. Victorian
hymn-writers, especially late Victorian hymn-writers, did not worship
at the shrine of jingoistic nationalism and triumphant imperialism. They
were deeply patriotic and they loved and revered their Queen. It is,
however, wrong to suggest, as Lionel Adey does, that they secularized
the Christian faith and turned it into worship of the nation.

A more widespread charge levelled against Victorian hymns is that
they are over-sentimental and offer an easy and comfortable escape
from the problems and pressures of the real world. Comparing
eighteenth and nineteenth century hymns, Susan Tamke finds the latter
to be blander and 'more mawkishly sentimental'.[29] Some Victorian
hymns do employ images and language more appropriate to the parlour
ballad, deliberately tugging at the heart-strings and striving for
emotional effect. Against this, however, we have to set the objectivity
and reserve of so much nineteenth-century hymnody.

One apparent manifestation of this over-sentimental approach was
the strong sense of dependence, and perhaps even of infantilism, incul-
cated in both adults' and childrens' hymns. It is there in Lyte's 'Father-
like he tends and spares us, / Well our feeble frame he knows' and in
Burns's 'That we may see with child-like eyes/ Truths that are hidden
from the wise'. Yet if Victorian hymns were encouraging adults to be
more child-like and to look on God as a kind and gentle father, they

were surely doing no more than following Jesus' own very clear lead and teaching. Critics have also suggested that children were also infantilized by the constant use of the word 'little' as in 'little ones to him belong/they are weak, but he is strong'. The modern hymn-writer Elizabeth Cosnett has singled out Mrs Alexander for particular condemnation in this regard, accusing her of having 'carried to its extreme the Victorian stress on the littleness of children'.[30] Seen from the late twentieth-century perspective where childhood has pretty well been whittled away by television and commercial and cultural pressures, with infants moving almost straight into a kind of pre-adolescence as a result, however, I wonder whether the Victorian idolization of the innocence and dependency of childhood looks either as repressive or unhealthy as it once did. One might well argue that it is our modern loss of any sense of human dependency and our attachment to the illusion that we have come of age and can determine our destiny that has been responsible for much of the acute social and cultural malaise of this current age. That is for another book than this one to pursue, I know, but it is just worth commenting here on the almost complete absence from Victorian hymns, for all the apparent optimism and self-confidence of the age, of this post-Enlightenment (and, dare one add, post-Christian) ideal of mature, adult humanity.

Closely related to their idolization of childhood is the charge that Victorian hymns sentimentalized Jesus and turned him into a rather weak and effeminate figure. Hymns about the nativity are particularly in the firing line here – notably Edward Caswall's 'See, in yonder manger low' with its prayer 'Teach, O teach us, Holy Child, / By Thy face so meek and mild', and Mrs Alexander's 'Once in royal David's City' with its portrayal of the infant Jesus as 'mild, obedient, good . . . little, weak and helpless'. In fact, it is important to point out that the phrase 'Gentle Jesus, meek and mild', memorably described by George Bernard Shaw as 'a snivelling travesty', was not of Victorian origin but formed the first line of a children's hymn written by Charles Wesley in 1763. Some early nineteenth-century Tractarians were tempted to use this kind of imagery about Jesus in their hymns – and it is interesting that it was more prevalent among those caught up in the Oxford Movement than among Evangelicals – but hymn-book editors were quick to eliminate it. The original opening verse of an Epiphany hymn submitted to *A & M* by John Chandler ran:

> In stature grows the heavenly child,
>   With death before his eyes;
> A Lamb unblemished, meek, and mild,
>   Prepared for sacrifice.

The compilers amended it to read:

> The heavenly Child in stature grows,
>   And growing learns to die;
> And still His early training shows
>   His coming agony.

In this case the compilers were acting as much to remove unwanted sacrificial imagery about Jesus as to eliminate the phrase 'meek and mild'. There was, in fact, a clear trend during the Victorian period away from the portrayal of Jesus as a sacrificial lamb, achieving salvation through the power of his blood and towards a much more 'healthy minded' (the phrase is constantly used) and manly picture of one who is a hero, friend and brother. Charlotte Elliott's 'Just as I am, without one plea/But that Thy blood was shed for me' was altered by Marianne Farningham in 1881 for a Congregational hymnal to fit in with this changing image and became 'Just as I am, Thine own to be, / Friend of the young, who lovest me'. This transition from redeemer to role model, which reached its apogee in early twentieth-century hymns like Frank Fletcher's 'O son of man, our hero strong and tender', was part of the move away from the blood-soaked imagery of eighteenth-century evangelicalism and of the general shift from atonement to incarnation noted at the beginning of this chapter.

   If Victorian hymns were progressively depicting the figure of Jesus in a less disturbing and more reassuring light, then they were often also providing comfort and consolation in another direction by looking backwards rather than forwards. Critics often point to their nostalgic escapism and their retreat from the problems and tensions of a complex industrial society and post-Enlightenment culture into the reiteration of ancient tradition. 'I think when I read that sweet story of old', 'Tell me the old, old story', 'The good old book!' all seem to take refuge in the past. There are Victorian hymns that look to the future – as we have seen there are several that invoke the theme of pilgrimage – but often they do so with a hesitation and uncertainty that is again out of kilter with the spirit of an age supposedly so optimistic and confident. There is nothing in Victorian hymnody that comes close to embracing the new and moving into the future in the manner of Sydney Carter's 'One more step along the world I go'.

An often cited aspect of this backward-looking perspective is the rural imagery of most Victorian hymns. Reading or singing them, one would have virtually no clue that they were written at a time when Britain was a rapidly urbanizing industrial society where most people lived in cities and towns. They are full of references to golden sheaves of corn, shepherds and purple-headed mountains. So, of course, is the Bible. Yet this does not excuse the almost total absence of references to the realities of contemporary life. Adey is quite justified in observing that 'Victorian hymns never exalted the manufacturers, inventions, transportation, and industrial cities that were the chief cause of England's wealth and influence.'[31] It is equally hard to quarrel with Susan Tamke's remark that 'In their hymns there is a strong thread of conservatism and romanticism. The images which they used were not those of contemporary reality, but of an idealized past.'[32] With the exception of the splendid railway hymn mentioned earlier (p. 54) and John Ellerton's 'Behold us, Lord, a little space' with its reference to 'the loom, the forge, the mart', I can think of no Victorian mainstream hymn that refers to the worlds of industry, commerce and urban life.

One could, of course, say the same of much twentieth-century hymnody. Those hymns which have tried to engage with modern inventions, like Richard Jones's 'God of concrete, God of steel', have not proved very popular. It is only at the tail end of the century that issues such as unemployment and violence to women have found their way into hymns. Susan Tamke is right to observe that 'hymns are one of the most conservative components of an already conservative institution'.[33] We are much happier singing in church about events recorded in the Bible than about contemporary social problems.

Yet Victorian hymn-writers did not altogether duck contemporary issues. As we have seen, theological controversies like the Colenso affair inspired hymns, although they were generally of a reactive and reactionary kind. The thorny subject of science and faith was tackled by the redoubtable Mrs Alexander in a hymn which began:

> Through paths of pleasant thought I ran,
>   False science sang enchanted airs;
> She told of nature and of man,
>   And of the Godlike gift he bears.

The tone here is again reactive. 'False science' is soon discarded in favour of a meditation on the true nature of the human condition as one of sin, guilt, pain and trial.

Shunning difficult and controversial topics and steering clear of engagement with major social and economic issues, many Victorian hymn-writers seem to opt rather for reassurance and comfort, dwelling on the domestic images of the hearth and the home. Several critics have seen this escapist tendency epitomized in Henry Baker's 'The King of Love my Shepherd is'. Erik Routley notes: 'Sir Henry Baker writes, not a pastoral paraphrase like George Herbert's or an eighteenth-century country-house paraphrase like Addison's, but an English parish-church paraphrase . . . This is the purest Anglican Herefordshire.'[34] Lionel Adey sees it as the hymn that above all others 'exemplifies the piety of the learned tradition in its subjective aspect' and expresses the two cardinal principles of Victorian faith – the coherence of God and the certainty of salvation.[35] He draws attention particularly to the lines:

> Perverse and foolish oft I strayed,
>   And yet in love he sought me,
> And on his shoulder gently laid,
>   And home rejoicing brought me.

Adey points to the clear influence here of the words of the General Confession in the Book of Common Prayer: 'We have erred and strayed from thy ways like lost sheep.' He also suggests that to the untold thousands who have sung this hymn in church or school, 'both "home" and "rejoicing" surely denote their present state of life, neither crisis nor consummation, but simply health, cheerfulness, self-acceptance. Home is where the heart has ease. Heaven is a continuance in that state.'[36] It is, he suggests, a hymn written by and for the comfortably off, which suggests that there is no radical discontinuity between this world and the next. Heaven is portrayed as home, and more specifically as an upper-middle-class home.

I wonder, however, whether this is being entirely fair. It is quite true that Baker led the untroubled life of a prosperous squarson and the gentle pastoral imagery of his hymns belongs to the secluded rural world inhabited by so many Victorian hymn-writers. Yet the inspiration for this particular verse, which departs markedly from the 23rd Psalm of which the hymn is otherwise a fairly close paraphrase, is surely the parable of the prodigal son, a theme that recurs again and again in Victorian hymnody. It is not a story that one would expect to appeal to the comfortably off and complacent. After all, it is the nose of the ultra-respectable, God-fearing, eminently Victorian elder brother that is put out of joint by the father's welcome of his feckless ne'er-do-well sibling.

Some of the most enduring Victorian hymns which at first sight might seem to offer empty exhortation from a position of comfort and ease turn out on closer examination to be the product of considerable heart-searching born out of lives of sacrifice and struggle. Take that master-piece of muscular Christianity, 'Courage, brother! do not stumble', which I dearly hope we can preserve in these days of inclusive language. It was written for working men by Norman Macleod, who had a highly demanding inner-city parish ministry in Glasgow during which he worked tirelessly for social reform and economic justice and fell foul of more conservative colleagues by opposing the narrow Sabbatarianism which so cramped the leisure pursuits of working-class communities in Scotland. There are unmistakable echoes of this struggle in the second stanza of his hymn.

> Perish policy and cunning,
>   Perish all that fears the light!
> Whether losing, whether winning,
>   Trust in God, and do the right.
> Some will hate thee, some will love thee,
>   Some will flatter, some will slight;
> Cease from man, and look above thee:
>   Trust in God, and do the right.

Several other hymns of exhortation and encouragement were also far from being the pious utterances of those in easy circumstances with an untroubled faith. 'Say not, the struggle naught availeth', was extracted from a poem by Arthur Hugh Clough, who was plagued by religious doubts. Another late Victorian favourite, Sarah Flower Adams's 'Nearer, my God, to Thee' is similarly shot through with a sense of difficulty and despair, with 'the sun gone down' and 'darkness . . . over me'.

Darkness is, indeed, a theme that haunts a surprising number of Victorian hymns. Matthew Arnold's celebrated statement in Dover Beach, 'we are here as on a darkling plain' is echoed by Lyte ('the dark-ness deepens'), Newman ('the night is dark, and I am far from home'), Thomas Binney ('I, whose native sphere is dark') and even by Anne Ross Cousin in 'The sands of time are sinking' ('Dark, dark hath been the midnight'). In these hymns darkness stands for difficulty, despair, per-plexity and also for doubt. Owen Chadwick, in his classic work, *The*

Victorian Church, asserts that 'the intellectual difficulties of the nineteenth century were little reflected in devotion'.³⁷ I beg to differ. It seems
to me that the Victorian crisis of faith was reflected in the hymns of the
age. It is true that some devout sceptics kept their doubts out of their
devotional writings. Chadwick points to the contrast between the theme
of a little book privately printed under the title *Between doubt and
prayer* by Edwin Hatch, one of the leading theologians of 1880s, and
the tone of his most celebrated hymn, 'Breathe on me, breath of God',
which 'contained more assurance of faith than many famous Arminian
hymns'.³⁸ Yet there were other eminent Victorian divines, including
those mentioned earlier in this paragraph, who were not afraid to put
their doubts as well as their faith into their hymns. Erik Routley
identifies Henry Twells, author of 'At even, when the sun was set',
as one who wrote searching, penitential, doubt-filled hymns which 'a
frowning contemporary would surely have been proud to have
written'.³⁹ In a perceptive analysis of the themes of Victorian hymns,
Horton Davis has pointed out that a high proportion of those with a
triumphalist message turn out to be translations or imitations of verses
from the early church: 'They were not as truly indigeneous as the hymns
of faith-in-doubt.'⁴⁰

    This motif of faith-in-doubt is particularly evident in two hymns that
were consistently in the upper reaches of the Victorian Top Ten. 'Strong
Son of God, immortal Love' was culled from Tennyson's great outpour-
ing of anger and doubt in the wake of the death of his close friend,
Arthur Hallam. *In Memoriam* provides that great affirmation 'There
lives more faith in honest doubt,/ Believe me, than in half the creeds'.
The verses which were taken up as a hymn have, perhaps, a rather
greater sense of faith but it is faith grounded in trust rather than in
certainty and once again the imagery of darkness is prominent:

> We have but faith: we cannot know;
> For knowledge is of things we see;
> And yet we trust it comes from Thee,
> A beam in darkness: let it grow.

Newman's 'Lead, kindly light' was, if anything, even more doubt-filled.
Certainly that was how it was perceived by many of his contemporaries.
While it found its way into virtually every Unitarian, rationalist and
labour church collection, it was regarded with considerable suspicion by
the compilers of several more orthodox church hymn-books. We have
already noted Edward Bickersteth's attempt to provide a more distinctly

Christian focus and a more up-beat ending where Newman had left a lingering sense of uncertainty (p. 105). Despite frequent requests, Newman refused to elucidate the meaning of the enigmatic closing reference to the angel faces 'which I have loved long since, and lost awhile'. Variously conjectured to refer to his Anglican friends or the souls of the departed, the angel faces came to symbolize for many the faith that had once shone more brightly in their hearts and now seemed to have dimmed. Like that great couplet in William Cowper's 'O, for a closer walk with God' that asks 'Where is the blessedness I knew / When first I saw the Lord?', the closing lines of 'Lead, kindly light' struck a deep chord because, to quote Owen Chadwick, 'hesitant faith was what so many souls felt themselves to possess'.[41]

Newman himself came to feel that the verses, which he had never intended for congregational singing, were too doubt-laden. In the early stages of his final illness he asked to hear Faber's hymn, 'Eternal Years'. After it had been sung to him by members of his Birmingham Oratory he said:

> Some people have liked my 'Lead, kindly light', and it is the voice of one in darkness asking for help from our Lord. But this (Eternal Years) is quite different; this is one with full light rejoicing in suffering with our Lord, so that mine compares unfavourably with it.[42]

Yet the fact is that for most of his contemporaries 'Eternal Years', full of assurance and light as it was, meant much less than the haunting ambiguities and darkness of 'Lead, kindly light'. It is no coincidence that the single most popular hymn in that so-called age of faith should reflect uncertainty and doubt in an honest and sensitive way.

6

'Sweet and low'

Victorian hymn tunes and their composers

In September 1873 the compilers of *Hymns Ancient and Modern* consulted twenty leading musicians over the question of whether double bar lines should be printed at the end of each line in the music edition. The list of those consulted reads like a roll-call of the great and the good in the Victorian musical establishment. It included the professors of music at Oxford and Edinburgh and the organists of three major cathedrals. The episode reminds us once again of how seriously the Victorians took the whole subject of hymns and hymn singing. The fact that such eminent and busy men were prepared to give their time to considering such a question also shows how the hymn tune was taken to be a valid and important musical genre. Nowadays tunes for hymns and worship songs are often produced by a specialist singer-songwriters and musicians working almost entirely in this field. In the nineteenth century writing hymn tunes was a much less marginal occupation. It engaged the talents both of a large group of amateurs and also of many of the most distinguished composers of the day, for whom, quite apart from any devotional considerations, it provided a useful source of income.

The practice of giving hymns specific tunes undoubtedly played a major role in raising the profile and standard of this particular musical form. Instead of being simply an all-purpose melody written, borrowed or adapted to fit a particular metre and suitable for a whole range of hymns, the hymn tune became a highly crafted marriage of music to words, designed to enhance the spiritual and emotional impact of a particular text. As a novel and potentially lucrative form of musical commission, it appealed to a wide range of composers by no means all of whom were strongly committed Christians. In the words of Erik Routley, 'the English hymn tune during the Victorian era was easily the most interesting of England's contributions to music at that time. It was the only genuinely English musical form available. All other music in England was Continental in sympathy and ethos.'[1]

The hymn tune in this sense, and as we have largely come to understand it, is, indeed, yet another Victorian invention. To quote Routley again, 'before about 1840 we still talk either of "psalm tunes" or of "Methodist hymns". Thereafter, it is, with an affectionate or patronizing air according to one's temperament, simply "hymns".'[2] As we have seen, the vigorous fuguing tunes associated particularly with Methodism played a key role in encouraging congregational hymn singing in the immediate pre-Victorian era. LYDIA, LYNGHAM and SAGINA, together with the thrilling DIADEM, composed in the year after the Queen's accession by James Ellor, an 18-year-old hat-maker, for the choir of the Wesleyan Chapel at Droylesden near Manchester, and perhaps the last great tune in this tradition, continued to be enormously popular, especially in Nonconformist circles. The great Baptist preacher, Charles Hadden Spurgeon, broke off in the middle of addressing a large congregation in a public hall in Yorkshire in the mid-1880s and announced 'Let's have that glorious tune CRANBROOK to the words "Grace, 'tis a charming sound".' When we think of Victorian hymn tunes, however, it is not the hearty strains of these melodies that come to mind but something at once more restrained and more sentimental, like J. B. Dykes' melody DOMINUS REGIT ME written for Henry Baker's 'The King of love my Shepherd is'. As Routley has memorably written, 'to speak of a "Victorian hymn tune" is to set off in any remotely musical mind the strains of John Bacchus Dykes' tune to "The King of Love". There is nothing more centrally Victorian in all English religion than those words set to that tune . . . that folk-genius Dykes gathered up there everything that this kind of Victorian music has to say.'[3]

It was the Anglican, and especially the High Anglican, take-over of the hymn-singing revolution initiated by Nonconformists and Evangelicals that brought both amateurs like Dykes and professional composers into the business of writing hymn tunes. Initially, the main interest of church musicians was focussed on cathedral music, the lamentable state of which was highlighted in a tract published in 1849 by S. S. Wesley. He castigated the clergy of the Church of England for having no real interest in music and claimed that not one single cathedral could raise the money needed for a basic minimum choir of just 12 voices. Although Wesley's plea, which was to become a life-long crusade, for church musicians to be properly remunerated and recognized, was never properly addressed, at least to his satisfaction, many of his other suggestions, such as establishing paid choirs and organists in all cathedrals and major parish churches and setting up training colleges to set standards in church music, were implemented. As we have seen, the choral revival brought enormous improvements in the musical standards of the established church. Several parish churches, especially the leading Tractarian places of worship in the capital, came to boast choirs that were at least the equal of those found in many cathedrals. At St Anne's, Soho, where Joseph Barnby became organist in 1871, the choir ran to 32 trebles, 8 altos, 12 tenors and 12 basses and confidently tackled complex pieces by continental composers. At a humbler level, most urban and suburban parish churches had robed choirs capable of tackling the home-produced introits, anthems and settings of the *Magnificat, Benedicite* and *Te Deum* which were to provide Victorian composers with another important field of work.

One might have thought that composers would have confined their attention to this kind of work and not bothered to engage in the seem- ingly more mundane and less satisfying occupation of turning out hymn tunes. Yet, as we have seen, hymn tunes were not deemed to be beneath the dignity of serious composers. Their composition was rather seen, quite rightly, both as a demanding discipline and as an eminently worthy occupation which carried the added bonus of providing much greater public exposure and more substantial long-term earnings than did most classical compositions. Undoubtedly these latter factors helped to persuade a number of professional musicians to take up writing hymn tunes. S. S. Wesley had complained in his tract on church music that while the artist Sir Edwin Landseer received 1000 guineas for a painting of a horse which had taken him eight days no composer would dare ask for 1000 farthings for a choral work which had taken the same time. With the proliferation and huge sales of hymn-books there was relatively good money (although never enough to satisfy Wesley) to be made from hymn tunes which did not take more than a day or so to write. The failure of congregations enthusiastically to embrace either the Gregorian plainchant championed by Frederick Oakeley, Richard Redhead and Thomas Helmore or the cathedral-style Anglican chant favoured by Wesley and Edward Hopkins also helped to promote the hymn tune as a respectable musical form. Although prose chants replaced the metrical versions of the psalms in most Anglican churches, in other respects the choral revival failed in its ultimate aim of pro- moting cathedral-style music throughout the Church of England. Most

Anglican congregations followed their Nonconformist counterparts in much preferring to sing hymns to modern tunes in the style of the immensely popular and highly sentimental parlour part-songs. The lush, chromatic harmonies associated with leading continental composers like Mendelssohn, Gounod and Spohr proved much more attractive than the austere simplicity of Gregorian chant. Professional British composers found themselves propelled by popular taste as well as in some cases by personal inclination to join a growing band of amateurs who were supplying the seemingly insatiable demand of publishers and editors for new hymn tunes.

The roll-call of amateur Victorian hymn tune writers is headed, in terms of social rank if not necessarily of musical skill, by the Queen's consort. Prince Albert wrote two hymn tunes, appropriately named COBURG and GOTHA, which found their way into several hymnals. At the other end of the scale, perhaps, is a figure like Jessie Seymour Irvine, who apparently while still in her teens and a member of the church choir at Crimond in Aberdeenshire where her father was minister, penned the tune now indissolubly linked with the most popular metrical setting of the 23rd Psalm.[4] Although there continues to be some debate about the circumstances of its composition, CRIMOND seems to have been written as an exercise for an organists' class that Jessie Irvine was attending in Banff. She stands in a strong Scottish tradition of talented amateurs who, as one might expect, tended to produce general-purpose metrical psalm tunes rather than the dedicated hymn tunes increasingly being composed in England. Two Glasgow merchants were particularly prominent in this sphere: Charles Hutcheson produced *Christian Vespers* (1832), a collection of hymn tunes harmonized in four parts and later, around 1849, wrote the much-loved tune STRACATHRO, and John Campbell published a similar volume in 1854 entitled *The Sacred Psaltery in Four Vocal Parts* containing the beautiful ORLINGTON which is still used in Scotland for the 23rd Psalm and also works very well when set to William Cowper's 'God moves in a mysterious way'. Alexander Ewing, an Aberdeen law graduate who later became a soldier and served with distinction in the Crimean War, composed the tune that bears his name for J. M. Neale's 'For thee, O dear, dear country'. His cousin, who bore the same name and was Bishop of Argyll and the Isles in the Scottish Episcopal Church, was left to negotiate with hymnal editors about the tune's use during the composer's absence on active service abroad. He objected strongly when it was assigned in the 1861 edition of *A & M* to 'Jerusalem the Golden', to which it has remained wedded ever since, and complained to Sir Henry Baker that the tune did not suit the words, being 'pathethic, not triumphant'.[5]

There was a notable crop of amateur hymn tune composers in Wales. Virtually all of them came of Nonconformist stock and were associated with chapel choirs or the singing societies that grew out of the temperance movement. John Roberts, a wood carver from Aberystwyth, was just 18 when he composed ALEXANDER and Rowland Huw Pritchard, a mill hand from Bala, two years older when he wrote the majestic HYFRYDOL. That classic tune in the minor mode, BRYN CALFARIA, was composed by William Owen, who worked in a North Wales slate quarry from the age of ten, while the lyrical GWALCHMAI, usually used for George Herbert's 'King of glory, King of peace' came from the pen of a teacher, Joseph Jones. Another notable hymn tune composer, John Roberts, who used the pseudonymn Ieuan Gwyllt, was minister of the Calvinistic Methodist Church at Capel Goch, Llanberis, and one of the founders of the *Gymanfa ganu*, the great singing festivals held across the principality. Those two most enduringly popular of all Welsh hymn tunes, BLAENWERN and CWM RHONDDA, which both date from the early 1900s and so strictly speaking count as Edwardian rather than Victorian, were the work of self-taught musicians, William Penfro Rowlands, a Pembrokeshire schoolteacher, and John Hughes, a clerk with the Great Western Railway at Pontypridd. Victorian Wales' greatest professional composer, Joseph Parry, who was professor of music at University College, Aberystwyth when he produced his haunting hymn tune ABERYSTWYTH in 1877, came from a similar background, having started work in a coal mine at the age of ten and switched to stoking the puddling furnace of an ironworks in his native Merthyr Tydfil two years later. It is surely the hard background from which so many of their composers came that gives Welsh hymn tunes their distinctive fervour and melancholy. In the words of John Hughes, who has made a study of the genre, 'Where Victorian hymn tunes in England were functional exercises in piety and worship, in Wales they were often powerful social statements.'[6]

Very different in both social background and musical style were the handful of English amateur composers who dabbled in hymnody. Sir Frederick Champneys, four of whose tunes appeared in *Hymns Ancient and Modern*, was an obstetrician who spent twenty-seven years as chairman of the Central Midwives' Board. Frederic Blunt, composer of LYNDHURST, was a successful London solicitor, while William Henry Gladstone, who wrote OMBERSLEY, now almost invariably used for

'Lord of all being throned afar', for 'Jesus shall reign where'er the sun' in 1872, followed his hymn-writing father into politics and was a Liberal MP for twenty years.

Some of the most popular and successful Victorian hymn tunes were written by Anglican clergy. Sir Henry Baker wrote a number of tunes for hymns appearing in *A & M*, including some of his own. ST CLEMENT, inseparably linked with 'The day Thou gavest, Lord, is ended', is generally credited to Clement Cotterill Scholefield, for ten years chaplain of Eton and subsequently vicar of Holy Trinity, Knightsbridge. However, in a recent article Mervyn Horder has persuasively argued that Arthur Sullivan, who was organist at St Peter's, Cranley Gardens, London, when Scholefield was a curate there, may have had a hand in it.[7] The two men were good friends and it was in *Church Hymns*, of which Sullivan was musical editor, that the tune first appeared. Scholefield contributed a further five tunes to *Church Hymns* and also submitted a number unsuccessfully to the compilers of *A & M*. Altogether, he wrote 41 hymn tunes. None of the others has anything like the quality or singability of ST CLEMENT and it is certainly tempting to speculate that Sullivan's role in its composition may have been more than simply editorial. Other prolific clerical composers of hymn tunes included William Henry Havergal, who devoted himself to church music after a carriage accident forced him out of parochial ministry, and Frederick Ouseley, founder of St Michael's College, Tenbury Wells, professor of music at Oxford and precentor of Hereford Cathedral.

It was a modest provincial clergyman with very little formal musical training who was to become the Victorians' favourite hymn tune composer. The tunes of John Bacchus Dykes figure prominently in virtually every hymn-book published between 1860 and 1900, irrespective of denomination, and in many of them they easily outnumber those of any other composer. No one better epitomizes the distinctive musical style of Victorian hymnody, with its lush chromatic harmonies, heavy use of repeated notes and stationary basses, close affinity to part song and parlour ballad and dramatic use of mood and melody to heighten the emotional and spiritual impact of the words. As we have already noted, Erik Routley regarded Dykes' DOMINUS REGIT ME as in many ways the archetypal Victorian hymn tune. Nicholas Temperley includes five of Dykes' tunes among the fourteen that he selects as representing 'the High Victorian hymn tune' in the second volume of his classic work, *The Music of the English Parish Church* and C. H. Phillips describes Dykes' work as 'the type *par excellence* of the Victorian hymn tune'.[8]

Dykes belonged to the same secure world of provincial Anglicanism that produced so many of the great Victorian hymn writers. Born in Hull in 1823, he was the fifth of fourteen children of the manager of the local branch of the Yorkshire District Bank. He seems to have picked up his love and aptitude for music from impromptu family concerts before bedtime every evening, and by the age of ten he was practising on the organ at the church where his evangelical grandfather was incumbent for fifty-seven years. He won a scholarship to Cambridge where he read classics and was able to make some more formal study of harmony and counterpoint. As a student he was renowned for composing and singing comic songs but a dramatic change of musical mood took place after his ordination. 'We tried hard,' a student friend noted, 'to get him to sing one of his humorous songs, with which he delighted our concert audiences in Cambridge, but he said he had made up his mind, on taking Holy Orders, to forswear them all for ever.'[9] Henceforth he was to devote his talents entirely to church music, predominantly writing hymn tunes but also some anthems and a fine unaccompanied setting of the funeral sentences 'I am the Resurrection and the life . . . ' Dykes was deeply moved by a performance of *Elijah* in 1847 and subsequently took Mendelssohn as his great mentor and model. His sister was alarmed to enter the drawing room of the vicarage of Tewkesbury where the family was staying in November that year to find her brother at the piano, having just heard of the composer's death, 'his eyes overflowing with tears, as he played one of the *Lieder ohne worte*'.[10]

After a curacy in Malton, Dykes moved to Durham where he was to spend the remaining years of his life, thirteen as precentor of the cathedral and thirteen as vicar of St Oswald's. A keen enthusiast for the Anglican choral revival, he introduced a new discipline and dedication into the somewhat slack regime of the cathedral choir and introduced a surpliced choir at St Oswald's. Pushed by a strongly ritualistic curate, he became involved in an unhappy controversy with the Bishop of Durham who demanded that his curates should never wear coloured stoles, use incense or turn their backs on the congregation during the celebration of communion. Dykes' gentle and eirenic temper was not suited to confrontation. He found relief from the strain of liturgical controversy by turning to his beloved music making. Many of his hymn tunes were inspired by incidents in his personal, family and devotional life. HOLLINGSIDE was named after the small cottage on the outskirts of Durham where he took his young wife in 1850, HORBURY was written when he made his first confession in 1859 and he composed tunes for two funeral hymns, one of them a translation from the German by Catherine Winkworth specifically for use at a child's funeral, in the immediate aftermath of the death of his ten-year-old daughter, Mabel, from scarlet fever in 1870. Particularly fond of writing for children, he gathered his own children and those of friends round the drawing room piano on Sunday evenings to try out new tunes. If they failed to 'take', he quickly dropped them.

Altogether, Dykes composed over 300 hymn tunes. They were always written with specific words in mind. 'I never think of setting a Hymn that is worthily set,' he explained, 'That would be silly caprice, or vanity or presumption. But if a Hymn does not appear to me worthily set, then, I own, I am often induced, I may say, sometimes almost compelled, to try to do my best for it . . . My own desire is this: – that each Hymn should be so set to music (by whomsoever God wills to select for that purpose) that its power of influencing and teaching may be best brought out.'[11] This modest outlook and determination that the music should serve the interests of the words was accompanied by a great generosity of spirit and a broad ecumenism. Dykes was happy for his tunes to be used in hymn-books of all denominations and rarely, if ever, asked for payment. *Hymns Ancient and Modern* was the first book to take up his tunes and it was there that he achieved his most spectacular ascendancy. He contributed seven tunes to the first music edition, among them the evergreen MELITA, NICAEA, HOLLINGSIDE and ST CUTHBERT. In the 1875 edition 56 hymns – one in eight of the total – were set to his melodies.

Table 2 shows the dominant position maintained by Dykes in hymn-books of three different denominations across a quarter of a century. He had far more entries than any other composer in the 1875 edition of *A & M*, the *Congregational Church Hymnal* of 1887 and the Presbyterian *Church Hymnary* of 1898. He was also among the top ten composers represented in the High Anglican *Hymnary* of 1872. I have taken these four hymn-books, two published in the middle of Victoria's reign and two towards the end, as being representative of a broad range of denominational persuasion and churchmanship. By noting the composers most prominently represented in each of them, it is possible to construct a league table of the most popular Victorian hymn tune writers. They form a relatively small group: a third of all the hymn tunes in both the *Hymnary* and the 1875 edition of *A & M* were contributed by just five men. Six names occur among the 'top ten' in all four books: Dykes (with a total of 183 appearances), Joseph Barnby (124), Henry

Gauntlett (123), Henry Smart (98), Edward Hopkins (92) and Arthur Sullivan (82). Two others, William Henry Monk and John Stainer, just fail to make the top ten in one book, but come well up the league table with scores of 77 each. These eight men can reasonably be regarded as the most successful practitioners of the art of the Victorian hymn tune.

Apart from Dykes, they were all professional musicians. This is also true of the other eight composers who feature in the lists opposite and who could be said to constitute a second division of Victorian hymn tune writers: Samuel Sebastian Wesley, Richard Redhead, George Elvey, Charles Steggall, John Goss, Frederick Ouseley, Herbert Oakeley and Josiah Booth. A glance at the brief biographies of all sixteen, which can be found in Appendix 3 (p. 257), reveals that they had much in common. All were English and male and all but one Anglicans, the exception being the Congregationalist Booth whose tunes were almost entirely confined to hymn-books of his own denomination. Despite their own strong musical traditions and deep-rooted attachment to hymn singing, when major Nonconformist churches produced their hymn-books it was generally to Anglican composers that they turned both for tunes and for musical editors. This was presumably a reflection both of the reputation of Anglican composers and also perhaps of the snob value and cachet in being associated with the Anglican musical establishment. It also, perhaps, reflected the fact that with very few exceptions Anglican churches were the only ones that could afford to employ professional musicians. The Wesleyan Methodists picked Gauntlett to edit the music for their major hymnal, the Con-gregationalists chose Hopkins and the Scottish Presbyterians Stainer. This is, of course, why the last two composers scored particularly highly in the *Congregational Church Hymnal* and the *Church Hymnary* respectively. The same reason underlies Monk's strong showing in *Hymns Ancient and Modern* and Barnby's in *The Hymnary*. Musical editors generally provided a considerable number of new tunes them-selves as well as commissioning and collecting the work of others.

Perhaps the most noticeable common feature uniting this group was a close involvement with the organ. It included six of the most important practitioners and popularizers of the instrument in nineteenth-century Britain: Goss and Stainer were organists at St Paul's Cathedral, Smart and Gauntlett tirelessly toured the country publicizing the wonders of the new pedal organ and advising churches who wished to instal one, Hopkins co-authored a definitive treatise on the instrument and Steggall was one of the founders of the Royal College of Organists and for fifty

Table 2

The most popular Victorian hymn tune composers

(Note: The figure after the name of each composer indicates the total number of hymns set to his tunes. It does not include arrangements but only original tunes, which may, of course, be used for more than one hymn.)

The Hymnary (1872) (646 hymns)	*Hymns Ancient and Modern* (1875) (473 hymns)	*Congregational Church Hymnal* (1887) (774 hymns)	*Church Hymnary* (1898) (650 hymns)
1 H. J. Gauntlett (71)	1 J. B. Dykes (59)	1 J. B. Dykes (53)	1 J. B. Dykes (48)
2 J. J. Barnby (64)	2 W. H. Monk (39)	2 E. J. Hopkins (48)	2 J. Stainer (42)
3 H. Smart (45)	3 H. J. Gauntlett (22)	3 J. Booth (32)	3 J. Barnby (32)
4= J. B. Dykes & E. J. Hopkins (23)	4 J. Stainer (21)	4 A. Sullivan (27)	4 A. Sullivan (28)
6 A. Sullivan (21)	5 H. Smart (14)	5 J. Barnby (24)	5= W. H. Monk & H. Smart (23)
7 S. S. Wesley (18)	6= A. Sullivan, E. J. Hopkins, F. A. G. Ouseley (6)	6 H. Gauntlett (20)	7= S. S. Wesley & E. J. Hopkins (15)
8 C. Steggall (13)		7 H. Smart (16)	
9 J. Goss (12)	9 R. Redhead (5)	8 W. H. Monk (15)	9 G. J. Elvey (13)
10= R. Redhead & H. S. Oakeley, J. Barnby (4)	10= H. S. Oakeley, J. Barnby (4)	9 S.S. Wesley (10)	10 H. J. Gauntlett (10)
		10 R. Redhead (9)	

years chief professor of the organ at the Royal Academy of Music where he was said to have trained more organists than any other teacher in the country. Twelve of the sixteen top hymn tune composers held positions as church organists, ten of them in London churches. The metropolitanism of those who wrote the tunes of Victorian hymns stands in marked contrast to the provincialism of those who supplied the words. It is also somewhat surprising when one considers the vitality of musical and choral life in the provinces. The only significant hymn tune writers living and working outside London were S.S.Wesley, who had been born in the capital but spent his working life as organist in provincial cathedrals and churches, Ouseley, founder of St Michael's College, Tenbury, professor of music at Oxford and precentor at Hereford Cathedral, Oakeley, professor of music at Edinburgh, and of course, Dykes.

Most of the group shared a 'churchy' background. Gauntlett and Oakeley came from clerical families while Ouseley and Dykes were themselves ordained. Eight had been boy choristers – Elvey at Canterbury Cathedral, Barnby at York Minster, Stainer at St Paul's, Redhead at Magdalen College, Oxford, and Hopkins, Wesley, Goss and Sullivan at the Chapel Royal. Most remained happily within the world of church music, and the distinctive ethos of Anglican cathedral music, throughout their lives, restricting their composing principally to hymn tunes, anthems, chants for prose psalms, settings of the *Magnificat* and *Nunc Dimittis* with occasional forays into the world of sacred oratorio. It is perhaps significant that the two who were least 'churchy' in terms of their musical outlook and range of compositions were on the whole better represented in Nonconformist than Anglican hymnals. Sullivan and Barnby stand apart from the rest of the group in having had one foot firmly planted in the world of secular music. Although they both served as organists in fashionable London churches, their most significant appointments and best-known compositions were secular rather than ecclesiastical. Sullivan, of course, achieved his fame through the Savoy Operas and was also a significant orchestral and choral conductor and composer. Barnby was director of music at Eton College and then Principal of the Guildhall School of Music and was better known for the Eton Boating Song and 'Sweet and Low' than for his hymn settings. Their hymn tunes, which were on the whole more bright and breezy than those of their more narrowly ecclesiastically-focussed contemporaries, seem to have appealed more to Nonconformist ears, and have certainly survived longer in Nonconformist hymn-books.

There was considerable variation in the relative importance of hymn tunes within these composers' overall work and in their output in this particular sphere. The most prolific by far was Henry Gauntlett, who gave up a career as a solicitor to devote himself to music in 1844 and concentrated for the next thirty years on playing the organ, first at St Olave's Church, Southwark, and then at Union Chapel, Islington, and composing hymn tunes, of which he claimed to have produced around 10,000. The financial possibilities from this line of employment had been brought home to him as a young boy when his father, the vicar of Olney, had offered him a farthing for every tune or chant he copied out. A few days later he knocked on the study door with a sheaf of a thousand tunes and chants for which he demanded a guinea. Gauntlett was the nearest that Victorian Britain came to the kind of professional sacred tunesmith who emerged in late nineteenth-century America and was under contract to produce so many melodies a week. The output of the other composers was much more modest in this field which was, of course, a relatively minor part of their total output. Stainer has been identified as the author of 157 tunes and Sullivan of 90, both of which are almost certainly higher figures than the average for the group as a whole.

In terms of musical style and approach there were two distinct groups within the ranks of these top hymn tune writers. The division fell broadly along age lines. The older composers, notably John Goss (born in 1800), Henry Smart (1813), George Elvey (1816), Richard Redhead (1820) and Charles Steggall (1826), broadly stuck to the idiom of traditional psalm tunes with their four-square robustness and solidity. Fine examples of this approach are Smart's REGENT SQUARE, which so clearly echoes the 'stately, dignified, measured beat and slow movement' of the old psalm tunes he so much admired, Steggall's CHRIST CHURCH, described by Routley as 'pure Croft . . . and perhaps the best hymn tune written in the nineteenth century', and Goss' PRAISE MY SOUL, which Bertram Barnby finds 'simple yet musicianly, stately yet jubilant, solemn yet warm-hearted'.[12] To some extent S.S.Wesley (born in 1810) also belongs to this group. Certainly his AURELIA has the same majestic state-liness and solidity that distinguish these other tunes. All of them work well in unison and eschew the intricate part-writing and harmony, the chromatic slides and other embellishments of the more emotionally and sentimentally charged later Victorian hymn tunes.

The younger composers, especially Barnby (born 1838), Stainer (1840) and Sullivan (1842), followed the lead of Monk and Dykes (both

born 1823) in casting aside the formal restraint and austerity of psalm
tunes and making hymn tunes more like secular ballads and part-songs.
Dykes' MELITA and VOX DILECTI, Monk's EVENTIDE, Barnby's O
PERFECT LOVE and Sullivan's SAMUEL were each specifically written for
a particular hymn and designed to bring out every ounce of its pathos
and sentiment. This approach brought severe criticisms from composers
of the older school who felt that it lacked manly robustness. Smart
remarked that Dykes' tunes 'have generally an effeminacy of character
which is not appropriate' while from the other side Barnby complained
that 'the terms effeminate and maudlin, with others, are freely used
nowadays to stigmatize such new tunes as are not direct imitations of
old ones'.[13] The debate that ensued is described in chapter 8.

A trawl through successive hymn-books of all denominations in the
latter half of Victoria's reign reveals the tunes of the older composers
being steadily supplanted by those of the younger breed. Table 2
confirms this trend. While Smart occupies third place in the list of
composers represented in the 1872 Hymnary with 45 entries, he is
down to fifth place with just 23 entries in the 1898 Church Hymnary
while Goss, Redhead and Steggall have disappeared completely from the
top ten in both the later volumes. Hymns Ancient and Modern exerted
an extremely important influence in promoting the new style of hymn
tune. Its musical editor, William Henry Monk, who is said to have
suggested the book's winning title, had a natural affinity for the
approach and style of the younger composers although he also kept one
foot firmly planted in the world of more traditional church music.
Throughout the time that he was associated with A & M he was
organist at St Matthias, Stoke Newington, a Tractarian church in the
van of the Anglican choral revival, where somewhat unusually the choir
sang much of the service in unison to encourage congregational participation. He was also for a period professor of vocal music at King's
College, London. His talents probably lay more in being able to spot a
good and singable tune and in editorship and arrangement than in the
field of original composition. Echoing the judgment of Dr Bernard
Massey that the chief characteristic of his work was 'a decorous
ordinariness', Bertram Barnby has written that 'given a good opening
phrase, Monk could construct a tune having the ring of inevitability.
This facility led him to rewrite old melodies to make them
"respectable": the foreign he Anglicized; the English he Victorianized'.[14]
His own work did not win plaudits from musical purists of the old
school. One, complaining of the 'puerile harmony' and 'bare faced-

plagiarism' of the tunes in *A & M*, singled out Monk's EVENTIDE for its accumulation of ill-constructed chords:

> We find in bar 3 a double minor seventh; in bar 5 an unresolved fourth-sixth; in bar 7 a minor seventh resolved upwards; in bar 11 a revival of the ill-sounding discord of major third and minor sixth; in bar 13 a strain commencing on a discord; and throughout the tune, wherever a discord will 'stick', there will such be found, viz. in 16 chords out of 40.[15]

A & M played a crucial role in popularizing the tunes of Dykes. Much of his work first appeared in its pages, including the seven tunes that he contributed to the first edition where Monk was assisted in the musical editorship by the more conservative Ouseley. The 1868 supplement showed a more adventurous musical approach. More than half the tunes were new, including 11 by Dykes and contributions from Barnby, Elvey and Stainer who was brought into the editorial process two years later to assist on the tunes committee. It seems that Stainer's main task consisted in dealing with the huge amount of unsolicited material sent in by amateur composers: 'My entire work hitherto has been one of protest. Tune after tune has reached me with which I feel thoroughly ashamed to have anything to do.'[16] Monk also found himself almost submerged under the weight of tunes sent in – in 1887 he reported that he was considering 1,120 submissions. With Monk's health failing, Steggall was brought in as music editor and it was he who supervised the production of the 1889 supplement.

Hymns Ancient and Modern became an important quarry for editors seeking tunes for their own hymnals. This is highlighted in the correspondence between Sir Henry Baker and Dr Henry Allon, editor of the *Congregational Psalmist* (see p. 75). Allon was particularly enthusiastic about Dykes' tunes which he regarded as inseparable from the hymns to which they are set. During the early cordial stages of their relationship, Baker happily gave Allon permission to use all the tunes that he wished from *A & M* and returned a cheque sent by the grateful Congregationalist 'for your own parochial use'.[17] He did not object to the tunes being renamed to give a more biblical ring – EWING was changed to SALEM and Latin names were Anglicized on the slightly strange grounds that 'the announcement of an unseemly name might disturb the gravity or quiet of worshipping feeling'.[18] However, following the appearance of Allon's article in the *British Quarterly* attacking the notion of established churches the *A & M* proprietors changed their tone and began to feel that he was asking for too much. A note from one of them in 1885 described his latest request as 'a monstrous demand . . . but when he says we gave ten more tunes to the Presbyterian Book, he rather "has us on the hip", has he not?'[19] The correspondence ended on a rather sour note with the proprietors putting an absolute ban on Allon using any tunes of which they held the copyright.

A & M was not, of course, the only showcase for new hymn tunes. The great proliferation of hymn-books in the late 1860s and early 1870s brought numerous opportunities for composers eager to enter the field. It also often enabled members of the relatively small London musical establishment to provide work for their friends. Sullivan seems to have been drawn into hymn tune writing by his friend, the clergyman and amateur composer, Robert Brown-Borthwick, in whose *Supplemental Hymn and Tune Book* (1868) several of his tunes appeared. Brown-Borthwick's other commissions for this collection included two of the most enduring and effective Victorian hymn tunes, GOSS' PRAISE MY SOUL and Hopkins' ELLERS. Sullivan wrote his immortal ST GERTRUDE for the *Hymnary* being edited by his close friend Barnby. While commissions undertaken for friends could, as in Sullivan's case, prove lucrative, they could also take on the character of unwelcome burdens and lead to a greater involvement in this particular genre than some composers might have wished. Responding to the criticism that he had written too many hymn tunes, Stainer pleaded the excuse 'that, almost without exception, they have been written at the request of musical and clerical editors and personal friends'.[20]

Along with drawing-room ballads and choral and orchestral works for municipal music festivals, hymn tunes and anthems provided one of the major sources of income for professional composers in the nineteenth century. Being relatively quick to write and capable of generating repeat fees if they were taken up in a number of hymn-books, they often appealed particularly to those who were making their way in the world of music and had not yet attained fame and fortune. The great majority of Sullivan's hymn tunes, for example, were written before he began his lucrative partnership with W.S.Gilbert in 1875. The extent to which the most popular composers were able to cash in on the huge sales of hymn-books containing their tunes depended to a large extent on how jealously they guarded the copyright and whether they charged a fee for every appearance of an existing tune in a new book or new edition. The most generous minded and free from any thought of reward was Dykes,

who did, not of course, depend for his living on his musical compositions. His refusal of any kind of payment for the reproduction of his
hymns in successive editions of *The Congregational Psalmist* led Allon
to enthuse about his 'courtesy and kindness'.[21] When Baker was shilly-
shallying over whether to give permission for the use of Dykes' tunes in
a new Irish Church hymnal in 1873, the composer wrote to him: 'I say
by all means give them the tunes if they want them . . . please say "yes"
and have done with it.'[22] Others who depended more on composition
for their income could also be generous, or careless, about copyright.
Henry Gauntlett parted with the rights on ten tunes for the original
edition of *A & M* for just five guineas while Joseph Barnby was forced
to buy back from the proprietors for the nine guineas that they had
originally paid him the copyright in three of his tunes so that he could
use them in his own *Hymnary*.

A very different attitude was displayed by one of the most 'churchy'
of Victorian composers, S. S. Wesley, who sent out a standard printed
letter to all those seeking permission to use one of his tunes:

> Sir, I can but be flattered by your wish to adopt my tune, but I must
> inform you that I do not compose music for pleasure solely.
>
> My profession being that of a musician, I can no more *give away*
> my compositions than a painter his pictures or a merchant his
> merchandise.
>
> For the privilege of printing one of my hymn-tunes, for this special
> occasion, I require . . .[23]

One can forgive much from the man who contributed AURELIA and
HEREFORD to the treasury of English hymn tunes and I suppose that one
should also make allowances for the unhappy circumstances of his
illegitimate birth which left him with a permanent chip on his shoulder.
Yet for one whose entire professional life was devoted to church music,
Wesley does seem to have been rather mean-spirited and mercenary
when it came to the subject of hymn tunes. He was also extraordinarily
dismissive of the work of others in this sphere.

> I never have seen one first-rate Hymn Tune, the production of an
> Englishman, during the last thirty years. Most of these persons who
> practise such composition have not even attempted – publicly – *any*
> other kind of church pieces. In my opinion the best that can be said of
> modern Hymn Tunes is that about two new tunes are pretty good.
> Not one is fine and great and the majority are contemptible and

unworthy of being used in any service of public worship with their love-song affectations and even faulty writing.[24]

Wesley made this outburst in a letter to Sir Henry Baker in 1868 explaining his reluctance to contribute tunes to *Hymns Ancient and Modern* because of the company he would be keeping there. Declining 'to rank amongst your contributors in the usual way by furnishing a tune or two at the ordinary rate of hack writers', he proceeded to demand sums far in excess of the 'going rate' of two to three guineas per tune if his material was to be used.[25] Baker was offered ten tunes, either new or already published, for the princely sum of 130 guineas. In the event, Wesley was paid twenty-five guineas for the use of just two tunes – one of them already published – in the 1868 *A & M* appendix. Stainer, by contrast, received £10 for three new tunes, Barnby nine guineas for four tunes, three of which were already published, Smart nineteen guineas for six new tunes and Elvey six guineas for three. Dykes was given a lump sum of £100 for twelve new tunes, the use of three already published and for his help in the musical editorship of the supplement, while Monk received £350 for his work in editing the music for the book and contributing some forty tunes of his own.

Another way for composers to make money out of the boom in hymn singing was to take on the musical editorship of a hymn-book. Several of the most popular writers of hymn tunes also engaged in this activity. Monk acted as musical editor for successive editions of *A & M*, Barnby for the *Hymnary* published by Novello, Sullivan for SPCK's *Church Hymns and Tunes*, Stainer for the *Church Hymnary*, Goss for *Hymns of Redemption* and the *Church Psalter and Hymnbook*, Gauntlett for the Anglican *Church Hymn and Tune Book*, the *Congregational Psalmist* and the *Wesleyan Methodist Hymn-book* and Hopkins for the English Presbyterians' *Church Praise*, the *Free Church of Scotland Hymnal*, the *Congregational Church Hymnal* and *The Hymnal of the Presbyterian Church of Canada*. Wesley, characteristically, pursued a rather different tack and produced his own volume, *The European Psalmist*, published in 1872. It contained 615 hymn tunes, 143 of which were his own compositions and the rest predominantly of continental origin. Among the latter was a tune by J. M. Haydn to which Wesley gave the name CALCUTTA and from which Paul Chappell has convincingly argued he may well have derived AURELIA. As might be expected, Wesley eschewed the work of his British contemporaries and deliberately provided new tunes for hymns that had already been set successfully by Monk and

Dykes, notably 'Abide with me', 'Holy, holy, holy', 'Jesu, lover of my soul' and 'Nearer, my God, to thee'. Wesley's own melodies were often over-elaborate and cumbersome – his setting of 'Onward, Christian soldiers' required the repetition of the chorus and then the further repetition of its last two lines. His book failed to dethrone the composers whose work he so despised from their position at the top of the hymnological hit parade.

A good number of Victorian hymn tunes were created out of melodies that had been written for quite another purpose. Mendelssohn's works provided a particularly rich quarry. Three of his four-part songs were turned into hymn tunes and given the quintessentially English names of SHERBORNE, ST SAVIOUR'S and ELLESMERE. In the early 1850s W. H. Cummings, the young organist of Waltham Abbey parish church, was leafing through a choral work that Mendelssohn had written for a festival to celebrate the 400th anniversary of the invention of printing. A melody from the second movement struck him as the perfect accompaniment for 'Hark! the herald angels sing' to which it has been wedded ever since. Other less exalted material was also pressed into service. The compilers of an 1830 hymnbook set Isaac Watts' 'Hark from the tombs, a doleful sound' to the tune Sir Henry Bishop had penned seven years earlier for the enormously successful parlour ballad 'Home, sweet home'. Sullivan's melody for 'The Lost Chord' was adapted and set to 'Jerusalem the Golden' with the composer's permission. E. F. Benson gives a delightful picture of the plagiarism involved in the production of the hymnal that his father, Edward Benson, hastily put together when he became the first headmaster of Wellington School in 1859:

> Well-known tunes, not in copyright, like 'Adeste Fideles' (sic) and Haydn's 'Austrian anthem' would be included, but these would not supply sufficient melodies. So a lady called Miss Moultrie, whom he held to have high musical gifts, was called in, and by request she composed a quantity of hymn tunes herself for this book, and when her own invention failed, she took such airs as the opening lines of one of Beethoven's Violin Sonatas, and Spohr's 'How blessed are the departed,' and chiselled them with ruthless carpentry into hymn tunes of the required length and rhythm, cutting out a bar here and a half-bar there and, where necessary, writing extra parts.[26]

The practice of taking secular folk songs and setting them to hymns was much less common in the Victoria era than it had been in the eighteenth century and was to be again in the twentieth. On the whole, Victorian editors preferred tunes which were more obviously 'churchy'. A Roman Catholic collection published in 1851 set 'Hail, Queen of Heaven, the ocean star' to the melody of a not wholly inappropriate Tyneside folk song, 'Sweet Mary, sweet Mary, my age is sixteen' which also turned up under the title COVENTRY in a Wesleyan Methodist tune book of 1858. Gauntlett used a number of folk melodies in *The Congregational Psalmist*, notably ASCALON which came to be almost universally associated with 'Fairest Lord Jesus'. Its origins as a Silesian peasant song were rather too secular and proletarian for a number of hymn book editors who gave it a wholly spurious pedigree as a Crusader hymn sung by German pilgrims on their way to Jerusalem. There was a similar reluctance to acknowledge that the tune used for William Hutchings' Sunday School hymn 'When mothers of Salem their children brought to Jesus' had been taken from a German drinking song.

Compiling and editing the music for a major denominational hymn-book could be tedious and time-consuming. In sifting through huge numbers of unsolicited mediocre melodies, one had to have a keen eye for plagiarism and mis-representation. Monk was constantly being sent an adaptation of the opening chorus from Weber's opera *Oberon* passed off as an original unpublished melody. He also received a hymn set to a tune said to be by Sullivan 'which was so deplorably bad that I wrote to him and he at once disowned it'. On returning it, he was promptly sent a melody apparently by Gounod, 'the same tune with the same terrible mistakes'.[27] In a rather pained letter to Baker, Monk complained about his lot: 'I shall have proofs every night for some time to come yet. You can afford to be generous: and if you could know how much gratuitous work my connection with the Church brings me, and how many occasions there are on which people cut themselves off from me – professionally – because I *am* a Churchman, you would not hesitate to be so.'[28] He went on to point out that the highest sum he had dared to ask for all his work on *A & M* was precisely what one leading light composer of the day had received for a single waltz tune. Sullivan was another who found the business of editing a hymn-book a drudge. 'I hope that the hymn-book will be a blessing to the Church. It's a curse to me' he complained in the midst of his labours over *Church Hymns and Tunes*. 'Had I known the wearisome labours of it, I would not have undertaken it for a *thousand pounds*.'[29]

The musical editorship of hymn-books did not bring substantial material rewards. Certainly it is difficult to feel that Monk, who was probably the best paid, was treated as generously as he should have been in view of the scale of his contribution to the quality and success of *A & M*. His annual remuneration was notably less than the amount that the proprietors voted themselves out of the profits – and they, of course, were all Anglican incumbents with comfortable stipends. He did at least receive £1000 for his work on the revised edition of 1875 and when he fell ill in 1884, the proprietors voted him an allowance of £200 a year, but this does not seem over generous when one discovers that two years later when he appealed for new tunes more than 600 came in and had to be assessed in just three months. Curiously, one eminent composer complained that the *A & M* proprietors were paying their musical advisers too much. In 1895 Charles Stanford told them that the guinea an hour fee they were proposing to give musical advisers for committee work 'is too much to pay the class of man whom we had in view'.[30] He offered his own services in the work of revision 'even if it meant loss of time and no remuneration' and proposed bringing in Sir Hubert Parry, Fuller Maitland, chief music critic of *The Times*, Barclay Squire of the British Museum and Harry Wooldridge, Robert Bridges' musical collaborator in the production of *The Yattendon Hymnal*, to assist. 'The musical work is so important that the best musical talent of England should if possible be secured in order that so great an undertaking may be of the very best.'[31]

Statements by even the least 'churchy' of those Victorian composers who engaged in writing hymn tunes suggest that they saw this aspect of their work in equally exalted terms. 'The test of a hymn tune', according to the flamboyant Joseph Barnby, 'is that it shall equally satisfy the worshipper, whether musician or amateur . . . There is no excuse for those who continue to use in God's house a class of music, which from its want of refinement, and even of ordinary musicianly qualities, would be scarcely admitted into any drawing room.'[32] Yet there is considerable evidence that many hymn tunes were turned out at considerable speed and without a great deal of deliberation. Gauntlett wrote ST ALPHEGE at his dinner table while a messenger waited to rush it to the editors of a hymn-book who had somehow mislaid their intended tune for 'Brief life is here our portion'. Stainer dashed off IN MEMORIAM in somewhat similar circumstances during a meeting of the *A & M* editorial board in the Langham Hotel, London. When the hymn 'There's a friend for little children' came up for discussion, the committee could not agree on a tune for it and so the composer took himself off to an adjoining bed-

room and came back a few minutes later with the melody that was
to be sung by children up and down the land. Some stories suggest that
W. H. Monk penned EVENTIDE for 'Abide with me' in ten minutes
following another *A & M* committee meeting and while a piano lesson
was going on in the same room. However, his widow has left a more
romantic account of its composition: 'Hand in hand we were silently
watching the glory of the setting sun until the golden hue had faded . . .
then he took paper and pencilled the tune which has gone all over the
world.'[33] Several other highly popular hymn tunes were also composed
in a matter of minutes. Albert Peace, organist of Glasgow Cathedral,
wrote ST MARGARET for George Matheson's poem 'O love that wilt not
let me go' while staying at Brodick Manse on the Isle of Arran: 'After
reading it over carefully, I wrote the music straight off, and I may say
that the ink of the first note was hardly dry when I had finished the
tune.'[34] Inspiration came to composers, as it did to authors, in many
different forms. Dykes worked out his tune LUX BENIGNA for Newman's
'Lead, kindly light' while walking along the Strand. Monk apparently
set Baker's 'O perfect life of love' in his sleep. He woke up in the middle
of the night with the tune perfectly formed in his head, wrote it down
and was able to sing it to the author, who was staying with him, over
breakfast.

Did those professional composers who wrote hymn tunes regard this
part of their output as hack work which could be dashed off relatively
quickly or did they see themselves rather as servants of the church working for the greater glory of God? Their position was, of course, different
from that of the great majority of those responsible for the words of
hymns who were not professional writers and who could be presumed
to be expressing their own faith and devotion in their verses. Composers
were paid to set words to music. Did it make a great difference to them
whether they were the words of a parlour ballad or a hymn to be sung
in church? The fact is, of course, that composers varied greatly in the
extent of their own Christian conviction. Some had a profound faith
and would have shared the somewhat idealized view of their calling
expounded by W. H. Gladstone: 'The spirit of one who writes for the
Church must not be that of a mere musician . . . He must be something
more. His office has some analogy to that of the preacher. He, too, has
to select, expound and illustrate his text, to dive into its inner meanings,
and clothe it in a vesture of song . . . such was the spirit in which one,
whose name has been endeared to thousands by his hymns – Dr Dykes –
approached his task. Dr Wesley confesses the same.'[35]

Gladstone might more justly have singled out John Stainer than S. S. Wesley as the supreme exemplar of this approach among professional musicians. Stainer had the same high spiritual motives as Dykes, whose work he passionately defended against attack from the musical establishment. He also showed the same modest reticence about providing new settings for hymns that already had perfectly good ones, declining Sir Henry Baker's request for a tune for 'Just as I am' since 'Smart's is beautiful'.[36] Deeply interested in the contribution of music to worship, he wrote learned articles on 'the rhythmical form of the Anglican chant', 'Music of the Bible' and 'Music considered in its effect upon, and in connexion with, the worship of the Church'. His commitment to hymnody was deep-rooted and sincere. It probably went back to his boyhood when his schoolmaster father would often come back tired from a day with his unruly charges and console himself by playing a hymn tune on his violin. It was significant that he inserted five hymns into his most famous choral work, *The Crucifixion*, so that the congregation could take part in it. Amidst all his grander and more serious compositions, hymn tunes seem to have given him the most satisfaction. 'I was one Sunday walking at some seaside place, and on turning a corner I heard a number of Sunday-school children singing a tune I had composed. I thought to myself "I want no higher reward than this for all my work." I can only tell you that I would not exchange it for the very finest monument in Westminster Abbey.'[37]

At the other end of the spectrum were those composers who lacked strong Christian convictions and for whom church music in general, and hymn tunes in particular, were a very minor part of their output. Arthur Sullivan was almost certainly the least religious of all the top Victorian hymn tune composers. It is true that he had a strong Anglican upbringing as a chorister in the Chapel Royal and played the organ in a number of fashionable London churches, but there is nothing in his life or his writings to suggest any real faith. Yet this worldly figure, at home in the casinos of Monte Carlo and the orchestra pit of the Savoy Theatre rather than in cathedral choir stalls or organ loft, had a fascination with hymn tunes and wrote some of the finest and most enduring of the Victorian age. He based his *Festival Te Deum* around ST ANNE, which *A & M* had firmly wedded to 'O God, our help in ages past', and introduced his own ST GERTRUDE into his great *Boer War Te Deum* just a year before his death. Sullivan's hymn tunes were often knocked out in a few minutes in country-house salons – ST GERTRUDE was written while he was staying at Hanford in Dorset and named after his hostess there,

Mrs Gertrude Clay-Ker-Seymour. Yet his tunes struck an instant and
enduring chord with congregations, especially Nonconformist ones.
ST GERTRUDE seemingly effortlessly achieved what Wesley's cumbersome melody and Dykes' ponderous arrangement of the theme of the
slow movement from a Haydn symphony had utterly failed to do and
turned 'Onward, Christian soldiers' into a smash hit, taken up by
brass bands, street hurdy-gurdies and fair-ground organs as well as by
enthusiastic congregations up and down the land.

Sullivan's enthusiasm, or lack of it, for writing hymn tunes has been
the subject of much debate among musicologists. Erik Routley, who was
fiercely critical of his work in this area, was in no doubt that it was
wholly uncongenial to the composer of the Savoy Operas and simply
taken on as a way of making money before he had established his
career:

> Sullivan's genius was not in the least religious; it was too light for the
> graver themes, as the hymn tunes themselves show. We can imagine
> the relief with which he escaped from his early occupation with
> church music, in which he was not at home, into that wholly con-
> genial field of light opera in which, along with his twin genius,
> W. S. Gilbert, he was to achieve his artistic immortality.[38]

Yet, as we know, light opera was not a wholly congenial field for
Sullivan and he desperately wanted recognition as a serious composer.
Samuel Rogal, an American musicologist, has suggested that his hymn
tunes were a way out of the pit both literally and metaphorically, providing spiritual release from the comic opera stage and also from his
own pain and loneliness: 'Arthur Sullivan found religion not within the
walls of a church or the tenets of a denomination, but from the balm
provided by his own genius for composing music for hymns and sacred
song.'[39] Having studied both Sullivan's life and his hymn tunes in some
detail, I am more inclined to agree with this latter view than with
Routley's. It is impossible to listen to or sing Sullivan's greatest hymn
tunes without feeling that they are the work of a man with deep spiritual
feelings, if not of conventional religiosity. It is certainly true that
Sullivan's hymn tunes are extraordinarily variable in quality – when
they are bad, they are very, very bad. When Sullivan had to set a text of
some theological complexity full of abstract imagery he floundered. His
CHAPEL ROYAL totally fails to plumb the powerful depths of 'O love that
wilt not let me go'. Presented with a strong narrative, on the other hand,
as he was with 'Hushed was the evening hymn' he was in his element,

producing in SAMUEL a tune of real sensitivity. He was also at home with an expression of anguished doubt, witness his setting of Newman's 'Lead, kindly light', LUX IN TENEBRIS, to my mind, the best that there is.[40]

Perhaps more than those of any other composer, Sullivan's settings of sacred verses epitomize the peculiar genius and the particular pitfalls of the Victorian hymn tune. Loved by congregations, and by many clergy, yet castigated by critics, and by most musicians, they manage to combine vulgarity, sentimentality, emotionalism and sheer singability with an enduring memorability and particular aptness to the words to which they are set. At one level, they are crude musical constructions involving easy and lazy devices such as repeated notes, stationary or marching basses and chromatic harmonies, all equally beloved of that most popular of all Victorian hymn tune composers, J. B. Dykes. At another, however, they display an unmistakable if undefinable touch of genius.

One of the most persistent criticisms of Victorian hymn tunes has been that they are altogether too histrionic and dramatic. Routley points to 'the assiduous, and sometimes anxious, and even frantic, desire of the Victorian hymn-tune writer to be sure that at every beat there will be something to catch the listener's attention . . . Just as in architecture, empty space is intolerable without some kind of decoration, so in music, silence and repose are emotionally taboo. All must be picturesque.'[41] It is certainly true that the tunes of the younger group of Victorian composers are clear expressions of the Age of Romanticism which gave them birth. Very few have the austere restraint of earlier psalm tunes. Yet the quest for the picturesque was not simply a matter of cultish whim or self-indulgence. What may seem to modern ears as excessive and slightly vulgar embellishments were put in to heighten the dramatic and emotional impact of the words. Technology may well have played a part here. The development of the four manual organ with a battery of stops opened up all sorts of musical effects. It was not just the younger composers who seized on its dramatic possibilities, as Dykes did so effectively with his rolling basses for 'Fierce raged the tempest o'er the deep' and 'Eternal Father, strong to save'. Whenever there was a reference to a storm in a hymn, psalm or anthem, Sir John Goss would sound forth a deep roll from the St Paul's Cathedral organ, much to the delight of the regular members of the congregation.

As well as being over-emotional, Victorian hymn tunes have also long been criticized for their sentimentality. Louis Benson, the distinguished

American hymnologist, categorized them as 'sentimental rather than strenuous, and often plaintive; supported in the inner parts by what might be called a sentimental use of close harmonies, in the manner of current part-song as over against the independently melodious counterpoint of the old psalm tunes. They express more the feeling of the Oxford Revival than its resolution, the spiritual sentiment of the individual rather than the sense of corporate worship.'[42] There is an undeniably individualistic and sentimental feeling to many Victorian hymn tunes, particularly perhaps to those of Dykes, but then so there is to the words that they so closely match in style and feeling. This is partly bound up with the unashamedly evangelistic purposes of some of the leading composers. Dykes once said that he wrote hymn tunes 'to impress, soften, humanise and win'.[43] In this context, it was wholly appropriate deliberately to pull on the heart-strings and strike a deliberately sentimental note, just as it was equally legitimate to use strong marching basses which sounded so stirring when played by the colliery bands that regularly accompanied the singing in Durham Cathedral. Hymn tunes were not being written to please musical purists or provide artistically perfect miniatures. They were designed to reinforce the gospel message and to get people who were largely musically illiterate singing their faith.

Did some composers have a rather more ambitious agenda and strive too hard to make their hymn tunes beautiful in a rather self-consciously religious way? This was certainly the view of Erik Routley who wrote that 'in the Victorian age, for the first time, composers looked at their work in hymn tunes with a conscious desire to make it beautiful'.[44] He applies this criticism particularly to Sullivan whom he sees as dropping his normal and natural creative exuberance when writing hymn tunes and anthems and adopting a self-consciously 'churchy' mantle which inhibited his melodic gifts and produced a dull and false religiosity. There may be an element of truth in this, although it can hardly be applied to tunes like ST GERTRUDE, BISHOPGARTH and COURAGE BROTHER which have all the vigorous vulgarity (and the rumpty-tumpty-ness) of choruses from the Savoy Operas. Undoubtedly, several Victorian hymn tunes, particularly and understandably, perhaps, those for children's hymns, do strike a note of seemingly rather forced sweetness and perfection. If not quite beautiful, then they do seem altogether too self-consciously pretty.

This was something that contemporary critics noticed. When J. W. Elliot's DAY OF REST was published, one detractor suggested that the composer had been working on two compositions – one for Christopher Wordsworth's hymn, 'O day of rest and gladness' and another for a children's song 'I had a little doggie, it used to sit and beg' – and that he had by mistake put the finished tunes in the wrong envelopes.[45] The implication that too many hymn tunes had the sugary qualities of sentimental parlour ballads is not wholly unjustified. There was a very fine dividing line between the Victorian hymn and the Victorian parlour ballad. A heavy air of religiosity hung over many 'secular' Victorian songs – one has only to think of such favourites as 'The Lost Chord', 'The Volunteer Organist' and the best-selling 'The Holy City', which had words by Frederic Weatherly, author of 'The Roses of Picardy' and 'Danny Boy', and music by Stephen Adams, the psedonymn of Michael Maybrick, who had been appointed organist of St Peter's, Liverpool at the age of 14. Several writers successfully straddled both genres. Adelaide Anne Procter, for example, who wrote 'My God, I thank Thee, who hast made' was also responsible for the words of 'The Lost Chord'. Barnby and Sullivan were not the only composers who worked in both fields. Even S. S. Wesley was known to set secular songs, including one with the distinctly racy title 'Young Bacchus in his lusty prime'.

We should not, in fact, be surprised if those well-schooled in setting drawing-room ballads also produced good hymn tunes. The qualities needed for these two activities are very similar. They require a close attention and sensitivity to the words, and especially to their mood and flow, and the ability to provide a strong and fresh melody which is eminently singable and yet does not grow stale with repeated use. Victorian composers excelled at enhancing and sustaining the mood of the texts that they set. This talent was displayed with particular effect in the case of secular songs and hymns with a strongly dramatic or didactic theme and content. The tune very much followed the text and to that extent was clearly viewed as its subordinate. The one weakness of this word-centred approach in the case of multi-verse hymns is that while the first stanza may be perfectly matched musically, subsequent verses may not be so well served. An example often cited is Dykes' tune GERONTIUS for 'Praise to the holiest in the height' which fits the first and last verses superbly with its high dominant coinciding with the word 'height' but works less well for the others.

The effect of this approach was to bond together particular hymns and melodies to the great enhancement of their popularity and power. It is now impossible to think of 'Praise, my soul, the King of heaven' without thinking at the same time of Goss's PRAISE MY SOUL, 'Eternal Father, strong to save' without Dykes' MELITA, 'Holy, Holy, Holy, Lord God Almighty' without his NICAEA or 'Abide with me' without Monk's EVENTIDE. Most of the great Victorian hymn tunes, and there are not a few of them, were crafted with great care and artistry to fit a particular set of words. This is pre-eminently true, for example, of Elvey's DAIDEMATA for 'Crown him with many crowns' and Redhead's PETRA for 'Rock of Ages'.

It is this matching of tunes to words that surely constitutes both the defining genius of Victorian hymn tune composers and their greatest gift to posterity. I suppose it is an acquired taste. Some doubtless prefer the words to stand on their own and would rather do without the 'heavy swell' effect created by the rolling bass and chromatic progressions in MELITA or the gentle pastoral reinforcement that DOMINUS REGIT ME gives to Baker's treatment of the 23rd Psalm. The fact is that, contrary to received wisdom, the dedicated Victorian tunes for particular hymns can often be a good deal less cosy and comfortable than the all-purpose folk melodies that have been tagged on to them in the twentieth century. 'I heard the voice of Jesus say' becomes easy listening when it is sung to the smooth and soothing strains of KINGSFOLD, chosen by Vaughan Williams for *The English Hymnal*, or DRINK TO ME ONLY WITH THINE EYES which has also come into recent favour. Dykes' VOX DILECTI is a much more 'difficult' and less instantly appealing tune but it is much closer to the spirit of the words, not least because of its highly effective and dramatic change from minor to major key in the middle of every verse to signal the shift from Jesus' invitation to the individual's response. Patrick Little has demonstrated in a recent scholarly article that another of Dykes' tunes, HORBURY, reflects the starkness and toughness of 'Nearer, my God, to thee' in a way that wholly belies glib generalizations about the cosy sentimentality of Victorian hymns.[46]

On the whole authors recognized and admired this ability on the part of composers. They were often profoundly grateful for it. Newman famously remarked when congratulated on the world-wide popularity of 'Lead, kindly light', 'It is not the hymn, but the tune, that has gained the popularity! The tune is Dykes's, and Dr Dykes was a great master.'[47] Yet sometimes authors did not feel that composers had served them so well. Francis Pott's Tractarian reserve was offended by the adulation which greeted his hymn 'Angel voices ever singing':

I am afraid some of its popularity arose from Sullivan having, contrary to my desire, set it in 'The Hymnary' to a trivial, pretty but altogether unfit tune of his own – which caught the ear of people who did not trouble themselves to see that the Hymn was of quite another character. In giving permission since for the printing of the hymn I have always made it a condition that Sullivan's tune shall not be in any way referred to.[48]

Most authors, however, did not share such misgivings about their hymns being made more popular by the tunes. John Ellerton expressed a more common sentiment when he thanked the editors of *A & M* for Joseph Barnby's HEBRON which had been commissioned for his 'Now the labourer's task is o'er': 'It seems to me nearly as perfect in its way as Sullivan's tune for 'Let no tears today be shed' – I mean as an interpretation of the words.'[49]

It is significant that Ellerton, the friend of working men and perhaps of all clerical hymn writers the one most attuned to the popular taste, should have singled out for special praise the two least 'churchy' of the major hymn tune composers. The quality for which he praised them was of course exactly what made Barnby such a master of the parlour ballad and Sullivan the king of the patter song. These two men, especially Sullivan, had in even fuller measure than their contemporaries that particularly Victorian virtue of finding the right tune for a given set of words. In the way that he used that gift in the field of hymnody Sullivan seems to me to be just as much a devoted servant of God and of his church as the more evidently and conspicuously pious S. S. Wesley. He was also a good deal more generous spirited. It was at his suggestion, not that of William Walsham How, who wrote the words, that all profits from the sale of the hymn for Queen Victoria's diamond jubilee on which they collaborated should go to the Prince of Wales Hospital Fund 'in both our names'.[50] This represented a considerable sacrifice since within three months of its publication in May 1897 the hymn was to net over £200 which would otherwise have gone to the composer.

How's 'O King of kings, whose reign of old' takes us to the heart of High Victorian hymnody. Intensely sentimental, patriotic, and more than a touch triumphalist, it also had a broad inclusiveness and sought to articulate the shared values of the community and a sense of the common good. 'When you sing it properly in church', How told a young boy who had written to say how much he liked it, 'you must try to think you are singing it to God, and thanking him for giving us so good a Queen.'[51] There is no reason to doubt the sincerity of Sullivan, who was deeply attached to Queen Victoria, when he told How, 'I have rarely come across so beautiful a combination of poetry and deep religious feeling.'[52] He produced a tune, BISHOPGARTH, which modern critics have not been kind about – Arthur Jacobs describes it as 'a weak tune, weakly harmonized' – but which his contemporaries loved.[53] Vigorous, muscular, uplifting and forward-looking, it inspired another eminent Victorian bishop, Edward Bickersteth, to pen a hymn two years after the jubilee which ensured that BISHOPGARTH would not be lost but would ring through the twentieth century as the stirring accompaniment of 'For my sake and the Gospel's, go and tell redemption's story'.

When Sullivan sent the tune to How, he wrote: 'It is not a part song, nor an exercise in harmony. It is a tune which everyone will, I hope, be able to pick up quickly and sing heartily.'[54] In that statement is contained both the credo of the major hymn tune writers in Victorian Britain and the secret of their success. They wrote unashamedly for congregations rather than choirs, for amateur singers. This was as true in the established church as in the Nonconformist denominations where there had always been more of a premium on congregational participation and hearty singing. For all the attempts of the Tractarians and those musicians in the van of the Anglican choral revival, church-goers never took to Gregorian chant and the office hymns of the early church. They wanted less austere and archaic fare. The compilers of *Hymns Ancient and Modern* acknowledged this as they gradually dropped the ancient from their collection and admitted more and more of the modern. Hearty singing was the order of the day across the land, whether in crowded city mission halls and Sunday Schools or lofty school chapels, like that at Repton where the headmaster enthusiastically embraced the new popular style of church music: 'Better to hear the praise of God heartily sung by the people to a vulgar tune, than an anthem of the highest order performed in the purest style by a dozen select singers.'[55]

7

'Hold the fort for I am coming'

American imports and gospel songs

It is hard to think of more quintessentially 'traditional' English Christmas hymns than 'Away in a manger', 'O little town of Bethlehem', 'It came upon the midnight clear' and 'We three kings of Orient are'. In fact, they were all written in North America in the latter half of the nineteenth century. So were such favourite Victorian hymns as 'Dear Lord and Father of Mankind', 'City of God, how broad how far', 'Stand up, stand up for Jesus', 'Take up thy cross, the Saviour said' and 'What a friend we have in Jesus'. North American imports made a considerable contribution to nineteenth-century British hymnody. Their influence was particularly marked in two very different areas. They introduced the revivalist gospel song and the hymn of social concern. While it was undoubtedly the former that had the greatest impact, spawning a host of British imitators, the latter also made its mark in a less spectacular way. The social gospel hymns may not have had the immediate appeal and instant singability of the catchy evangelistic choruses but they helped to show that liberals could sing their faith as much as evangelicals and catholics. They also serve to remind us that there are other strains to American Christianity than the tradition of simplistic and triumphalist fundamentalism that runs from Moody and Sankey to contemporary tele-evangelists.

The strong liberal vein in nineteenth-century American hymnody is perhaps most clearly represented in the work of a group of Unitarian poets and intellectuals. Their hymns reflect a keen interest in science and cosmology as well as a strong commitment to the social gospel. Oliver Wendell Holmes wrote 'Lord of all being, throned afar' shortly after taking up the chair of anatomy at Harvard in 1847, while John White Chadwick's 'Eternal ruler of the ceaseless round' was written for the graduating class of the Divinity School at Cambridge, Massachusetts, in

1864. In that year an important Unitarian collection appeared entitled *Hymns of the Spirit*. It was edited by Samuel Johnson, author of 'City of God, how broad, how far' and Samuel Longfellow, whose brother Henry was responsible for this stirring 'Psalm of Life':

> Tell me not in mournful numbers
> 'Life is but an empty dream!'
> For the soul is dead that slumbers,
> And things are not what they seem.
>
> Life is real! life is earnest!
> And the grave is not its goal;
> 'Dust thou art, to dust returnest'
> Was not spoken of the soul.

Other prominent American Unitarian hymn-writers included Frederick Hosmer, author of 'Thy kingdom come! on bended knee', and Julia Ward Howe, who wrote 'Mine eyes have seen the glory of the coming of the Lord' in order to provide more edifying words for the tune of 'John Brown's body lies a mouldering in the grave'. James Russell Lowell, poet, academic, editor of the *Atlantic Monthly* and the *North American Review*, penned that great anthem of strenuous, muscular, liberal Christianity, 'Once to every man and nation':

> New occasions teach new duties;
> Time makes ancient good uncouth;
> They must upward still, and onward,
> Who would keep abreast of Truth.
>
> Lo, before us gleams her campfires!
> We ourselves must Pilgrims be,
> Launch our Mayflower, and steer boldly
> Through the desperate winter sea.

Those verses were not, in fact, written for congregational singing but quickly found their way into hymn-books. The same was true of much of the work of Ray Palmer, a New York Congregational minister who produced one of the best-known translations of Bernard of Clairvaux's great eleventh century Latin poem, 'Jesu, thou joy of loving hearts'. Writing later about what became his most popular hymn, 'My faith looks up to Thee, Thou Lamb of Calvary' he commented, 'There was not the slightest thought of writing for another eye, least of all of writing a hymn for Christian worship.'[1]

Another reluctant hymn-writer was the Quaker journalist and anti-slavery crusader, John Greenleaf Whittier. Although over fifty of his poems were turned into hymns, including 'Immortal love, for ever full' and 'O brother man, fold to thy heart thy brother', he insisted 'I am not really a hymn-writer for the good reason that I know nothing of music. Only a very few of my pieces were written for singing. A good hymn is the best use to which poetry can be devoted, but I do not claim that I have succeeded in composing one.'[2] Whittier actually wrote a long poem 'The Brewing of Soma' to express his distaste for over-hearty congregational singing of the kind found at revivalist meetings which he compared to the drug-induced frenzies of ancient Indians. It is ironic that the verses beginning 'Dear Lord and Father', which were plucked out of the poem first by American Unitarians and then by English Congregationalists, should have become one of the most popular of all congregational hymns in the late twentieth century.

'Dear Lord and Father' first appeared in an English hymn-book in 1884 when William Garrett Horder included it in his *Congregational Hymns*. The verses of Whittier, Lowell and Longfellow particularly appealed to this liberal Congregationalist for their stress on the social gospel and call to earnest good works, qualities which he found lacking in most British hymns.[3] His *Treasury of American Sacred Song* (1896) and *Worship Song* (1898) did much to promote their popularity in Britain. Horder saw the United States as the home of both the best and the worst of contemporary hymnody. While he greatly admired the work of American liberals, he detested the quietism and passivity being preached by many of the sacred songs from the burgeoning evangelical camp. His particular *bête noir* was James Proctor's 'It is finished'.

> Nothing either great or small – Nothing, sinner, no;
> Jesus did it all, Long, long ago.
> > 'It is finished!' Yes, indeed, finished every jot;
> > Sinner, this is all you need; tell me, is it not?
>
> Till to Jesus' work you cling by a simple faith,
> 'Doing' is a deadly thing – 'doing' ends in death.
> > Cast your deadly 'doing' down – down at Jesus' feet;
> > Stand in Him, in Him alone, gloriously complete.

The spirit of those verses, which were set to music by Ira Sankey and popularized in his *Sacred Songs and Solos*, recalls the sense of submission and resignation found in the work of British writers like Frances

Havergal and Anna Waring (see p. 92). While their hymns are addressed to God and have him as their object and focus, however, 'It is finished' has a rather different orientation. As such it is unmistakeably a sacred song, as opposed to a hymn, in terms of the useful distinction drawn by an American writer at the turn of the century: 'A true hymn is worship; a sacred song is not. The ultimate objective point contemplated in a hymn is God himself; in a sacred song it is the hearer. A hymn co-ordinates with prayer. A sacred song co-ordinates with exhortation.'[4] With its strong measure of exhortation and evangelism, and its distinctive catchy tune, the sacred gospel song was a largely American invention, originating in the rural camp meetings and missions of the early part of the nineteenth century, supplying the needs of the burgeoning Sunday School movement and coming into full bloom with the mass rallies and hugely popular song-books of Dwight Moody and Ira Sankey.

Women writers were well represented in this particular genre, perhaps because of their considerable involvement in Sunday schools. Priscilla Owens produced a string of songs for the Baltimore Sunday School where she taught for fifty years, including 'We have heard the joyful sound – Jesus saves, Jesus saves' and 'Will your anchor hold in the storms of life?' Two unmarried sisters, Anna and Susan Warner, who lived in some style in their lawyer father's mansion on Constitution Island in the Hudson River, held Bible classes followed by tea and gingerbread every Sunday afternoon for cadets from the nearby West Point Military Academy, who were rowed over to the island by a servant. Both sisters were to find their way into the children's section of every late Victorian hymn-book, Anna with 'Jesus loves me, this I know' and Susan with 'Jesus bids us shine with a pure, clear light'.

The most prolific of all nineteenth-century American sacred song writers produced some work which clearly deserves the epithet of hymnody. Frances Jane van Alstyne, better known by her maiden name, Fanny Crosby, was converted to evangelical Christianity during the singing of Isaac Watts' hymn 'Alas and did my Saviour bleed' at a Methodist meeting in New York. Despite being totally blind, she went on to have a full-time career as a writer, employing 216 different pen names and producing a total of over 8,000 religious verses. She had regular contracts with a number of publishers, one of whom commissioned her to write three songs every week. While many of her efforts, which include 'Blessed assurance, Jesus is mine' and 'Safe in the arms of Jesus', belong clearly to the category of sacred song, others, like

'To God be the glory', should surely count as hymns if we follow the definition given above.

No man came near to matching this output, although the two who were probably closest did score over Fanny Crosby by writing tunes as well as words. Robert Lowry was unusual in the largely lay world of gospel song writing in being both an ordained minister and an academic. Professor of Rhetoric at Lewisburgh University, Pennsylvania, he was responsible for both the words and music of 'Shall we gather at the river' and 'Where is my wandering boy tonight?', and the tune of 'I need thee every hour' the words of which were supplied by Annie Sherwood Hawks, a member of the Brooklyn Baptist Church where he was pastor. More typical, and more prolific, was Philipp Bliss, a Congregational Church Sunday School superintendent in Chicago, who like Fanny Crosby earned his living from writing songs for Sunday Schools. He was responsible for the words and music of 'Whosoever heareth! Shout, shout the sound', 'Man of sorrows! What a name' and 'Hold the fort for I am coming'. This last song, based on a semaphore signal flashed by General Sherman to a besieged supply depot in Georgia at the height of the US Civil War, was to become the theme song of the Moody and Sankey crusades in Britain in the mid-1870s and prompted the 7th Earl of Shaftesbury to observe that 'If Mr Sankey has done no more than teach the people to sing "Hold the Fort" he has conferred an inestimable blessing on the British Empire.'[5]

'Hold the fort', which was the first number in Sankey's *Sacred Songs and Solos*, epitomizes a central theme in the theology of the late nineteenth-century gospel song. It is full of images of war and battle, suggesting that Christians are engaged in a fight against the world. A similar militaristic tone characterizes the work of another American Baptist song writer, William Sherwin, best known for his rousing 'Sound the battle cry! See, the foe is nigh; Raise the standard high for the Lord'. In 'Hold the fort' there is also a sense of a siege mentality with the true church portrayed as a faithful remnant bravely holding out against the encroaching forces of the Devil, and his allies the theological liberals, in anticipation of the Second Advent. This is coupled with a strong sense that salvation and security are to be achieved by withdrawing from the world with its evil ways. In many gospel songs this idea is expressed through the imagery of storm-tossed sailors being rescued through the agency of lighthouses and lifeboats. Among Bliss's other great successes were 'Brightly beams our Father's mercy from his lighthouse evermore' and 'Light in the darkness, sailor' with its rousing chorus:

Pull for the shore, sailor! pull for the shore,
Heed not the rolling waves, but bend to the oar;
Safe in the lifeboat, sailor, cling to self no more:
Leave the poor old stranded wreck and pull for the shore.

Although they hammered home the traditional evangelical themes of sin, repentance, personal conversion and salvation through the cross, the American gospel songs harped rather less on the awfulness of sin and the atoning power of Jesus' blood than several earlier British hymns had. None had quite the sin-stained and blood-soaked imagery of Anne Ross Cousin's 'O Christ what burdens bowed thy head', for example. Sandra Sizer, in her fine study *Gospel Hymns and Social Religion*, has shown how far the language in gospel songs was toned down from that of Isaac Watts. Where he would portray the human condition as being that of a miserable worm, they preferred to speak of a wanderer.[6] The gospel story of the prodigal son returning to his father was a favourite theme, taken up in songs like Ellen Gates' 'Come home, come home, you are weary at heart' and Robert Lowry's 'Where is my wandering boy tonight?'

The overall message of the gospel songs was comforting and reassuring. It is true that some had an exhortatory tone, like 'Yield not to temptation, for yielding is sin', which was the work of another tune and song writer, Horatio Richmond Palmer, who ran the New York Church Choral Union and held various academic music posts. The majority, however, instilled a mood of dependence and passivity, portraying the human condition as one of being object rather than subject, tossed in the billows, shipwrecked, and then rescued and saved entirely by the actions of Jesus. The message that 'little ones to him belong, they are weak, but he is strong' pervaded many of the adult songs as well as those specifically addressed to children. The Godhead was portrayed in much less remote and awesome terms than in most Victorian hymns. The Father was seen less as immortal, invisible and only wise, and more as a kindly figure to whom to turn when you are tempest-tossed, while the Son, instead of being addressed as the sure foundation of the church or the first-born of creation, was hailed as a help-mate, as in the Canadian Joseph Scriven's 'What a friend we have in Jesus'. Heaven featured even more prominently in late nineteenth-century gospel songs than it did in Victorian hymns. Conceived of in terms of an Arminian notion of universal atonement rather than a harsher Calvinistic ethic of predestination and election, it was seen as a happy home where families and loved ones would be united when 'In the sweet by and by, we shall meet on that beautiful shore'.

It was, hardly surprisingly perhaps, the songs that stressed the themes of assurance and security that came to be most popular. In another fine modern study of this genre, appropriately titled *Holding the Fort*, John Kent has shown that there were less comforting songs about the atonement which spoke of God's rejection of impenitent sinners. They appeared in the early Sankey collections but were gradually dropped from later volumes, having clearly failed to take on and gain wide usage. Writing about their reception in Britain John Kent comments: 'The section of the middle classes which clung to *Sacred Songs and Solos* as its only real hymn-book for thirty years or more did so more because it was able to transform and sentimentalize the contents by multiplying songs about a travel agent's idea of Heaven, than because of the attraction of the salvation-rejection songs about the atonement.'[7]

The traffic in gospel songs across the Atlantic was not all one way. Some of the most popular items sung at American camp meetings and revivalist rallies were of British origin. As one might expect, hymns by evangelical women writers struck a particular chord. Both Charlotte Elliott and Frances Havergal featured prominently in Sankey's collections. Catherine Hankey's 'Tell me the old, old story' was really made by its inclusion in *Sacred Songs and Solos* where it was given a suitably sentimental tune. Another British hymn-writer who owed much of her popularity to Sankey was Elizabeth Cecilia Clephane, a devoted member of the Free Church of Scotland who suffered from poor health and died at the age of 38. While travelling on a train from Glasgow to Edinburgh in 1874, he came across her poem 'There were ninety and nine that safely lay' in a newspaper that he had bought in the hope of finding news from America. Impressed with the poem's treatment of the theme of the Good Shepherd, he cut it out and put it in his pocket. Two days later, at an evangelistic rally in Edinburgh, Moody asked him for an appropriate solo with which to close the service.

> At this moment I seemed to hear a voice saying: 'Sing the hymn you found on the train! . . . Placing the little newspaper slip on the organ in front of me, I lifted my heart in prayer, asking God to help me so to sing that the people might hear and understand. Laying my hands upon the organ I struck the chord of A flat, and began to sing. After the first verse I was glad I had got through, but overwhelmed with fear that the tune for the next verse would be greatly different from

the first. But again looking to the Lord for help in this most trying moment, He gave me again the same tune for all the remaining verses, note for note.[8]

Several of the most successful gospel song tunes were improvised in equally hasty circumstances. They were produced both by amateur composers and by professional tunesmiths who were part of the burgeoning popular music industry that was to culminate in the emergence of Tin Pan Alley. The American popular music industry began in the 1830s, boosted by the spread of pianos and harmoniums and developments in printing which made sheet music widely and cheaply available. As in Britain, there was a fine dividing line between parlour ballads, which often had a strong religious tinge, and gospel songs and hymns. The most prolific suppliers of sacred tunes included Robert Lowry, Philipp Bliss and William Kirkpatrick, a Philadelphia carpenter who produced no less than 87 books of gospel song tunes, including the melody for 'Will your anchor hold?' and CRADLE SONG for 'Away in a manger'. Another talented amateur, William Howard Doane, ran a firm manufacturing wood-turning equipment in Cincinatti, Ohio, where he was also a Baptist Sunday School super-intendent. It was for his tune REFUGE and at his request that Fanny Crosby wrote 'Safe in the arms of Jesus'. He also composed the tune that was to turn 'Tell me the old, old story' into one of the best-loved of all gospel songs. Having heard the words recited by an English major-general at a YMCA convention in Montreal in 1867, Doane wrote the music 'one hot afternoon while on the stage coach between the Glen Falls Hotel and the Crawford House in the White Mountains. That evening we sang it in the parlours of the hotel. We thought it pretty, although we scarcely anticipated the popularity which was subsequently accorded it.'[9]

Opinions have varied as to the 'prettiness' or otherwise of this and other gospel song melodies. Lionel Adey not altogether unjustly describes the tune of 'The sweet by and by' as having 'the jingling senti-mentality of a public-house chorus at closing time'.[10] What is indis-putable, however, is the role played by the music in popularizing this particular genre of sacred song. Musically, if not theologically, the gospel songs were deeply incarnational, using the idioms and rhythms of the public house chorus, the music hall and the parlour ballad. Cloyingly sentimental and jingling they may have been but they were also eminently singable. It was to be predominantly through their tunes that these American imports were to enter Victorian Britain and to win a place in the affections of a people who were distinctly chauvinistic and distrustful of anything from across the Channel, let alone from the other side of the Atlantic. Instrumental in persuading the British to accept this particular piece of American cultural imperialism was the figure of Ira Sankey.

Although, like Gilbert and Sullivan, the names of Moody and Sankey are always coupled in a way that gives the wordsmith prominence over the music man, in this particular partnership there is no doubt that the singer had more impact than the preacher. A large part of the reason for this was simple audibility. While Moody's sermons were often difficult to hear in vast auditoria without the benefits of microphones and amplification, Sankey's songs, accompanied on the harmonium or belted out by huge massed choirs, echoed round the great halls where the evangelists held their rallies and left a lasting impression on those who heard them.

Dwight Moody and Ira Sankey were products of the evangelical revival in mid-nineteenth century America. They met at an international YMCA convention in Indianapolis in 1870 when Moody was 33 and Sankey just 30. Arriving late for a seven o'clock morning prayer meeting that Moody was taking, Sankey squeezed in next to a Presbyterian minister who said to him: 'The singing here has been abominable; I wish you would start up something when that man stops praying, if he ever does.'[11] Sankey obliged by singing 'There is a fountain filled with blood' and at the end of the meeting Moody asked if he would join him in his evangelistic work. The next day Sankey received a summons from the evangelist to be on a certain street corner that evening at six o'clock. When he arrived, he was immediately called on to stand on a large box which Moody had borrowed from a nearby store. His singing of 'Am I a soldier of the Cross?' drew a crowd that remained to listen to a twenty-five-minute sermon from Moody. Singing 'Shall we gather at the river', Sankey then led the assembled throng through the streets to the Opera House where the meeting was to be continued.

The partnership thus born in song was essentially one between two great performers. Moody was first and foremost a preacher; Sankey, although he composed some tunes of his own, was primarily a singer and choir leader. He had no qualms about the fact that his talents lay in presenting the work of others rather than in original composition. Nor did he have any illusions about his music-making, which was self-consciously evangelistic in aim and without any aesthetic or liturgical pretensions. Its purpose, he said, was to reinforce the teaching and preaching message of the words rather than to praise God. Moody had a rather higher view of his partner's craft, holding that 'music and the bible are the two important agencies with which to reach the world, and I've made as much of singing as I have of preaching'.[12] It is perhaps a little unkind to say of him, as Louis Benson did, that 'unable to tell one tune from another, Moody selected the Lowry-Bliss type of music because he observed its emotional appeal to the masses'.[13] What both men undoubtedly possessed was an unerring populist streak and a feel for the kind of melody that would appeal to the working and lower-middle-class audiences who flocked to their evangelistic rallies.

Moody and Sankey made their first visit to Britain in June 1873. They spent the first five weeks in York and went on to Sunderland before beginning a six-month mission in Scotland in November. During the latter part of 1874 they held rallies in large cities in the North and Midlands before moving down to London early in 1875. Their meetings, held in public halls or specially erected tents, were unlike anything seen before in the British Isles and attracted considerable attention. At Manchester's Free Trade Hall they drew up to 17,000 each evening and attendance at the Agricultural Hall, Islington regularly topped 21,000. Altogether, it has been estimated that around one-and-a-half million people attended their London rallies alone and it was not surprising that they were invited back to Britain for further visits in 1881–82 and 1891–92.

Music played a key role both in creating the mood and in reinforcing the message of Moody and Sankey's rallies. Their technique of using a mixture of solo and choral items to build up the atmosphere has continued to be employed by mass evangelists ever since and perhaps reached its apogee in the Billy Graham crusades of the 1950s and 1960s. At each venue Sankey recruited a large mixed-voice choir from local churches and rehearsed them in gospel songs. As people arrived for an evening meeting, the choir was singing, gradually building up to a climax to herald the appearance of Moody. The evangelist's prayers and sermon were interspersed with solos and choruses, the most powerful and emotionally charged being saved for the time when people were being called forward to make their declaration for Christ. A contemporary account of one of the London meetings in 1875 indicates the range of material that was sung:

During the hour of waiting some of the best known of Mr Sankey's hymns were sung by an excellent choir, especially the beautiful one 'Tell me the old, old story'. The pianissimo rendering of some of the passages in this was exceedingly telling, and could be heard distinctly over the whole building. With admirable punctuality, Mr Moody made his appearance on the platform at exactly half-past seven, by which time the whole hall was filled. With some abruptness, and in a decidely provincial accent, he gave out the verse 'Praise God, from whom all blessings flow', adding 'All sing; let's praise God for what He's going to do'. The congregation responded heartily, every man and woman appearing to join full-voiced in the doxology. Then followed a brief prayer, after which Mr Moody gave out the 100th Psalm, again adding 'Let all the people sing' and certainly all the people did. It was a fine sight to see that vast assemblage rise, and a treat to hear their powerful unison. After a brief silent prayer, Mr Moody offered a special supplication for London. It was a great city, he said, but God was a great God. 'Thou God of Pentecost,' he said, 'give us a Pentecostal blessing here in London'. Then followed a solo by Mr Sankey, 'Jesus of Nazareth passeth by' and for the first time was heard the clear notes of that rich voice ringing through the recesses of that spacious building. One excitable gentleman caused a little contretemps by proposing a chorus, evidently not wishing that Mr Sankey should have it quite to himself, but Mr Moody was an admirable manager, and easily restrained the interrupter's unseasonable zeal. After 'Rock of Ages' had been sung to the tune of 'Rousseau's Dream', the climax of the evening was reached. Mr Moody read a passage from 1 Cor. i.17, with following verses, and commenced his address.[14]

While those attending the Moody and Sankey rallies clearly got to sing old home-grown favourites from metrical psalmody and the eighteenth-century evangelical hymn writers, it was the new American material that particularly caught their ears. The gentleman who called out for a chorus in the particular rally reported above was not to be disappointed since it ended with a rousing rendition of 'Hold the fort'. Sankey concentrated on a basic repertoire of around thirty gospel songs, all of which were of recent American provenence. They were largely unknown in Britain although some had been introduced by Peter Phillips, an itinerant American ballad singer known as 'the Singing Pilgrim' who had toured the country during the 1860s. The transatlantic material was initially greeted with some suspicion. After the first meeting in York, which was attended by less than fifty people who took seats as far away from the pulpit as possible, Sankey noted: 'It was with some difficulty that I could get the people to sing, as they had not been accustomed to the kind of songs that I was using.'[15] Before long, however, initial inhibitions and apprehensions were overcome and the catchy new gospel songs were being enthusiastically sung both inside and outside the meeting halls.

Reactions to the songs and hymns introduced into Britain by Moody and Sankey were predictably varied. As one would expect, evangelicals were generally enthusiastic, though by no means universally so – Henry Venn Elliott, for instance, commented reprovingly, 'I cannot think that souls get to heaven by exciting or marching music.'[16] From the High Church camp there was predictable unease about the aggressively non-sacramental approach of the lay evangelists and the sentimental emotionalism of their music. 'Some of the melodies of Moody and Sankey are popular enough,' W. H. Monk conceded, 'but it is quite another question whether they are worthy of association with God's worship. Are they and the hymns they accompany not rather the exponents of a somewhat unwholesome and sentimental feeling, too personal and effeminate for public worship?'[17] A clergyman lecturing on the subject of 'hymns and hymnology' complained that the gospel songs 'do not exhibit reverence and their poetry no one has defended. On nearly every page is there the twang of Yankee Doodle. Why have they got such a hold on the people? One reason is that the melodies or refrain are catching – in fact you can't refrain from catching them, and that is what the great musical unwashed like.'[18] Liberals were divided, some deploring the stress on substitutionary atonement and the message of passivity in Sankey's songs, others, like the great Birmingham Congregationalist, R. W. Dale, rejoicing that they were stirring the hearts of the masses.

> Mr Sankey's solos evidently touched very many hearts; and the effect produced by the manner in which the vast audiences united in such songs as 'Hold the fort, for I am coming', 'Safe in the arms of Jesus' and 'The great Physician now is near' was sometimes very thrilling. The 'songs' have been sharply criticized. It is very easy to criticize them; it might be more profitable to consider why it is that both the music and the words are so popular and effective . . . Mr Sankey's melodies – whatever their demerits – are caught by thousands of

people of all kinds, cultivated and uncultivated, men, women, and children, and are sung with a will . . .

The same principles are applicable to the hymns. Critics have said that they are 'childish', that they have no 'literary merit', that there is something ridiculous in hearing a congregation of grown people singing with enthusiasm, 'I am so glad that Jesus loves me'. Well, the fact that hymns which are so simple even to childishness are sung by grown people with so much earnestness, that hymns with no 'literary merit' kindle new fire in the hearts of men and women who know something of Shakespeare, Milton and Wordsworth is surely worth investigating. Is it the 'childishness' which accounts for their power? Is it the absence of 'literary merit'? I think not. Give the people a collection of hymns characterized by equal fervour, expressing with the same directness the elementary convictions and the deepest emotions of the Christian heart . . . and they will become equally popular and more enduring. But our hymn books are too stiff and cold. People want to sing not what they *think* but what they *feel*.[19]

Dale's plea did not fall on deaf ears. As we have already seen, even before the arrival of Moody and Sankey, hymnal compilers, not least those responsible for *Hymns Ancient and Modern*, were beginning to introduce items from the mission halls. By the end of the century a select body of American gospel hymns had found their way into most British denominational hymn-books, although not into *A & M*. Perhaps rather surprisingly it was in 'stiff and cold' Presbyterian Scotland, with its stubborn attachment to unaccompanied metrical psalmody and deep suspicion of all other forms of music in worship, that Moody and Sankey made their greatest impact on both the content and style of congregational singing. At their first meeting in Edinburgh, Sankey, knowing the Scots' unease about 'human hymns' in public worship, invited those present to join in the 100th Psalm. Later he rather tentatively embarked on a solo rendering of 'Jesus of Nazareth passeth by'. It was received so warmly that after the sermon and closing prayer he felt emboldened to launch into 'Hold the fort', in some trepidation inviting the congregation to join in the chorus 'which they did with such heartiness and such power that I was convinced that Gospel songs would prove as useful and acceptable to the masses in Edinburgh as they had in the cities of York and Newcastle'.[20]

Almost more amazing than Sankey's ability to get the Scots to sing choruses was his almost single-handed success in converting them to the benefits of the instrument they had previously dismissed as 'a kist o' whistles' with a devil in every pipe. For the second meeting of the evangelists' opening Edinburgh crusade, held at Barclay Free Church, he ordered an organ so that the solos and hymns might have the kind of accompaniment that he was used to giving them. The driver of the cart bringing it to the church took a turn too quickly with the result that the instrument was shot into the street. Others might have taken this as a warning sign from the Almighty but Sankey was undaunted and had the damaged organ installed in the church. He was subsequently to use an organ or harmonium at every meeting in Scotland. Far from provoking an outrage, this seems to have proved a major factor in winning Scots round to the instrument that had already proved itself so beneficial in encouraging and supporting congregational hymn-singing in England. Certainly there was an upsurge in the installation of organs in Scottish churches from 1873-4.

The acceptance of both organs and gospel songs in Scotland was undoubtedly helped by the blessing given to both innovations by Horatius Bonar. Sankey was somewhat unnerved to find Bonar sitting close to him as he took his place behind the harmonium at the third meeting of the Edinburgh crusade. Fearful that the influential and respected Free Church minister might regard the music as an entertainment rather than a spiritual blessing, he launched 'fear and trembling' into a solo rendering of 'Free from the law, oh, happy condition'. His anxieties were relieved when 'at the close of Mr Moody's address, Dr Bonar turned towards me with a smile on his venerable face, and reaching out his hand he said: "Well, Mr Sankey, you sang the Gospel tonight." And thus the way was opened for my mission of sacred song in Scotland.'[21] In fact, the American musician and the Scottish minister were to strike up a close friendship and a fruitful partnership of their own. Unable to use any of his own hymns in his own church because the Kirk Session allowed nothing but metrical psalms, Bonar was only too pleased to have Sankey set and sing them. The first gospel song tune that Sankey ever wrote was for Bonar's 'Yet there is room'. He penned it shortly after his arrival in Edinburgh in November 1873 and some months before setting Elizabeth Clephane's 'There were ninety and nine that safely lay'.

'Yet there is room' was the only British contribution to Sankey's first song book which appeared in September 1873, superseding Peter Phillips' *Hallowed Songs* which they had used in the early months of their British mission. Costing sixpence and containing just sixteen songs, the booklet netted profits of over £7000 which the evangelists refused to take for themselves and passed on to charitable and religious causes. In 1875 the collection was widened to thirty items and given the title *Sacred Songs and Solos*. Later that year another, larger, book was issued, *Gospel Hymns and Sacred Solos*, which incorporated material from an earlier collection put together by Philipp Bliss and Major D. W. Whittle, a travelling American evangelist who had first given Bliss the idea for 'Hold the fort'. Sankey published a number of other titles, including a volume of *New Hymns and Solos* for the 1891 British mission, but none came near ousting *Sacred Songs and Solos* from its place as the bible of the gospel song movement. Constantly expanded and reprinted, although always retaining 'Hold the fort' as the opening song, it had swollen by 1903 to include 1,200 songs and was far out-selling even *Hymns Ancient and Modern*. In Britain alone it sold over eighty million copies in the fifty years following its first publication. As well as becoming the staple hymn-book of mission and gospel halls, independent evangelical churches and many Sunday Schools, it found a place in many parlours, perched on the harmonium amidst books of ballads.

As it expanded, *Sacred Songs and Solos* became broader in content. The 1875 edition was almost entirely made up of recent American gospel songs with ten of the thirty items being written and composed by Philipp Bliss. By 1903, although American authors still predominated, High Church Anglican hymn-writers like Neale, Baring-Gould and Alford were represented along with Heber and Lyte and more pre-dictable figures from the evangelical and dissenting worlds like Mont-gomery, Midlane, Charlotte Elliott and Frances Havergal. The best represented British author was Horatius Bonar, with twenty-six hymns in the 1903 edition. The music had a more emphatic American bias, although Sullivan and Barnby were well represented and Monk, Gauntlett and Dykes made a number of appearances. Overall, the tunes were less 'churchy' than those found in Victorian hymn-books with the saloon-bar chorus being a more obvious influence than the part song and drawing-room ballad. Vulgar and unsophisticated they may have been but there was no doubt as to their popularity and Vic Gammon may well be right to argue that they filled the vacuum left with the collapse of the west gallery tradition and brought about a renewed popular participation in church music.[22]

In so far as Britain produced a home-grown gospel song movement, it largely came out of the Salvation Army, founded by William Booth five years after the start of Moody and Sankey's first British crusade. In fact, many of the songs that were taken up by the Army and popularized by its songsters, tambourines and brass bands were American. They included two rousing numbers unaccountably ignored by Sankey, Fanny Crosby's 'We are marching on with shield and banner bright', written for a Sunday School in 1867, and 'We're bound for the land of the pure and the holy' penned by William Hunter, a Methodist minister from Pennsylvania, and included by Booth as the first song in the *Revival Hymn Book* which he compiled in 1866 for his Christian mission in the East End of London.

Like Sankey, Booth produced a stream of ever-expanding revivalist song books, several of which were targeted specifically at children. His original 1866 collection had 118 songs. The 1878 revised edition of the *Christian Mission Hymn Book*, which was the first to bear the title *Songs of the Salvation Army*, had 650. Two years later the Salvation Army started producing penny song books and printing a new song every week in its newspaper, *The War Cry*. Brass band parts followed in 1900 by when *The Salvation Army Song Book* had 870 songs and 216 choruses. A high proportion of its contents were American in origin. 'When upon life's billows you are tempest tossed' with its stirring chorus 'Count your blessings', which became almost a Salvation Army anthem, was the work of Johnson Oatman, a minister in the Methodist Episcopal Church who also managed to run an insurance business in New Jersey and to turn out more than 5000 gospel songs. The tune was by Edwin Excell, another prolific writer, who after his conversion in 1883 published 90 collections of gospel songs and composed tunes for some 2000 revivalist hymns. Another Army favourite, 'When the trumpet of the Lord shall sound' was the work of a Pennsylvania Methodist Sunday School teacher, James Black.

Late Victorian Britain did produce a number of gospel song writers, virtually all of whom were Salvation Army officers. Richard Slater, converted at a holiness meeting in Regent Hall in 1882, worked in the Army's music department from 1883 to 1913 and wrote more than 500 songs, 18 of which are still in the current (1986) edition of the *Salvation Army Song Book*. Thomas Marshall, who served in a variety of posts in the Army between 1883 and 1898, including that of Booth's personal secretary, produced 450 songs, including 'We're the soldiers of the Army of Salvation'. James Bateman, a former music-hall singer who followed a Salvation Army band from a public house and spent six years as an officer in the 1880s, was responsible for 'Come, shout and sing, make Heaven ring'. William Pearson, a former Primitive Methodist lay preacher who managed the Salvation Army Book Stores, for a number of years produced a new song each week, including the ever-popular 'Come, join our Army, to battle we go' which was said to have been written in 1875 after he had heard the town hall chimes in Bradford play 'Ring the bell, watchman'.

William Booth himself wrote several hymns, among them 'O boundless salvation! deep ocean of love'. His son, Herbert, produced 86, including 'Summoned home! the call has sounded', and two other children, William Bramwell and Evangeline, are also represented in the current Army *Song Book*. It was, however, as an unashamed apologist for using popular music in the service of evangelism that Booth made his greatest impact on late Victorian hymnody. 'To "sing with understanding" ', he wrote, 'surely means not so much with musical correctness as with the solemn consciousness of the eternal truth of that which is sung, for we sing of salvation and aim to save souls as well as by proclaiming the gospel of the Grace of God . . . Let us have a real tune, a melody with some distinct air in it – which takes hold of people and goes on humming in the mind – that is the sort of tune to help you – it will preach to you and bring you believers and converts.'[23] Shamelessly adopting the idiom and often the tunes of the contemporary music hall, he had no time for the view that certain kinds of music were too vulgar or worldly to be harnessed to the gospel message. 'Not allowed to sing that tune or this tune? Indeed! Secular music, do you say? Belongs to the devil, does it? Well, if it did, I would plunder him of it . . . Every note and every strain and every harmony is divine and belongs to us.'[24]

Booth's resolve to hijack the popular hits of the day and turn them into choruses of salvation seems to have come out of a visit he made to a revivalist meeting in a Worcester theatre in 1883. He was much taken by a gospel song 'Bless his name, he set me free' which was sung on the stage by a converted sea captain called George 'Sailor' Fielder. Booth was momentarily taken aback when Fielder told him afterwards that the tune was that of the popular music-hall song 'Champagne Charlie is my name'. After reflecting on the impact it had made on the audience, he turned to his son, Bramwell, and said 'That settles it. Why should the Devil have all the best tunes?'[25] William Booth was not, in fact, the first person to use that famous phrase. It had been coined more than a century earlier by Rowland Hill, preacher at the Surrey Chapel in London, who turned 'Rule Britannia' into a sacred song which began 'When Jesus first at Heaven's command'. Other eighteenth-century evangelicals regularly took over secular tunes. Charles Wesley wrote a hymn to fit the melody of 'Nancy Dawson' which a group of drunken sailors had sung in an effort to drown out one of his open-air services, and borrowed a melody written by Purcell to Dryden's 'Fairest isle, all isles excelling' for his own 'Love divine, all loves excelling'.

No one, however, adopted the Devil's tunes for evangelistic purposes as systematically and successfully as Booth and his followers in the infant Salvation Army. None of the popular music styles of the day was safe from their attentions. Stephen Foster's American minstrel songs were taken over, with 'Way down upon the Swanee River' becoming 'Joy, freedom, peace and ceaseless blessing' and 'Gone are the days when my heart was young and gay' resurfacing as 'Gone are the days of wretchedness and sin'. George Scott Railton, who pioneered the Salvation Army's first forays into the United States and Germany and was then territorial commander in France, wrote 'Shout aloud salvation and we'll have another song' to fit the catchy tune of 'Marching through Georgia'. The music hall favourite 'The daring young man on the flying trapeze' was given new lyrics beginning 'I'm washed in the blood of the Lamb', the drinking song 'Here's to good old whisky, drink it down', became 'Storm the forts of darkness, bring them down' and the traditional air 'Ye banks and braes of Bonnie Doon' was given a new lease of life as a gospel song beginning 'All things are possible in him/That can in Jesus' name believe'. The *Church Times* asked disdainfully 'Can anyone suppose that St Paul would have thought of adapting Christian hymns to the melodies used by the votaries of Dionysus or Aphrodite?'[26] Booth had a ready answer for such critics who complained about the 'consecration of tunes hitherto called secular'. He told them: 'I have sought to print just that music which has been sung amidst the most overpowering scenes of salvation in this country and America during the last thirty years.'[27]

The Salvation Army was just one product of a general evangelical awakening in Britain at end of the nineteenth century which brought a new religious enthusiasm, reminiscent in some ways of the spirit of the camp meetings of early Primitive Methodism. Communal singing of revivalist hymns and gospel songs played a major role in the holiness movement, which encouraged Christians to look for a second decisive experience beyond conversion, and particularly in the annual Keswick Conventions, which began in 1875. The Keswick hymn book, *Hymns of Consecration and Faith*, included a significant proportion of hymns by evangelical women writers, notably Frances Havergal, Charlotte Elliott and Fanny Crosby. In keeping with the emotional American-style devotional atmosphere of Keswick, the hymn settings in the book were 'generally soft and low'.[28]

Revivalist hymns and gospel songs began to find their way into mainstream denominational hymn-books in the closing years of the century. The 1887 *Congregational Hymnal*, for example, contained Annie Hawks' 'I need thee every hour' with its tune by Lowry and it also included Sankey's setting of Horatius Bonar's 'Yet there is room'. While *Hymns Ancient and Modern* and other major Church of England hymnals largely spurned this kind of material, several smaller Anglican publications, of both a High Church and an evangelical hue, took it up in an effort to reach the urban working classes. A hymn-book issued by the Cowley Fathers for a mission to the East End of London included some gospel songs along with rousing classics like 'Rock of Ages' and 'Onward, Christian soldiers' and a selection of more Catholic hymns on the sacraments, saints and martyrs.

Another distinct hymnodic genre which emerged in the latter part of Victoria's reign was also strongly influenced by the American gospel song movement. Temperance hymns used highly-charged emotional language and catchy Sankey-style tunes to hammer home their message of the evils of the demon drink. Alcohol was not, in fact, the only target of these hymns which sought to create a counter-culture to the world of public houses, gin palaces and music halls. The *National Temperance Hymnal* contained at least one song which tackled another widespread addiction:

> What gives the breath an awful smell,
> And hinders one from feeling well?
> A single word the tale will tell – Tobacco![29]

With the temperance hymns we have moved a long way from the liturgical purposes of *Hymns Ancient and Modern* and the evangelistic aims of *Sacred Songs and Solos*. The fact that the hymn form was increasingly being used not just to worship God and bring sinners to repentance but to promote social reform and encourage more responsible behaviour is a testament to the recognition of its effectiveness and popularity well beyond the church world. By the end of Victoria's reign the idiom of the hymn and the gospel song was being employed by a wide variety of social and political campaigners in an effort to popularize and reinforce their particular message. The trend towards more secular public education meant that genuine gospel songs were unlikely to be encountered by children who had no church attachment. Darlington School Board combed the Sankey hymn-book for material that might be appropriately sung by pupils at its elementary schools but could find only one, 'Work for the night is coming', that would not offend the secularists. However, the new socialist Sunday Schools and Labour churches realized the powerful pull of this new transatlantic import and set their high-minded, ethical socialist creed to tunes that could have come out of the mission hall or Salvation Army citadel. They also displayed a strong attachment to more traditional hymnody. John Trevor, founder of the Labour Church movement, who had left his Unitarian pulpit in Manchester in 1891 because he felt he was not reaching the poorest classes through the chapel, decreed that three hymns should be sung at the services of his new 'churchless' church. The first *Labour Church Hymn Book*, published in 1892, contained verses by Whittier and Lowell, alongside William Morris' romantic socialist poems and Newman's 'Lead, kindly light'. It also included two hymns to be sung to the national anthem, one patriotic, 'God bless our native land' and the other more class-conscious, 'God save the working man'.

Revivalist hymns and gospel songs held a strong appeal for several of the pioneers of trade unionism and Labour politics. Joseph Arch, himself a staunch Methodist, recruited farm workers to his Agricultural Labourers' Union to the strains of 'Hold the fort for I am coming' played by a brass band.[30] When Ramsay MacDonald fought his first parliamentary election in 1894 as the Independent Labour Party candidate for Southampton, he sent his agent a copy of the *Labour Church Hymn Book*, with 'those that seem to be the favourites' marked, and expressed the hope that the campaign should include 'music, singing, exhortative readings and short discussions'.[31] Socialist leaders also felt the pull of more traditional church music. During a meeting of the Trades Union Congress in Norwich in 1894, a group of delegates were walking through the Cathedral Close at sunset. Suddenly Keir Hardie broke into the 23rd Psalm. 'We all joined in', one of the delegates later noted, 'Christians and agnostics, blending our voices, not so much in any devotional spirit as out of deference to the influence of the place.'[32]

It was perhaps the ultimate tribute to the strength of the cultural power and influence of hymns in late Victorian Britain that they were being sung not just in churches and chapels, in parlours and school classrooms, at street corners and in tents but also at the gatherings of those who had rejected Christianity in favour of the new creeds of positivism and secularism. The 'temple' of high-minded, rational atheism, the South Place Ethical Society, issued its own hymn-book, *Hymns of Modern Thought*, in 1900. Alongside verses from the American liberal tradition like Chadwick's 'Eternal Ruler of the ceaseless round' and Whittier's 'O brother man, fold to thy heart thy brother', it printed emasculated versions of more traditional hymns from which all christological and mythological references had been edited out. The following year, the last of Victoria's reign, the *Labour Church Record* published a curious amalgam of Isaac Watts, the American social gospel tradition and twentieth-century religious pluralism that was yet clearly still cast in the language and form of a hymn:

> When I survey the unrighteousness,
> Cause of all things that hurt, oppress,
> I feel, though I be sacrificed,
> That one must follow Buddha, Christ.[33]

8

'Lead, kindly light'

How the Victorians viewed hymns

'The songs of the English-speaking world are for the most part hymns. For the immense majority of our people today the only minstrelsy is that of the hymnbook.'[1] With these words, W. T. Stead, staunch Congregationalist and tireless crusader for moral causes ranging from ending child prostitution to bringing about world disarmament, introduced a book that points perhaps more clearly than any other to the extraordinarily powerful hold that hymns had on the Victorians. He had the brilliant idea of writing to well-known figures and asking them what hymns had helped them in their lives. The results were published in 1896 in a little volume entitled *Hymns that Have Helped*.

> The hymn may be doggerel poetry, it may contain heretical theology, its grammar may be faulty and its metaphors atrocious, but if that hymn proved itself a staff and a stay to some heroic soul in the darkest hours of his life's pilgrimage, then that hymn has won its right to a place among the sacred songs through which God has spoken to the soul of man.[2]

As a professional journalist who successively edited the *Northern Echo*, the *Pall Mall Gazette* and the *Review of Reviews*, Stead knew how to turn out a stirring phrase. His early newspaper days at Darlington had given him a vivid insight into the popularity of gospel hymns among working men: 'It was a sight to see and not to forget, – a string of cabmen at a north-country station sitting on a fence, singing the hymns of the Salvation Army in the intervals between the trains.'[3] The sight of middle-class men in the Home Counties singing hymns outdoors had similarly struck a French visitor to England in the 1860s – 'On a Sunday I saw two men in frock coats and black hats singing psalms on the green of a village forty miles from London . . . They were surrounded by some twenty people improving themselves by the performance . . . I was told this was no uncommon sight, especially when the afternoon sermon had been good.'[4] As Stead pointed out in one of his purplest passages, the Victorians' love affair with hymns was not just confined to the British Isles but extended throughout the Empire.

> At this moment, on the slope of the Rockies, or in the sweltering jungles of India, in crowded Australian city, or secluded English hamlet, the sound of some simple hymn tune will, as by mere magic spell, call from the silent grave the shadowy forms of the unforgotten dead, and transport the listener, involuntarily, over land and sea, to the scene of his childhood's years, to the village, school, to the parish church.[5]

The appeal of Victorian hymns to the native peoples of the Empire is a huge subject which really warrants a book in itself. Even now Christians in Africa are still enthusiastically singing from editions of *Hymns Ancient and Modern* and the *Church Hymnary* that have long been discarded in Britain because of their archaic language and outmoded sentiments. Hymns were among the first English texts to be translated into African languages. Scottish visitors to the Livingstone Inland Mission on the Congo were thrilled to hear Bonar's 'A few more years shall roll' being sung in Kishi Kongo. As at home, the singing of hymns marked important rites of passage and national events. When the King of Tonga and his people adopted a constitutional form of government in 1862 they chose to mark their liberation 'from cannibal horrors' by singing 'Jesus shall reign, where'er the sun'.

Stead limited his research to the home front and did not attempt to survey the wider imperial scene. From the eminent contemporaries whom he approached about the hymns that had helped them he received an almost unanimously positive response. Only four replied in negative terms. The Archbishop of Canterbury refused to nominate any favourite hymns and somewhat airily directed Stead to a hymn-book that he himself had compiled. The Dean of St Paul's declined to take part in the survey on the grounds that Stead's selection would be 'unsectarian'. Lord Rosebery replied that he eschewed 'confession in general', and Herbert Spencer made clear that he found hymns more of a curse than a blessing: 'If parents had more sense than is commonly found among them they would never dream of setting their children to learn hymns as tasks. With me the effect was not to generate any liking for this or that hymn, but to generate a dislike for hymns at large.'[6]

The other recipients of his enquiries, however, provided not just a list of their favourite hymns but in many cases also deeply affecting accounts of how these had helped in particular times of sorrow and joy. The Queen herself circumspectly did not name any individual hymn but confided that the categories that had helped her most were those associated with marriages and funerals. Other members of the Royal Family were less reticent. The Prince of Wales wrote from Sandringham that 'among serious hymns there is none more touching nor one that goes more truly to the heart than "Nearer my God to Thee",' while the Duke of Cambridge, in keeping with his position as Commander-in-Chief of the British Army, nominated 'Onward, Christian soldiers'.[7] The Dean of Canterbury, F. W. Farrar, confided that 'I can scarcely ever join in "For ever with the Lord" without tears.'[8] Stead did not confine his enquiries to the great and the good. He also sought the views of the working men of Darlington, one of whom told him, 'We, sir, have our helps as well as those above us. I can assure you that the sweet songs of the sanctuary of the soul have given us weary ones many a solace and a lift.'[9] This particular correspondent was especially fond of hymns from Dr Martineau's Unitarian collections while another wrote in praise of Sankey's sacred songs.

Interestingly, the hymn mentioned more than any other by the contemporary celebrities whom Stead approached was Newman's 'Lead, kindly light'. Among those who singled it out were the agnostic Thomas Hardy, the High Churchman W. E. Gladstone, the scholar of comparative religion Max Müller, the radical MP Justin McCarthy, the Roman Catholic Marquis of Ripon and the diplomat Sir Evelyn Wood. Stead noted that it was frequently sung at séances while spiritualists were waiting for a materialization or manifestation from beyond the grave (presumably because of the reference in the last verse to the 'angel faces') and pointed out that at a recent meeting of the World Parliament of Religions at Chicago the only activities that all those present had been prepared to join in were the saying of the Lord's Prayer and the singing of 'Lead, kindly light'. As we have already noted, Newman's tentative and inconclusive verses were especially popular with those on the fringes of faith. It appeared in the midst of an otherwise almost exclusively Unitarian selection in the 1891 *Essex Hall Hymn Book* and was also one of the few contributions from orthodox Christians in the first *Labour Church Hymnal* of 1892. Stead received and published several moving accounts of how this hymn had helped those sunk deep in gloom or despond. 'Abide with me' also received a good many mentions.

Apart from these two works by recently deceased authors, the most frequently mentioned hymns in Stead's survey came from the eighteenth century, perhaps confirming the point that there is a hundred-year time lag in the popular appreciation of hymns. 'Rock of Ages' scored highly. Among those who nominated it as their favourite was W. E. Gladstone, who also cited Walter Scott's translation of the *Dies Irae* and Newman's 'Praise to the holiest'. Surprisingly, perhaps, the verses of Charles Wesley did not feature very prominently in Stead's volume. Gladstone apparently spoke for many of his contemporaries when he described them as overrated – 'He wrote more than Homer; 7,000 hymns of thirty lines each, say; do the sum, gentlemen, and be appalled.'[10] The work of other eighteenth-century evangelical paraphrasers was more popular, with the Duke of Argyll leading a chorus of approval for Philip Doddridge's 'O God of Bethel', and both H. H. Asquith and John Bright opting for Isaac Watts' 'Our God, our help in ages past'. Bishop Ken's evening hymn 'Glory to Thee, my God, this night' was also mentioned by several of Stead's correspondents, including the editor of the *Daily Telegraph* and the Archdeacon of Manchester.

Alongside the results of Stead's quizzing of eminent Victorians we can put the findings of more systematic surveys of favourite hymns conducted towards the end of the nineteenth century. One of the most extensive was undertaken among readers of *Sunday at Home* in 1887. Nearly 3500 people took part in this particular poll and it may, I think, be taken as reasonably representative of the tastes in hymnody of late Victorian middle-class evangelicals. Not surprisingly, 'Lead, kindly light' scored less well in this company than it did among Stead's intellectuals and free-thinkers, although it was still fifteenth in overall popularity. The top ten included three eighteenth-century favourites ('Rock of Ages' at No. 1, 'Jesu, lover of my soul' at No.3 and 'How sweet the name of Jesus sounds' at No. 5) and three hymns by contemporary evangelical women writers (Charlotte Elliott's 'Just as I am' at No. 4 and 'My God and Father, while I stray' at No.6 and Sarah Adams' 'Nearer, my God, to thee' at No. 7). 'Abide with me' took second place and the last three of the top ten slots were occupied by Keble's 'Sun of my soul, Thou Saviour dear', Bonar's 'I heard the voice of Jesus say' and Neale's 'Art thou weary, art thou languid?'[11]

These last three hymns featured even more prominently in an interesting survey conducted in 1899 by John Brownlie, a Church of Scotland minister who was a keen hymnologist. He compared the contents of the 24 most widely used hymnals in Britain and the United

States of America in order to produce a list of the most commonly occurring hymns. Somewhat surprisingly, only one item, 'Sun of my soul, Thou Saviour dear', found a place in every hymnal. Nine hymns appeared in 23 of the 24 books surveyed – 'Art thou weary, art thou languid?', 'I heard the voice of Jesus say', 'Jesu, lover of my soul', 'Just as I am', 'As with gladness men of old', 'From Greenland's icy mountains', 'Hark! the herald angels sing', 'Holy, holy, holy, Lord God Almighty' and 'Our blest Redeemer, ere he breathed'. A further 7 hymns appeared in 22 books – 'All hail the power of Jesus' name', 'Awake, my soul, and with the sun', 'Jesus shall reign where'er the sun', 'O day of rest and gladness', 'O worship the king', 'Rock of Ages' and 'Saviour, blessed Saviour, listen while we sing' – and 12 in 21 : 'Abide with me', 'Brightly gleams our banner', 'Christ the Lord is risen today', 'For ever with the Lord', 'Hail to the Lord's Anointed', 'How sweet the name of Jesus sounds', 'Hushed was the evening hymn', 'Jerusalem the golden', 'Jesus, the very thought of thee', 'There is a green hill far away', 'There's a friend for little children' and 'We plough the fields and scatter'.[12]

Another way of gauging the popularity of hymns is to look at the number of times they were set to music. In this respect 'Abide with me' was almost certainly first in the field, being set by Monk, Barnby, Goss, Hopkins, Steggall and S. S. Wesley, who described it as his favourite hymn and composed three tunes for it including the dark and melancholy recitative-like unison chant ORISONS. 'Lead, kindly light' was also popular among composers, being given serviceable tunes by Dykes, Wesley and Charles Purday and set as anthems by Stainer and Sullivan.

Taking all these pieces of evidence together, is it possible to construct a Victorian top ten? Eighteenth-century evangelical hymns would undoubtedly figure prominently, with 'Rock of Ages', 'Jesu, lover of my soul' and 'Our God, our help' conceivably occupying the top three places. 'Glory to thee, my God, this night' would almost certainly also have found a place, as it had for the previous 150 years among Anglican church-goers at least. The remaining six places would probably have been taken up by more recent works, led by 'Abide with me' and 'Lead, kindly light' and followed, perhaps, by 'Sun of my soul', 'Just as I am', 'I heard the voice of Jesus say' and 'Art thou weary, art thou languid?'. Interestingly, the two Victorian hymns that regularly top favourite hymn polls today would have come lower down the popularity stakes a hundred years ago. Whittier's 'Dear Lord and Father of mankind' was only just coming into use in Britain as a result of Horder's championship and was not to find its way into any Anglican book until well into the twentieth century. 'The day thou gavest, Lord, is ended', which John Ellerton had written for a liturgy for missionary meetings in 1870, did not really 'take off' until Queen Victoria chose it for her Diamond Jubilee celebrations in 1897. Fifty years later the young Princess Elizabeth, shortly to become Queen Elizabeth II, was to give a similar boost to the 23rd Psalm set to CRIMOND when she chose it for her wedding to Prince Philip.

By the end of Victoria's reign the communal singing of these and other favourites had become a popular recreational activity. As we have already noted, hymns were regularly sung at public meetings, political gatherings and trade-union rallies. They were also often heard in public houses, not so much from the lips of the regulars as from chapel-goers who toured the drinking dens on Saturday evenings seeking to redeem their habitués from their evil ways. During the 1890s the gentlemen choristers of one Staffordshire parish church processed after Sunday evensong to the 'Duke of Wellington' where, in a continuation of the custom practised by the old west gallery musicians and lovingly described by Thomas Hardy in *The Mayor of Casterbridge*, they would 'seat themselves round the mahogany table in His Grace's front parlour, lay down their top-hats, and, for the edification of the erring sheep in the public bar, sing a hymn. They would then each drink a half-pint of ale provided . . . in return for this assurance of divine mercy upon publicans and sinners.'[13]

Much of the public hymn singing in the late nineteenth century seems to have achieved the hearty quality favoured by Arthur Sullivan and Adolphus Pears (see p. 168). As one might imagine, this was particularly the case among members of the armed forces. In 1887 the Chaplain to the Fleet wrote to the compilers of *Hymns Ancient and Modern* asking for marks of expression to be put in the words-only edition:

In Greenwich Hospital chapel we have an excellent organ but it is oftentimes drowned altogether by the voices of 1000 boys of the school. In each of our five training ships we have from 500 to 900 older boys (with harmoniums only) and in some of our large ships there are about 700 men. Now imagine what a volume of sound there is when a favourite hymn is chosen such as 'Hark, hark my soul, Angelic songs are swelling' or 'All hail the power of Jesus' name' and think how differently such a congregation would sing 'Fierce raged the tempest o'er the deep' with this guide to remind them when to give the appropriate expression.[14]

The most full-blooded hymn-singing continued to emanate from Nonconformist chapels. A journalist visiting Spurgeon's Tabernacle in 1873 was struck by the unison singing of the whole congregation without any accompaniment. A Methodist minister's daughter who had emigrated to America returned for a vist to Bradford in 1888: 'I went to an intense Methodist service and heard a thousand Yorkshire men and women sing "There is a land of pure delight" and "Lo, He comes with clouds descending!" as I shall never hear them again.'[15] A correspondent to the *Primitive Methodist Magazine* in 1896 was similarly moved by the singing in the chapel of a mining village:

> There was a little scraping and twanging of fiddle-strings before all the stringed instruments – of which there were a dozen – were brought into accord with the organ, but then such a glorious outburst of music as could not help the spirit of devotion. How these North folk sing. We felt the Divine enchantment of the hour. The glory of the Lord was in His sanctuary. Forgotten in the ecstatic bliss of mystic communion with heaven were the bare, unsightly walls, the hard seats, the dreary pit, perhaps beneath our very feet, in which men crawl like beasts for six days in the week, heaving coals, naked to the waist, while the perspiration makes white channels down their grimy bodies; forgotten the hardship, the dull, aching monotony, and the familiar thought of death . . . the vision of God and the Celestial City are seen by these men in that outburst of song in which the soul was finding expression.[16]

Hymns also exerted a strong emotional power in more private and domestic contexts. They were a key element in that quintessentially Victorian institution, the death-bed scene. Many eminent Victorians breathed their last with the words of a hymn either on their own lips or being sung to them by their nearest and dearest. Queen Victoria repeated the last verse of 'Lead, kindly light' to her son, the Duke of Albany, as he lay dying and she asked for Newman's hymn to be read to her in her own final hours. It may very well have been her favourite hymn. She had wanted to invite Newman to tea on the strength of it but Prince Albert dissuaded her from entertaining so controversial a figure who might enrage the Protestant susceptibilities of her subjects. Newman himself asked to hear F. W. Faber's hymn 'Eternal Years' during his final illness. A harmonium was brought into the passage out-side his bedroom in the Birmingham Oratory and one member of the community played it while another sang and a third knelt by his bed saying the words. Hymns played a prominent role in many other affect-ing death-bed scenes. Prince Albert asked for 'Rock of Ages', Edward Baines, the prominent Nonconformist and Liberal MP for Leeds, called on his family to gather round him and sing Robert Grant's 'When gathering clouds around I view', Sir Walter Scott recited the *Dies Ira* and *Stabat Mater Dolorosa*, Dora Wordsworth, daughter of the poet, repeated 'Just as I am' and Henry Baker died whispering the stanza of his own 'The king of love my shepherd is' which begins 'Perverse and foolish oft I strayed'.

Funerals provided another important occasion for singing hymns. From a random and by no means exhaustive trawl through newspaper accounts, 'Lead, kindly light' and 'Abide with me' would appear to have been among the most popular funeral hymns with Ellerton's 'Now the labourer's task is o'er', How's 'For all the saints' and Newman's 'Praise to the holiest in the height' close runners-up. Watts' 'Our God, our help in ages past', sung at the funerals of the Queen and her longest serving Prime Minister, Mr Gladstone, was also a favourite for occasions of both public and private mourning. Gospel songs featured in the funerals of a number of prominent Victorian evangelicals. As the hearse carrying the coffin of the 7th Earl of Shaftesbury left Westminster Abbey, the band of the Costermongers' Temperance Society struck up 'Safe in the arms of Jesus'.

As well as accompanying souls out of this world and into the next hymns were also sometimes responsible for converting sinners from worldliness to a lively Christian faith. Eighteenth-century evangelical hymns were particularly credited with effecting spectacular conversions, although many also attributed their turning to Christ to the influence of a gospel song or chorus in the Sankey mould. For some, hymnody was a decisive factor in bringing about a quickening of faith and change in denominational allegiance. A notable example was Thomas Gill, a prodigious evangelical Anglican hymn-writer who had started life as a Unitarian. According to a contemporary, 'Delight in the divine songs of Watts was his earliest intellectual enjoyment, and in after years the contrast between their native force and fullness and their shrunken and dwindled presentation in the mutilated version in Unitarian hymn-books began that estrangement from his hereditary faith which gradually became complete.'[17] A number of Victorian clerics made much of the power of hymns to change men's hearts. In a volume of stories from church history aimed at children, for example, J. M. Neale pointed out how the Emperor Louis I was moved from lethargy and indifference to pious faith through hearing the imprisoned Theodulph of Orleans singing the Latin original of 'All glory, laud and honour' as he rode past his prison window in a procession in 821.

While most clergy across the denominations came to see the value of hymns as evangelistic and liturgical aids, a minority were uneasy about the enormously important role that they had come to have by the end of the century both in worship and in shaping popular belief. In an important study published in 1903 and entitled *A Worshipful Church* John Hunter, a Congregational minister who served in York, Hull and Glasgow, expressed concern that the hymn-singing cult had become altogether too dominant and that congregations were in danger of being 'choir-ridden rather than priest-ridden'.[18] Similar concerns were being voiced among High Anglican clergy. Giving evidence in 1905 to the Royal Commission on alleged disorders in the church, Charles Gore, newly consecrated Bishop of Birmingham, deftly turned the tables on the commissioners who were seeking to sniff out, and snuff out, Romish ritualistic practices in the Church of England, by telling them that 'indiscriminate hymn-singing has really altered the whole type of our services'.[19] Anglican worship, he complained, had become 'flooded' with evangelical and revivalist hymns which were wholly alien to the spirit of the Prayer Book. This, he ventured to suggest, was far a more serious disciplinary matter than the ritualism of a few High Church priests – 'by the use of metrical forms any kind of doctrinal innovation could be introduced'.[20] The eminent Congregationalist, A. M. Fairbairn, expressed similar misgivings a few years later when he wrote of his gratitude 'that my childhood was nurtured on the Book of Psalms, rather than on the jingling verses that celebrate the "Sweet Saviour", or protest how I love "my Jesus" '.[21]

It is, perhaps, significant that these protests about the unfortunate theological and doctrinal consequences of the huge popularity of hymn-singing arose at the end of the Victorian era when the influence of the highly sentimental imported American gospel songs and native Salvation Army material was at its height. Those Victorian clergy who sought to define the essence of a good hymn – and not a few of them did – tended to stress factors like restraint and earnestness and to deplore any display of what they took to be self-indulgent emotionalism. L. C. Biggs, editor of the 1867 annotated edition of

Hymns Ancient and Modern, listed three key requirements for a good hymn – devotional quality, intellegibility and earnestness. Hymns should bring 'the soul of the singer into communion with God'. He also made a plea, which was to be repeated many times, for simplicity; 'an involved construction, a foreign phraseology, an allusion unexplained or misunderstood, will at once paralyse the devotional power of a hymn'.[22] The leading Victorian practitioners shared this view. William Walsham How felt that 'a good hymn should be like a good prayer – simple, real, earnest and reverent'.[23] John Ellerton identified five key qualities: sincerity, vigour, simplicity, brevity and musicality – 'the metre, therefore, ought not to be too complex, or greatly varied. The rhythm ought not to be rugged, nor the diction bald and prosaic. We cannot always expect real poetry, even in a good hymn; but we have a right to expect words that lend themselves well to the simple and solemn music which alone is fit for congregational worship'.[24] Good middle-of-the road Anglican that he was, Ellerton deplored any lapse from the principles of restraint and moderation, such as he found among several Roman Catholic writers:

> Theatrical displays of emotion . . . disgrace many hymns, both Roman and Protestant, on our Lord's suffering. The thoughts with which a devout and intelligent believer in our own day dwells upon the Passion can never clothe themselves in the sensuous language of Faber and Caswall; they 'lie too deep for tears'. In our Prayer-book there are no overstrained expressions either of sorrow or of joy; no invitations to weep, or prayers for 'a fount of tears': why should such things be found in our Hymnal?[25]

In fact, Caswall was equally uneasy about the subjectivity and emotionalism of many modern hymns. For him, as for several other Anglo- and Roman Catholics, the only wholly satisfactory hymns to sing in church, in translation if need be, were the ancient Latin office hymns. They had a commendable objectivity, being designed 'to take the individual out of himself; to set before him, in turn, all the varied and sublime objects of the faith; and to blend him with the universal family of the Faithful. In this respect they utterly differ from the hymn-books of modern heretical bodies, which dwelling, as they do, almost entirely on the state and emotions of the individual, tend to inculcate the worst of all egotisms.'[26] Those of a more Protestant persuasion, how-ever, felt that there were altogether too many ancient hymns being sung and not enough reflecting contemporary concerns and interests. In the preface to his *Hymns of Praise and Power* (1874) the Unitarian James Martineau charged the Oxford Movement with having nurtured a retrospective and historical piety characterized in hymns which gave an exaggerated prominence to the objective and mythological elements of the Christian faith accumulated during the formulation of the creeds in the early centuries of the church's development.

By far the most widespread and persistent contemporary clerical complaint against Victorian hymns was their excessive subjectivity and sentimentality. Bishop Christopher Wordsworth articulated a common complaint when he wrote that 'The pronouns *I* and *my* are rarely found in any ancient hymn. But in modern hymns the individual often detaches himself from the body of the faithful and in a spirit of sentimental selfishness obtrudes his own feelings concerning himself.'[27] Several of the most popular hymns earned severe rebukes in this regard. John Ellerton suggested that 'Abide with me' was perhaps best kept only for funerals since it was 'almost too intense and personal for ordinary congregational use'.[28] John Heywood, editor of the *Anglican Psalter Noted*, criticized the congregational use of 'Lead, kindly light' on the grounds that it described a highly personal and unusual state of mind and was totally meaningless when sung communally in church. John Brownlie similarly argued that George Matheson's 'O love that wilt not let me go' was altogether too introspective for congregational use: 'It is a song for one singer, and for a singer in very special circumstances and mood of mind.'[29] An anonymous correspondent to the *Church Times* in November 1897 called for the dropping from the standard Church of England repertoire of 'all the subjective or morbid hymns, especially those beginning with a capital "I"'. He went on to complain 'It is not infrequent to hear "Lead, kindly light", "My God, my Father, while I stray", "Art thou weary, art thou languid" etc. given out in the middle of Mattins in a congregation largely composed of robust young men, and maidens, and rosy-faced children.'[30]

This kind of criticism spanned all the main denominations. A hymnal supplement published by the Congregational Union in 1874 was castigated by several clergy for 'the number of hysterically sentimental hymns'.[31] Its appearance may well have been one of the factors that persuaded the leading Birmingham Congregational minister, R. W. Dale, to publish *The English Hymn Book* in protest against 'the sensuous sentimentalism which has been encouraged by some recent Hymn-writers' and to promote the 'manly simplicity' of the English tradition of faith and feeling.[32] Prebendary J. H. Lester, secretary of the

Lichfield Church Mission, experienced a similar reaction on reading through a draft hymn book for mission churches sent out by the compilers of *Hymns Ancient and Modern*: 'If there had been fewer hymns of an 'up-in-the-sky' sentiment and more that touched upon the experiences of common life, it would, I think, serve the true purpose of the Church better – viz. of attracting and attaching to the Church plain men and women who are meeting the dangers and difficulties of life without the comfort of religion.' He called for 'simple English-bred words, sentences direct in construction, and metaphors drawn from actual life'.[33] Charles Kingsley, the Anglican country clergyman and novelist, made a similar complaint: 'How often is the tone in which hymns speak of the natural world one of dissatisfaction, distrust, almost contempt. "Change and decay in all around I see" is their keynote.'[34] Henry Shuttleworth, a minor canon of St Paul's Cathedral and Professor of Pastoral and Liturgical Theology at King's College, London, who was a prominent Christian Socialist and author of several books on church music, told W. T. Stead: 'I hate with a holy hatred all sentimentalist maunderings, all feeble religiosities, all diseased raptures and sorrows. To help men, hymns should be manful.'[35]

One of the most eloquent pleas for more 'manly' hymns which would preach less pie-in-the-sky and more of a humanitarian and social gospel was made by a hymn-writer who had himself been accused of over-emotionalism and subjectivity. Asked what he thought of modern hymns, George Matheson replied that they lacked humanitarianism.

> There is any amount of doctrine . . . but what of the secular life – the infirmary, the hospital, the home of refuge? . . . I don't think our hymns will ever be what they ought to be until we get them inspired by a sense of the enthusiasm of, and for, humanity . . . Hymnists speak of the surrender to Christ. They forget that Christ is not simply an individual. He is Head of a body, the body of humanity; and it no longer expresses the idea correctly to join yourself to Christ only, you must give yourself to the whole brotherhood of man to fulfil the idea. I like 'Lead, kindly Light'; it is universal . . . Another good hymn is 'Trust in God and do the Right' written by Dr Norman Macleod, a good and practical hymn. 'We give Thee but Thine Own' sounds the real humanitarian note to the fatherless and widows. Hymnology is feeble and ineffective when it ignores the humanitarian side of religion.[36]

Victorian hymn-tunes also came in for much contemporary criticism for their sentimentalism and effeminacy. Leading the attack, predictably, were those who deplored the vulgarity and secular associations of the part- song style and looked back longingly to the age of plainsong, metrical psalmody and chorales. For Thomas Helmore, whose life's ambition had been to restore plainchant as the main vehicle for Anglican worship, 'most modern hymn tunes are nauseous; and there are some others I utterly abhor, as being so tainted with the natural expression of frivolous, or even corrupt associations, that in their very essence they are wholly unsuitable for divine worship . . . If any plead in favour of their use that they attract the ungodly, let them believe me that they repel the well-nurtured and holy, corrupt the religious feeling of the masses, undermine the just sense of what is true in worship and chaste in Art, the handmaid of Religion.'[3] In a paper published in 1863 Edwin George Monk, organist of York Minster and composer of ANGEL VOICES (though no relation or great admirer of the William Henry Monk), criticized the effeminate vulgarity of contemporary hymn tunes in equally trenchant terms:

> A good tune, whether strong, or tender, or jubilant in character, should possess something beyond mere vigour, or tenderness, or joyfulness; it should be devout, unsecular, soul-stirring . . . Few only of the popular tunes now in use will answer to this description. Let us, therefore, dread the tendency to which I have alluded; and encourage in its stead, sober, broad, and elevating melodies, supported by masculine, church-like, and untheatrical harmonies.[38]

The tunes that so offended the ears of some musicians often found stout defenders among the clergy who were well aware of their popularity and ability to enhance the impact of the words. William Walsham How fought a vigorous rearguard action in 1897 when the musical tide was beginning to turn away from sentimentalism. The editors of A & M were proposing to excise the tune ALSTONE, written by Christopher Willing, *maestro al piano* at Her Majesty's Theatre, London, and later chorus master at Covent Garden Opera. For generations of children it was indissolubly linked to Mrs Alexander's 'We are but little children weak'. How strongly opposed this move, arguing that while the tune 'may not be high class music, it has entered into the whole church life of the land'.[39] He also protested at the proposed dropping of ST CLEMENT for 'The day, thou gavest', prompting the response from A & M's editor, W. H. Frere, 'It is quite true that people like waltz-tunes but does the Bishop seriously hold that that is a reason for providing them?'[40] In the event, How's advocacy of popular tunes won the day and both ALSTONE and ST CLEMENT remained in the hymn-book.

One prominent late-Victorian musician was prepared to antagonize many of his professional colleagues by vigorously defending modern hymn tunes. In the preface to the volume in which he collected his own 157 hymn tunes Sir John Stainer paid a glowing tribute to the work of John Bacchus Dykes:

> It is impossible to speak of Dr Dykes without enthusiasm; he devoted his musical genius (for genius he certainly had) entirely to the service of the Church, with splendid results with which we are happily so familiar . . . It requires some courage at the present moment to announce oneself as a disciple of Dykes, because modern hymn tunes are likely to have to pass through the fire of severe criticism. They are, it is said, 'sentimental' and 'weak' ; these epithets are mild and polite compared to many others hurled against them. No doubt many tunes that are over-sweet may, after twenty-five years' use, begin to cloy. But it must not be forgotten that the critics of hymn tunes nearly always fall into the insidious snare of judging of the old by the best specimens, and of the modern by the worst.[41]

Stainer went on boldly to state his conviction that many ancient hymn tunes were of a very poor standard and to plead that different criteria be employed for judging a hymn tune from those used for other pieces of music.

> The true estimate of a hymn-tune cannot be found by principles of abstract criticism or by any internal evidence that it exhibits an artist's handicraft. There is something indefinable and intangible which can render a hymn-tune not only a winning musical melody, but also a most powerful evangeliser.[42]

These remarks appalled W. H. Hadow, a leading academic musicologist and editor of *The Oxford History of Music*. He found it monstrous that Stainer should suspend his usual critical musical faculties when dealing with hymn tunes. In a savage review of Stainer's collection in the High Church paper, *The Guardian*, in October 1900, he praised plainsong melodies, German chorales and French and Swiss psalm tunes and tore into modern British hymn tunes for their cloying sentimentality and second-rate musicality: 'They seek the honeyed cadence and the perfumed phrase . . . they can touch the surface of emotion, but can never sound its depths.'[43]

One recently published hymn-book shone out for Hadow like a beacon amidst the thick treacly fog of contemporary sentimentality. *The Yattendon Hymnal* had been produced in 1895-99 by the future poet laureate Robert Bridges in an attempt to wrest hymnody from vulgar popularism and bring to it the highest cultural, literary and musical standards. In some ways it harked back to the purist antiquarianism of the Oxford Movement. More than that, however, it represented the revolt of a cultured literary mind against the sentimental vulgarity of Victorian hymnody. Like Hadow, Bridges felt that those writing hymns and composing tunes, and also those who acclaimed their work, had suspended the critical faculties that they would apply if they were engaged in any other field of creative endeavour. For him the essential factor in defining what constituted a good hymn was not its popular appeal, evangelistic effectiveness or emotional impact but whether it satisfied the criterion of good taste.

Robert Bridges was born in 1844 into a family of Kentish yeoman farmers and had a conventional upper-middle-class Victorian upbringing in which hymns played a large part. His boyhood Sunday evenings were spent memorizing sacred lyrics, including Keble's *The Christian Year* which made a particular impression on him, and then singing them round the piano. At Eton he developed a deep love of early English church music and at Oxford he fell under the spell of the Oxford Movement, although not of its more emotionally charged hymns. Of F.W. Faber, 'a Romanized clergyman', he wrote rather disparagingly, 'I have nothing to say, except that a maudlin hymn of his . . . provoked my disgust.'[44]

Bridges toyed with the idea of taking holy orders but instead became a doctor. In 1882, however, he gave up his medical practice and moved to a large house at Yattendon near Newbury. Here he took up the post of choirmaster in the parish church where he reinstated plainchant and sixteenth-century psalm tunes. He resigned after nine years, no longer able to bear the vicar's sermons, and devoted himself to providing a hymnal for the choir and for more general use. *The Yattendon Hymnal* appeared in four parts between 1895 and 1899. Beautifully printed on hand-made paper with a deliberately archaic type face, it was as much an exercise in antiquarianism as in hymnody. Only three tunes dated from after 1750. The great majority were from sixteenth- and seventeenth-century composers, notably Louis Bourgeois, Johann Crüger, J. S. Bach, Thomas Tallis, Orlando Gibbons and Jeremiah Clark. Bridges wrote many of the words himself, feeling that most

Victorian verses were unworthy of such great music and being determined to avoid distorting the chorales and psalm-tunes to make them fit English metres as previous editors had done. His own hymns include 'Happy are they, they that love God', 'The duteous day now closeth', 'Love of the Father, love of God the Son' and the magnificent 'All my hope on God is founded'.

In terms of his dates Bridges stands as the last Victorian hymn-writer. However, his stress on musical and literary purity rather than singability, emotional power and didactic impact places him rather in the tradition of early twentieth-century hymnody. *The Yattendon Hymnal* was a reaction against nearly all that Victorian hymn-writers and hymn tune composers stood for. Bridges felt that what they were offering to God was of poor quality. This came home to him when he attended his daughter's confirmation in Exeter.

> The service was ruined by the introduction of some of the most maudlin and washy hymns with their tunes out of *Hymns Ancient and Modern*. I was earnestly praying the Preserver of Souls that my dear little girl might be safe-guarded through life from the unholy spirit that all parsons seemed to be invoking, and that she might have the Spirit of Wisdom, and understanding, and the Spirit of Might, instead of that Spirit of bosh and ignorance, and weakness – which sounded in the air and was apparent in nearly all the faces of the clergy.[45]

In addition to producing a hymn-book to embody the higher standards that he felt were needed, Bridges also preached his message in *A Practical Discourse on some Principles of Hymn-Singing*.

> Music being the universal expression of the mysterious and supernatural, the best that man has ever attain'd to, is capable of uniting in common devotion minds that are only separated by creeds, and it comforts our hope with a brighter promise of unity than any logic offers. And if we consider and ask ourselves what sort of music we should wish to hear on entering a church, we should surely, in describing our ideal, say first of all that it must be something different from what is heard elsewhere; that it should be a sacred music, devoted to its purpose, a music whose peace should still passion, whose dignity should strengthen our faith, whose unquestion'd beauty should find a home in our hearts, to cheer us in life and in death.[46]

In case any readers were left uncertain as to what such music was, he elaborated by telling them that plainsong melodies, whose unbarred rhythms 'dance at liberty with the voice and sense' were infinitely to be preferred to those modern hymn tunes 'plumping down on the first note of every bar whether it will or no' have any clear advantages' (sic).[4]

The trouble was, of course, that the Victorians liked tunes that plumped down on the first note of every bar. They liked their hymns to have strong singable melodies and if they had a touch of sentimentalism and vulgarity, so much the better. Bridges spoke with the unmistakable voice of cultural élitism, asking that churches 'should have at least one service a week where people like myself can attend without being offended or moved to laughter'.[48] As Lionel Adey has observed, *The Yattendon Hymnal* 'represents the most conscious endeavour to merge worship with literary culture'.[49] It stands at the turning point between nineteenth- and early twentieth-century hymnody, anticipating the high literary and musical standards of the *English Hymnal* of 1906 and *Songs of Praise* of 1925 and 1931. To that extent, it exerted an important influence. Yet its immediate impact was minimal. It was not taken up in more than a handful of parish churches and remained largely a collector's item for antiquarians. The popularity of Dykes and Stainer, and the gospel hymns associated with Moody and Sankey, vulgar and sentimental as they might be, continued undiminished.

Bridges was not the only cultured and literary Victorian to feel uneasy about the hymns of which most of his contemporaries seemed so fond. Matthew Arnold, educationalist, critic and defender of high culture against what he took to be the rising tide of philistine barbarism, also took the view that they epitomized 'bad music and bad poetry'. In his *Literature and Dogma* he wrote 'Hymns, such as I know them, are a sort of composition which I do not at all admire . . . I regret their prevalence and popularity among us.'[50] John Ruskin was another scathing critic of this particular contemporary genre. In an essay written in 1877 and entitled 'Rock Honeycomb' he compared the restraint and dignity of the psalms as translated in the sixteenth century by Sir Philip Sidney with the vacuous blandness of modern hymns which seemed designed 'to obtain such a concatenation of pious sayings as may, on the whole, be sung without offence, and by their pleasant sound soothe and refresh the congregation after kneeling till they are stiff'.[51]

Ruskin was particularly disturbed by the unreality of hymns and the gap between their pious platitudes and the actual feelings of those singing them.

In my own parish church, only the Sunday before last, the whole congregation, and especially the children, sang, in greet glee and contentment, a hymn which declared their extreme eagerness to die, and be immediately with God: but if, in the course of the tune, the smallest bit of plaster had fallen from the ceiling, implying any degree of instability in the rafters thereof, very certainly the whole symphonious company would have scuttled out as fast as they could . . .

The entire system of the modern English canticle is half paralytic, half profane, consisting partly of the expression of what the singers never in their lives felt, or attempted to feel; and partly in the address of prayers to God, which nothing could more disagreeably astonish them than His attending to.[52]

Other prominent members of the Victorian literary establishment were much more enthusiastic about hymns. Tennyson, whose views on the difficulty of writing a good hymn have already been quoted (p. 81), was enthusiastic about the literary quality of one of the most popular contemporary hymns. According to Francis Palgrave, on reading 'Abide with me' the Poet Laureate 'was deeply impressed by its solemn beauty; remarking that it wanted very little to take rank among the really perfect poems of our language'.[53] Thackeray also seems to have been susceptible to the emotional power of Victorian hymns. He was apparently moved to tears by the singing of 'There is a happy land' by a group of ragged children as he was passing through a London slum.

It is in the work of novelists that we are given some of the most telling glimpses of the centrality of hymns in Victorian culture and also some of the most perceptive analyses of their strengths and weaknesses. We have already noted the importance of hymns in the stories of early Victorian writers like George Eliot, Anne and Charlotte Bronte and Elizabeth Gaskell. The language, music, message and social nuances of hymnody remained an important theme for mid- and late-Victorian novelists – there is indeed scope for a whole study devoted to this single subject. Some novelists inserted hymn titles and references primarily to add flavour and colour to their scenes and characters and establish their authenticity, as in Sally Pratt McLean's *Cape Cod Folks* where two fishermen are portrayed singing J. M. Neale's 'Art thou weary, art thou languid?' as they sit mending their nets. For others, like Thomas Hardy, hymns played a much more significant role, acting almost as a *leitmotif* weaved in and out of the narrative to symbolize and sustain a particular mood or theme.

In general it seems to me that mid-Victorian novelists were more inclined to be ambivalent or hostile to the influence of hymns on their contemporaries, while those writing in the late Victorian period, and even more those who grew up at the end of the nineteenth century and wrote in the early twentieth, were much more sympathetic. Certainly there is no doubting the antagonism of the doyen of mid-Victorian novelists, Charles Dickens. His revulsion at the many hymns expressing the narrowness and smugness of Puritanism is well expressed by the words that he put into the mouth of the hero of his short story *George Silvester's Explanation*, first published in 1868, describing the horrors of worship in a small exclusive brethren chapel:

> The service closed with a hymn, in which the brothers unanimously roared, and the sisters unanimously shrieked at me, that I by wiles of worldly gain was mocked, and they on waters of sweet love were rocked; that I with mammon struggled in the dark, while they were floating in a second ark. I went out from all this with an aching heart and a weary spirit.[54]

An earlier novel with a strong social message, Charles Kingsley's *Alton Locke* (1850) was also less than flattering about the quality of congregational hymn-singing, at least in its Nonconformist incarnation. The eponymous hero, a Cockney tailor and poet, brought up as a Baptist by his widowed mother, had been attracted to King David as a boy because of 'the hymn writing side of his character', and himself wrote a hymn with universalist implications about Jesus' love for all. His outlook changed radically, however, when he walked into the drawing-room of an Anglican Deanery and finds the daughter of the house singing Italian airs:

> I had no idea that music was capable of expressing and conveying emotions so intense and ennobling. My experience was confined to street music and to the bawling of chapel. And, as yet, Mr Hullah had not risen into a power more enviable than that of kings, and given to every workman a free entrance into the magic world of harmony and melody.[55]

Another more famous mid-Victorian work of fiction subjected two well-known hymns to the ridicule of parody. I suspect that authors before Lewis Carroll may well have used this device but his *Alice in*

Wonderland (1865) contains the earliest parodies of hymns which I have come across. 'How doth the little crocodile / Improve his shining tail' and 'Twas the voice of the lobster' are clear take-offs of Isaac Watts's 'How doth the little busy bee / Improve the shining hour' and ''Tis the voice of the sluggard', and testaments, in their own way, to the enduring place of improving hymns in the Victorian nursery.

Carroll's choice of hymns to parody, in the knowledge that they would be recognizable to the great majority of his young readers, is further testimony to the popularity of eighteenth-century hymnody in the Victorian period. Other novels from even later in the nineteenth century point to the continuing strong hold of the verses of Watts, Wesley and Toplady on the popular imagination. W. E. Tirebuck's *Miss Grace of All Souls*, written in 1895 and set in a northern mining village during a lock-out, portrays the Ockleshaw family singing 'Rock of Ages', provoking Ned, their radical son, to suggest that they should change the title to 'Rock o'Ages, cleft for masters' because 'that's what aw seem to hide in it for'.[56] Eighteenth-century verses also featured prominently, alongside more contemporary hymns, in two seminal autobiographical novels by authors who both experienced strongly evangelical upbringings and largely lost their faith in adulthood, Samuel Butler's *The Way of All Flesh*, and Edmund Gosse's *Father and Son*.

The Way of All Flesh was largely written in the 1870s although it was not published until 1903, the year after the author's death. As might be expected from one who himself grew up in a rectory in the 1840s (his father was rector of Langar in Nottinghamshire), Samuel Butler was well versed in the tensions involved in introducing hymn-singing into a typical English country parish. Mrs Pontifex's determination to give an organ to Battersby Church provides the novel with one of its main story-lines and we have already had cause to quote its portrayal of the impact of *Hymns Ancient and Modern* (p. 47). Through the largely autobiographical character of Ernest Pontifex, son of the rector of Battersby, Butler powerfully evoked the enormous influence of hymns and hymn-singing in his own childhood. As for so many other Victorian children, hymns were associated especially with death. When he was ill, young Ernest was told by his mother that he need not be afraid of dying since 'Grandpapa is now in heaven singing beautiful hymns with grandmama Allaby to Jesus.' When he himself got to heaven, which he assuredly would 'if he would only be sorry for having done his lessons so badly and vexed his dear papa, and if he would promise never, never to vex him any more,' his grandparents would be there to meet him 'and would be very good to him and teach him to sing ever such beautiful hymns, more beautiful by far than those which he was now so fond of'.[57] Butler was doubtless also drawing on his own childhood experiences when he described Sunday evening at Battersby rectory where the children were allowed as a special treat to sing hymns to visitors.

> In the course of the evening they came into the drawing room, and, as an especial treat, were to sing some of their hymns to me, instead of saying them, so that I might hear how nicely they sang. Ernest was to choose the first hymn, and he chose one about some people who were to come to the sunset tree. I am no botanist, and do not know what kind of tree a sunset tree is, but the words began, 'Come, come, come come to the sunset tree for the day is past and gone.' The tune was rather pretty and had taken Ernest' fancy, for he was unusually fond of music and had a sweet little child's voice which he liked using.[58]

That particular sing-song ended, like so many events in the Pontifex household, in a display of paternal cruelty with Ernest's father sending the boy up to his room and beating him because he could not pronounce the letter 'c' and so sang 'tum' instead of 'come'. Yet through the atmosphere of relentless and crushing oppression that characterizes Samuel Butler's depiction of a Victorian childhood in *The Way Of All Flesh*, hymn-singing shines out as one of the few pleasurable activities. As a boy Ernest was kept going through long church services by the organ voluntaries and the hymns, and it was not surprising that later as a young curate he should introduce the children under his care to the joys of hymn-singing (see p. 49).

Edmund Gosse's *Father and Son* also demonstrates the centrality of hymns for those brought up in evangelical Victorian homes and the ambiguity of the reaction that they provoked. At times, it recalls the revulsion of Dickens, as in the recollection of the author's experience of worship among the Plymouth Brethren in the 1850s: 'At the Chapel, we sang, drearily and slowly, loud hymns of experience and humiliation.'[59] Gosse's mother nurtured the hope that he would be another Charles Wesley but his rebellious streak came out in a display of youthful impiety, clearly prompted by singing Heber's 'From Greenland's icy mountains'. Fascinated by the notion of heathens bowing down to wood and stone, he hoisted a small chair on to the dining-room table, knelt down on the carpet in front of it and 'said my daily prayer in a loud voice, only substituting the address "O Chair!" for the habitual one'.[60] The failure of this flagrant piece of idolatory to provoke any divine reaction began the process of questioning that was eventually to lead Gosse to abandon belief in the Christian faith. The highly didactic and selective nature of his father's choice of hymns also had the effect of sowing seeds of rebellion in his young mind.

> My Father and I used to sing lustily together. The Wesleys, Charlotte Elliott ('Just as I am, without one plea'), and James Montgomery ('For ever with the Lord') represented his predilection in hymnology. I acquiesced, although that would not have been my independent choice. These represented the devotional verse which made its direct appeal to the evangelical mind, and served in those 'Puseyite' days to counteract the High Church poetry founded on *The Christian Year*. Of that famous volume I never met with a copy until I was grown up, and equally unknown in our circle were the hymns of Newman, Faber and Neale.
>
> It was my Father's plan from the first to keep me entirely ignorant of the poetry of the High Church, which deeply offended his Calvinism; he thought that religious truth could be sucked in, like mother's milk, from hymns which were godly and sound, and yet correctly versified; and I was therefore carefully trained in this direction from an early date. But my spirit had rebelled against some of these hymns, especially against those written – a mighty multitude – by Horatius Bonar; naughtily refusing to read Bonar's 'I heard the voice of Jesus say' to my Mother in our Pimlico lodgings. A secret hostility to this particular form of effusion was already, at the age of seven, beginning to define itself in my brain, side by side with an unctuous infantile conformity.[61]

Yet for all his dislike of contemporary hymns, Gosse had a curious affection for certain highly evangelical eighteenth-century verses. When his dying mother asked him to recite one of his favourite hymns, he chose Toplady's 'What though my frail eyelids refuse'. The passage in which he describes singing it to her in his high treble voice, and hearing her repeat the verses, 'her eyes brimming with tears and her alabastrine fingers locked tightly together', is one of the most moving in the book.

> To this day, I cannot repeat this hymn without a sense of poignant emotion, nor can I pretend to decide how much of this is due to its merit and how much to the peculiar nature of the memories it recalls.

But it might be as rude as I genuinely think it to be skilful, and I should continue to regard it as a sacred poem.[62]

Three great English novelists who grew up in the Victorian era wrote with particular force about the power and impact of hymns. Thomas Hardy, Rudyard Kipling and D. H. Lawrence shared a strong Christian upbringing and a position of agnosticism in later life. Although all three in adulthood discarded much of their childhood faith, they retained for the hymns with which they had been brought up a deep attachment that went beyond a mere wistful yearning for the simple certainties of childhood.

Thomas Hardy's abiding attachment to church music undoubtedly owed much to his birth into a family that for generations had been the mainstay of the west gallery bands in Stinsford and Puddletown churches in Dorset. His special affection for metrical psalmody and the gallery tradition has already been noted. It provided a major part of the plot in his novels *The Mayor of Casterbridge* and *Under the Greenwood Tree* and is clearly evident in such poems as 'Afternoon Service at Mellstock *c.* 1850' and 'Apostrophe to an Old Psalm Tune'. Another less well-known poem, 'The Chapel-Organist', tells the story of a female organist in a Nonconformist Chapel who is dismissed when she is seen to be pregnant and ends up killing herself. In lines that allow Hardy to pour out a litany of his favourite psalm tunes she makes clear that, for her, music means more than any man:

> Yet God knows, if aught He knows ever, I loved the Old-Hundredth, Saint Stephen's,
> Mount Zion, New Sabbath, Miles-Lane, Holy Rest, and Arabia, and Eaton,
> Above all embraces of body by wooers who sought me and won![63]

As we have seen, Hardy never lost his love of metrical psalmody and never quite forgave the hymn-singing revolution in general, and *Hymns Ancient and Modern* in particular, for having ousted it from English parish churches. Yet hymns, and even the dreaded book that had so emasculated his beloved psalms and their tunes, came to exercise their own magic spell on him. His own well-thumbed copy of *A & M*, now preserved in the Dorset County Museum, shows just how fond he was of much of its contents. Hardy put asterisks against many hymns indicating that they were personal favourites. Among those thus marked are 'Sun of my soul, Thou Saviour dear', 'O perfect life of love', 'The King of Love my Shepherd is', 'Lord of our life and God of our salvation', 'The Church's one foundation', 'Ten thousand times ten thousand', 'Just as I am', 'For ever with the Lord', 'I heard the voice of Jesus say' and 'Lord, when thy kingdom comes, remember me'. At the back of the book he pencilled a list of his wife's favourite hymns and against certain hymns he wrote the name of a friend or relative, presumably indicating that it had a special significance for them. A. E. Housman's name is pencilled against 'Praise the Lord! Ye heavens adore him', Swinburne's beside the compilers' translation of the *Dies Irae* and his wife's next to 'Angel voices ever singing'. He also noted significant occasions at which particular hymns were used. The provenance of hymn tunes was a matter of considerable interest to him. He frequently pencilled in the name of the composer against a tune, sometimes adding a brief biography or note on the circumstances of composition. On one occasion he wrote to his second wife's mother, 'I have a tune in my head which I cannot get rid of – it is called "Houghton" by Dr Gauntlett. I wonder if you ever play it?'[64]

It is not surprising that there are both references to and quotations from individual hymns in several of Hardy's novels. In *Tess of the D'Urbervilles* William Dewy saves himself from being gored to death by a bull by playing the Nativity Hymn ('While shepherds watched') on his fiddle. The effect is immediate: 'lo and behold, down went the bull on his bended knees, in his ignorance, just as if 'twere the true 'Tivity night and hour'.[65] In a poem entitled 'The Dead Quire' the singing of the same hymn brings back to life the long-dead members of the Mellstock choir who are heard joining in and voicing 'the old holy air'. In *Two on a Tower* the choir of the village church struggle to get to grips with 'Onward, Christian soldiers' which the parson has begun to sing 'in notes of rigid cheerfulness'. It is interesting to note that for the Wessex edition of this novel, published in 1912 thirty years after the original version, Hardy changed this reference, substituting for Sabine Baring-Gould's rousing hymn Tate and Brady's version of the 53rd psalm to the tune DEVIZES. It is unclear whether the change was made as a late protest against the ousting of metrical psalms by hymns or because the author realized that the opening line of this particular Tate and Brady version, 'The Lord look'd down from Heav'n's high tower' was particularly apt to the theme of the book.[66]

Hardy's poetry and prose provide some of the most poignant literary expressions of the Victorian crisis of faith and they are full of wistful longing for the long-lost certainties of childhood. Especially touching scenes in the two novels which perhaps deal most directly and painfully with the loss of religious faith involve the hero and heroine respectively hearing a hymn as outsiders and being deeply moved by its message and associations. The first is the opening sequence of *A Laodicean*, which has already been quoted (p. 46–47). George Somerset's initial reaction to the red brick Baptist Chapel that he comes across while walking back through the fields from sketching ancient churches is wholly negative: 'the chapel had neither beauty, quaintness, nor congeniality to recommend it'. As he gets closer, however, he is overcome by the singing coming from inside: 'in the heaving of that tune (NEW SABBATH) there was an earnestness which made him thoughtful'. The sound of the hymn brings back all kinds of memories from his youth and inspires him with an intense sense of beauty and goodness.[67]

Even more telling, perhaps, is the passage in *Far From the Madding Crowd* which portrays Bathsheba, slowly recovering from the fever and depression that had overtaken her, walking in the village one August evening and hearing singing coming from the church. The choir are learning a new hymn, which happens to be Hardy's favourite, 'Lead, kindly light'.

> Bathsheba was stirred by emotions which latterly she had assumed to be altogether dead within her. The little attenuated voices of the children brought to her ear in distinct utterance the words they sang without thought or comprehension -
>
> > Lead, kindly Light, amid the encircling gloom,
> > Lead Thou me on.
>
> Bathsheba's feeling was always to some extent dependent upon her whim, as in the case with many other women. Something big came into her throat and an uprising to her eyes – and she thought that she would allow the imminent tears to flow if they wished. They did flow and plenteously, and one fell upon the stone bench beside her. Once that she had begun to cry for she hardly knew what, she could not leave off for crowding thoughts she knew too well. She would have given anything in the world to be, as those children were, unconcerned at the meaning of their words, because too innocent to feel the necessity of such expression.[68]

That passage sums up the mixture of emotions that hymns – and that hymn in particular – stirred up in the soul of this Victorian agnostic: the triggering of memories, the reminder of the lost innocence of childhood, the haunting ambiguity and lingering sadness of those closing lines that spoke so powerfully to so many of his doubt-filled contemporaries:

> And with the morn those angel faces smile,
> Which I have loved long since, and lost awhile.

It is fitting that one of Hardy's own poems should have found a place in a hymn-book just before his death. In 1925 he gave Percy Dearmer permission to include his hymn from *The Dynasts*, 'To Thee, Whose eye all nature owns' in *Songs of Praise*. Set to a fifteenth-century melody supposedly sung by English troops at the Battle of Agincourt, it enabled literary and liberal congregations, untroubled by obscure language and unorthodox theology, to

> quire to highest height
> The Wellwiller, the kindly Might
> That balances the Vast for weal,
> That purges as by wounds to heal.[69]

Rudyard Kipling's verses appealed to a rather wider range of hymnal editors. Several early twentieth-century hymn-books contained in their 'national' section his 'God of our fathers, known of old' and his children's hymn 'Father in heaven, who lovest all' (sometimes prefaced with the verse beginning 'Land of our birth, we pledge to thee') which first appeared in his 1906 novel 'Puck of Pook's Hill'. Susan Tamke sees this latter hymn (which is, strictly speaking, Edwardian) as summing up the Victorian ideal of the Christian child – 'patriotic, hardworking, steadfast, honest, controlled and clean, God-fearing, strong but helpful to the weak, and possessing the simple virtues of delight, mirth, forgiveness and love'.[70]

Like Hardy, Kipling had been brought up in a hymn-singing household and retained a strong love for this particular literary and musical form in adulthood even though he largely abandoned orthodox Christian belief. Both his grandfathers were Methodist ministers and because his parents lived in India, he spent his formative childhood years, from the age of 6 to 11, in Southsea with strictly Calvinistic relatives for whom hymns and Bible readings were the only kind of literary activity to be looked on with favour. One of his biographers has commented that when he took up poetry in later life, he tended to write in one of two styles. His lighter verse was based on music-hall and barrack-room ballads while 'his more serious effects were made in a sonorous and didactic style that derived directly from *Hymns Ancient and Modern*. [1] The most hymn-like of all Kipling's poems, the extra-ordinary 'Hymn Before Action' which he sent to *The Times* at a time of considerable international tension in February 1896, was actually based on Samuel Stone's 'The Church's one foundation'. His original title for the poem, which *The Times* declined to print, was 'A Little Sermon' and it struck the same note of national penitence as the better-known 'Recessional' which he penned the following year. After a sombre open-ing announcing that 'The earth is full of anger, / The seas are dark with wrath', the hymn appealed to 'Jehovah of the Thunders', 'Lord God of Battles' and, more surprisingly, 'Mary pierced with sorrow' to deliver the world, and Britain in particular, from 'panic, pride and terror'. Kipling wrote to a friend: 'Some day I want that Hymn added to *Hymns Ancient and Modern* for official use. Who had I better tackle – a bishop or a priest? They must have an editor of sorts.' [2] None of his verses reached *A & M*, however. Somewhat surprisingly, Nonconformist editors, for all their greater unease about imperialism and establishment values, were much more inclined to include his work than Anglicans, although even they jibbed at the decidedly unorthodox theology of the 'Hymn Before Action'.

References to well-loved hymns feature prominently in several of Kipling's writings. The couplet from Heber's 'From Greenland's icy mountains' about the heathen in his blindness bowing down to wood and stone, which had so intrigued the young Edmund Gosse, provided the inspiration and the first line for Kipling's 1896 poem 'The 'Eathen'. In a short story published in 1891, 'At the End of the Passage', he described how four young Englishmen involved in building a railway across India lifted their spirits while sweltering in the almost unbearable heat of their remote imperial outpost in the midst of a cholera epidemic, and with a dust storm raging around them, by singing Bishop Ken's evening hymn, 'Glory to thee, my God, this night'. It conjured up for each of them 'the most sacred recollections . . . summer evenings in the country . . . stained-glass window . . . bats, roses, milk and midges. Also mothers. I can just recollect my mother singing me to sleep with that when I was a little chap.'[73]

For D. H. Lawrence, too, hymns evoked the long-lost innocence, wonder and simple faith of childhood and triggered fond early memories of home and maternal love:

Softly, in the dusk, a woman is singing to me;
Taking me back down the vista of years, till I see

A child sitting under the piano, in the boom of the tingling strings
And pressing the small, poised feet of a mother who smiles as she sings.

In spite of myself, the insidious mastery of song
Betrays me back, till the heart of me weeps to belong
To the old Sunday evenings at home, with winter outside
And hymns in the cosy parlour, the tinkling piano our guide.[74]

In 1928, just two years before his death, Lawrence wrote a fascinating newspaper article on the subject of 'Hymns in a Man's Life'.
Although it belongs clearly to the twentieth century, I want to quote
from it in this chapter rather than the next because it is about the
experience of someone who grew up as a Victorian. Lawrence was born
in 1885 and brought up as a Congregationalist, two circumstances for
which he expressed himself eternally grateful because of the exposure
that he was thereby given to hymns as a child. His article is both a
searching exploration and a wonderful celebration of the power that
hymns exercised on the imagination of children brought up in the last
quarter of the nineteenth century:

> Nothing is more difficult than to determine what a child takes in, and
> does not take in, of its environment and its teaching. This fact is
> brought home to me by the hymns which I learned as a child, and
> never forgot. They mean to me almost more than the finest poetry,
> and they have for me a more permanent value, somehow or other.[75]

Amplifying this last remark, Lawrence confessed that the poems of
Shakespeare, Keats and Wordsworth were not woven as deep into his
consciousness as 'the rather banal Nonconformist hymns that penetrated through and through my childhood'.[76] For him the real power of
hymns lay in their capacity to evoke wonder, the element which is the
basis of a child's perceptions: 'Hymns live and glisten in the depths of
man's consciousness in undimmed wonder, because they have not been
subjected to any criticism or analysis'.[77] He recalled the quintessentially
Victorian hymns which had particularly stirred his childish imagination.
Keble's 'Sun of my soul, thou Saviour dear' was sung as the last hymn at
the board school he attended. 'It did not mean any Christian dogma or
any salvation. Just the words penetrated me with wonder and the
mystery of twilight.'[78] He was similarly captivated by John Gurney's
'Fair waved the golden corn / In Canaan's pleasant land' and by a gospel
song 'O Galilee, sweet Galilee'.

To me the word Galilee has a wonderful sound. The Lake of Galilee! I don't know where it is. I never want to go to Palestine. Galilee is one of those lovely, glamorous worlds, not places, that exist in the golden haze of a child's half-formed imagination. And in my man's imagination it is just the same. It has been left untouched. With regard to the hymns which had such a profound influence on my childish consciousness, there has been no crystallising out, no dwindling into actuality, no hardening into the commonplace. They are the same to my man's experience as they were to me nearly forty years ago.[79]

Another favourite was Monsell's 'O worship the Lord in the beauty of holiness':

I don't know what the 'beauty of holiness' is, exactly. It easily becomes cant, or nonsense. But if you don't think about it – and why should you? – it has a magic. The same with the whole verse. It is rather bad, really, 'gold of obedience' and 'incense of lowliness'. But in me, to the music, it still produces a sense of splendour.

I am always glad we had the Bristol hymn-book, not Moody and Sankey. And I am glad our Scotch minister on the whole avoided sentimental messes such as 'Lead, kindly light', or even 'Abide with me'. He had a healthy preference for healthy hymns.

> At even, ere the sun was set,
>   The sick, O Lord, around Thee lay.
> Oh, in what divers pains they met!
>   Oh, in what joy they went away!

And often we had 'Fight the good fight with all thy might'.

In Sunday School I am eternally grateful to old Mr Remington, with his round white beard and his ferocity. He made us sing! And he loved the martial hymns:

> Sound the battle-cry,
> See, the foe is nigh.
> Raise the standard high
> For the Lord.

Thirty six years ago men, even Sunday School teachers, still believed in the fight for life and the fun of it. 'Hold the fort, for I am coming.' It was far, far from any militarism or gunfighting. But it was the battle-cry of a stout soul, and a fine thing too.

> Stand up, stand up for Jesus,
> Ye soldiers of the Lord.

Here is the clue to the ordinary Englishman – in the Non-conformist hymns.[80]

It is ironic that those words were penned by the author of *Lady Chatterley's Lover* and *Sons and Lovers*, the man who from his grave was to shock Nonconformist middle-class England and sound the death knell for the provincial puritanism it represented. For all that he was the herald of sexual liberation and kitchen-sink fiction, D. H. Lawrence also supremely articulated and epitomized another very different and no less pervasive strain in twentieth-century British culture in his deeply sentimental attachment to hymns as vehicles of nostalgia and triggers for memories.

9

'Abide with me'

Victorian hymns in the twentieth century

Shortly before his death in 1892 Alfred Tennyson engaged in a little futurology. 'What will people come to in a hundred years?' he asked the head of an Oxford college. 'Do you think they will give up all religious forms and go and sit in silence in churches listening to the organs?'[1] In fact, if anything, we have become noisier rather than quieter in our worship as the twentieth century has progressed. Although there is now in some quarters at least a belated recognition of the value of silence in worship, the sound of hearty singing is still perhaps the most characteristic feature of church services across virtually all denominations. Contemporary charismatic and evangelical movements may have brought back west gallery-style music in the form of praise bands and introduced new worship songs and choruses, but Victorian hymns, sung to traditional organ accompaniments, have proved remarkably durable and at the tail end of the twentieth century still provide the popular image of music in church, at least for non church-goers if perhaps less for regular attenders at worship.

Victorian hymns, like other products of their age, have enjoyed a fluctuating reputation during the present century. Initially derided and scorned for their sentimentality and poor taste, they have come to be cherished as precious period pieces and suffused with a warm nostalgic glow. Consistently popular with the public at large, they continue to top polls of favourite hymns taken by television and radio programmes while constituting a source of acute embarrassment to theologians and modernizing clergy, and quietly (or not so quietly) being dropped from hymn-books or emasculated in the cause of inclusive language and political correctness. In some quarters at least they seem to have become an endangered species and I have myself suggested, not altogether in jest, that the time may have come to slap preservation orders on at least a core of the best to prevent them disappearing from common usage in the coming century.

The twentieth century began with a strong reaction against most things Victorian, and hymns were no exception. The attitude displayed by Robert Bridges and exemplified in *The Yattendon Hymnal* even had an effect on the compilers of the 1904 edition of *A & M* who jettisoned a good many of the best-loved hymns from earlier editions. Some were dropped on theological grounds – Faber's 'O Paradise, O Paradise' and T. J. Potter's 'Brightly gleams our banner' were thought to suggest too easy a passage to heaven for certain souls in contradiction of the doctrine of general resurrection – but others, such as Pott's 'Angel voices ever singing', A. T. Gurney's 'Christ is risen' and Mrs Alexander's 'His are the thousand sparkling rills', were cut for no apparent reason. The *A & M* archives contain numerous letters from disgruntled clergy who sent back their copies in protest at these and other omissions. There was also a wholesale purge of Victorian hymn tunes – 170 were dropped, including Barnby's FOR ALL THE SAINTS and Sullivan's ST GERTRUDE, while many of those left in had their harmonies stripped away, a process likened by Kenneth Finlay to 'removing a flimsy and highly coloured frock from a tailor's dummy'.[2] The new edition was a commercial disaster and indicated that the compilers had lost their rapport with both clerical and popular Anglican taste. *Hymns Ancient and Modern* was never again to have the influence or dominant position that it had enjoyed in the first forty years of its life.

The book that was to become its main challenger as the leading Anglican hymnal for most of the twentieth century first appeared in 1906 as an almost consciously anti-Victorian statement. *The English Hymnal* put into general practice many of the principles which had underlain *The Yattendon Hymnal*. Its editors had a distinct preference for early office hymns and mediaeval verses, accompanied wherever possible by tunes of the time. They also turned several notable seventeenth-century poems into hymns, notably those of George Herbert. Neither the literary editor, Percy Dearmer, nor his musical colleague, Ralph Vaughan Williams, made any secret of their dislike for much Victorian hymnody. Vaughan Williams preferred traditional folk melodies to nineteenth-century part-songs, replacing Dykes's VOX DILECTI for 'I heard the voice of Jesus say' with KINGSFOLD and Stainer's IN MEMORIAM for 'There's a friend for little children' with INGRAVE (although this latter substitution was made for copyright reasons). He also shared Bridges' enthusiasm for sixteenth-century

French and German melodies. 'The day thou gavest' was set to a tune by Louis Bourgeois from the 1543 Genevan Psalter and ST CLEMENT relegated to an appendix, once famously described by Vaughan Williams as his 'chamber of horrors', into which he dumped several of the most popular tunes of Monk, Sullivan, Barnby and Dykes.

The compilers of *The English Hymnal* could not, of course, eliminate Victorian hymns altogether, nor did they want to do so. Several of *A & M*'s great couplings, like 'Holy, Holy, Holy' with NICAEA and 'Eternal Father' with MELITA, were included. So, rather more surprisingly, were five songs culled from Sankey's *Sacred Songs and Solos*: 'Ho! my comrades', 'I hear Thy welcome voice', 'Safe in the arms of Jesus', 'Tell me the old, old story' and 'There were ninety and nine'. It was a tribute to the widespread penetration of gospel songs into Church of England worship that such material could find a home in a refined high Anglican hymnal, albeit segregated in in a section entitled 'Mission Services'.

By no means all editors of early twentieth-century hymn-books shared the animus against Victorian hymns felt by Vaughan Williams and Dearmer. Most English Nonconformist and Scottish Presbyterian hymnals continued to make them their staple diet. Indeed, collections like the 1927 revised edition of *The Church Hymnary* (Presbyterian), the 1933 *Baptist Church Hymnal (Revised)* and the 1933 *Methodist Hymn Book*, were heavily weighted in favour of Victorian material.

Certain other institutions also continued to favour Victorian hymns through much of the twentieth century. Perhaps the most significant were the public schools. The first edition of *The Public School Hymn Book*, which appeared in 1903, was dominated by late-nineteenth century tunes and verses. Later editions in 1919 and 1949 successively reduced the amount of Victorian material and *Hymns For Church and School*, published in 1964 and still in use in many independent schools, belatedly introduced the popular seventeenth-century devotional poems first taken up by *The English Hymnal* and *Songs of Praise* and a smattering of more recent hymns. Even during the radical days of the late 1960s and early 1970s, however, when South Bank or 'death of God' theology was being preached from their pulpits, school chapels continued to resound to the stirring strains of high Victorian hymnody in its most triumphant incarnation. Lindsay Anderson got it absolutely right in his cult film *If* (1968) when he had the school hymn, 'Stand up, stand up for college' set to the vigorous tune ELLACOMBE, generally associated with J. M. Neale's 'The Day of Resurrection'. Several

Victorian and Edwardian lyrics continue to do service as school hymns. 'Through the night of doubt and sorrow' seems particularly popular for this role. The girls of Francis Holland School in London still sing Kipling's 'Father in heaven, who lovest all', a choice which caused some amusement to journalists covering a recent visit by an old girl, the actress Joan Collins, to open a new swimming pool. One noted that the actress joined in the hymn lustily. ' "Teach us delight in simple things" she sang, as her chauffeur waited outside in her stretch-limo to whisk her off to a book-signing session in Harrods.'[3] Individual school hymn-books still in regular use often remain the last resting-place for former Victorian favourites which have now largely disappeared from mainstream denominational collections. The latest edition of the excellent *Hymns and Prayers for Dragons*, for example, produced as recently as 1989 for use at the Dragon School, Oxford, contains Jane Borthwick's 'Come, labour on!' and Sabine Baring-Gould's 'Now the day is over, night is drawing nigh'.

Public schools have also played a significant role in keeping certain Victorian hymns alive through the twentieth century by providing them with particularly vigorous and singable tunes, almost invariably written for unison singing. Outstanding examples are WOODLANDS, written by Walter Greatorex, director of music at Gresham's School, Holt, from 1911 to 1936, for Henry Butler's 'Lift up your hearts!' and REPTON, which enormously enhanced the popularity of Whittier's 'Dear Lord and Father of mankind' when it was plucked in the early 1920s by Dr George Gilbert Stocks, music master of Repton School, from Sir Hubert Parry's oratorio, *Judith*. Vaughan Williams' thrilling SINE NOMINE which largely supplanted Barnby's tune for How's 'For all the saints' and in so doing probably extended the lifetime of that hymn for at least fifty years, can also surely be put into this category. As Jonathan Gathorne-Hardy has commented: 'One can quite often detect hymn themes or treatments in English composers of a certain generation as thousands of public school Sundays and assemblies stir in their subconscious – in Vaughan Williams (Charterhouse) particularly, but also in Britten and Lennox Berkeley (Gresham's).'[4]

It is not just composers who have carried throughout their lives memories of hymns sung in their school chapels. George Orwell's 'extraordinary knowledge of hymns, which he remembered more exactly than any other agnostic I have ever met' was attributed to his school-days at Eton by his biographer and friend, George Woodcock.[5] Another old Etonian, the cricket commentator and broadcaster, Brian

Johnston, retained enough knowledge of the contents of the standard edition of *Hymns Ancient and Modern* to announce in one cricket commentary that 'the score is now 332. That's "There is a green hill far away".' Seven years as a scholarship boy at Bancroft's School in Essex gave the actor Denis Quilley a similar facility: 'I'm an expert on hymns – if you give me a number I'll tell you the hymn. My family and I used to play a funny game with car registration plates – "Oh, there's Onward Christian Soldiers just gone by!".'[6]

Public school chapels have also been important agencies in promoting that interesting and important corpus of post-Victorian hymns which includes such powerful expressions of the social gospel as Henry Scott Holland's 'Judge eternal, throned in splendour', Chesterton's 'O God of earth and altar' and Clifford Bax's 'Turn back, O man, forswear thy foolish ways'. Overall, the Edwardian era, and particularly the years during and immediately after the First World War, saw a reaction against the perceived quietism and passivity of some popular Victorian hymns and a renewed stress on social activism and involvement in the world. For the 1916 *Congregational Hymnary*, for example, Howell Lewis, a Welsh Congregationalist, wrote 'Lord of light, whose name outshineth' specifically to counter the heretical tendency he found in a hymn such as Charlotte Elliott's 'My God and Father, while I stray' that what God required above all in those who followed him was a mood of humble resignation. A similar agenda informed Percy Dearmer's *Songs of Praise*, first published in 1925. This collection, which was widely taken up by local education authorities for use in both primary and secondary school assemblies, had a strong literary flavour, introducing verses from a number of Victorian poets, including Hardy and Swinburne, who would hardly qualify as conventional Christians, and incorporating a good deal of American material. In other respects it was almost aggressively anti-Victorian. This was especially true on the musical side. Not a single Sullivan tune was included ('Onward, Christian soldiers' was set to an arrangement by Gustav Holst of an old English march) and only five by Dykes, reducing his representation to less than one tune in a hundred as against the 1875 edition of *A & M* where he had one in eight.

At the popular level, however, the hymn tunes of the culturally despised Dykes and Sullivan and their contemporaries remained firm favourites. This is perhaps most clearly shown by the way in which they provided the melodies for so many of the best-known soldiers' songs from the First World War. 'We've had no beer' and 'Raining, raining,

raining' took over Dykes' LUX BENIGNA and NICAEA, 'We are Fred Karno's Army' gave a new lease of life to S. S. Wesley's AURELIA and 'When this lousy war is over' showed the power of CONVERSE. In a neat tit-for-tat for General Booth's take-over of music hall songs for evangelistic purposes the soldiers in the trenches secularized Sankey and Salvation Army choruses so that 'Wash me in the blood of the Lamb' became 'Wash me in the water that you washed your dirty daughter in' and 'In the blood, in the blood' was transformed into 'The Quartermaster's Stores'. Subsequent parodies and adaptations for strictly secular use have shown the continuing potency and popularity of Victorian hymn tunes throughout the twentieth century. They have cropped up in some strange places, including on a record issued by the satirical magazine *Private Eye* in the early 1960s where a satirical hymn to the media, 'When I am feeling like a laugh / I read *The Daily Telegraph*' was set to MELITA, and in two television commercials (for Quality Street chocolates using 'When the roll is called up yonder' and for Volkswagen cars using CONVERSE) which were both banned after protests.

Another indicator of the continuing strong hold of Victorian hymns on the popular imagination has been their use at public occasions. I suppose the best known example is the singing of 'Abide with me' at the FA Cup Final. This practice began in 1927 at the suggestion of the secretary, Sir Alfred Wall, and with the strong approval of King George V who shared with his wife, Queen Mary, a particular affection for Lyte's hymn. It was significantly a Victorian hymn that the bandmaster of the Titanic struck up as that ill-fated liner began to sink after hitting an iceberg on the night of 14 April 1912 – either, as legend has it, Sarah Adams' 'Nearer, my God to Thee', or, as some recent commentators have suggested, 'He leadeth me!' to the tune AUGHTON.[7] The idea of singing a hymn came spontaneously into people's minds on other less tragic occasions. When Edwin Scrymgeour, the only British MP elected on a Prohibitionist ticket, had unseated Winston Churchill from his Dundee constituency in 1922, he announced that come prohibition, all ales and spirits in the city would be emptied into the River Tay. The assembled crowd promptly reacted by singing 'Shall we gather at the river?'

It was perhaps partly because of this popularity with the vulgar throng that musical and literary purists heaped increasing opprobrium on Victorian hymns. The attack on their tunes was especially fierce as a host of composers and critics followed Vaughan Williams's lead.

According to one recent American scholar, Sullivan's ST GERTRUDE may have been the missing tune on which Edward Elgar based his Enigma Variations. If so, this was a rare compliment from one who shared the general distaste felt by the musical establishment for the whole genre. More common was the kind of sustained critical assault found in George Gardner's *Worship and Music* published in 1918. This book, which had the explicit endorsement of Charles Gore, Bishop of Oxford, deplored the 'vulgar lusciousness' of Dykes' melodies and the 'thin and rowdy sentimentalism' of Barnby's work.[8] In 1925 Percy Dearmer's son Geoffrey wrote a paper on 'The Fall and Rise of the Hymn Tune' which identified *Hymns Ancient and Modern* as representing the low-point and 'plunging religious music into an abyss'.[9] The introduction to the music in the 1927 handbook to the *Revised Church Hymnary*, written by G. Wauchope Stewart, a leading musical authority in the Church of Scotland, expressed the view that Victorian tunes 'are too often of a weak and sentimental character, depending for their appeal not on bold and clearly outlined curves of melody or on strong and forceful rhythms, but on chromatic harmonies which are apt to cloy and become loathsome in their own deliciousness'.[10] In 1932 the Archbishop of Canterbury, Cosmo Gordon Lang, forcefully condemned Scholefield's ST CLEMENT, sparking off a long correspondence in *The Times* in which many sided with him in wishing to see a 'feeble waltz' dismissed from service.

The greatest hymnologist of the twentieth century, Erik Routley, had an ambivalent attitude towards Victorian hymn tunes. In his book *The Musical Wesleys* he wrote rather dismissively: 'Take a hundred assorted hymn tunes from the period 1861-1900, and there will be a good case against ninety-seven of them.'[11] In a series of articles in the Hymn Society Bulletin in 1948 he attempted to rehabilitate the reputation of leading Victorian composers but gave the impression of damning most of them with distinctly faint praise. S. S. Wesley's AURELIA was dismissed for its 'depressing and threadbare quality' and Dykes was portrayed as embodying a 'reposeful, gracious, secure cosiness'. About Sullivan Routley could hardly bring himself to say a single good word.[12]

Sullivan was also singled out for criticism in the context of a more general attack on Victorian hymn tunes in Arthur Hutchings' important and scholarly study, *Church Music in the Nineteenth Century* (1967). Describing Victorian hymnody as 'semi-sophisticated popular music in which we may meet phrases and bits of tune or harmony unconsciously borrowed from famous poets and musicians', Hutchings especially deplored its self-conscious religiosity:

It is not in the deeply religious Dykes that one finds revolting sanctimosity but in the charmingly worldly Sullivan . . . if he had not felt the need to be a different Sullivan on Sundays, he might have contributed something enduring to church music . . . Sullivan's church music is best forgotten; from it we can but illustrate only the nadir of sanctimonious vulgarity.[13]

Although Dykes escaped relatively lightly at the hands of Hutchings, he was severely treated by other critics. Geoffrey Faber, in his seminal book on the Oxford Movement, *Oxford Apostles* (first published in 1933), commented of Newman's 'Lead, kindly light' that 'It needs an effort to dissociate the poem from the dreary drawling tune fitted to it by the Reverend John Bacchus Dykes.'[14] Many subsequent writers have shared this verdict. C. H. Phillips in *The Singing Church* (1979), for example, describing Dykes' output as 'the type *par excellence* of the Victorian hymn-tune', singled out LUX BENIGNA as 'rhythmically unadventurous', over-emotional and making too much use of the dominant seventh – 'a chord of fatal fascination to the Victorian'.[15]

There have been few more wholesale condemnations of Victorian hymnody than that found in Kenneth Long's 1971 study, *The Music of the English Church*. Dykes, Gauntlett, Sullivan, Stainer and Barnby are here bracketed together under the heading 'Victoriana' with the dismissive comment that 'most of their music has long since been discounted by sensitive musicians'.[16] After complaining of 'the comforting warm glow of spurious religiosity induced by trivial and sentimental ear-ticklers', Long enumerates the specific faults of these composers' hymn tunes as 'a static bass, enfeebled chromatic harmony, stilted rhythms, rigid four-bar phrases, meretricious tunes, and a complete disregard for the rhythms, inflections, meaning and mood of the words'.[17] More fundamentally, he finds 'a basic insincerity . . . the deliberate attempt to write down to popular taste . . . the music is not only highly emotional but the emotions are patently stage emotions, the tears are crocodile tears, and the humility and self-abasement are never allowed to obscure the fact that the sun never sets on the British Empire'.[18] Alluding to Gauntlett's estimated 10,000 tunes, he comments tartly that 'not surprisingly, Homer not only nods but sleeps pretty soundly for some 9,990 of them'.[19] Dykes is castigated for 'weaknesses that make musicians blush . . . slipping and sliding over treacherous chromatics' while Barnby's church music is dismissed as 'simply mawkish'.[20] Sullivan, by contrast, receives a much less severe ticking-off, being guilty only of 'the far more healthy fault of sheer vulgarity'.[21]

Given this background of sustained criticism it is not surprising that fewer and fewer Victorian hymn tunes have appeared in successive editions of several major hymn-books. Table 3 shows the number of original tunes by leading Victorian composers that have appeared in a representative sample of hymnals published over the last seventy years.

	RCH 1927	MHB 1933	AMR 1950	CH3 1973	HP 1983	BPW 1991
Dykes	26	26	31	9	21	11
Monk	14	11	15	2	8	8
Sullivan	12	12	3	5	3	1
Stainer	14	12	15	2	8	3
Barnby	11	16	4	0	4	4
Smart	15	13	8	4	8	5

Table 3

Victorian hymn tunes in twentieth-century hymn-books

The books from which these figures have been extracted are the 1927 *Revised Church Hymnary* (Presbyterian), the 1933 *Methodist Hymnbook*, the 1950 *Hymns Ancient and Modern Revised*, the 1973 (third) edition of *The Church Hymnary*, the 1983 *Hymns and Psalms* (Methodist) and the 1991 *Baptist Praise and Worship*. A comparison of the figures for 1927 and 1973 and for 1933 and 1983 thus shows the changing fortunes of the major Victorian composers in the hymn-books of two denominations published respectively in the early and later parts of the twentieth century. The picture is of a clear decline in both cases, although notably steeper in the case of the Presbyterians than the Methodists. This latter discrepancy is probably in large part explained by the fact that the third edition of *The Church Hymnary* was compiled in the 1960s when Victorian hymns were particularly out of favour, with their words as well as their music coming under severe attack, as instanced by Horton Davis' comment, in his 1962 study on *Worship and Theology in England 1850-1900*, that many of them deserved to be seared with the judgment of Richard Neibuhr that 'a God without wrath brought men without sin to a kingdom without judgment through the ministrations of a Christ without a cross'.[22] By the early 1980s when *Hymns and Psalms* was being compiled, the pendulum had swung somewhat back in favour of Victorian hymnody. Certainly the 1973 edition of *The Church Hymnary* marked the nadir of the fortunes of nineteenth-century hymn tune composers. As a reviewer commented, 'There are now no tunes left by Barnby, and only two by Stainer. How are the mighty fallen, especially if they happened to be Victorians!'[23]

Although Table 3 is selective and incomplete, it points to a clear decline in the number of Victorian hymn tunes included in hymn-books published during the first three-quarters of the twentieth century, with a slight rally, or at least a levelling out, over the last two decades. This reflects a general and understandable falling-off in the number of Victorian hymns chosen by successive hymn-book editors and a determination to find room for newer words and tunes. In several cases where Victorian hymns have been retained their original tunes have been replaced by much better later compositions, as with 'For all the saints'. Table 3 also reveals some lingering denominational preferences. Both Monk and Dykes, for example, have their strongest showing in the one Anglican book surveyed, the 1950 revised edition of *Hymns Ancient and Modern*. *A & M Revised* was, in fact, something of a Victorian treasure-trove. It introduced a number of important texts which had not previously figured in *A & M*, including Christina Rossetti's 'In the bleak mid-winter', J. S. B. Monsell's 'O worship the Lord in the beauty of holiness' and Newman's 'Firmly I believe and truly'. The 1950s did, indeed, constitute an Indian summer for Victorian hymnody. Of the hymns in the companion to *The English Hymnal* which was compiled at the beginning of that decade for use in Tonbridge School Chapel, and which was still very much in use throughout my time as a pupil there during the swinging sixties, more than three-quarters came from the nineteenth century, and less than 5% from the twentieth. No doubt my own exposure to such an overwhelmingly Victorian diet at an impressionable age partly accounts for my own taste and fascination for this particular area.

Recent surveys of the hymns that people most enjoy singing, as distinct from those that hymn-book editors think they should be singing, show the extraordinary durability and enduring popularity of Victorian favourites. Table 4 lists the top ten hymns chosen in three substantial recent polls taken on both sides of the Atlantic. The preponderance of nineteenth-century material is striking in all of them – seven out of the top ten in both Peter Harvey's 1994 survey and the American *Anglican Digest* poll of the same year and four out of ten, more than for any other century, in the BBC radio and television survey conducted in 1995.

Almost certainly all of these three poll findings are heavily weighted in favour of the older age group. Yet when younger people choose hymns, those from the Victorian era continue to score remarkably highly. Each year I ask the students taking my hymnody class at Aberdeen University, the majority of whom are in their early twenties, to list their favourite ten hymns. Collating the results of this survey over the last three years produces a top ten which includes three Victorian hymns ('Dear Lord and Father of mankind', 'Abide with me' and 'O love that wilt not let me go'), three from the eighteenth century, two from the early twentieth century and two modern worship songs. The *Puffin Book of Hymns*, a collection published in 1992 and chosen by children for children, contains the words of 90 hymns and carols of which 30 date from the nineteenth century (including translations). The most widely-used book for assemblies in British primary schools over the last 25 years, the BBC's *Come and Praise*, contains ten Victorian hymns in its total of 72 items. Ysenda Maxtone Grahame, in her recent study of the Church of England, *The Church Hesitant*, observes that 'schoolgirls love the hymn which goes "For those in peril on the sea". It has an exciting, seasick tune and makes you think of distressed sailors with pails and wet ropes on deck. They also love the slightly foody hymn, "Jerusalem the golden, with milk and honey blest", and the soppy one towards the end of the hymn-book which goes, "But thy couch was the sod, O thou son of God, in the desert of Galilee" (Emily Elliott's 'Thou didst leave thy throne').'[24]

The continuing popular attachment to Victorian hymns is evident from the fact that they are far more likely than either earlier or more recent material to feature in those services and occasions where the choice of what is to be sung rests with lay people rather than with professional clergy. They remain the most favoured category of hymn for weddings and funerals. Of the 39 hymns listed in the 1994 edition of the Joint Liturgical Group's *Funeral Service Book*, 22 are Victorian. I cannot recall a single funeral that I have conducted, either in church, undertakers' rooms or crematorium, that has not included at least one

Table 4
Some recent top hymn surveys

Poll 1: Harvey 1994

1 Dear Lord and Father of mankind
2 Praise, my soul, the King of heaven
3 The day Thou gavest, Lord, is ended
4 When I survey the wondrous Cross
5 Love Divine, all loves excelling
6 O Jesus, I have promised
7 Abide with me
8 Guide me, O Thou great Jehovah
9 At the name of Jesus
10 Just as I am, without one plea

Poll 1 was conducted by the late Peter Harvey, a retired Anglican priest. Over 13,000 votes were cast by clergy, readers, churchwardens, organists and choir members. A further five Victorian hymns appeared in the top twenty – 'The King of Love my Shepherd is' (11), 'There is a green hill far away' (16), 'Onward, Christian soldiers' (17), 'Let all mortal flesh keep silence' (18) and 'Lead us, heavenly Father, lead us' (19).

Poll 2: *Anglican Digest* 1994

1 Abide with me
2 The Church's one foundation
3 Amazing Grace
4 I sing a song of the saints of God
5 Ye watchers and ye holy ones
6 Holy! Holy! Holy!
7 Eternal Father, strong to save
8 Lift high the Cross
9 Breathe on me, breath of God
10 Onward, Christian soldiers

Poll 2 involved 3,000 readers of the *Anglican Digest*, the most widely read publication of the Episcopal Church in the United States. The results appeared in the Transfiguration 1994 issue of the *Anglican Digest*, Vol. 36, No. 4, p.6.

Poll 3: BBC 1995

1 Dear Lord and Father of mankind
2 The day Thou gavest, Lord, is ended
3 How great thou art
4 Abide with me
5 Guide me, O Thou great Jehovah
6 Great is thy faithfulness
7 Praise, my soul, the King of heaven
8 Love Divine, all loves excelling
9 When I survey the wondrous Cross
10 Shine, Jesus, shine

Poll 3 brought together the choices of over 8,500 people who responded to the BBC's request to name their three favourite hymns. The results were broadcast on 28 May 1995.

Victorian hymn or hymn tune and in the great majority everything sung has come from the nineteenth century – a reflection, I hasten to say, of the express wishes of the mourners and not of any influence on my part. The same is true of virtually all the funerals reported in detail in the press because of either the eminence or the particularly tragic circumstances of the death of the deceased. To give just three recent examples: the funeral service for the former Labour Party leader, John Smith, held in Edinburgh on 20 May 1994 included Caroline Noel's 'At the name of Jesus' and Norman Macleod's 'Courage, brother! do not stumble'. Those who gathered at Wincle parish church in Cheshire on 31 January 1996 to mourn the death of Johanne Masheder, murdered by a drug-crazed Buddhist monk during the last leg of a backpacking trip in Thailand, sang 'Dear Lord and Father of mankind' and 'The King of Love my Shepherd is'. The funeral service held in Ealing Abbey on 16 February 1996 for Philip Lawrence, the London headmaster stabbed to death in front of his own school, included 'For all the saints who from their labours rest'.

Victorian hymns still also remain apparently indispensable adjuncts to solemn public and state occasions on both sides of the Atlantic. An analysis by Samuel Rogal of the hymns sung in funeral services for American dignitaries during the greater part of the present century reveals the clear favourites to be 'Abide with me' (sung at the funerals of Herbert Hoover and Adlai Stevenson), 'Eternal Father, strong to save' (John F. Kennedy and his brother Robert), 'Lead, kindly light' (Douglas MacArthur and Dwight D. Eisenhower) and 'Faith of our fathers' (MacArthur, Stevenson and Eisenhower).[25] In Britain the national service to commemorate the fiftieth anniversary of the D Day landings included 'Abide with me' and 'Praise, my soul, the King of heaven', and at the British Legion Festival of Remembrance in the Albert Hall on 11 November 1995, marking the fiftieth anniversary of the end of the Second World War, all four hymns sung were Victorian – 'The day thou gavest', 'Dear Lord and Father', 'Eternal Father, strong to save' and 'Saviour, again to thy dear name we raise'. The 1996 Festival also included four Victorian hymns – 'The day thou gavest', 'Stand up, stand up, for Jesus', 'Now thank we all our God' and 'Abide with me'. The church too, for its big public ceremonies, still relies heavily on the nine-teenth-century repertoire. Those attending the enthronement of Dr David Hope as Archbishop of York on 8 December 1995, for example, sang their way through Walter Chalmers Smith's 'Immortal, invisible, God only wise', J. M. Neale's 'To the name that brings salvation',

Matthew Bridges' 'Crown him with many crowns' and John Henry Newman's 'Firmly I belive and truly'.

It is a measure of the abiding hold of Victorian hymns on the British psyche that references to them continue to be woven into contemporary English literature. Headline writers regularly quote from their first lines in the knowledge that they will strike a chord with their readers – a recent feature on *The Times* arts page about cultural initiatives in the north of England was headed 'Hills of the north rejoice'.[26] Dictionaries of quotations continue to include the first lines of relatively obscure Victorian hymns. I was surprised to be asked by the editor of the new Collins Dictionary of Quotations, published in 1996, to supply biographical details on the authors of 'Work, for the night is coming', 'What a friend we have in Jesus' and 'Have you been to Jesus for the cleansing power?' Late twentieth-century novels may not quote from hymns anything like as often as those written one hundred years or so ago, but when they do it is almost invariably from Victorian rather than contemporary ones. I have not come across a single modern novel which mentions a twentieth-century hymn. There are, however, a fair sprinkling of nineteenth-century hymnological references. Sometimes these are in the title, as in Michael Campbell's tale of adolescent homosexuality in public schools, *Lord Dismiss Us*, published in 1968, or James Herriot's immensely popular *All Creatures Great and Small*. In *Wise Virgin* (1982) A. N. Wilson has the young Tibba Fox make up a curse to fit the tune of 'Immortal, invisible, God only wise' and H. E. Bates includes a poignant and extensive quotation of 'O love that wilt not let me go' in his short story *The House with the Apricot*. I have even come across a misquotation of one of our best-loved Victorian hymns at the hands of one of our best-selling contemporary novelists. It occurs in the scene in Joanna Trollope's *The Men and the Girls* (1992) when Beatrice Bachelor sits in the lounge of the Randolph Hotel, Oxford, waiting to take tea with the man who has knocked her off her bike:

> She looked at herself in the hall mirror without affection, and hummed a little tune, 'O Lord and Father of mankind'. How irritating hymns were, burrowing about persistently in one's subconscious when one didn't subscribe to a word of them.[27]

I may say that I wrote to Joanna Trollope, expressing the view that Miss Bachelor, atheist as she might be, was surely well-educated enough to get the opening line of that particular hymn right. I received a most gracious reply from the novelist assuring me that she will be especially careful about any future hymnological references in her works. I felt rather like Lord Reith who once upbraided Winston Churchill for mis-quoting 'Eternal father, strong to save' in his memoirs. I am well used to having errors in my own work pointed out – I am sure that the eagle-eyed will notice some in this book – and I took some not very laudable satisfaction in spotting a mistake in another's for a change.

The capacity of hymns experienced and learned in childhood to stir and stay with those who have moved in adulthood to agnosticism or atheism remains as potent now as it was for Thomas Hardy and D. H. Lawrence earlier this century. Arthur Scargill, the militant former leader of the National Union of Mineworkers, must surely have surprised and touched his many detractors when on *Desert Island Discs* he chose George Matheson's 'O love that wilt not let me go' because of its abiding associations with his mother's love. In another programme in the same series the American novelist and radio personality, Garrison Keillor, chose 'Abide with me' as the one record that he would choose above all others to take to a desert island. The reason he gave was that it had been sung at every family funeral he could remember. It could, of course, be said that we have come close here to moving to a vein of pure nostalgia where Victorian hymns are clung to because of the associations and memories that they trigger and the long-lost simple faith and comforting certainties that they seem to embody. This must surely be a factor in the abiding popularity of highly sentimental Victorian Sunday School hymns which are hardly ever now sung by children at school or church but which remain high on the list of requests to radio and television programmes. When Lord Soper, the Methodist preacher and peer, chose 'I think when I read that sweet story of old' for a *Songs of Praise* programme marking his ninetieth birthday in 1993, the BBC was inundated with requests for it to be repeated on *Praise Be!* Indeed, Thora Hird revealed in the latter programme that she had never received more letters about a single hymn.

Victorian hymns can all too easily become vehicles for cosy nostalgia and encourage a wholly backward-looking faith. John Bell, the leading contemporary Scottish hymn writer, has pointed to the damage done to the cause of reform and moving on in the life of churches by the deadening effect of the line 'Change and decay in all around I see' from 'Abide with me' which, in his view, had encouraged a demonizing of the whole notion of change in Christian circles. Susan Tamke's perceptive remarks about the naturally conservative influence of hymns perhaps apply with particular force to those from the Victorian era:

Because familiar hymns make a special appeal to the memory, hymns are one of the most conservative components of an already conservative institution. It is the old hymn, the hymn of childhood, which comforts most and thus is most readily sung. Thus, hymns not only reflect conservative attitudes but also help to perpetuate them.[28]

There is also a danger that Victorian hymns are becoming part of the burgeoning heritage industry and being viewed as rather quaint period pieces, suitable for slightly arch treatment on Radio 2's Sunday schedule along with drawing room ballads and palm court favourites and for mild and affectionate sending up in the right hand bottom corner of *The Times* letters page. To some extent, this view is encouraged by the commercial marketing of CDs and cassettes of Victorian hymns. A recent advertisement for 'Jesus bids us shine', a compilation of favourite Victorian children's hymns sung by the choir of the Salvation Army Music School in Belfast, invited prospective purchasers to 'bring back those Sunday School memories'. Films and television dramas frequently use Victorian hymns to create a period feel. A recent example was in BBC 1's adaptation of *Little Lord Fauntleroy* in January 1995 where 'Praise, my soul, the King of heaven' was used with great effect to evoke the atmosphere of a Victorian church service.

The presentation of Victorian hymns in the media is not just, however, in terms of old-world charm and easy listening. In one four-month period in 1996, BBC Radio 4 used 'Dear Lord and Father of mankind' to illustrate a documentary on schizophrenia, 'Onward, Christian soldiers' to introduce a feature on church-state relations during the premiership of Margaret Thatcher, and 'Abide with me' to preview the FA Cup Final.[29] In many respects, radio and television have given traditional hymns a new lease of life, kept them fresh and vital and contributed considerably to their continuing popularity and usage in churches. BBC Television's flagship religious programme, *Songs of Praise*, which regularly commands audiences in excess of six million, presents both well-tried favourites and lesser-known Victorian hymns not just as museum pieces but as meaningful and appropriate expressions of contemporary faith. It is perhaps significant that its current (1997) title sequence features the first lines of three nineteenth-century hymns, three from the eighteenth century and just two from the twentieth century. BBC Radio, and especially Radio 2, also treats Victorian hymnody seriously and with integrity. *Sunday Half Hour* provides a generous weekly serving of nineteenth-century fare, consistently well sung and sensitively handled. Recent one-off documentaries and series on Radio 2 have explored the development of hymn singing in Britain and specific aspects of Victorian hymnody and gospel music. The commercial recording industry is also turning its attention to this field with some commendable results. The 'Hymn Makers' series from Kingsway Records which provides first-class recordings on CD and cassette accompanied by extensive notes has recently moved from the eighteenth century into the nineteenth with recent issues on Fanny Crosby and Mrs C.F.Alexander. The biggest mail order music club in Britain has a number of hymn compilations in its current catalogue, heavily weighted in favour of Victorian items and promoted in a style which, if slightly too full of hype and hyperbole, stresses the vitality of the material rather than its nostalgic old world charms. The Huddersfield Choral Society's 'Hymns Album' is described as having a sound that is 'absolutely thrilling – big, bold and thoroughly moving', while the London Community Gospel Choir's 'Gospel Greats', which includes 'What a friend we have in Jesus', 'There is a green hill far away' and 'Count your many blessings' among its nineteenth-century items, is 'great for the soul, finger-clicking and toe-tapping good'. Modern publishers are also serving some Victorian hymn-writers well, particularly those of an evangelical hue. I recently came across a very well produced paperback of Horatius Bonar's hymns, produced by Christian Focus Publications and entitled *Longing for Heaven*. Intended for private devotional use, it is apparently selling well.

There has, indeed, been a discernible shift of mood among many musicians, liturgists and hymn-book compilers over the last decade or so in favour of Victorian hymnody. Recent books on church music tend to be much less scathing about the genre than their predecessors. I suspect that an important harbinger of this new mood was Nicholas Temperley's *The Music of the English Parish Church*, published in 1979, which staunchly defended Victorian hymn tunes against their many detractors. Perhaps too the poor quality of much contemporary Christian music has made people realize that the Victorian hymn tune composers were not really so bad after all. Lionel Dakers, former director of the Royal School of Church Music, notes in his *Parish Music* (1991) that the work of certain late twentieth-century church musicians 'reveals a degree of mediocrity and poverty of musical invention which would be hard to equal anywhere, even in the worst excesses of many Victorian hymns'.[30] In similar vein Andrew Wilson-Dickson writes of

Victorian hymns in *The Story of Christian Music* (1992): 'While both tunes and words of many were instantly forgettable, a very few of them have a rightly valued place in the spiritual life of almost every English-speaking Christian.'[31] This may be damning with faint praise but at least it is more positive than the remarks made by those writing about church music in the 1960s and 1970s. The Hymn Society of Great Britain and Ireland has also taken a noticeably more charitable view of Victorian hymns over the last decade or so, publishing several important articles in their defence in its Bulletin, notably Donald Webster's 'Victoriana Revisited' in 1987. The reputation of Arthur Sullivan as a composer of hymn tunes has been considerably enhanced in recent years by the tireless advocacy of the Sullivan Society, the production of a fine compact disc of his sacred work recorded by Ely Cathedral Choir, and the painstaking work of Richard Cockaday in identifying and collecting his hymn tunes.

The words of Victorian hymns are also perhaps more appreciated now among literary critics than they once were. This has in part come about as the result of a general realization of the literary value of hymnody and a readiness, at long last, to treat it as a serious art form. An important contribution to this process was made by the late Donald Davie in the introduction to his *New Oxford Book of Christian Verse* (1981) and his more recent *The Eighteenth Century Hymn in England* (1993). Another significant scholar working in this field is Richard Watson, Professor of English at Durham University, whose inaugural lecture was devoted to the subject of Victorian hymns. Important scholarly works are beginning to appear on individual Victorian hymn-writers, such as Leon Litvack's *J. M. Neale and the Quest for Sobornost* and Michael Chandler's *The Life and Work of John Mason Neale 1818–1866*. Theologians and liturgists are also belatedly recognizing the importance of hymnody. Brian Castle, Vice-Principal of Ripon College, Cuddesdon, has rightly pointed to the fact that it is through hymns that most people learn theology, and has argued for much greater use to be made of them not just in worship but in study groups and church education and training programmes. He is as not as enthusiastic as I am about the particular merits of Victorian hymns as vehicles for teaching and transmitting doctrine, but he does write extremely movingly in his recent book *Sing a New Song to the Lord* about the power of Robert Bridges' 'All my hope on God is founded' to stimulate theological discussion and reflection. There is a growing movement within the Church of England to establish a core liturgy which will include classic hymns alongside prayers from the *Book of Common Prayer* and other sources.

It is even possible to detect a swing back to Victorian hymns and tunes in the latest editions of some major denominational hymn-books. The *New English Hymnal* of 1986, for example, restores 25 tunes and nearly 50 hymns from the Victorian period which were not included in the original 1906 edition. The New Standard Edition of *Hymns Ancient and Modern* (1983) has a strong nineteenth-century bias and J. M. Neale, with 32 entries, remains the most frequently appearing author. Victorian hymns still constitute the largest single chronological category in the Methodists' *Hymns and Psalms* (1983), *Baptist Praise and Worship* (1991), *The Song Book of the Salvation Army* (1986) and, just, in the United Reformed Church's *Rejoice and Sing* (1991). *The New Redemption Hymnal* (1986), used by the Elim Pentecostal Church, the Apostolic Church and the Assemblies of God in the British Isles, has a solid core of Victorian classics and still contains 200 items from the Sankey collection. Roman Catholics, who have not been as strongly wedded to Victorian hymnody as most Protestant denominations, are showing a new interest and enthusiasm for the genre. Dissatisfaction with the liturgical, literary and musical paucity of much of the material in their own hymnals has led several Catholic churches, including the Cathedrals at Liverpool and Leeds, to adopt the *New English Hymnal*. In an article about this interesting development the master of music at Liverpool is quoted as describing 'Praise, my soul, the King of heaven' as an 'Anglican pot-boiler' while his counterpart at Leeds refers to 'All my hope on *thee* is founded' but even if they are being patronized and misquoted, it is good to see Victorian hymns being given a new lease of liturgical life in a church which has hitherto largely neglected them.[32]

It might seem that Victorian hymns stand in good stead with the churches as we approach the new millennium. While their general popularity with the public is probably as high as it has ever been, however, their continued use in worship is threatened by a number of current movements and developments in the churches. Interestingly, the attack has shifted from their tunes and it is now their words that are under severe denominational, ecclesiological, liturgical, theological and cultural assault.

The main denominational and ecclesiological assault comes from the fast-growing independent house churches and fellowships which are increasingly making the running in the dynamic world of charismatic renewal and evangelical revival. These new churches, whose style of worship is profoundly influencing many congregations in mainstream denominations, particularly the Church of England, prefer using contemporary choruses and worship songs to traditional congregational hymns. Some of the material coming out of this stable is of a very high order. Several of the hymns of Graham Kendrick, for example, deserve to stand alongside the work of Charles Wesley as classics of evangelical hymnody. Sadly, however, there is a tendency in many of the new churches to worship with an exclusive diet of modern material, perhaps supplemented with some of the great eighteenth-century evangelical hymns. The great corpus of Victorian hymnody, together with the important and much under-rated material produced by twentieth-century writers such as Fred Kaan, Fred Pratt Green, Brian Wren and Albert Bayly, is largely neglected. One of main hymn-books used by these new churches, *Celebration* (1986), has just 18 Victorian hymns among its 376 items. *Songs and Hymns of Fellowship* (1986), another favourite book for those involved in the modern charismatic and evangelical movements, is little different, with just 58 out of its 645 hymns and songs coming from the nineteenth century. The top-scoring Victorian author in this collection is Frances Havergal with just four hymns, a slightly poorer showing than that achieved by J. B. Dykes, whose six tunes make him the best represented composer from any period, including the present day. This squeezing out of Victorian hymns is reflected in the pages of *Mission Praise*, almost certainly now the single most popular hymn-book in Britain, which has crossed numerous denominational divides and is to be found in the pews of Anglican, Presbyterian, Baptist, Methodist and even Roman Catholic places of worship as well as in the new independent churches. While 30% of the hymns in the original 1983 edition came from the nineteenth century, the proportion in the much larger 1990 edition is down to 25%, with over 60% coming from the late twentieth century.

It may be that there will be a swing back to greater use of Victorian hymns in the new churches as their members gain greater maturity and feel the need for some more substantial fare than is provided by many of the contemporary songs and choruses. Andrew Maries, one of the leading musicians associated with the charimastic movement, has commented that 'traditional hymns are now widely used in house and community churches. Previously, worship has been led to a large extent by recently converted Christians, and by others who are ignorant of the Church's hymnic heritage.'[33] The trouble is that the books being used in these churches do not provide much in the way of older material to

draw on even if the inclination is there. Those who are newly converted
to Christianity are unlikely to have had much exposure to the great
treasures of English hymnody in their childhood and it may be difficult
for them to gain access to material which could so enrich and deepen
their spiritual development.

The current assault on Victorian hymnody is not just coming from
new churches. It also arises from a liturgical tide in the mainstream
denominations which is sweeping away old hymns in the name of
relevance, accessibility and contemporaneity. This process has gone
furthest in the Church of England where it is becoming increasingly
common for hymn-books to be dispensed with and congregations to
sing from photocopied service sheets containing exclusively modern
material. Hardly a month goes by without the press reporting a row
between a trendy (and usually evangelical) vicar and a traditionalist
organist and choir. These are reported with particular relish in *The
Daily Telegraph*. Brief mention of three typical incidents will suffice.
In May 1994 the organist at Cromer Parish Church in Norfolk was
reportedly sacked for urging parishioners to oppose the 'bludgeoning in'
of *Mission Praise* in place of *Hymns Ancient and Modern*. A story in
November 1995 under the headline 'Choir quits after rector says: Abide
with me or leave' reported the wholesale resignation of the organist and
choir of Bedworth Parish Church in Warwickshire because of the vicar's
'trendy ideas' which included dropping the recessional hymn at the end
of the service and introducing a folk group with guitars and ukeleles. In
October 1996 the musical director and half the members of the choir at
St Mary's Church in Wroxham, Norfolk, resigned in protest at having
to sing a hymn in praise of jet planes refuelling in mid-air at the annual
harvest festival. Once again, the *Telegraph* sub-editors enjoyed themselves, this time providing the headline 'Hymns ancient and too
modern'.[34]

The one surviving sanctuary of almost undiluted Victorian hymnody
within the Anglican liturgy is progressively disappearing as more and
more churches give up evensong. Where it survives, this remains an
oasis, or ghetto, of Victoriana for the simple reason that the great
majority of evening hymns date from the nineteenth century. A recent
survey of the most popular evening hymns, on the basis of the frequency
of their appearance in the thirty most widely used hymn-books in the
United States, produced the following almost exclusively Victorian top
ten (the one exception being Bishop Ken's evening hymn).

1   'Abide with me' (26 appearances)
2   'Glory to thee, my God, this night' (25)
3   'Saviour, again to thy dear name we raise' (22)
4   'The day Thou gavest, Lord, is ended' (21)
5   'Sun of my soul, thou Saviour dear' (18)
6 = 'Now the day is over'
     'At even, when the sun was set' (17)
8   'O gladsome light' (16)
9   'God, who mad'st the earth and heaven' (14)
10 'Softly now the light of day'
     'Saviour, breathe an evening blessing' (13)

It is, perhaps, worth noting in passing that another Victorian evening hymn, Robert Bridges' 'The duteous day now closeth' appears in a list of 100 top hymns drawn up by the Commission on Music of the National Council of Churches of the USA. This list also includes Tennyson's 'Strong Son of God, Immortal Love', which has almost entirely disappeared from hymn-books in Britain and 'Lord of all being throned afar' which would certainly not appear in a UK list of top hymns.

Victorian hymns are high on the hit list of the politically correct, who castigate them for their hierarchical message and sexist and militaristic language. We have already noted the somewhat intemperate and unjustified attack by Bishop David Konstant on the long-discarded verse of 'All things bright and beautiful' about 'the rich man in his castle, the poor man at his gate' (p. 123). Sensitivity about supposedly exclusive language has led the editors of several recent hymnals to drop the stirring 'Courage, brother! do not stumble', born out of Norman Macleod's liberal faith and remarkable ministry in inner-city Glasgow, and William Merrill's great call to social action, 'Rise up, O men of God'. Duffield's 'Stand up, stand up for Jesus' was not included in *Rejoice and Sing* and appears on the list of hymns to be dropped from the next edition of the *Church Hymnary* because of its supposedly militaristic language. For similar reasons, several churches have banished 'Onward, Christian soldiers' from their hymn-books, including the Presbyterian Church of the USA in 1989, the United Reformed Church in Britain in 1991 and the Anglican Church of Canada at its 1995 Synod. Others, not wanting to lose the tune, have sought to re-write Sabine-Gould's great pilgrim hymn in a more acceptable contemporary idiom. Bishop Derek Rawcliffe produced a version for the twentieth

anniversary festival of the Lesbian and Gay Christian Movement at
Southwark Cathedral in November 1996 which began 'Onward,
Christian homos' and David Wright offered a pacifist version in the
aftermath of the Falklands War:

> Onward, Christian pilgrims,
> Working hard for peace,
> Day by day we're praying
> That all wars may cease.
> Christ our royal master
> Bids us love our foes;
> Do good to those who harm us,
> And violence oppose![35]

The trouble with this kind of exercise, however worthy and well-
intentioned, is that it ignores and destroys the message and integrity of
the original. 'Onward, Christian soldiers' is a great poetic expression of
the (highly orthodox and biblical) idea of the church militant. It is about
moving onward in faith rather than standing still, engaging in the world
rather than withdrawing from it, and proclaiming the unity of
Christians rather than parading their differences. It is firmly christological in focus and puts the cross of Jesus at the centre of the Christian
life. As such, one might have thought that it would appeal to those
committed to an active, progressive faith and attached to the social
gospel. Its language is not so much directly militaristic as carefully and
calculatedly allegorical and metaphorical – '*like* a mighty army' and
'marching *as* to war'. It also speaks very directly and positively to those
many souls in our fractured and broken society who do have to contend
with evil forces and demonic influences.

It is not just hymns deemed politically 'incorrect' that are in danger of
disappearing from use. Others are being excluded from hymnals on the
grounds that they are inaccessible, ambiguous and contain 'difficult'
language. A prime example is 'Lead, kindly light'. I have been surprised
at the vehemence of the opposition to this hymn shown by my fellow-
members on the committee charged with producing the next edition of
The Church Hymnary. I suspect that much of the problem lies in the
two tunes to which it is usually sung – LUX BENIGNA and SANDON, both
of which are perhaps rather *too* Victorian for all but those of us who are
devotees of the genre. Sullivan's LUX IN TENEBRIS provides a deeply
sensitive setting of Newman's words which should be within the range
of most congregations (see Appendix 2). It seems to me well worth

reinstating to preserve what is a comparatively rare animal – although not perhaps as rare in the nineteenth century as in the twentieth – a hymn of doubt in faith. To pluck Newman's verses from our hymn-books would be to deprive the many who face and wrestle with honest doubt of a powerful poetic soul-mate. It would also be to diminish our worship by removing a piece of extraordinarily subtle spiritual writing at a time when we are at last beginning to discover the importance of allusion, metaphor and ambiguity in spirituality and devotion. It is worth noting that 'Lead, kindly light' stands alongside 'Nearer, my God, to thee', 'Once to every man and nation' and 'O love that wilt not let me go' in the list of hymns which American Episcopalians most regret leaving out of their latest (1982) hymnal.[36]

Behind this assault on inaccessible and 'difficult' hymns, which is part of a much wider debate about the appropriate language for worship, lies the demand of our post-literary culture that everything should be instantly understandable and relevant and nothing left mysterious or ambiguous. Victorian hymns fail this requirement completely. They fit uneasily into the age of the soundbite when image is all and content counts for little. Instead of being 'up-front' and 'user friendly', they ooze subtlety and mystery and are packed with ambiguities and nuances. They are full of 'difficult' phrases and ideas which only begin to unpack themselves with repeated usage and growing familiarity. Future generations will have their imaginations starved and their spiritual potential stunted if 'difficult' hymns are dropped wholesale from the hymn-books or suffer severe mutilation and alteration in the interests of modernity and easy accessibility.

It is hard to know which is the worse fate. At least the hymns that are discarded remain in their former glory and complexity, perhaps to be rediscovered by future generations with more respect for nuance and numinance. Those that are rewritten to remove perceived archaism and obscurity often end up being robbed of their resonance and reduced to banality. At the hands of the editors of *Hymns for Today's Church*, who felt that the word 'behest', like 'thou', was beyond the grasp of modern church-goers, the opening lines of John Ellerton's evening hymn are turned into a soft-focus travel advert:

> The day you gave us, Lord, is ended,
> The sun is sinking in the west.

This particular book, which came out in 1982, contains many such crass revisions. I suppose that we should at least be thankful that it never quite sank to the depths of another modern hymnal which rendered the refrain of 'Eternal Father, strong to save' into a couplet of which even Gilbert and Sullivan would have been ashamed:

> O hear us when we cry to you
> For those who sail the ocean blue.[37]

The process of up-dating traditional hymns often leaves them robbed not just of their poetry and mystery but also of the more difficult and uncomfortable elements in their teaching. Brian Abel Ragen, assistant professor of English at Southern Illinois University, has made an interesting study of recent revisions of eighteenth and nineteenth-century hymns made in American hymnals. He found that the overall effect has been to reduce, if not entirely remove, the emphasis on sin, penitence and individual responsibility, to put the focus on the worshipper rather than on Christ, and to promote a comfortable 'feel-good factor':

> The revisions of traditional hymns in recent American hymnals reveal a troubling attitude towards the members of the congregation: they are evidently imagined not to be very bright, not able to deal with any sort of difficulty, and more interested in feeling good about themselves than in the doctrine of Christianity. They cannot deal with vivid imagery . . . They cannot sing settings as complex as those their parents and grandparents sang with joy. And evidently they cannot pay attention to anything longer than the average TV commercial, for hymns are getting shorter and shorter . . . In fact, if the progression we see continues, it seems clear that eventually no hymn will be more than two stanzas long. Perhaps this development is just another proof of the diminishing attention span of the average American. Then again, since there is so much we must avoid saying, perhaps it is simply impossible to find more than two consecutive stanzas that do not say something offensive, like 'man', 'men', 'he', 'thee', 'thy', 'thou', 'soldier', 'sword', 'prince', 'Lord', 'servant' or 'sinner'.[38]

The modern penchant for up-dating or discarding some of the great hymns of the past has not gone unchallenged. I myself have suggested in newspaper articles over the last five years that we may need to put preservation orders on certain hymns to prevent them from being vandalized and have proposed a new pressure group called CATCH (Campaign for Traditional Church Hymns).[39] I was delighted to discover that others had beaten me to it and that there was already in existence a group called SERAPH (The Society for the Encouragement, Recital and Appreciation of Proper Hymns). More recently, David Wright has launched a campaign for real hymns based on the highly successful Campaign for Real Ale.[40] There has also been condemnation in the press for clergy who throw out or modernize favourite hymns. It is interesting how the wheel turns full circle. A hundred and fifty years ago, at least if we are to believe Thomas Hardy, there was popular outrage when modernizing clergy ousted metrical psalms and gallery bands with *Hymns Ancient and Modern*. Now 'trendy vicars' are in the firing line for getting rid of *A & M* and replacing hymns with choruses. 'All hymns bright and beautiful, those clerics changed them all' ran a recent headline in the *Sunday Times*.[41] The columnists of *The Daily Telegraph* can also be relied upon to join in the chase:

> Clergymen who are philistine have to be told so. 'The beauty of holiness', as John Samuel Monsell called it, is part of the Church of England's inheritance, and we cannot watch in silence while it is supplanted by wanton ugliness.
>
> Quite how one conveys to an earnest, cloth-eared vicar that he is getting it all wrong is a difficult question. The man has been to theological college. He may have developed the spiritual resources to cope without 'Jerusalem', 'Immortal, invisible, God only wise', 'Dear Lord and Father of mankind', 'Lead, kindly light, amid the encircling gloom' and 'Abide with me, fast falls the eventide'. Perhaps the most tactful thing we can do is to tell him that in our weakness, we need these pillars of our faith.
>
> We should not mistrust the emotion that great hymns inspire in us. Our hearts need to be reached as much as our heads . . . Either the world is meaningless or it is a mystery, and one of the best ways the Christian mystery comes to us is through the work of great composers and hymn writers.[42]

Those of us who are enthusiasts for Victorian hymnody do need to be able to sort out the wheat from the chaff and to resist the temptation to cling on to certain stranded wrecks which would be better broken up. It is good for us to be confronted with the withering judgment of a leading contemporary hymn-writer like John Bell, who has recently written that 'The Victorians dumped on us a legacy of forced piety, sentimentalism and deceptive images of God in their hymns. Their tunes, with mushy harmonies or pedantic melodies, were little better.'[43] These remarks may be just in the case of much that was written in the nineteenth century.

Yet there are particular strengths and insights in Victorian hymns that continue to make them a worthwhile and enriching element in Christian worship today. At first sight, they may appear to fit uneasily into our increasingly fragmented and disposable pick-and-mix culture. Yet this may be precisely why we need them. As the perceptive religious commentator Clifford Longley has observed, part of the malaise of contemporary society springs from our collective loss of metaphysical imagination and of 'the mental stock of meaningful things in life like glory, honour, dignity, sacrifice, tragedy . . . and God'.[44] Victorian hymns are richly stocked with metaphysical images. They embody and articulate the values of effort, earnestness and excellence which Frances Lawrence, the widow of the London headmaster murdered outside his school, commended in her moving manifesto for national moral revival. They breathe an atmosphere of order and calm. This is not the same as shallow comfort and complacency. As we have seen, doubt and ambiguity are to be found in many Victorian hymns. There is, however, an underlying and overarching sense of moral order and purpose about them. This is, perhaps, most evident in the structure and progression of their often derided and under-rated tunes which stand in sharp contrast to the frenzied confusion and jerky sensationalism of much modern music, including that used for contemporary Christian worship.

We are acutely conscious of the brutalized nature of contemporary society. The research of behavioural scientists and acoustic experts is now clearly demonstrating what common experience has long told us, that there is a close relationship between the kind of music that we sing and listen to and our social attitudes and behaviour. Lengthy exposure to loud and discordant pop music does not just produce tinnitus and deafness; it also deadens the senses in other respects and encourages introversion, self-centredness and anti-social behaviour. It may sound very simplistic and authoritarian to prescribe a diet of Victorian hymns as part of a programme to restore moral purpose and social cohesion to alienated and desensitized young people. Yet there is evidence from at least one secondary school pointing to the beneficial effects that the singing of Victorian hymns can have on pupils' attitudes and performance. Central to the ethos and the corporate identity of Malbank School in Nantwich, Cheshire, which emerged as the top comprehensive school in Britain in a survey carried out by *The Times* in 1996, is the annual Remembrance Day service at which all 1216 pupils sing 'Abide with me' and then observe one minute's silence. It is a source of particular pride to the head, who takes some pleasure in confounding those sceptics, including the local vicar, who feel that massed 'teenagers will neither sing out nor stay completely silent'.[45] It ought also to be a source of enormous encouragement to those of us who feel that Victorian hymns can still inspire, instruct, uplift, challenge and encourage, and who hope that they may be allowed to abide with us for many, many years to come.

Appendix 1

100 Victorian hymns that should be in any self-respecting modern hymnal

Note: This list of hymns written and published between 1837 and 1901 excludes Christmas hymns and carols. Translations are in brackets. Tunes are given where they are Victorian and deserve to be used.

Abide with me – EVENTIDE

(All creatures of our God and King)

(All my hope on God is founded)

All things bright and beautiful – ALL THINGS BRIGHT

Alleluia! Alleluia! Hearts to heaven and voices raise – LUX EOI

Alleluia! Sing to Jesus – HYFRYDOL

Almighty Father of all things that be – CHILTON FOLIAT

And now, O Father, mindful of the love

Angel voices ever singing – ANGEL VOICES

At the name of Jesus – EVELYNS

(Be still, my soul)

Blessed assurance – BLESSED ASSURANCE

Breathe on me, breath of God

Bright the vision that delighted – LAUS DEO

Christ is coming! Let creation from her groans and travails cease

Christ is made the sure foundation

City of God, how broad, how far

(Come down, O love divine)

Come, ye faithful, raise the anthem

Come, ye thankful people, come – ST GEORGE

Courage, brother! do not stumble – COURAGE BROTHER

Crown him with many crowns – DIADEMATA

Dear Lord and Father of mankind – REPTON

Eternal Father, strong to save – MELITA

Eternal light! Eternal light

Eternal Ruler of the ceaseless round

Father, hear the prayer we offer

For all the Saints who from their labours rest

For my sake and the Gospel's, go – BISHOPGARTH

For the beauty of the earth

Forty days and forty nights

From thee all skill and science flow

God be with you till we meet again – GOD BE WITH YOU

God is working his purpose out

(Happy are they, they that love God)

(Hark a thrilling voice is sounding) – MERTON

Hark what a sound, and too divine for hearing

Hushed was the evening hymn – SAMUEL

(I bind unto myself today)

I heard the voice of Jesus say – VOX DILECTI

Immortal, invisible, God only wise – JOANNA

In the cross of Christ I glory – ST OSWALD and ALL FOR JESUS

(Jerusalem the golden) – EWING

(Jesu, thou joy of loving hearts)

Jesus calls us o'er the tumult – ST ANDREW

(Jesus lives! Thy terrors now) – ST ALBINUS

Just as I am – SAFFRON WALDEN

Lead, kindly light – LUX BENIGNA, SANDON and LUX IN TENEBRIS

Lead us, heavenly father, lead us

(Let all mortal flesh keep silent)

Lift up your hearts ! We lift them, Lord to thee

Lord, enthroned in heavenly splendour – ST HELEN

Lord, thy word abideth

Make me a captive, Lord – LLANLLYFNI

Mine eyes have seen the glory of the coming of the Lord

My God, how wonderful thou art – WESTMINSTER

Nearer my God to thee – HORBURY and PROPIOR DEO

(Now thank we all our God)

(O come, o come, Emmanuel)

O Jesus, I have promised – THORNBURY

O love that wilt not let me go – ST MARGARET

O perfect Love, all human thought transcending – O PERFECT LOVE

O praise ye the Lord – LAUDATE DOMINO

(O sacred head, sore wounded)

O worship the Lord in the beauty of holiness

(On Jordan's bank the Baptist's Cry)

Onward, Christian soldiers – ST GERTURDE

Praise to the holiest in the height – GERONTIUS

(Praise to the Lord, the Almighty, the King of creation)

Ride on, ride on, in majesty

Safe in the arms of Jesus – REFUGE

Saviour, again to thy dear name we raise – ELLERS

Shall we gather at the river – SHALL WE GATHER

Stand up, stand up for Jesus – MORNING LIGHT

Take my life and let it be – CONSECRATION

Take up thy cross, the Saviour said

Tell me the old, old story – TELL ME THE OLD, OLD STORY

Ten thousand times ten thousand – ALFORD

The Church's one foundation – AURELIA

(The Day of Resurrection)

The day thou gavest, Lord, is ended – ST CLEMENT

The King of love my shepherd is – DOMINUS REGIT ME

(The royal banners forward go)

(The strife is o'er, the battle done)

There's a wideness in God's mercy

There is a green hill far away

Thine arm, O Lord, in days of old

Thou didst leave thy throne and thy kingly crown

(Through the night of doubt and sorrow)

Thy hand, O God, has guided – THORNBURY

Thy kingdom come, on bended knee

To God be the glory – TO GOD BE THE GLORY

(To the Name of our Salvation) – REGENT SQUARE

(Wake, O wake, with tidings thrilling)

(We plough the fields and scatter)

What a friend we have in Jesus – CONVERSE

(When morning gilds the skies, – LAUDES DOMINI

Who is on the Lord's side – ARMAGEDDON

Will your anchor hold in the storms of life – WILL YOUR ANCHOR HOLD

(Ye choirs of New Jerusalem) – FULBERT

The following twelve tunes, written and published between 1837 and 1901 for pre-Victorian hymns, should also surely find a place in every hymnal:

ABERYSTWYTH (for Jesu, Lover of my soul)

CHURCH TRIUMPHANT (for The Lord is King! Lift up thy voice)

CRIMOND (for The Lord's My shepherd)

CROSS OF JESUS (for Come, thou long expected Jesus)

GWALCHMAI (for King of glory, King of peace)

HEREFORD (for O Thou who camest from above)

MELCOMBE (for New every morning is the love)

NICAEA (for Holy, Holy, Holy)

PETRA (for Rock of Ages)

PRAISE MY SOUL (for Praise, my soul, the King of heaven)

RIVAULX (for Father of heaven, whose love profound)

ST CUTHBERT (for Our blest Redeemer, ere he breathed)

Appendix 2

Victorian hymns and tunes that deserve rehabilitation

a) Hymns

'Fierce raged the tempest o'er the deep' – it is easy to dismiss this as a classic period piece which has now had its day, yet the Methodists are surely right to retain it to Dykes' ST AELRED in *Hymns and Psalms*. Storm winds still drift us from the shore and we need to hear Christ's words 'Peace! Be still' every bit as much as now as did our forefathers. It is also good to have a hymn about the miracle of the stilling of the storm.

'For my sake and the Gospel's, go' – still well known and much used in the Church of Scotland, especially at ordinations, but almost entirely abandoned in England despite its impeccably Anglican credentials. It was written by Edward Bickersteth, Bishop of Exeter, to fit Sullivan's superb tune BISHOPGARTH which deserves to be preserved at all costs. The tune, at least, has not been completely lost south of the border, being used in *Hymns and Psalms* in preference to the more common GOLDEN SHEAVES for 'To thee, O Lord, our hearts we raise'. Bickersteth's words are also worth keeping, not least for the stirring couplet about the communion of Saints: 'In concert with the holy dead/The warrior church rejoices'.

'Gather us in, thou love that fillest all' – George Matheson's wonderfully inclusive hymn strikes an original and modern note with its interfaith spirit. As far as I am aware, the only hymnbook in which it has ever appeared is the *BBC Hymn Book* of 1951 where it is set to a fine tune by Cyril Taylor, TAMBARAM.

'Go, labour on, spend, and be spent' – Horatius Bonar's exhortation to work and work and work again is still sung by Methodists – at least it appears in *Hymns and Psalms* but it could usefully be taken up by other denominations.

'God of the living, in whose eyes' – John Ellerton's verses can be found in both their original and revised versions, together with a discussion of the controversy that surrounded them, on pages 155–58 of Bernard Braley's *Hymn Writers*, Vol. 1. Unaccountably and unpardonably missing from the expanded list of hymns recommended for funerals by the Churches' Group on Funeral Services at Cemeteries and Crematoria (Canterbury Press 1994) and from most modern hymnals (the third edition of the *Church Hymnary* is a shining exception), it could, when sung to MELITA, bring considerable comfort and consolation to mourners and is particularly appropriate for use, as Ellerton intended, at funerals of non church-goers.

'Hail, gladdening light' – Keble's translation of the ancient lamp-lighting hymn is still in a number of hymn-books but is little sung now. It should be heard much more to Stainer's fine chant SEBASTE.

'His are the thousand sparkling rills' – I fear that the flowery language of the first line will be enough to kill off any chances of rehabilitation for Mrs Alexander's hymn. Yet we have few enough hymns for Good Friday and this is in fact a very penetrating and profound treatment of the Passion. The best tune for it is A. H. Brown's SAFFRON WALDEN.

'Jesus us bids us shine' – I will be accused of gross sentimentality for pleading for the restoration of this long-time Sunday School favourite. Despite the unfortunate and inappropriately individualistic message conveyed by the line 'You in your small corner, and I in mine', I find its imagery and message still very fresh and meaningful. It is an indispensable accompaniment to children's addresses on the theme of letting our lights shine and on the appropriateness of thinking of the light of Christ in terms of a candle flame rather than the harsh glow of the fluorescent tube.

'O Jesu, thou art standing' – I am surprised that these verses by William Walsham How have apparently completely disappeared from use. Inspired by Holman Hunt's painting 'The Light of the World', they portray Jesus as the one standing at the door, knocking and waiting. It is a beautifully written hymn, complemented by R. F. Dale's tune ST CATHERINE, and can be found in the 1950 *Hymns Ancient and Modern Revised* at No.355.

'O lead my blindness by the hand' – I doubt that we will ever again have a hymn-writing Prime Minister but I would urge the claims of W. E. Gladstone's hymn on its merits rather than its curiosity value. In the *BBC Hymn Book* it is set to a particularly suitable tune, RYBURN, by Norman Cocker.

'On the Resurrection morning' – I cannot find Sabine Baring-Gould's verses in any book since the 1933 *English Hymnal* which is a great pity since it is one of the very few hymns, if not the only one, to tackle the difficult doctrine of bodily resurrection. For theological reasons alone, it should be reinstated. It goes particularly well to S. S. Wesley's HORNSEY to which it is set in the Appendix of the *English Hymnal*.

'Strong Son of God, Immortal Love' – The first stanzas of Tennyson's *In Memoriam* represent one of the classic expressions of the Victorian crisis of faith and seem to me equally valid in our own uncertain times. It goes particularly well to J.B. Dykes' RIVAULX.

'Thou to whom the sick and dying' – Godfrey Thring's pastorally sensitive hymn about illness and dying was in *Hymns Ancient and Modern Revised* and the 1951 *BBC Hymn Book* but I cannot find it in any current hymnal.

b) Tunes

LUX IN TENEBRIS – Sullivan's extraordinarily sensitive setting of Newman's ambiguous poem of doubt-in-faith was in the first edition of the *Church Hymnary* but has been in few hymnals since. It transformed 'Lead, kindly light' for my Aberdeen students who had hitherto found it dull and maudlin. Although perhaps ideally suited to choirs and certainly worthy of coming back into the anthem repertoire, it is also surely within the capabilities of many congregations.

ORLINGTON – John Campbell's magnificent tune is still much used in Scotland. It deserves much greater exposure south of the border. It goes particularly well to Cowper's 'O for a closer walk with God'.

PENTECOST – Ian Mackenzie is surely right to say that William Boyd's tune for 'Fight the good fight' 'burned and crunched with a sense of profound inner struggle, not a macho display of prowess'.[1]

VENI SPIRITUS – Stainer's tune is surely infinitely preferable for 'Breathe on me, breath of God' to the lugubrious TRENTHAM, so rightly described by Bertram Barnby as suggesting the sentiment 'Oh what a dreary day'.

Appendix 3

The top fifteen Victorian hymn tune composers

Joseph Barnby (1838–96) – chorister at York Minster, organist at St Andrew's, Wells Street and St Anne's, Soho, director of music at Eton and principal of Guildhall School of Music.

Josiah Booth (1852–1929) – organist at Banbury and at Park Congregational Church, Crouch End.

John Bacchus Dykes (1823–76) – curate at Malton, precentor of Durham Cathedral, vicar of St Oswald's, Durham.

George Jacob Elvey (1816–93) – chorister at Canterbury Cathedral, organist at St George's, Windsor.

Henry John Gauntlett (1805–76) – organist at his father's church in Olney at the age of nine, started as a solicitor, organist of St Olave's, Southwark, Christ Church, Newgate Street, Union Chapel, Islington and St Bartholomew the Less, Smithfield.

John Goss (1800–80) – chorister at Chapel Royal, organist at St Luke's, Chelsea, and St Paul's Cathedral.

Edward John Hopkins (1818–1901) – chorister at Chapel Royal, organist at Temple Church.

William Henry Monk (1823–89) – organist at St Matthias, Stoke Newington, professor of vocal music at King's College, London, music editor of *Hymns Ancient and Modern*.

Herbert Stanley Oakeley (1830–1903) – professor of music at Edinburgh University and composer to Queen Victoria.

Frederick Arthur Gore Ouseley (1825–89) – curate in Pimlico and Knightsbridge, founder of St Michael's College, Tenbury, professor of music at Oxford University, precentor of Hereford Cathedral.

Richard Redhead (1820–1901) – chorister at Magdalen College, Oxford, organist of Margaret Street Chapel and St Mary Magdalene, Paddington.

Henry Smart (1813–79) – organist at Blackburn Parish Church, St
  Giles, Cripplegate, St Luke's, Old Street and St Pancras Parish
  Church, blind from the age of 51.

John Stainer (1840–1901) – chorister at St Paul's Cathedral, organist at
  St Benet's and St Paul's, Upper Thames Street, London, St Michael's
  College, Tenbury, Magdalen College, Oxford, St Paul's Cathedral,
  professor of music at Oxford University.

Arthur Seymour Sullivan (1842–1900) – chorister at Chapel Royal,
  organist at St Michael's, Chester Square, and St Peter's, Cranley
  Gardens (both London), principal of the National Training School for
  Music, conductor of the Glasgow Choral Union, the Covent Garden
  Promenade Concerts and the Leeds Festival, composer of operettas
  and oratorios.

Samuel Sebastian Wesley (1810–76) – chorister at Chapel Royal,
  organist at Leeds Parish Church and Hereford, Exeter, Winchester
  and Gloucester Cathedrals, leading composer of anthems and other
  church music.

Notes

Where publication details are not given, these will be found in the Bibliography which follows these Notes. Titles are generally referred to here in abbreviated form.

Preface

1. This estimate was given by Bertram Barnby in an article entitled 'Choir Stalled' in *The Guardian*, 9 April 1977.
2. Davis, *Worship and Theology in England*, p. 210.
3. Tamke, *Make a Joyful Noise Unto the Lord*, p. 2. Other important studies of Victorian hymnody from a cultural, literary and historical perspective include Susan Drain's *The Anglican Church in Nineteenth Century Britain* and Lionel Adey's two volumes, *Hymns and the Christian Myth* and *Class and Idol in the English Hymn*. There has, in fact, been a much greater scholarly appreciation of the cultural significance of Victorian hymnody in North America than in Britain. This may have something to do with the fact that Americans remain less embarrassed about singing Victorian hymns than their transatlantic cousins or it may simply reflect the greater seriousness with which they take the whole subject of hymnody – witness, for example, the very high scholarly standard of articles in the journal of the Hymn Society in the United States and Canada, *The Hymn*.

1 'Praise, my soul, the King of heaven'

1. Hutchings, *Church Music in the Nineteenth Century*, p. 12.
2. Quoted in Woods, *Good Singing Still*, p. 50.
3. Quoted in Temperley, *The Music of the English Parish Church*, Vol. I, p. 138.
4. Quoted in Woods, op. cit., p. 102.
5. The best books for anyone wishing to read further about west gallery music are those by Woods and Temperley mentioned above. Rather older and more difficult to find, but still regarded as a classic and full of anecdotes, is K. H. MacDermott's *The Old Church Gallery Minstrels* . There has been a significant revival of interest in and performance of west gallery music in recent years, thanks partly to the work of the West Gallery Association

which may be contacted at Ironbridge Gorge Museum Trust, The Wharfage, Ironbridge, Telford, TF8 7AW.

6. Eliot, 'Amos Barton' (1857), published in *Scenes of Clerical Life*, pp. 42–43.
7. Gibson (ed), *Complete Poems of Thomas Hardy*, p. 252.
8. Hardy, *Selected Short Stories and Poems*, pp. 105–8.
9. Gibson (ed), op. cit., p. 429.
10. Hardy, *The Mayor of Casterbridge*, p. 256.
11. Gaskell, *Cousin Phillis*, pp. 231–32.
12. Gaskell, *Ruth*, p. 152.
13. Quoted in *Hymns and Psalms*, MPH 1983, p. x.
14. G. Booth (ed), *Primitive Methodist Hymnal*, 1889, p. iv.
15. 'A letter to a country gentleman on the subject of Methodism' quoted in Woods, *Good Singing Still*, p. 94.
16. John Wesley's Journal, 9 August 1768, quoted in Routley, *The Musical Wesleys*, p. 9.
17. Routley, *The Musical Wesleys*, p. 197.
18. Eliot, *Adam Bede*, p. 42.
19. Ibid., p. 46.
20. Ibid., p. 373.
21. Ibid., p. 463.
22. C. Bronte, *Shirley*, p. 161.
23. Cunningham, *Everywhere Spoken Against*, p. 87. This book offers some interesting insights into the portrayal of hymn singing in Victorian novels.
24. *The Poems of Anne Bronte*, p. 84.
25. Hardy, *Desperate Remedies*, p. 259.
26. J. H. Ewing, *Mrs Overthreway's Remembrances* quoted in N. Taylor (ed), *For Services Rendered*, Lutterworth Press 1993, p. 160.
27. How, *Bishop Walsham How*, p. 46.
28. Temperley, *The Music of the English Parish Church*, Vol. I, p.128.
29. Hennell, *John Venn*, p. 267.
30. Temperley, op. cit., p. 223.
31. Quoted in Clarke, *A Hundred Years of Hymns Ancient and Modern*, pp. 18–19.
32. Quoted in Knight, *The Nineteenth Century Church*, p. 85.
33. Eliot, *Scenes of Clerical Life*, pp. 43, 47.
34. Ibid., p. 47.
35. Bradley, *The English Middle Classes*, p. 48.
36. A. Heber, *The Life of Reginald Heber, Bishop of Calcutta*, John Murray 1830, Vol. I, p. 352.
37. Quoted in Braley, *Hymn Writers*, Vol. 1, p. 69.
38. Ibid., pp. 69–70.
39. Chadwick, *The Victorian Church*, Vol. I, p. 67.

40. Battsicombe, *John Keble*, p. 84.
41. Benson, *The English Hymn*, p. 437.
42. Quoted in Rainbow, *The Choral Revival in the Anglican Church* , p. 90.
43. *The Collected Hymns, Sequences and Carols of John Mason Neale*, p. viii.
44. F. Helmore quoted in Rainbow, *The Choral Revival*, p. 91.
45. Towle, *John Mason Neale*, p. 208.
46. Quoted in Rainbow, *The Choral Revival*, p. 91.
47. Butler, *The Way of All Flesh*, pp. 316–8.
48. Temperley, *The Music of English Parish Church*, Vol. I, p. 266.

2 'The playing of the merry organ, sweet singing in the choir'

1. Quoted in Jones, *Congregationalism in England*, p. 223.
2. La Trobe, *The Music of the Church*, pp. 92, 342.
3. Quoted in Routley, *The Musical Wesleys*, p. 120.
4. Quoted in Rainbow, *The Choral Revival*, p. 41.
5. Temperley, *The Music of the English Parish Church*,Vol. I, p. 245.
6. The nature of this debate is well described in Rainbow's book, which is the standard work on the nineteenth-century choral revival. See also Hutchings, *Church Music in the Nineteenth Century* and Fellowes, *English Cathedral Music*.
7. Temperley, op. cit., p. 258.
8. Church Congress Report, 1874, p. 97.
9. The controversy over the organ in Leeds is detailed in R. Davies, A. R. George and G. Rupp (eds), *A History of the Methodist Church in Great Britain*, Vol. 2, Epworth Press 1978, pp. 314–15.
10. Jones, *Congregationalsim in England*, p. 225.
11. *The Parish Choir*, Vol. II, 1847, p. 87.
12. *The Parish Choir*, Vol. I, 1846, p. 145.
13. Rainbow, *The Choral Revival*, pp. 119–21.
14. Hardy, *Under the Greenwood Tree*, pp. v–vi.
15. Eliot, *Scenes of Clerical Life*, pp. 41–42.
16. A good example of this argument is to be found in Vic Gammon's 'Babylonian Performances: the Rise and Suppression of Popular Church Music, 1660–1870'. Gammon does not himself use the phrase 'cultural imperialism' but it was used by a number of speakers at a conference on west gallery music held at Clacton in May 1995 and jointly organized by the West Gallery Association and the Music Department of Anglia University. A paper given at this gathering by Christopher Turner related the decline of the gallery tradition much more to overall social and cultural changes.
17. Hutchings, *Church Music*, p. 119.
18. MacDermott, *The Old Church Gallery Minstrels*, p. 5.

19. La Trobe, *The Music of the Church*, p. 114.
20. Woods, *Good Singing Still*, pp. 18–19.
21. See, for example, Woods, p. 19.
22. Temperley, *The Music of the English Parish Church*, Vol. I, p. 156.
23. MacDermott, *The Old Church Gallery Minstrels*, p. 7.
24. La Trobe, *The Music of the Church*, p. 72.
25. Gammon, 'Babylonian Performances', p. 80.
26. Temperley, *The Music of the English Parish Church*, p. 170.
27. Davis, *Worship and Theology in England*, p. 210.
28. Hardy, *A Laodecian*, p. 9.
29. Butler, *The Way of All Flesh*, pp. 52–53.
30. Hardy, *Under the Greenwood Tree*, pp. v–vi.
31. R. Palmer (ed), *The Painful Plough*, CUP 1972, p. 14.
32. Gammon, ' Babylonian Performances', p. 78.
33. Butler, *The Way of All Flesh*, p. 201.
34. Gosse, *Father and Son*, p. 200.
35. Gaskell, *North and South*, p. 414.
36. C. Bronte, *Villette*, p. 37.
37. Quoted in Braley, *Hymn Writers*, Vol. 1, p. 154.
38. W. L. Alexander, 'Lectures on the Public Psalmody of the Church' in *The Scottish Congregational Magazine*, August 1848, p. 254.
39. Baynes, *Lyra Anglicana*, p. vi.

3 'There is a book, who runs may read'

1. Fowler, *The Life and Letters of John Bacchus Dykes*, p. 198.
2. *The English Churchman*, 14 August 1862.
3. Litvack, *J. M. Neale*, p. 119.
4. *A & M* Archives. Letter from Francis Murray, 23 July 1858.
5. Quoted in Adey, *Class and Idol*, p. 52.
6. *Hymns of Progress*, The Modern Press 1883, p. i.
7. Ibid., pp. 15, 17.
8. Gathorne-Hardy, *The Public School Phenomenon*, p. 131. Gathorne-Hardy chooses a slightly curious trio of hymns to make his point – 'Jesu, Lover of my soul', 'God moves in a mysterious way' and 'Rock of ages'. I would question whether any of these were as characteristic or distinctive public school hymns as 'Lift up your hearts! We lift them, Lord, to Thee', 'Lord, enthroned in heavenly splendour' or 'O Jesus, I have promised'.
9. *Hymns of Progress*, p. ii.
10. *Hymns for the Christian Church and Home*, John Green 1840, p. viii.
11. Ibid., p. viii.
12. The controversy over *The Rivulet* is well covered in Erik Routley's *Hymns and Human Life*, pp. 117–21.

13. *A & M* Archives. Letter from Francis Murray to W. Denton, undated (1862).
14. *The Guardian*, 20 and 27 October 1858.
15. *A & M* Archives. Letter from Sir H. Baker, 15 December 1858.
16. Ibid. Letter from W. Priest, 29 March 1860.
17. Ibid. Letter from J. H. Lester, undated.
18. Ibid. Letter from W. Priest, 29 March 1860.
19. *The Ecclesiologist*, October 1861.
20. *A & M* Archives. Letter from J.R. Mackarness, 29 January 1872.
21. Ibid. Letter from E. Husband, 22 February 1875.
22. Quoted in Drain, *The Anglican Church in Nineteenth Century Britain*, pp. 383–84. Susan Drain's book provides a very readable and detailed study of the making of *A & M*. Also to be recommended is W. K. Lowther Clarke's *A Hundred Years of Hymns Ancient and Modern*.
23. *A & M* Archives. Letters from the Archdeacon of Shrewsbury, 13 February 1868 and the Archdeacon of Bedford, 7 January 1868.
24. Ibid. Letter from W. Pulling, 15 May 1878.
25. Ibid. Letter from F. Pott, 28 October 1859.
26. Ibid.
27. Drain, *The Anglican Church*, p. 356.
28. *A & M* Archives. Letter from E.Grinstead, 13 May 1897.
29. *Ibid*. Report of Sub-Committee on hymns on heaven and kindred subjects.
30. *The English Churchman*, 14 August 1862.
31. *Church Times*, 10 December 1897.
32. Drain, *The Anglican Church*, p. 493.
33. Fowler, *The Life and Letter of John Bacchus Dykes*, p. 123.
34. *The Ecclesiastical Gazette*, 16 February 1880.
35. Report of the Joint Committee of the Upper and Lower Houses of the Convocation of Canterbury, January 1894.
36. *A & M* Archives. Report of the debate in Convocation, April 1894.
37. *Church Times*, 24 September 1897.
38. *A & M* Archives. Memo dated 23 January 1893.
39. Milgate (ed), *The Life and Work of Thomas Hardy*, p. 404.
40. *A & M* Archives. Letter from E. Bickersteth, 20 July 1870.
41. Gammon, 'Babylonian Performances', p. 82.
42. *A & M* Archives. Letter of 24 September 1875. *The Complete Poems of Thomas Hardy*, p. 431.
43. *A & M* Archives. Letter from Dr Thring, 25 July 1874.
44. Quoted in Binfield, 'Hymns and an Orthodox Dissenter', p. 89.
45. Ibid., p. 89.
46. *A & M* Archives. Letter from Dr Allon, 10 December 1874.
47. Ibid. Letter from Dr Allon, 7 July 1879.
48. Binfield, 'Hymns and an Orthodox Dissenter', p. 90.

49. Ibid., p. 92.
50. A & M Archives. Letter from Alexander Brown, 25 July 1873.
51. Ibid. Letter from A. H. K. Boyd, 7 July 1885.
52. Brownlie, *Hymns and Hymn Writers*, p. 7.
53. Ibid., p. 5.

4 'For all the Saints who from their labours rest'

1. Quoted in Elliott-Binns, *Religion in the Victorian Era*, p. 374.
2. Quoted in Jefferson, *Hymns in Christian Worship*, p. 90.
3. *Alfred, Lord Tennyson. A Memoir by his Son*, Macmillan 1899, Vol. IV, p. 183.
4. Quoted in Litvack, *J. M. Neale*, pp. 22–23.
5. Preface to Faber's first collection of hymns quoted in G. B. Tennyson, *Victorian Devotional Poetry*, Harvard University Press 1981, p. 182.
6. Quoted in Bradley, *The Penguin Book of Hymns*, p. 377.
7. Moffatt and Patrick (eds), *Handbook to the Church Hymnary*, p. 365.
8. On the Winkworth sisters see Peter Skrine's Inaugural Lecture as Professor of German at the University of Bristol delivered on 20 May 1991 and published by the Hymn Society of Great Britain and Ireland as an Occasional Paper, Second Series, No. 2, in June 1992.
9. Quoted in Wallace, *Mrs Alexander*, p. 153. Valerie Wallace's recent biography is to be recommended to anyone wishing to find out more about this remarkable Victorian lady.
10. Moffatt and Patrick (eds), *Handbook*, p. 78.
11. Litvack, *J. M. Neale*, p. 25.
12. The phrase comes from Henry Stapleton, Dean of Carlisle, who has made a special study of Samuel Stone and written an unpublished paper, 'Samuel J. Stone of All Hallows, London Wall', 1988.
13. Campbell, *Hymns and Hymn Makers*, p. 98.
14. Quoted in Chadwick, *The Spirit of the Oxford Movement*, p. 95.
15. Moffatt and Patrick (eds), *Handbook*, p. 190.
16. Ibid., p. 204.
17. Ibid., p. 32.
18. Frost, *Historical Companion to Hymns Ancient & Modern*, p. 561.
19. Moffatt and Patrick (eds), *Handbook*, p. 76.
20. Purcell, *Onward Christian Soldier*, p. 74.
21. Macmillan, *The Life of George Matheson*, p. 181.
22. These extracts are to be found in Bernard Braley's essay on Ellerton in *Hymn Writers*, Vol. 1, pp. 186–87.
23. Ibid., p. 191.
24. A & M Archives. Letter from Francis Pott, 21 February 1868.
25. Ibid. Letter from Horatius Bonar, 9 November 1887.

26. Ibid. Letter from William Whiting, 9 March 1874.
27. Ibid. Letter from Christopher Wordsworth, 25 May 1868.
28. Quoted in D. G. Hill, 'Prefaces and Other Marginal Matters' in *Hymn Society Bulletin,* No. 203, April 1995, p. 135.
29. *A & M* Archives. Letter from W. D. Maclagan, undated (1874).
30. Quoted in Perry, *Preparing for Worship*, p. 51.
31. *Collected Hymns of John Mason Neale*, p. 4.
32. These and other extracts from different versions of the hymn are given in Owen Chadwick's masterly essay on 'Lead, kindly light' which forms chapter 4 of his *The Spirit of the Oxford Movement*.
33. Ibid., p. 93.
34. Ibid.
35. Ibid., p. 95.
36. Ibid., p. 88.
37. 'Strong Son of God' first appeared as a hymn in the 1887 *Congregational Church Hymnal,* 'Sunset and Evening Star' in the 1889 edition of *Hymns Ancient and Modern*.
38. At least no Victorian editor went as far as Percy Dearmer who in *Songs of Praise* (1931) made a hymn ('The world's great age begins anew') out of verses by Shelley, who had been thrown out of Oxford for writing an atheistic tract!
39. *A & M* Archives. Letter from William Bright, 21 July 1874.

5 'Tell me the old, old story'

1. L. Adey, 'The Secularization of the Victorian Hymn' in *Hymn Society Bulletin*, No. 147, January 1980, p. 116.
2. Adey, *Class and Idol*, p. 34.
3. Quoted in Drain, *The Anglican Church*, p. 70.
4. Adey, *Class and Idol*, p. 122.
5. Ibid., p. 102.
6. Ibid., p. 109.
7. Quoted in Tamke, *Make a Joyful Noise*, p. 83.
8. Castle, *Hymns*.
9. This particular line comes from a hymn in the 1860 Harrow School hymnal.
10. Castle, *Sing A New Song to the Lord*, p. 35.
11. Gammon, 'The English Funeral Hymn in the Eighteenth and Nineteenth Centuries' in *Social History Society Newsletter*, Vol. 12, No. 1, Spring 1987, p. 4.
12. Stead, *Hymns that Have Helped*, p. 49.
13. Routley, *Hymns and Human Life*, p. 133.

14. Quoted in B. Braley, 'John Ellerton and "God the Living"' in *Hymn Society Bulletin*, No.168, July 1986, pp. 157–58.
15. Young, *Chapel*, p. 79.
16. J. M. Neale, 'They whose course on earth is o'er'.
17. C. F. Alexander, 'The roseate hues of early dawn'. Another good example in the same genre is Godfrey Thring's 'The radiant morn hath passed away'.
18. H. Bonar, ''Tis not for man to trifle'.
19. C. Elliott, *The Invalid's Hymn Book*, 2nd edn 1841, Hymn 1, verse 1; A.A. Procter, 'My God, I thank thee', verse 3.
20. *The Times*, 5 September 1995. The bishop's denunciation provoked some spirited defences of Mrs Alexander in the correspondence columns of *The Times*, notably on 7 and 14 September 1995. It also inspired Bel Littlejohn to produce this new version of the verse in the spirit of New Labour: 'God made them high and lowly/ And vowed that through an ongoing consultative process He would eventually adopt a dynamic new policy agenda to iron out the very real divisions in our society whilst still making proper provision for the rewarding of hard work and initiative' (*The Guardian*, 8 September 1995). Also worthy of quotation are Auberon Waugh's reflections in *The Daily Telegraph*, 5 September 1995: 'The rich man almost certainly no longer lives in his castle. He has lost his money – at Lloyd's, or through some imprudent investment, or sold the castle to the daughter of a local bus conductor. If he still lives in his castle, he is reduced to penury by the cost of maintaining it. He has sold the lodge at his gate to a much richer man who uses it at weekends . . . The new arrangement, of poor man in his castle, rich man at his gate, was not ordained by God but by Mrs Thatcher and the Tory radicals. It offers nothing to sing about.' Who said that Victorian hymns were dead?
21. S. Wilson, 'Religious and Social Attitudes in Hymns Ancient and Modern (1889)' in *Social Compass*, Vol. XXII, 1975, pp. 211–36.
22. Routley, *Hymns and Human Life*, p. 147.
23. *The Spiritual Songster. A Choice and Unique Collection of Song and Hymn for the Awakening of Spiritual and Progressive Ideas in the Mind of Humanity*, Newcastle 1893, Hymn 100.
24. Dearmer, *Songs of Praise Discussed*, p. 172.
25. *Hymns Ancient and Modern* (1904 edn), p. iv.
26. Wilson, art. cit., p. 218; Adey, *Class and Idol*, p. 74.
27. Chadwick, *The Victorian Church*, Vol.II, p. 290.
28. Keating, *Kipling the Poet*, p. 116.
29. Tamke, *Make a Joyful Noise*, p. 141.
30. E. Cosnett, 'A (Female) Bookworm Reads Some Hymns' in *Hymn Society Bulletin*, No. 205, October 1995, p. 177.
31. Adey, *Class and Idol*, p. 211.

32. Tamke, *Make a Joyful Noise*, p. 155.
33. Ibid., p. 158.
34. Routley, *The Musical Wesleys*, pp. 197–98.
35. Adey, *Class and Idol*, p. 66.
36. Ibid.
37. Chadwick, *The Victorian Church*, Vol. II, p. 469.
38. Ibid.
39. Routley, *A Panorama of Christian Hymnody*, p. 96.
40. Davis, *Worship and Theology in England* , p. 207.
41. Chadwick, 'Lead, Kindly Light' in *The Spirit of the Oxford Movement*, p. 97.
42. Bellasis, *Cardinal Newman as Musician*, p. 38.

6 ' *Sweet and low*'

1. Routley, *The Musical Wesleys*, p. 195.
2. Ibid., p. 197.
3. Ibid.
4. On the debate over whether Jessie Irvine did, in fact, write CRIMOND see the article by the late Ronald Johnson entitled 'How far is it to Crimond?' in the *Hymn Society Bulletin*, No. 176, July 1988, p. 38 and Jack Webster's column in the *Glasgow Herald*, 17 September 1991.
5. *A & M* Archives. Letter from Ewing to Baker, 26 October 1862.
6. John Hughes, 'The Victorian Hymn Tune in Wales' (unpublished paper), p. 4. This important subject can also be profitably pursude in Alan Luff's *Welsh Hymns and their Tunes*.
7. Mervyn Horder, 'A Note on ST CLEMENT', *Hymn Society Bulletin*, No. 200, July 1994, p. 67, reprinted in the magazine of the Sir Arthur Sullivan Society, No. 41, Autumn 1995.
8. Temperley, *The Music of the English Parish Church*, Vol. II, pp. 15–17; Phillips, *The Singing Church*, p. 171.
9. Fowler, *The Life and Letters of John Bacchus Dykes*, p. 42.
10. Ibid., p. 40.
11. Ibid., p. 199.
12. Routley, *The Musical Wesleys*, p. 139; Bertram Barnby, 'Singing the Faith' (unpublished manuscript), p. 176.
13. Smart to Curwen, quoted in David Hill, 'The Hymn Tunes of Henry Smart' in *Hymn Society Bulletin*, No. 195, April 1993, p. 215; J. Barnby, *Hymn Tunes*, London 1869, preface.
14. Bernard Massey, 'William Henry Monk 1823–89' in *Hymn Society Bulletin*, No. 179, April 1989, p. 99; Bertram Barnby, op. cit., p. 179.
15. *A & M* Archives. Letter from S. G. Hatherly in *The Record*, 30 January 1865.

16. Charlton, *John Stainer*, p. 133.
17. A & M Archives. Henry Allon to Henry Baker, 10 December 1874.
18. Ibid. Henry Allon to Henry Baker, 15 June 1867.
19. Ibid. George Huntingford to Henry Baker, 13 August 1885.
20. Charlton, *John Stainer*, p. 134.
21. A & M Archives. Letter from Dr Allon to Henry Baker, 10 December 1874.
22. A & M Archives. Letter from J. B. Dykes to Henry Baker, undated (1873).
23. A copy is in A & M Archives.
24. A & M Archives. Letter from S. S. Wesley to Henry Baker, 15 February 1868.
25. Ibid.
26. E. F. Benson, *As We Were*, Hogarth Press 1985, p. 7.
27. A & M Archives. Letter from W. H. Monk to Secretary, 30 April 1886.
28. Letter from Monk to Henry Baker, 25 January 1869.
29. Quoted in Jacobs, *Arthur Sullivan*, pp. 74–75.
30. A & M Archives. Letter from W. H. Frere to G. White, 12 November 1895.
31. Ibid.
32. *The Church Hymnary*, Novello 1872, p. viii.
33. A & M Archives. Letter from Hope Isidora Monk to Mr Murray, 28 October 1891.
34. Moffatt and Patrick (eds), *Handbook*, p. 146.
35. Quoted in Baker and Welsby, *Hymns and Hymn Singing*, pp. 86–87.
36. A & M Archives. John Stainer to Henry Baker, 17 September 1875.
37. Lightwood, *Hymn Tunes*, p. 204.
38. *Hymn Society Bulletin*, No.20, July 1942, p. 7.
39. Samuel Rogal, 'The Hymn Tunes of Arthur Seymour Sullivan' in James Helyar (ed), *Gilbert and Sullivan. Papers presented at the International Conference held at the University of Kansas in May 1970*, University of Kansas Press 1971, p. 179.
40. Sullivan's setting of 'Lead, kindly light', LUX IN TENEBRIS, can be heard sung by Ely Cathedral Choir on a CD and cassette produced in 1992 by Cantoris Records and entitled *That Glorious Song of Old* (CRMC2368).
41. Routley, *The Musical Wesleys*, p. 199.
42. Benson, *The Hymnody of the Christian Church*, p. 262.
43. Notes taken during conversation with Paul Chappell.
44. Routley, *The Musical Wesleys*, p. 198.
45. Clarke, *A Hundred Years of Hymns Ancient and Modern*, p. 53.
46. Patrick Little, 'J. B. Dykes' HORBURY' in *Hymn Society Bulletin*, No.185, October 1990, pp. 232–35.
47. Moffatt and Patrick (eds), *Handbook*, p. 196.
48. A & M Archives. Letter from Francis Pott to Mr Murray, November 1887.
49. A & M Archives. Letter from John Ellerton to Henry Baker, 8 June 1874.

50. How, *Bishop Walsham How*, p. 352.
51. Ibid., p. 359.
52. Ibid., p. 352.
53. Jacobs, *Arthur Sullivan*, p. 377.
54. Lightwood, *Hymn Tunes*, p. 311.
55. Steuart Adolphus Pears, *Remarks on the Protestant Theory of Church Music* (1852), quoted in Baker and Welsby, *Hymns and Hymn Singing*, p. 86.

7 'Hold the fort for I am coming'

1. Quoted in David Hill, 'Prefaces and other Marginal Matters' in *Hymn Society Bulletin*, No. 203, April 1995, p. 138. Nineteenth-century liberal American hymnody is well covered in the chapter on 'The Literary Movement in America' in Louis Benson's *The English Hymn*, pp. 460–82. Also useful is Alfred Putnam, *Singers and Songs of the Liberal Faith*.
2. Quoted in Moffatt and Patrick (eds), *Handbook*, p. 541.
3. Lowell's poems also appealed to Thomas Hughes, who quoted from them extensively in chapter headings in *Tom Brown's School Days* (1857).
4. Breed, *The History and Use of Hymns*, p. 336.
5. Kent, *Holding the Fort*, p. 218.
6. Sizer, *Gospel Hymns*, passim.
7. Kent, op. cit, p. 223.
8. Quoted in Pollock, *Moody without Sankey*, p. 122. In a recent letter to me David Wright, the Norwich-based hymnologist, floats the idea that the unusual rhythm for this tune may have been suggested to Sankey by the rhythm of a six-wheel rail coach running on jointed track. I am assured by railway enthusiasts that the rolling stock used in Scotland in this period would, indeed, have produced the BANG, BANG, BANG – PAUSE rhythm that is found in the tune. Maybe this is yet another example of the influence that the railways had on Victorian hymnody!
9. Sankey, *My Life and Sacred Songs*, pp. 249–50.
10. Adey, *Class and Idol*, p. 62.
11. Sankey, *My Life*, p. 5.
12. Pollock, *Moody without Sankey*, p. 223.
13. Benson, *The Hymnody of the Christian Church*, p. 265.
14. Account of Moody and Sankey meeting in the Agricultural Hall, Islington, by C. H. Davies, quoted in Parsons, *Religion in Victorian Britain*, Vol.3, p. 275.
15. Sankey, *My Life*, p. 18.
16. Elliott-Binns, *Religion in the Victorian Era*, p. 214.
17. Quoted in Baker and Welsby, *Hymns and Hymn Singing*, p. 101.
18. 'Hymns and Hymnology. Jottings of a lecture by Revd Wiseman, with

various additions and alterations by John Crichton Dick Boyd' (hand-written in December 1897, typed and made available to me by Mrs J. F. A. Newth).

19. Quoted in Briggs and Sellers, *Victorian Nonconformity*, p. 147.
20. Sankey, *My Life*, p. 23.
21. Ibid., p. 25.
22. Gammon, 'Babylonian Performances', p. 78.
23. Quoted in Taylor, *Companion to the Song Book of the Salvation Army*, pp. xiv–xv.
24. Quoted in Wilson-Dickson, *The Story of Christian Music*, p. 140.
25. Quoted in Ian Bradley, 'Blowing for the Lord', *History Today*, Vol. XXVII, No.3, March 1977, p. 191.
26. Ibid., p. 191.
27. Booth, *Salvation Army Music*, preface.
28. Quoted in Bebbington, *Evangelicalism in Modern Britain*, p. 174.
29. Quoted in Routley, *Hymns and Human Life*, p. 303.
30. Cunningham, *Everywhere Spoken Against,* p. 99.
31. R. Samuel, 'The Discovery of Puritanism, 1820–1914' in J. Garnett and C. Matthew (eds), *Revival and Religion since 1700*, Hambledon Press 1993, p. 244.
32. William Stewart, *J. Keir Hardie*, Cassell 1921, p. 97.
33. Quoted in Inglis, *Churches and the Working Classes*, p. 238.

8 'Lead, kindly light'

1. Stead, *Hymns that Have Helped*, p. 2.
2. Ibid.
3. Quoted in Tamke, *Make a Joyful Noise*, p. 2.
4. Hippolyte Taine, *Notes on England*, translated by W. F. Rae, Strahan, London 1872, p. 234.
5. Stead, *Hymns that Have Helped*, p. 5.
6. Ibid., p. 7.
7. Ibid., p. 66.
8. Ibid., p. 9.
9. Ibid., p. 7.
10. J. E. Ritchie, *The Real Gladstone: An Anecdotal Biography,* T. Fisher Unwin 1898, p. 212.
11. The results of the survey can be found in Appendix II of Stead, *Hymns that Have Helped*, pp. 113–15.
12. Brownlie, *Hymns and Hymn Writers*, pp. 331–33.
13. Adey, *Hymns and the Christian Myth*, p. ix.
14. *A & M* Archives. Letter from Chaplain to the Fleet, 17 December 1887.
15. Amelia Barr, *All the Days of My Life: An Autobiography,* New York 1913,

pp. 415–56.
16. *Primitive Methodist Magazine*, 1896, p. 830.
17. Moffatt and Patrick (eds), *Handbook*, p. 350.
18. Hunter, *A Plea for a Worshipful Church*, p. 22.
19. Prestige, *The Life of Charles Gore*, p. 295.
20. Ibid.
21. Fairbairn, *Studies in Religion and Theology*, p. 272.
22. Biggs, *Annotated Edition of Hymns Ancient and Modern*, p. 39.
23. Campbell, *Hymns and Hymn Makers*, p. 130.
24. Quoted in 'John Ellerton on Good Hymnody' in *Hymn Society Bulletin*, No.203, April 1995, p. 151.
25. Ibid., p. 150.
26. Caswall, *Lyra Catholica*, pp. viii–ix.
27. Moffatt and Patrick (eds), *Handbook*, p. xvi.
28. Quoted in Julian, *A Dictionary of Hymnology*, p. 7.
29. Brownlie, *Hymns and Hymn Writers*, p. 225.
30. *Church Times*, 26 November 1897.
31. Quoted in Peel, *These Hundred Years*, p. 287.
32. Benson, *The English Hymn*, p. 456.
33. *A & M* Archives. Letter from Prebendary J. H. Lester, undated, 1885.
34. Stead, *Hymns that Have Helped*, p. 15.
35. Ibid., p. 115.
36. Macmillan, *The Life of George Matheson*, p. 185.
37. Helmore, *Plainsong*, pp. 86–87.
38. Quoted in Gatens, *Victorian Cathedral Music*, p. 78.
39. *A & M* Archives. Letter from Bishop How, 12 June 1897.
40. *A & M* Archives. Letter from W. H. Frere to Bishop How, 21 June 1897.
41. Quoted in *The Guardian* review of Stainer's collection, 31 October 1900, p. 1531.
42. Ibid., p. 1532.
43. Ibid.
44. Quoted in Phillips, *Robert Bridges*, p. 20.
45. Ibid., p. 198.
46. Ibid., pp. 162–63.
47. Ibid., p. 163.
48. Article for the Church Music Society written in 1911 and quoted in Braley, *Hymn Writers*, Vol.3, p. 112. Braley's essay on Bridges in this volume and Catherine Phillips' study are recommended to anyone seeking more information on this fascinating figure.
49. Adey, *Class and Idol*, p. 225.
50. Quoted in Benson, *The Hymnody of the Christian Church*, p. 134.
51. E. T. Cook and A. Wedderburn (eds), *The Complete Works of John Ruskin*, Vol. XXXI, George Allen 1907, pp. 114–15.

52. Ibid., pp. 115–16.
53. *A & M* Archives. Letter from F. T. Palgrave, 17 January 1884.
54. Dickens, 'George Silvester's Explanation' (1868) in *Christmas Stories and Other Stories*, p. 628.
55. Kingsley, *Alton Locke*, p. 128.
56. Quoted in Keating, *The Working Classes in Victorian Fiction*, p. 237.
57. Butler, *The Way of All Flesh*, p. 77.
58. Ibid., p. 78.
59. Gosse, *Father and Son*, p. 60.
60. Ibid., p. 66.
61. Ibid., p. 91.
62. Ibid., p. 73.
63. Hardy, *Complete Poems*, p. 634.
64. Hardy, *Collected Letters*,Vol.6 (1987), p. 89.
65. Hardy, *Tess of the D'Urbevilles*, p. 143.
66. Hardy, *Two on a Tower*, Macmillan 1906, p. 21; compare Wessex Edition, Macmillan 1912, p. 21.
67. Hardy, *A Laodicean*, p. 9.
68. Hardy, *Far From the Madding Crowd* , pp. 448–49.
69. *Songs of Praise*, Enlarged Edition, OUP 1931, No. 684.
70. Tamke, *Make a Joyful Noise*, p. 90.
71. Carrington, *Rudyard Kipling*, p. 351.
72. *The Letters of Rudyard Kipling*, Vol.2, p. 234. There is an interesting analysis of the theology and sentiments of the 'Hymn Before Action' in Keating, *Kipling the Poet*, pp. 111–13.
73. Kipling, *Life's Handicap*, p. 194. There is a more extensive quotation of this passage, and commentary on its significance, in Donald Davie, *The Eighteenth Century Hymn in England*, pp. 1–3.
74. *The Complete Poems of D. H. Lawrence*, Vol. 1, p. 148.
75. 'Hymns in a Man's Life' (first published in the *Evening News*, 13 October 1928). Reproduced in *D. H. Lawrence. Selected Literary Criticism*, p. 6.
76. Ibid.
77. Ibid., p. 8.
78. Ibid., p. 9.
79. Ibid., p. 7.
80. Ibid., pp. 10–11.

9 *'Abide with me'*

1. *Alfred, Lord Tennyson. A Memoir by his Son*, Macmillan 1899, Vol. IV, p. 184.
2. Kenneth Finlay, 'A Famous Failure and a Historical Sequel' in *Hymn Society Bulletin*, January 1945, p. 2.

3. *The Daily Telegraph*, 20 September 1996, p. 6.
4. Gathorne-Hardy, *The Public School Phenomenon*, p. 132.
5. George Woodcock, *The Crystal Spirit: A Study of George Orwell*, Penguin 1970, p. 81.
6. *The Guardian*, 6 February 1996, Schools Section, p. 3.
7. The main advocate of the view that it was the latter hymn that was sung as the *Titanic* went down, and not 'Nearer, my God, to thee', was the late Sir Ronald Johnson.
8. Quoted in Benson, *The Hymnody of the Christian Church*, p. 253.
9. Ibid.
10. Moffatt and Patrick (eds), *Handbook*, pp. xxv–xxvi.
11. Routley, *The Musical Wesleys*, p. 198.
12. See, for example, Routley's article in the *Hymn Society Bulletin*, Vol. 2, No. 7, July 1949, pp. 103–10. I have myself attempted to restore Sullivan's reputation among hymnologists and refute some of Routley's criticisms in my article 'Sullivan's Hymn Tunes Reconsidered' in the *Hymn Society Bulletin*, No.193, October 1992, pp. 172–77.
13. Hutchings, *Church Music in the Nineteenth Century*, pp. 151, 18, 109.
14. Faber, *Oxford Apostles*, p. 315.
15. Phillips, *The Singing Church*, p. 171–72.
16. Long, *The Music of the English Church*, p. 359.
17. Ibid., p. 360.
18. Ibid.
19. Ibid., p. 361.
20. Ibid., pp. 361, 366.
21. Ibid., p. 366.
22. Davis, *Worship and Theology in England*, p. 208.
23. *Hymn Society Bulletin* , No. 129, February 1974, p. 48.
24. Grahame, *The Church Hesitant*, pp. 216–17.
25. Samuel J. Rogal, 'A Survey of Hymns in Funeral Services for American Dignitaries, 1921–1969' in *The Hymn* (Journal of the Hymn Society in the US and Canada), Vol. 45, No. 3, July 1994.
26. *The Times*, 12 December 1995. My favourite recent hymnological headline does, I must confess, invoke an eighteenth-century rather than a Victorian classic. A *Times* leader of 14 February 1996 on the state of the contemporary church was headed 'Rock of Ages cleft for me, are you becoming too PC?'
27. Joanna Trollope, *The Men and the Girls*, Black Swan 1992, p. 74.
28. John Bell, 'Change and decay' in *Life and Work*, October 1996, p. 18; Tamke, *Make a Joyful Noise*, p. 158.
29. *News of Hymnody*, July 1996, p. 8.
30. Dakers, *Parish Music*, p. 63.
31. Wilson-Dickson, *The Story of Christian Music*, p. 137.

32. Betty Saunders, 'Anglican hymnbooks infiltrate Roman pews' in *Church Times*, 16 September 1994.

33. Donald Webster, 'A Hymn-Book Survey 1980–93', Hymn Society Occasional Paper, Second Series, No. 4, October 1994, p. 29.

34. *The Daily Telegraph*, 1 May 1994; 13 November 1995; 10 October 1996.

35. Derek Rawcliffe's hymn was printed in *The Independent*, 15 November 1996; David Wright's was quoted in *The Sunday Times*, 5 May 1996, and is reproduced with the author's permission.

36. *Anglican Digest* (Eureka Springs, Arkansas), Vol. 36, No. 4, Transfiguration 1994, p. 7.

37. Tyler Whittle, *Solid Joys and Lasting Treasures*, Ross Anderson Publications, Bolton 1985, p. 198. Another of my own particular *bete-noirs* is the alteration made to 'Through the night of doubt and sorrow' in one inclusive language hymnal where 'brother clasps the hand of brother' has been altered to 'person clasps the hand of person'.

38. Brian Abel Ragen, 'Hymns Ancient and Modern, English and American' (unpublished and undated paper), pp. 8–9. See also the same author's 'A Wretch Like Who?' in *America*, 29 January 1994, pp. 8–11.

39. Ian Bradley, 'The campaign for real hymns', *The Daily Telegraph*, 16 October 1990; 'Abide with us', *The Sunday Telegraph*, 12 September 1993; 'A sense of wonder cut short by hymn book vandals', *The Guardian*, 20 November 1993; 'All jubilant with song', *Church Times*, 26 May 1995; 'Praise Hymn',*The Sunday Telegraph*, 28 May 1995.

40. *The Times*, 22 April 1996.

41. *The Sunday Times*, 5 May 1996.

42. Andrew Grimson, 'Don't drag hymns down to earth', *The Daily Telegraph*,11 October 1996. See also the leading article entitled 'Hymns Bright and Dutiful' in *The Times*, 14 October 1995.

43. *Life and Work*, October 1996, p. 18.

44. Clifford Longley, 'Lest we forget', *The Daily Telegraph*, 22 April 1994.

45. Bruce Kemble, 'Secrets of a comprehensive success', *The Times*, 6 September 1996.

Appendix 2

1. Mackenzie, *Tunes of Glory*, p. 170.

Bibliography

There are obviously many editions of the works of the Victorian novelists. Those listed here are the ones I have used, which are generally easily available. Unless otherwise stated, books and journals are published in the UK.

Adey, Lionel, *Hymns and the Christian Myth*, University of British Columbia Press, Vancouver 1986
—, *Class and Idol in the English Hymn*, University of British Columbia Press, Vancouver 1988

Baker, David and Welsby, Joan, *Hymns and Hymn Singing*, The Canterbury Press 1993
Barnby, Bertram, *In Concert Sing*, The Canterbury Press 1996
Battiscombe, G., *John Keble. A Study in Limitations*, Constable 1963
Baynes, R. H. (ed), *Lyra Anglicana*, Houlston and Wright 1863
Bebbington, David, *Evangelicalism in Modern Britain*, Unwin Hyman 1989
Bellasis, E., *Cardinal Newman as Musician*, Kegan Paul 1892
Benson, Louis, *The Hymnody of the Christian Church*, John Knox Press, Richmond, Virginia 1927
Benson, Louis, *The English Hymn – Its Development and Use in Worship*, John Knox Press, Richmond, Virginia 1962
Biggs, L. C. (ed), *Annotated Edition of Hymns Ancient and Modern*, 1867
Binfield, C., 'Hymns and an Orthodox Dissenter: In Commemoration of Bernard Lord Manning 1892-1941' in *Journal of the United Reformed Church History Society*, Vol.5, No.2, July 1993
Booth, William, *Salvation Army Music*, Salvation Army 1890
Bradley, I., *The English Middle Classes are Alive and Kicking*, Collins 1982
—, (ed), *The Penguin Book of Hymns*, Penguin 1990
Braley, Bernard, *Hymn Writers*, 3 vols, Stainer and Bell 1987, 1989, 1991
Breed, David, *The History and Use of Hymns and Hymn Tunes*, New York 1903
Briggs, John and Sellers, Ian, *Victorian Nonconformity*, Edward Arnold 1973
Bronte, Anne, *The Poems of Anne Bronte* ed E. Chitham, Macmillan 1979
Bronte, Charlotte, *Shirley* (1849), OUP Clarendon Edition 1979
—, *Villette* (1853), OUP Clarendon Edition 1984

Brownlie, John, *The Hymns and Hymn Writers of the Church Hymnary*, Henry Frowde 1899
Butler, Samuel, *The Way of All Flesh* (1903), Wordsworth Classics Edition 1994

Campbell, D., *Hymns and Hymn Makers*, Guild Library 1912
Carrington, Charles, *Rudyard Kipling*, Macmillan 1955
Castle, Brian, *Hymns: The Making and Shaping of a Theology for the Whole People of God*, Peter Lang, Frankfurt 1990
—, *Sing a New Song to the Lord*, DLT 1994
Caswall, Edward, *Lyra Catholica*, 1849
Chadwick, Owen, *The Victorian Church*, 2 vols, A. & C. Black 1966, 1970; SCM Press 1987
—, *The Spirit of the Oxford Movement*, CUP 1990
Chandler, Michael, *The Life and Work of John Mason Neale 1818-1866*, Gracewing/FowlerWright 1995
Charlton, Peter, *John Stainer and the Musical Life of Victorian Britain*, David and Charles 1984
Clarke, W. K. Lowther, *A Hundred Years of Hymns Ancient and Modern*, William Clowes 1960
Cunningham, V., *Everywhere Spoken Against: Dissent in the Victorian Novel*, Clarendon Press 1975

Dakers, Lionel, *Parish Music*, The Canterbury Press 1991
Davie, Donald, *The Eighteenth Century Hymn in England*, CUP 1993
Davis, Horton, *Worship and Theology in England 1850-1900*, Princeton University Press 1962
Dearmer, Percy, *Songs of Praise Discussed*, OUP 1933
Dickens, Charles, *Christmas Stories and Other Stories*, Chapman and Hall 1891
Drain, Susan, *The Anglican Church in Nineteenth Century Britain: Hymns Ancient and Modern 1860-75*, Edward Mellen Press 1989

Eliot, George, *Scenes of Clerical Life* (1858); Penguin Edition 1973
—, *Adam Bede* (1859); Penguin Edition 1994
Elliott-Binns, L.E., *Religion in the Victorian Era*, Lutterworth Press 1946

Faber, Geoffrey, *Oxford Apostles*, Penguin 1954
Fairburn, A. M., *Studies in Religion and Theology*, 1910
Fellowes, Edmund, *English Cathedral Music*, Methuen 1941
Fowler, J. T., *The Life and Letters of John Bacchus Dykes*, John Murray 1897
Frost, M. (ed), *Historical Companion to Hymns Ancient and Modern*, William Clowes 1962

Gammon, Vic, '"Babylonian Performances": the Rise and Suppression of Popular Church Music 1660-1870' in E. and S. Yeo (eds), *Popular Culture and Class Conflict 1590-1914*, Harvester Press 1981
Gaskell, Elizabeth, *Cousin Phillis*, (1864); Penguin Edition 1976
—, *Ruth* (1853); Dent Everyman Edition 1967
—, *North and South* (1855), Penguin Edition 1994
Gatens, William, *Victorian Cathedral Music in Theory and Practice*, CUP 1986
Gathorne-Hardy, Jonathan, *The Public School Phenomenon*, Hodder 1977
Gosse, Edmund, *Father and Son* (1907), Penguin Edition 1989
Grahame, Ysenda Maxtone, *The Church Hesitant*, Hodder 1993

Hardy, Thomas, *The Complete Poems of Thomas Hardy* ed James Gibson, Macmillan 1976
—, *The Collected Letters of Thomas Hardy* ed Richard L. Purdy and Michael Millgate, 7 vols, OUP 1978-88.
—, *Selected Short Stories and Poems*, Dent 1992
—, *Desperate Remedies* (1871), Wessex Edition, Macmillan 1912
—, *Under the Greenwood Tree* (1872), New Wessex Edition, Macmillan 1964
—, *Far from the Madding Crowd*, Wessex Edition, Macmillan 1912
—, *A Laodecian* (1881), Wessex Edition, Macmillan 1912
—, *Two on a Tower* (1882), Wessex Edition, Macmillan 1912
—, *The Mayor of Casterbridge* (1886), New Wessex Edition, Macmillan 1974
—, *Tess of the D'Urbervilles* (1891), Wessex Edition, Macmillan 1912
Helmore, Thomas, *Plainsong*, Novello 1877
Hennell, M., *John Venn and the Clapham Sect*, Lutterworth Press 1958
How, F. D., *Bishop Walsham How: A Memoir*, Isbister, London 1898
Hunter, J., *A Plea for a Worshipful Church*, Dent 1903
Hutchings, Arthur, *Church Music in the Nineteenth Century*, Herbert Jenkins 1967

Inglis, K.S., *Churches and the Working Classes in Victorian England*, Routledge 1963

Jacobs, Arthur, *Arthur Sullivan: A Victorian Musician*, Scolar Press, 2nd edn 1992
Jefferson, H.A.L., *Hymns in Christian Worship*, Rockcliff 1950
Jones, R. Tudur, *Congregationalism in England 1662-1962*, Independent Press 1962
Julian, John, *A Dictionary of Hymnology*, John Murray, 2nd edn 1907

Keating, Peter, *The Working Classes in Victorian Fiction*, Routledge 1971

Keating, Peter, *Kipling the Poet*, Secker and Warburg 1994
Kent, John, *Holding the Fort*, Epworth Press 1978
Kingsley, Charles, *Alton Locke, Tailor and Poet* (1850), new edn Macmillan 1876
Kipling, Rudyard, *Life's Handicap*, Macmillan 1913
Kipling, Rudyard, *The Letters of Rudyard Kipling* ed Thomas Pinney, 2 vols, Macmillan 1990
Knight, F., *The Nineteenth Century Church and English Society*, CUP 1995

La Trobe, J. A., *The Music of the Church, considered in its Various Aspects, Congregational and Choral*, London 1831
Lawrence, D. H., *The Complete Poems of D.H. Lawrence* ed Vivian de Sola and Warren Roberts, 2 vols, Heineman 1964
Lawrence, D. H., 'Hymns in a Man's Life' in Anthony Beal (ed), *D. H. Lawrence. Selected Literary Criticism*, Heinemann 1955
Lightwood, J. T., *Hymn Tunes and Their Story*, Charles Kelly 1906
Litvack, L., *J. M. Neale and the Quest for Sobornost*, Clarendon Press 1994
Long, Kenneth, *The Music of the English Church*, Hodder 1971
Luff, Alan, *Welsh Hymns and their Tunes*, Stainer and Bell 1990

MacDermott, K. H., *The Old Church Gallery Minstrels*, SPCK 1948
Mackenzie, Ian, *Tunes of Glory*, Handsel Press 1993
Macmillan, D., *The Life of George Matheson*, Hodder 1910
Milgate, M. (ed), *The Life and Work of Thomas Hardy*, Macmillan 1984
Moffat, James and Patrick, Millar (eds), *Handbook to the Church Hymnary*, Revised Edition, OUP 1927

Neale, J. M., *The Collected Hymns, Sequences and Carols of John Mason Neale DD*, Hodder 1914

Parsons, Gerald (ed), *Religion in Victorian Britain*, 4 vols, Manchester University Press 1988
Peel, Albert, *These Hundred Years. A History of the Congregational Union of England and Wales*, Independent Press 1931
Perry, M., *Preparing for Worship*, Marshall Pickering 1995
Phillips, C. H., *The Singing Church*, Mowbrays 1979
Phillips, Catherine, *Robert Bridges. A Biography*, OUP 1992
Pollock, John, *Moody without Sankey*, Hodder 1983
Prestige, G. L., *The Life of Charles Gore*, Heinemann 1935
Purcell, W., *Onward Christian Soldier: Life of Sabine Baring-Gould*, Longmans 1957
Putnam, Alfred, *Singers and Songs of the Liberal Faith*, Boston 1875

Rainbow, Bernarr, *The Choral Revival in the Anglican Church 1839-1872*, Barrie and Jenkins 1970
Routley, Erik, *Hymns and Human Life*, John Murray 1953
—, *The Musical Wesleys*, Herbert Jenkins 1968
—, *A Panorama of Christian Hymnody*, Liturgical Press, Minnesota 1979

Sankey, Ira, *My Life and Sacred Songs*, Hodder 1906
Sizer, Sandra, *Gospel Hymns and Social Religion*, Temple University Press, Philadelphia 1978
Stead, W. T., *Hymns that Have Helped*, Masterpiece Library 1896

Tamke, Susan, *Make a Joyful Noise Unto the Lord: Hymns as a Reflection of Victorian Social Attitudes*, Ohio University Press, Athens, Ohio 1978
Taylor, Gordon, *Companion to the Song Book of the Salvation Army*, Salvationist Publishing 1989
Temperley, Nicholas, *The Music of the English Parish Church*, 2 vols, CUP 1979
Towle, E. A., *John Mason Neale. A Memoir*, Longmans, Green & Co. 1907

Wallace, V., *Mrs Alexander: A Life of the Hymnwriter*, The Lilliput Press, Dublin 1995
Wilson-Dickson, Andrew, *The Story of Christian Music*, Lion 1992
Woods, R. G., *Good Singing Still*, West Gallery Music Association, Ironbridge 1995

Young, K., *Chapel*, Eyre Methuen 1972

Index of Hymns and Tunes

Index of Names